Applied Economics

in

Banking and Finance

APPLIED ECONOMICS IN BANKING AND FINANCE

FOURTH EDITION

I. PARTINGTON

OXFORD UNIVERSITY PRESS
1989

Oxford University Press, Walton Street, Oxford O X2 6DP
Oxford New York Toronto
Delhi Bombay Calcutta Madras Karachi
Petaling Jaya Singapore Hong Kong Tokyo
Nairobi Dar es Salaam Cape Town
Melbourne Auckland
and associated companies in
Berlin Ibadan

Oxford is a trade mark of Oxford University Press

Published in the United States
by Oxford University Press, New York
© I. Partington, Fourth Edition, 1989

British Library Cataloguing in Publication Data

Partington, I (Ian), 1941–
Applied economics in banking and finance – 4th ed.
1. Great Britain. Finance
I. Title
332'. 0941
ISBN 0 – 19 – 828329 – 6
ISBN 0 – 19 – 828330 – X (Pbk)

Library of Congress Cataloging–in–Publication Data
Partington, I. (Ian)
Applied economics in banking and finance
I. Partington.–4th ed.
p. cm.
Rev. ed. of : Applied economics in baking and finance
H. Carter and I. Partington. 3rd ed. 1984.
Includes bibiographical references.
1. Finance–Great Britain. 2. Banks and banking–Great
Britain. 3. Finance. 4. International finance. I. Carter, H. Applied
economics in banking and finance. II. Title.
HG186.G7C37 1990 89-25586
332'.0941–dc20
ISBN 0-19-828329-6 : ISBN 0-19-828339-X (Pbk.)

Typeset by Anamika Trading Co., Bombay – 400 028, India.

Printed and bound in
Great Britain by Biddles Ltd,
Guildford & King's Lynn

Preface

The fourth edition of *Applied Economics in Banking and Finance* had been prepared at a time of considerable change. Monetarism, at least as interpreted and practised by the UK Government, seems to have lost much of its appeal and credibility, and alongside this development has been a renewed emphasis on credit flows (the assets side of the balance sheet) as opposed to the money stock (the liabilities side). To say that we have moved 'back to Radcliffe' is probably going too far but a great deal of contemporary commentary, especially by economics journalists, is redolent of that period. The institutional changes – both within Britain and on the international scene – have also been substantial : building societies moving towards banking status, heightened competition between all the major financial intermediaries, the Big Bang of 1986, international moves towards agreement on capital adequacy of banks, growing financial imbalances between the major economies. One of the consequences of such change is that not only do textbooks quickly date (one might argue that all textbooks are dated by the time they are published) but also the structure of textbooks in the banking and financial field can be framed less confidently than in the past : the traditional, highly compartmentalised format has to some extent been replaced by a more integrated approach, such as that found in Chapter 6 where the intention has been to present a less fragmented picture for the reader, especially the newcomer to this area of economics.

The aims of the fourth edition remain largely those of the first : to provide a source of reference and information about the present financial system in the UK and, where appropriate, its historical origins; and the presentation of relevant and basic theoretical inputs which can be applied both to the data and the policy framework. The aim has been to provide the kind of reference material and detail which many students seek but is not to be found in existing texts. Advanced theoretical developments have been eschewed in favour of simpler presentations which it is hoped capture the essential points without diverting the student for whom this book is intended. One might also defend this decision on the grounds that there is no revealed wisdom and, as the past ten years have demonstrated, Keynes's dictum about politicians and defunct economists seems perhaps now to have a special relevance. Institutional integration and theoretical fluidity is mirrored in this edition by the enlargement and combination of subject material, but in order to assist the student the decimal subdivision of chapters has been extended.

Advanced Economics in Banking and Finance has been available for over ten years and appears to have met a need both at home and abroad, as well as in differing kinds of educational establishment, though these have been mainly in the higher education sector. Students and colleagues can be effective, if gentle, critics and it is to be hoped that the fourth edition continues to meet their needs in the light of many helpful comments. In this connection, the contributions of both Shaun Lang (Lancashire Polytechnic) and William Tandoh require special mention. The mistakes, of course, are all mine.

Ian Partington
Oxford Polytechnic
August 1989

Contents

I

The financial system

1.1 Introduction

In 1988 the British economy produced goods and services to the value of £358 billion. Of this total over 40 per cent consisted of the production of goods such as cars, food, and machinery, and the remainder of various services such as banking, health, and education. Almost 60 per cent of the total spending in the economy consists of the purchase of *consumer* goods and services, and the rest is spending by firms and government on *capital* goods such as roads, factory buildings, plant, and equipment. Spending by consumers and production by firms involves millions of separate economic decisions without any formal co-ordinating activity, and it is perhaps remarkable that the economic system appears literally to 'deliver the goods' – at least for many in the community.

Fundamental to the working of a modern economy is the existence of a *financial system* within which money, in its various forms, is an essential lubricant of the system; without it, production and exchange would be difficult and cumbersome. For example, the production of a motor car will require the financial system to play its part. In the mass production of motor vehicles the initial and continuing expenditure of funds for the purchase of investment goods (the factory and its production line, replacement of worn-out machinery, tools) is vital if production is to commence at all and to continue, and also if later production is to incorporate technical improvements or changes in the style of the product. The provision of investible *funds* is a key function of a financial system. This particular function is made the more important by the fact that modern methods of production often call for a volume of funds greater than those likely to be generated by the producing firm itself in its early stages of production. This situation usually obtains in those firms and industries which are highly capital-intensive, or where the production period is very lengthy, e.g. aircraft production. A financial system must therefore meet the needs of such enterprises by locating, securing, and channelling funds for firms which wish to invest.

The need for financial provision relates not only to producers but also to consumers. Again, to refer to the sale and purchase of motor cars, there are few private consumers who have sufficient accumulated savings with which to buy a car outright. Consequently many people are only able to purchase by borrowing either from a commercial bank or from a finance company by the means of hire purchase. In this way, part of the current output of motor cars is purchased not from current income of consumers but from, in effect, the future income of consumers. Although there are no published figures which identify the amount of credit which the personal sector (individuals, sole traders, unincorporated businesses, and private non-profit-making bodies) obtains in order to purchase motor vehicles, it is possible to observe a relationship between *credit* obtained through various agencies by the personal sector, and consumer *spending* on new and second-hand motor cars: In general, a shift in such consumer spending is seen to be reflected in the volume of bank and hire purchase finance. In other words, what is suggested in our illustration is that the close relationship between the changes in borrowing and changes in spending on new and second-hand cars indicates the importance of the provision of finance in this area of consumer spending. Without such financial provision it is probable that the volume of sales of such consumer goods would be lessened. Indeed it is likely that a considerable proportion of consumer expenditure on final output relies on external financing, i.e. funds provided by agencies other than the individual or firm which wishes to spend. For example, about one-third of total spending in the UK is on such items as house purchase, the buying of customer durables (cars, televisions, refrigerators, etc.); much of this expenditure will require external financing and, accordingly, will rely on the financial system which enables such financing to take place. An important part of the financial system is the banking system in the UK. To illustrate the point, it is interesting to note that between August 1987 and August 1988 total bank lending in sterling rose by almost £53 billion, whereas the output of the economy rose by £7 billion.

1.2 Finance and the circular flow

A simplified view of the workings of the economy might begin with representing production and spending as a *circular flow* of the kind expressed in *Table 1.1* and *Figure 1.1*. In this approach (or *model*) there are two major groups of economic unit:

Table 1.1

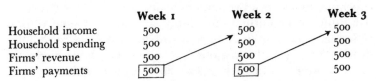

	Week 1	Week 2	Week 3
Household income	500	500	500
Household spending	500	500	500
Firms' revenue	500	500	500
Firms' payments	500	500	500

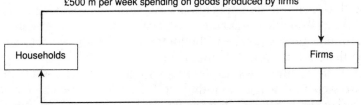

£500 m per week spending on goods produced by firms

Households   Firms

£ 500 m per week wages, salaries, and dividends paid to households

Figure 1.1

households and firms (there is no government or foreign trade). The households provide labour services to the firms, and the households are also the holders of the firms' equity capital, i.e. they are the firms' shareholders. In return for such services the households are paid wages, salaries, and dividends each week which are used to buy the final output of the firms. The revenue which the firms receive from the sale of output is then used to generate next week's output through payments for the necessary inputs, including further labour services from the households. Thus the firms' revenue of the previous week generates the income of the households in the following week. In this economic environment the expectations of both households and firms as to future income and sales could be held with certainty, and their behaviour – spending and production – would also be stable since expectations would be fulfilled within each weekly cycle.

Clearly many aspects of this simple economic model are remote from reality, in particular :
(a) The households do not save from their income.
(b) Firms are not investing in new capital equipment, either to add to their stock of capital, or to replace worn-out equipment.

There are clearly a number of very good reasons why households and individuals would wish to save a proportion of their income; as a means of planning future spending on expensive items, as a precaution against the need for unexpected future expenditures, to ensure adequate income during retirement, or simply from a desire to pass on wealth after death. Whatever the reasons it is clear that households are likely to save out of each week's flow of income they receive, and we must at some stage incorporate this into the model as well as examine its implications. Similarly, it would be much more reasonable to assume that firms will not only wish to maintain their equipment, buildings, etc. but also wish to add to their stock of capital equipment.

Table 1.2 indicates an alternative relationship between the two sectors. It will be seen that week 4 represents no change on week 3 (in Table 1.1), but the figures have been broken down, showing that household income derives from the sale of labour services (£400 million) and the receipt of dividends (£100 million). However, in week 5 we have assumed that households

Table 1.2
(£ m)

	Week 4	Week 5	Week 5a
Household income	500	500	500
Consumption	500	450	450
Saving	0	50	50
Accumulated saving	0	50	50
Consumer good sales	500	450	450
Capital good sales	0	0	50
Firms total revenue	500	450	500
Firms borrowing	0	0	50
Wages	400	360	400
Dividends	100	90	100
		= 450	

wish to save £50 million out of that week's income and accordingly cut down their consumption spending to £450 million. If such a change occurred the firms producing consumer goods would find that they had unsold stocks of consumer goods to the extent of £50 million and would presumably reduce output. If they did this, there would be further consequences for households; they would receive less income, since firms would be employing less labour provided by the households, and paying out less in dividends now that profits were lower as a result of reduced sales.

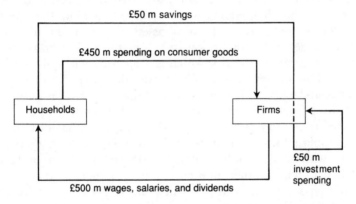

Figure 1.2

As an alternative course of events (*Table 1.2* and *Figure 1.2*), in week 5a we find that households plan to save £50 million from their income of that week and that firms also wish to *borrow* £50 million in that week in order to spend on capital goods. The result is that although the output of consumer goods has fallen to £450 million, this has just been offset by the new demand for £50 million capital goods. The firms are still obtaining receipts of £500 million and are thus able to sustain payments of £400 million for labour, together with £100 million in dividends to shareholders. Total firms' expenditure is maintained at £500 million and household income is also maintained at that level. If we continued the illustration on the assumption that households continued saving, we would observe the households accumulating wealth (their savings) each week.

Before modifying the simple circular flow model which has so far been outlined, we draw attention to certain features which will be partially considered in this chapter and developed in later ones.

First, the desire by households (and firms) to save poses the question as to the form such saving might take; in other words, the desire to save is likely to manifest itself as a *demand* for some form of asset. The form of asset chosen may be a tangible asset (gold sovereigns, jewellery, antiques) or a financial asset (sometimes referred to as a paper asset). In our illustration we assumed that households were prepared to hold the equity capital of the firms, i.e. financial assets. However, this may not be an acceptable assumption in reality since some households may be averse to the risk which is associated with this type of asset. The market value of shares can fall or rise : for example, between August and November 1987 the market value of shares fell by 27 per cent. Furthermore, not all households have the same needs and preferences with respect to the form their accumulated savings or wealth should take : some households may wish to accumulate money balances, i.e. cash or bank deposits, whilst other households may prefer to hold, say, building society deposits, or other assets presenting different degrees of risk and return. It is also worth noting that our simple model (*Table 1.2*) shows the household sector accumulating financial wealth through saving. This raises the question of the form which savings may take when wealth is actually *increasing*. The increase in wealth itself may alter the preference regarding the sort of assets to be held; for example, low-wealth households in the UK may well hold a greater *proportion* of their wealth in the form of bank deposits than high-wealth households (the latter perhaps wishing to hold more in the form of ordinary shares in commercial and industrial companies).

Secondly, the firms producing consumer goods in our simple model wished to spend in excess of receipts (in week 5a), i.e. to run a deficit of £50 million. If such firms are to obtain the additional funds, it follows that they must be capable of providing potential lenders with a financial asset suitable to the needs of the lenders. The requirement to meet the needs of potential lenders is probably one of the reasons for the *variety* of assets which companies may issue from time to time, e.g. ordinary shares, preference shares, debentures.

Thirdly, the needs of both the *demanders* of assets (savers) and the *suppliers* of assets (the firms wishing to invest in capital goods) are likely to create a *market* for such assets to enable both sets of needs to be met. This development is analogous to the establishment of other markets, e.g. foodstuffs, raw materials, which in such cases meet the needs of consumers and producers. The development of product markets has resulted in the appearance of specialist firms operating in such markets, and in a similar way the development of financial markets has produced specialist firms, for example the various types of bank.

Fourthly, *Table 1.2* shows that the accumulated wealth (assets) of the households is matched by the accumulated debt of the firms (week 5a), and furthermore that the accumulation of *financial* assets is paralleled by the production of *real* assets in the form of capital goods. One might therefore expect that a community's stock of financial assets will tend to grow as its stock of real capital grows.

Fifthly, so far the simple system we have constructed consists of three identifiable flows. There is the flow of spending on investment and consumer goods being produced and sold, and there is also the flow of saving taking place each week. In week 5a, for example, the flow of spending on consumer goods is £ 450 million, the flow of spending on investment goods is £ 50 million, and the saving flow is £ 50 million. It is worth pointing out at this stage the difference between a 'flow' concept and a 'stock' concept – a distinction which is important in economics. If an individual is said to have an income of £ 100, this description will convey no meaning unless a *time* dimension is added. Thus an income of £ 100 per week, per month, per year, etc. does have meaning but only because the time period has been specified. The use of the word 'flow' can perhaps be understood more clearly if one considers the flow of water through a pipe. Again, to say that the flow of water is 100 gallons has no meaning unless one adds the time dimensions, e.g. 100 gallons per minute. On the other hand if an individual is said to have a total wealth holding of £ 100 this *does* have meaning, and it is because wealth is a stock concept, i.e. a quantity which exists at a point in time. Thus one conceives of saving as a flow concept, e.g. £ 5 per week, whereas one's accumulated savings from the past constitute a stock concept since they are one's wealth. Similarly one's income is a flow concept, e.g. £ 50 per week, whereas the money which one has is a stock concept, e.g. £ 5 of currency held at 10.00 a.m. on Tuesday.

Finally, all the transactions which we have identified in the model will require *money* to act as the final means of payment, regardless of whether it is goods or assets which are being traded. The simple economic system embodied in the model will therefore require a certain stock of money to enable the system to function and all the transactions to be made.

1.3 The circular flow and the flow of funds

In the previous section we identified two sectors which interacted with each other: households (the personal sector) and firms (the industrial and commercial sector). In practice, three other sectors can be identified: the public sector (central and local government and the public corporations), the financial sector (banks and other financial firms), and the overseas sector.[1]

First we shall establish in outline the relationships between the sectors (excluding the financial sector), showing the major transactions which the four sectors are likely to undertake. The personal sector, for example, obtains receipts in the form of an inflow of income and this is disbursed as the following: spending on consumer goods, saving, and payment of taxes to the public sector. The industrial and commercial sector obtains *inflows* of receipts through consumer spending (sales revenue), investment spending (firms making capital goods receive the spending of other firms who are wishing to invest, e.g. manufacturing industry buys steel girders from the steel industry in order to erect more factories), the sales of exports, and finally the sales of goods and services to the public sector.

---

[1] This is rather less easy to define than the other sectors since it largely reflects changes in the balance of payments rather than a tangible area of activity. For this reason it will not be dealt with in any depth at this stage.

The receipts of the industrial and commercial sector are disbursed as *outflows:* payments to households (wages and salaries, dividends), spending on imported goods and materials, and the payment of taxes to the public sector. It should be noted that the two lists of inflows and outflows are not intended to be comprehensive but are illustrative of the major flows associated with each sector. Later chapters will provide much more detail, in particular relating to the public and overseas sectors (Chapters 6 and 7). The various flows identified can be converted into a flow diagram (*Figure 1.3*).

The superficial resemblance between *Figure 1.3* and a diagram showing a domestic water system is perhaps not inappropriate, since it can be seen that the four sectors are linked to

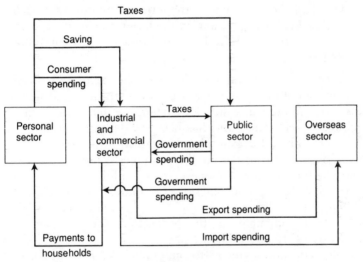

Figure 1.3

each other and the various flows feed into and out of each other. As with the earlier model (*Figure 1.2*) the personal sector (households) receives payments from the industrial and commercial sector (firms), and this income is disposed of in the form of three flows: consumer spending which goes back to the firms, saving which is used by the firms, and taxes which flow to the public sector. Similarly, the public sector is linked with the personal and industrial sectors by the flow of tax payments, and government and other public sector spending. The overseas sector is connected to the industrial sector by virtue of import and export spending. We can make a number of general points about this model:

(a) *Figure 1.3* portrays a *closed system.*
(b) Since the inflows and outflows feed into each other within a closed system it follows that the *total* outflows from the sectors must be equal to the *total* inflows to the sectors.
(c) Although total inflows must equal total outflows, for an *individual* sector this need not be the case.
(d) Clearly there are two important possibilities which could apply to the sectors. One is that the total disposals of income by each sector is exactly equal to total income, and the other is that sectors may wish to spend more or less than their income. In the former situation each sector 'balances its budget', and in the latter one or more sectors are in surplus whilst at least one other sector has a 'budget deficit'.

Table 1.3 and *Table 1.4* show each of the sector inflows and outflows identified in *Figure 1.3* but with the addition of illustrative numerical values for each of the items. In *Table 1.3* each of the sector accounts has been divided into receipts and payments. Thus, for example, the industrial and commercial sector obtains receipts from three sources: sales of consumer goods to the personal sector (£ 10,000 million), export sales (£ 1,000 million), and sales to the public sector (£ 1,500 million). Total receipts are £ 12,500 million, and this is disbursed in payments to the personal sector as wages and dividends (£ 10,000 million), payments for imports (£ 1,000 million), and tax payments to the public sector in the form of VAT and corporation tax (£ 1,500 million); total payments are £ 12,500 million. Furthermore it is clear that *all* sectors have 'balanced budgets' since no sector has a surplus or deficit.[2]

However, in *Table 1.4* we have assumed that sector behaviour has changed such that the personal sector has decided to reduce its consumer spending and save £ 1,000 million. This can be observed in the personal sector account which shows a fall in

[2]The term 'balanced budget' in this context simply refers to a sector's accounts. It is not the same as a 'balanced Budget' which refers to the central government accounts.

Table 1.3
($£$ m)

Personal sector		Industrial and commercial sector	
Income from		Sales revenue	10,000 *b*
emloyment	10,000 *c*	(consumer goods)	
Government		Exports	1,000
subsidies	1,500 *e*	Government spending	1,500 *f*
	11,500		12,500
Consumer spending	10,000 *a*	Payments to	
Income tax	1,500	personal sector	
		(factor earnings)	10,000 *d*
	11,500	Imports	1,000
		VAT	500
		Corporation tax	1,000
Surplus/deficit	nil		12,500

Public sector			
		Surplus/deficit	nil
Income tax	1,500		
Corporation tax	1,000		
VAT	500		
	3,000	*Overseas sector*	
		Exports	
		(foreign spending)	1,000
		Imports	
Public spending	3,000 *g*	(foreign receipts)	1,000

Surplus/deficit	nil	Surplus/deficit	nil

$a = b$; $c = d$; $e = f$; $e + f = g$

consumer spending from $£$ 10,000 million to $£$ 9,000 million. This spending, together with income tax payments of $£$ 1,500 million, accounts for the $£$ 10,500 disbursements by the personal sector in relation to receipts of $£$ 11,500 million, giving a 'budget surplus' of $£$ 1,000 million in the form of saving. Although the result of this is a reduced level of sales of consumer goods by the industrial and commercial sector (sales obviously fall from $£$ 10,000 million to $£$ 9,000 million), a part of the industrial and commercial sector is intending to invest and accordingly requires funds to finance such investments. Such funds are available from the personal sector (saving), and the

spending of these funds on investments offsets the decline of
£ 1,000 million in consumer goods output. This offsetting rise
in investment spending allows the earnings of the personal
sector derived from employment within the industrial and
commercial sector to be sustained at £ 10,000 million. If the
investment spending had not taken place as assumed, the
industrial and commercial sector would, *in the short run,* have
been forced to borrow £ 1,000 million in order to finance the
production and holding of unsold consumer goods as a result of
the reduced consumer spending by the personal sector.

It is important to realize that the above exposition is not
intended to be a totally realistic account of the responses which
would be likely to take place in the sectors. Rather the
intention is to show in a rudimentary form the basic relationships between the sectors which necessarily apply on the basis of
the system shown in *Figure 1.3.* In particular :

(a) The system *as a whole* cannot move into deficit or
surplus.

Table 1.4
(£ m)

Personal sector		*Industrial and commercial sector*	
Income from		Sales revenue	
employment	10,000 *c*	(consumer goods)	9,000 *b*
Government		Exports	1,000
subsidies	1,500	Government spending	1,500
	11,500		11,500
		Investment	1,000
Consumer spending	9,000 *a*	Payments to	
Income tax	1,500	personal sector	
		(factor earnings)	10,000 *d*
	10,500	Imports	1,000
		VAT	500
Surplus (saving)	1,000	Corporation tax	1,000
			12,500
		Deficit (borrowing)	1,000
Public sector		*Overseas sector*	
As for *Table 1.3*		As for *Table 1.3*	
a = b ; *c = d*			

(b) A deficit/surplus in one sector must have an opposite sur-
plus/deficit change mirrored in another sector or sectors.
Thus if one sector chooses to move from a 'balanced budget'
position (as the personal sector did in *Table 1.4*) this alters the
spending flows between the sectors (a fall in receipts by the
industrial and commercial sector) and also has a *financial*
repercussion. This repercussion took the form of borrowing by
the industrial and commercial sector in our example.

(c) Each sector is an aggregation of a great deal of different
economic activity. For example, the personal sector will
comprise millions of individuals and small firms. Some
individuals and firms might be increasing their borrowing,
paying back past debt, increasing their saving, and investing more. Therefore it should be remembered that the
overall change in deficit/surplus position of a sector could
disguise considerable *individual* change within that sector.

1.4 The UK accounts

So far we have been using hypothetical data in the accounts to
ensure simplicity so that we can concentrate our attention on
the underlying ideas. Nevertheless appropriate data for the
United Kingdom have been published in a suitable form, and
Table 1.5 is a condensed version of the figures for 1985. The
presentation of the information in this table has been made
comparable with the presentation of the hypothetical data used
earlier in *Table 1.3* and *1.4*. The summary of surpluses and
deficits at the bottom of *Table 1.5* illustrates two of the general
points made earlier. First, the sum of the surpluses and the sum
of the deficits cancel out, i.e. for the system as a whole there can
be neither a surplus nor a deficit position; second, the surplus
sectors match the deficit sectors (ignoring the compilation error
of 3,276 million).

1.5 The problem of surpluses and deficits

In our presentation of the sector accounts we have made only
limited reference to the financial repercussions of a change in
the behaviour of one or more of the sectors. We had considered
the possibility of one sector (the personal sector) moving into
surplus with an accommodating change in another sector (the

Table 1.5
UK flow of funds accounts : income and expenditure, 1985
(£ m)

Personal sector [a]		Overseas sector	
Income from employment		Exports and other	
and trading	225,209	receipts	155,057
Other income	77,633	Imports and other	
		payments	158,659
	302,842		
Consumption	213,208	Deficit [b]	3,602
Investment	16,556		
Taxes and other outlays	62,930		
	292,694		
Surplus	10,148		
Public sector		Company sector [c]	
Taxes and other receipts	157,566	Income from trading	
Income from employment		and employment	61,461
and trading	17,980	Other income	12,162
Other	9,666		
	185,212		73,623
Consumption	74,012	Investment	23,473
Investment	12,874	Taxes and other	
Grants, subsidies, and		outlays	43,231
other items	108,016		66,704
	194,902	Financial companies	
Deficit	9,690	and institutions deficit	499
		Surplus	6,420
Surplus		Deficit	
Personal sector	10,148	Public sector	9,690
Company sector	6,420	Overseas sector	3,602
		Error [d]	3,276
	16,568		16,568

[a] The personal sector includes sole traders, partnerships, and unincorporated private businesses as well as individuals who might wish to invest.
[b] This is a deficit for the overseas sector (foreign countries) and not for the UK. This figure is in effect the UK's current account surplus.
[c] Including financial institutions.
[d] This is the residual error in the national income accounts.
Source : United Kingdom National Accounts (CSO Blue Book) (1986).

industrial and commercial sector moving into deficit), but we
had not fully examined the financial consequences of such
changes. It is now appropriate to consider in slightly more
detail these repercussions, and we can do so by examining the
two basic changes: a sector moving into a budget deficit
position and a sector moving into a budget surplus position.

1.5.1 A SECTOR WITH A BUDGET DEFICIT

It has already been established that if a sector moves into deficit
then quite simply that sector is, for some reason, spending more
than it is receiving. Why might this be so? Within the
framework of the model which we have built, there could be
two reasons. One is that a sector wishes to purchase more
output from the economic system than that sector's income can
sustain. Another reason could be that the sector wishes to buy
financial assets, and when this form of spending is added to that
sector's purchases of output, total spending exceeds the sector's
receipts. An example of the first case might be where the
personal sector decides to purchase consumer durables on a
large scale such that for a period the personal sector's desired
expenditure exceeds its income. Such a deficit would involve
the personal sector in borrowing. In the second case, a sector or
major group may for example anticipate a fall in interest rates
and in accordance with this expectation decide to purchase
financial assets which yield the *current* interest rate. In order to
finance such purchases the sector borrows funds short-term at
the current rate with the intention of renegotiating the
borrowing later when interest rates have fallen. The final
result, after the change in interest rates, might be a situation
where the sector is holding £x million additional securities
which yield say, 10 per cent, and is indebted as a result of
borrowing £x million with an interest cost of say, 8 per cent.
A further illustration might be a situation where a sector
anticipates a borrowing need in the future and expects that
funds might be scarce at that future date. In these circumstances the sector may attempt to purchase short-term financial asssets *now* by using medium-term borrowed funds, and at
a later date when the funds are actually required the financial
assets acquired earlier could then be sold.

Whatever the particular intentions or needs of the deficit sector, we can generalize about the way such a sector might move into deficit. There are three possible methods: by selling assets which have been accumulated in past periods, which allows the sector to purchase a value of output in excess of current income; by creating liabilities against itself which a surplus sector is prepared to buy, and thus provide funds for the deficit sector; or by a combination of the two. Clearly a potential deficit sector will be able to move into deficit only if it is capable of selling assets which it happens to have accumulated, i.e. some other sector is prepared to purchase such assets; or if a surplus sector exists and is prepared to accept, willingly (or unwillingly)[3] the liabilities of the deficit sector. Furthermore, whichever method is used – sale of existing assets or production of new assets by the deficit sector – there will be an effect in financial markets (such as the London Stock Exchange) where such assets are traded, not least on the prices of such assets.

1.5.2 A SECTOR WITH A BUDGET SURPLUS

A sector which intends to move into a surplus position is one which is intending to spend less than its income. Some of the reasons for such behaviour have already been considered (Section 1.2); these relate to the desire to save. Whatever the reasons, if a sector is intending to move into a surplus position it is faced with three possible courses of action: it might accumulate assets which it purchases from deficit sectors; it might pay off past debts (in effect eliminating liabilities incurred in the past by buying back its own assets); or a combination of both. Whichever method is used, the potential surplus sector moves into surplus by obtaining some form of financial asset.

It is arguable that the position of the potential surplus sector is more flexible than the potential deficit sector, since a sector which wishes to move into surplus can always do so, at least in the short run, whereas the potential deficit sector may not always be in such a position. One can clarify this by referring back to budget deficit position already considered in Section

[3] If I refuse to pay for goods which I have had delivered from a shop, then in effect the shopkeeper is – unwillingly – accepting a liability which I have created against myself, which is the debt I owe the shopkeeper.

1.5.1. We showed that a deficit position could be achieved if that sector were able to sell assets. Obviously there are no reasons why such an opportunity is *necessarily* open to such a sector; either it may not have accumulated assets from the past or it may be unable to sell the assets which it wishes to create (e.g. a company may be unable to issue more shares or sell debentures because the market finds such assets unacceptable). However, similar limitations are *not* faced by the potential surplus sector. Even if a potential surplus sector has no debts to pay off or financial assets are not available from asset markets, such a sector would be able to move into surplus by accumulating the one financial asset which will be available, and that financial asset is money itself. In other words a sector wishing to move into surplus can, in the last resort, always accumulate money balances.

Earlier in the chapter we noted that for 1985, for example, the personal sector in the UK was in surplus to the extent of £10,148 million (*Table 1.5*), and this surplus made some provision towards the deficits of the public and external sectors. Official statistics are available which reveal how the surplus was utilized by individuals and firms which comprise the personal sector. *Table 1.6* presents the financial transactions of the personal sector in 1985. The table shows the increases in financial assets and liabilities during the year. Because the personal sector contains millions of individual transactors it is no surprise that some are increasing their liabilities whilst others are increasing assets. For our flow of funds analysis it is the *net* position which matters in relation to the position of the other sectors.

Table 1.6 reveals that in 1985 the personal sector chose to accumulate wealth largely in the form of contributions to life assurance and private sector pensions (£17·7 billion), building society deposits (£12·9 billion) and bank deposits (£5·2 billion), whereas most of the increase in personal sector indebtedness was clearly in the form of borrowing for house purchase and loans from the banks other than for house purchase (£25·8 billion). Overall the personal sector accumulated more assets than liabilities to the extent of £10·1 billion, which is its sector surplus identified in *Table 1.5*. The accumulation of assets by the personal sector will have a corresponding liability in the

Table 1.6

Financial transactions of the UK personal sector, 1985

Assets	£m	%	Liabilities	£m	%
Notes and coin	483	1.1	Local authority debt	937	2.9
Treasury bills and government securities	1,596	3.8	Bank loans	6,904	21.5
National Savings and tax instruments	2,553	6.1	Other loans (mainly mortgages)	18,876	58.8
Bank deposits	5,172	12.2	Trade and retail credit	320	1.0
Building society deposits	12,938	30.6	Other	19	0.1
Life assurance and pensions funds	17,727	41.9	Balancing item	5,071	15.8
UK and overseas securities and unit trusts	749	1.8			
Other items including accruals adjustment	1,057	2.5			
	42,275			32,127	
			Personal sector surplus	10,148	
	43,823			43,823	

Sources : Derived from *United Kingdom National Accounts* (CSO Blue Book) (1986); Bank of England *Quarterly Bulletin* (June 1986)

account(s) of other sectors. To illustrate the point, the personal sector accumulated (i.e. bought) assets issued by the public sector – Treasury bills and government securities such as bonds (£1·6 billion), National Savings and tax instruments (£2·5 billion) – and thus helped to finance the deficit of the public sector. These assets will, however, be expressed as additional *liabilities* in the accounts of financial transactions by the public sector.

1.6 Summary

By using a simple model of an economic system this introductory chapter has tried to show that within modern economies, especially the so-called 'private enterprise' economies, a financial system is likely to be needed to ensure the smooth operation of that economy.

(a) Expenditure and income flows between sectors of the economy may be such that some sectors are in surplus and others in deficit. These flow 'imbalances' will involve these sectors in decisions regarding their *stocks* of assets and liabilities.

(b) Changes in the preferences of sectors with respect to their assets/liability position (i.e. changes in their *stock* position) may have an effect on the *flows* of expenditures and income in the economy. For example, in 1985 the personal sector deposited £12·9 billion with the building societies, and this rise in building society deposits would have contributed to the increase in new mortgage commitments of £27·5 billion by the building societies in that year. Assuming spare capacity in the building industry, such an increase in mortgage commitments would, in turn, encourage housing starts and eventual house completions. In fact, housing starts rose by 8,000 in 1985. Such increased activity would have helped to sustain employment and incomes in the building industry.

(c) Although deficits and surpluses of sectors sum to zero in aggregate, there is the problem of communication and transmission between those sectors which are in surplus or deficit. Funds are required to flow from surplus to deficit sectors and, corresponding to this flow, deficit sectors will find it necessary to produce liabilities which are acceptable assets to surplus sectors.

(d) If we assume that tendencies towards surplus and deficit reflect sector preferences [4] (i.e. the personal sector wishes to save and the industrial and commercial sector wishes to invest), then inadequate links between sectors in an economy may thwart the achievement of sector objectives. For example, the personal sector may limit its savings or simply hoard money balances because of inadequate or unsatisfactory outlets for such funds.

(e) Although our analysis has so far been of a rudimentary nature, it is becoming evident that there are at least two possible functions which the financial sector can perform. One is to provide efficient transmission of funds between sectors by acting as an intermediary so as to ensure that surplus sectors

---

[4] As opposed to *errors* of budgeting by a sector.

(demanders of assets) obtain the assets they prefer, and that deficit sectors obtain the funds they require by generating the appropriate sort of liability. For example, insurance companies provide savings opportunities for the personal sector and at the same time such companies have considerable influence on the nature of the liabilities which they themselves hold. As we shall see in Chapter 6, the Bank of England is very obliging in providing government securities which suit the preferences of investment managers of insurance companies and other financial firms. The operations of banks and building societies are other examples of financial sector activity since they provide specialized methods by which those with surpluses can have such surpluses transmitted to those who wish to go into deficit. A second function of the financial sector is to produce the appropriate signals (e.g. a market interest rate) which will allow potential transacting sectors to make correct decisions about their present or future borrowing or lending. The interplay of competition amongst borrowers and lenders, and the rapid transmission of information in modern financial markets, are important elements in the production of financial 'signals'.

2
Wealth, money, and non-money assets

2.1 Introduction

In Chapter 1 our primary intention was to develop a simple model of an economic system within which the role of a financial system could be outlined in a rudimentary way. In Chapter 2 we shall be considering the financial system in more detail by looking at the nature of the output of such a system.

The 'output' of the financial system may be thought of as consisting of two kinds. On the one hand the various firms operating within the financial system provide their customers with a variety of services which use their specialist knowledge and skills; the modern operation of the banks is an obvious example of such a provision (see Chapter 4). On the other hand the financial firms and institutions within the system are involved in the production of a slightly less obvious form of output, and that is the production of *financial assets* or *claims*. As a result of such direct and indirect financial activity within the financial system, the total of financial claims in existence is very substantial. For example, the market value of UK company securities in 1987 amounted to £1,285 billion; company security value was almost four times as great as national income. However, this is only a small fraction of the total financial claims which exist, since it does not include many other forms of financial asset, such as government securities, bank deposits, assets of pension funds, and so on.

2.2 Forms of wealth

Financial assets represent part of the wealth of individuals and institutions which hold such assets. Such wealth is, however,

only one constituent of the total wealth of individuals and
institutions since wealth can take a real (i.e. physical) form, for
example property, stocks of goods, raw materials, land and
machines. Therefore if one is asked to add up the value of one's
own wealth, such things as a house and a motor car would be
included as well as the amount of money one has in a bank and
also the shares one might own. Thus, for the individual,

$$\text{wealth} = \text{real assets} + \text{financial assets}$$

But an individual is also likely to have liabilities (debts) such as
a mortgage or a bank loan, and in assessing the individual's *net
worth* these liabilities need to be taken into account :

net worth (individual) = real assets + financial assets – liabilities

If one wishes to extend this approach to the whole community
the result is quite interesting. It is important to realize that
although *financial* assets have a corresponding liability, real
assets do not. For example, an individual's mortgage with a
bank or building society is that person's financial liability, but
for the bank or building society it is represented as an asset in its
balance sheet – an asset which is *equal* to the liability of the
individual. So for all individuals, groups, and institutions, that
is the community,

net worth (community) = real assets + financial assets –
                        financial liabilities

But since, every financial asset is someone else's liability, for the
community as a whole, net worth will equal real assets only
since financial assets and liabilities cancel each other out.
Thus

net worth (community) = real assets

The position is somewhat curious. Financial assets held by
the individual will be rightly regarded as part of his wealth
(and if financial assets exceed financial liabilities then part of
his net worth), but for the community as a whole the financial
assets 'wash out' when assets and liabilities are aggregated. This
phenomenon has given rise to controversy amongst economists,
because although it would appear that financial claims are not
part of net worth it would be hard to argue that they do not
have any economic significance.

2.3 The growth of financial wealth

The existence in an economy of those who wish to borrow, and those who are willing and able to lend, in effect creates a market for financial claims (assets) of one kind or another. Such claims may pass from borrower to lender *directly*, as, for example, when a company makes a direct offer of further shares to existing shareholders; or the process may be *indirect*, for example when a company raises additional funds by engaging a merchant bank's services including the underwriting facility which usually attends such an arrangement. In the case of the latter example, if the ultimate lenders – e.g. institutional investors, the personal sector – are not prepared to purchase the shares offered them, then the underwriters will be obliged to provide the necessary funds to their client company.

Over time such transactions between deficit and surplus sectors will result in the accumulation of financial wealth. In this section we will examine briefly the growth of assets of various kinds. Using some early estimates made by J. Revell[1] as the basis of our account, we can establish that the nominal growth of assets during the years 1956 – 61 was substantial. The value of total assets (physical assets plus financial assets) in 1957 amounted to £174,000 million, of which £68,400 million consisted of physical assets and £105,700 million were financial assets, whereas in 1961 total assets amounted to £237,700 million of which £91,900 million were physical assets and £145,800 million were financial assets. Examining the ratio of financial assets to physical assets one finds that the ratio has not varied greatly during these five years. However, the ratio does indicate that in 1957, for example, the value of existing financial claims was 54 per cent *higher* than the value of physical assets. At first sight this does seem rather curious, since the analysis in Section 1.2 indicated that the growth of financial claims would rise with the growth of physical assets, e.g. investment goods, in the economy. In Chapter 1 we had assumed that the corporate sector would add to its capital stock by borrowing funds from the personal sector and in return provide the personal sector with some form of financial claim or asset. Accordingly the issue of financial claims would match the

[1] J. Revell, *The Wealth of the Nation* (Cambridge University Press, 1967).

growth of real assets. It is evident from the data to which we have referred in this section that the growth of financial claims is greater than the growth of physical assets, and clearly we need to offer some explanation for this. Leaving aside the problem of the valuation of the different types of asset in an economy (since this in itself is likely to produce a discrepancy), we can suggest two reasons for the different results.

First, one can question the assumption that the issue of a financial claim will arise solely through the process of capital accumulation as was assumed in Chapter 1. Quite simply, many individuals, firms, and indeed governments will go into debt for the purpose of adding to their level of consumption or current spending. If this occurs there will be the issue of a financial claim but no corresponding increase in the capital stock. To use a rather simple illustration, if one borrows in order to sustain day-to-day spending, then one is adding to the total of financial assets in the community (i.e. a liability to oneself but an asset to the person or institution which has provided the funds), but since the funds are being spent on consumer goods, the financial asset/liability remains even though the consumer goods which have been bought (e.g. food) no longer exist. Similarly, governments may borrow in order to finance the purchase or production of goods and services which are consumed and cease to exist, although the debt nevertheless remains. Probably the best example of this would be when a government borrows in order to finance a war. In this case the purpose of the borrowing is to purchase goods, some of which will ultimately be destroyed by war activity. In 1939 the UK national debt amounted to about £7,000 million, whereas by 1952 it had increased to almost £26,000 million; this almost fourfold increase was largely a result of the borrowing during the war of 1939 – 45.

A second reason for the 'imbalance' between the value of financial claims and the value of physical assets in an economy is that the process of raising funds for use, say, by a firm may well result in several financial firms being involved in the provision of the funds and at different stages. However, at each stage in the transmission of such funds there will be an entry in the balance sheet of each of the financial firms. Therefore if one adds up all the entries in the various balance sheets the result would be a figure in excess of the actual sum raised. This aspect of the behaviour of financial firms will be dealt with in more detail in Chapter 3.

Detailed information about the accumulation of wealth in the UK has been available in published data since about 1966 and can be found in *Financial Statistics*. Data are limited in coverage but at present identify the assets and liabilities of the personal sector and the wealth of the private sector of the economy (excluding the banks). *Table 2.1* represents a summary of the personal sector balance sheets using selected data

Table 2.1

Balance sheets of the personal sector (£b at 31 December)

	1979	1981	1983	1985
Total tangible assets	347.6	404.2	510.2	639.4
of which :				
Residential building	270.5	319.9	410.4	527.8
Total financial assets	243.7	331.0	475.2	622.8
of which :				
Equity in life assurance and				
pension funds	78.0	118.4	193.6	272.5
Building society shares				
and deposits	42.2	56.4	77.1	103.6
UK ordinary shares and				
unit trusts	32.0	39.7	58.9	75.0
Total financial liabilities	78.0	106.4	149.7	204.3
of which :				
Loans for house purchase	48.9	66.3	94.7	131.4
Bank loans and advances				
(excluding housing)	11.5	18.5	29.6	40.5
Net wealth	603.0	722.3	937.5	1,165.0

Source : Financial Statistics

from 1979. Although the personal sector is very large (and includes by definition small unincorporated businesses as well as households) the data probably indicate the preferred behaviour of individuals and groups, since one may presume that changes in the holdings of assets and accumulation of liabilities is not a random process. The data reveal, for example, that the most important real (tangible) asset of the personal sector is residential accommodation, i.e. houses, flats, etc. Financial assets held by the sector have increased *relative* to real assets. In 1979, for example, for every £1 of financial assets held by the personal sector, £1·10 was held as real assets; in 1985, for every £1 of financial assets held, £0·84 was held as real assets. Of the financial assets held, it is interesting to observe that in 1979 only 13 per cent were in the form of ordinary shares and unit trusts, and this figure was little changed by 1985. It is also clear that the personal sector 'invests' heavily in life assurance and pension rights, as well as having substantial holdings of funds with the building societies.

2.4 Money

At the beginning of this chapter we suggested that the financial system produces output in the form of services and alongside this goes the generation of a variety of financial claims. We can continue with this approach when we consider a special kind of asset; money. In Chapter 5 and 8 we shall be examining in considerable detail the mechanics of money creation and regulation. In this section our main purpose is to attempt to identify money, in particular some of its special characteristics, and also the way 'money' might be defined for statistical purposes by central banks.

Having already conceived of the financial system as 'producing' output in the form of assets, let us continue with this approach and establish who are the producers of money in the economy. Part of the answer to this question is very straightforward if one is considering only cash, i.e. notes and coins in circulation. In the UK the origin of notes and coin is of course the central bank, the Bank of England, and the Royal Mint. Notes and coin are unambiguously 'money' because they are *legally* the means by which we can settle our debts. Even though there are upper limits to the quantity of coins which constitute legal tender, this does not really alter the substance of the point which has been made. The community is prepared to use and hold notes and coin not only because these are the statutory means of settling debt but also because the general application and acceptability of this rule ensures that holders of notes and coin can, when required, convert such cash into goods and services. In other words cash represents instant purchasing power – the command over real resources.

Is cash an asset ? It is clearly a financial asset as far as the individual is concerned. But the existence of cash also provides the whole community with an asset other than that of simply a financial asset. Cash (and money generally) can be regarded almost as part of the capital stock of the community, since it enables transactions to occur, production of goods and services to take place more efficiently than in the absence of money, and employment of labour and specialization (division of labour) to be developed and continued. Cash and other moneys are the lubricant of the economic system, allowing the community to satisfy its wants and needs more efficiently. That is not to say that such activities would not be possible without money, but it certainly makes the whole process much easier and more efficient. The paper and metal which compose cash are of little intrinsic value,[2] but it is nonetheless a valuable kind of capital for the whole community; we hold money not for its *own* sake but rather for the services it can ultimately provide in use.

In our enquiry into the source and nature of money, we would be taking a very limited view if we considered only cash. From one's own personal experience it is obvious that cash represents only the 'small change' of the system since the bulk of one's spending – rent or mortgage payments, insurance premiums, large household bills – is done by the use of bank deposits drawn on by the use of the cheque. With the growing use of credit cards such as the Visa and Access, even the items of spending which used to be done by cash are frequently undertaken by the use of a credit card, and settlement is finally made by the use of cheque drawn on a bank deposit.

Bank deposits represent the major component of the money stock in modern economies, and in comparison with cash such deposits differ significantly in that their source is *not* the central bank but banks which are usually part of the private sector, i.e. the so-called deposit banks, and in addition such deposits do not rank as legal tender. Yet these assets produced by the banking system are widely used as money and provide an immensely convenient way of conducting transactions. In this respect these bank deposits are an asset to the community in the same way as cash.

---

[2] Average cost of producing a UK banknote is 3p.

However, the inclusion of bank deposits as part of our definition of the money stock of the community does raise some awkward problems. As we have already said, these deposits are not legal tender and are not issued with the authority of the state. Indeed they are in many countries the result of the business activity of private sector profit-making firms. Furthermore, one can observe a wide variety of 'bank deposits' originating from the private sector part of the financial system. So which deposits are part of the money stock and which are not ? Where can one draw the dividing line ? Clearly it is necessary to look more closely at which kind of asset from amongst the many types produced by the financial system we can define as money and which we cannot. The following sections will consider this particular problem.

2.4.1 THE FUNCTIONS OF MONEY

What one might term the 'traditional' approach to the problem of the nature of money is to consider money from the point of view of what it *does* rather than what it *is*. In other words, if one can isolate the primary functions which money performs in an economy (i.e. what money does), then the problem of the nature of money is solved, since anything which performs these functions is money by definition.[3] Using this approach, money can be said to have four functions: it can act as a medium of exchange, a store of value, a unit of account, and a standard for deferred payments.

2.4.1.1 Medium of exchange

This is the most important function which money performs in an economy. A non-monetary economy would be one in which economic transactions are performed by a process known as barter. Goods and services which are produced and intended for exchange can only be so traded by a simple swap. Goods and services are exchanged directly for goods and services. In anything other than a very primitive economy this arrangement would be immensely inconvenient and also likely to be inefficient. The basic problem with a barter system is that a

---

[3] A common analogy is that an elephant is defined by what it is, whereas an umbrella is defined by what it does. Both methods of identification are legitimate, of course.

successful swap rests on what is called the 'double coincidence of wants'. This is the necessity for the two parties to an exchange (if an exchange is to take place) to want what the other party is offering, i.e. if one produces food and requires shoes, then for a successful transaction to occur, someone else who produces shoes and requires food is needed – hence, the reference to 'double coincidence'. If such a coincidence does not exist, then for trade to take place there would have to be probably several intermediate transactions, e.g. if A produces food and wants shoes and B produces shoes but wants clothes, then A or B must search around for another transactor C who, say, produces clothes and wants food. This would allow A to trade with C, and then for A to trade with B. Clearly barter is a clumsy basis for trade and unlikely to be a system which encourages economic development. However the use of money can solve the problem quite simply since goods can be traded for money and then money traded for goods. The requirement of the double coincidence of wants is obviated where money acts as a medium of exchange.

Although this advantage of using money is very obvious, the history of money shows that the successful use of money in its role as a medium of exchange rests on the substance used as money being *generally acceptable* in the performance of that function. Clearly an individual will only accept money as payment for goods or services if that individual is convinced that others will do likewise both now and in the future. Without such general acceptance the particular money-substance, whether it be a coin, banknote, or bank deposit, will function imperfectly or not at all. Once confidence in the money-substance is lost, even if that money-substance is deemed legal tender, individuals within the community will either find some alternative money-substance or resort to barter. This type of change in people's attitude towards money is usually in modern times a result of rapid inflation. If inflation is proceeding very rapidly, then this will be reducing the value of money swiftly and noticeably. It is therefore possible that individuals will be reluctant to use money since any delay in using or obtaining money as payment will result in a significant loss of purchasing power when purchase is finally made. Under such circumstances one either abandons the use of money or increases the rate of spending and increases the rate at which one receives money income (paid by the hour for example).

2.4.1.2 Store of value

Money is a liquid store of value in that it provides individuals with a means of holding and accumulating their wealth in a form which can, at any time, be converted immediately into goods and services. When money is being used as a store of value it is effectively being treated by the holder as a substitute for an alternative financial asset. One is able to make this assertion since the alternative to holding money as a store of value would be to hold another form of financial asset, say a building society deposit, or a government security, and both of these would provide an explicit yield to the holder in the form of interest payments as well as being a store of value. The holding of money, as an alternative to an interest-yielding asset, involves the holder in a sacrifice of the interest which would otherwise have been gained; but one can argue that the holding of money must provide an *implicit* yield rather than an *explicit* yield. Two such implicit yields are that of convenience and certainty. Storing value in the form of money allows the holder to convert his asset into goods and services instantly and with the certainty that the money value, at least in nominal terms, has been retained. An untimely sale of a bond may result in having to sell at a capital loss, or the holding of a time deposit may be inconvenient if one is unable to convert that deposit into purchasing power when needed. On the other hand, we can say that money has the supreme quality of being absolutely liquid in the sense of providing instant purchasing power.

As with its function as a medium of exchange, the usefulness of money as a store of value depends upon the value of money remaining fairly stable or at least not declining too quickly. Under conditions of inflation, using money as a store of value involves not only the forgoing of an interest payment, but also the loss of *real value* as a result of rising prices between the time when the money balance was accumulated and the time when it is spent.

2.4.1.3 Unit of account

The role of money as a unit of account is linked with its being used as a medium of exchange. Even within an economy which uses barter as the means of trade there is likely to develop some method by which the commonly traded goods can be assigned a value. One can imagine the problems of trading many commodities in circumstances where there is not a common means by which the value of a commodity can be established so that the traders know the relative quantities of each commodity to be exchanged.

To take as an example, let us suppose that there are four commodities A, B, C, and D which are traded in an economy. For traders to trade successfully they will have to know the value of all commodities in terms of each other (their relative prices) and therefore a collection of price ratios would need to be established, i.e. how much of one commodity is to be exchanged for another. Quite simply we can establish how many ratios would have to be worked out, by producing the possible combinations of the four commodities (*Table 2.2*) : Thus one would need to know how much A exchanges for so much B, how much A exchanges for so much C, and so on. The combinations which are in parentheses are those which have been included, but the opposite way round, i.e. AB and BA. It is clear from the above illustration that four commodities will require the working out (and remembering) of six price ratios.

Table 2.2

Price ratios for six commodities

AB	(BA)	(CA)	(DA)	(EA)	(FA)
AC	BC	(CB)	(DB)	(EB)	(FB)
AD	BD	CD	(DC)	(EC)	(FC)
AE	BE	CE	DE	(ED)	(FD)
AF	BF	CF	DF	EF	(FE)

Now let us assume that another commodity E begins to be traded in the economy. We can see that this results in another *four* price ratios having to be established. If a further commodity F were added, this would result in an additional *five* ratios having to be worked out. The nature of the problem is clear: four commodities require six price ratios, five commodities require ten ratios, six commodities require fifteen ratios, seven commodities require twenty-one ratios, and so on. Clearly any community which traded or wished to trade in more than, say, fifteen commodities would require so many price ratios to be worked out that trade would indeed be a tiresome business.

However, a barter economy can still function without the use of money if it decides (and this is likely to happen naturally rather than as a conscious, collective decision) to adopt a unit of account. To take our earlier illustration, let us suppose that commodity A is chosen as the unit of account. By this we mean that all price ratios will be established in terms of a single commodity. The result of this is to simplify greatly the problem of setting price ratios. Thus so much of commodity A would be treated as the basic accounting unit, and all other commodities would be priced in terms of that unit. An example is set out in *Table 2.3*. Once such an arrangement has been established then the problem of working out the price ratios of the other goods is fairly simple. It is evident that 3 units of B will exchange for $2^1/_4$ units of E, and 4 units of D exchange for $1^1/_2$ units of F. It will be noted in this example, that by introducing a unit of account (commodity A) the number of price ratios which have to be set and remembered is reduced from fifteen to five. For a barter economy the establishment of a unit of account would indeed represent a great leap forward since the limitations on trading a larger number of goods are eliminated. It is to be emphasized that commodity A is not used as a trading medium, i.e. the other commodities are not actually exchanged for commodity A, which is then used for purchasing other commodities; rather commodity A is used to price the other goods which are then bartered for each other. However, it would seem to be an obvious next step in the development of such an economy if it identifies a convenient commodity which could in fact be used as a medium of exchange. Such a change would then eliminate the need for the 'double coincidence of wants'.

Table 2.3

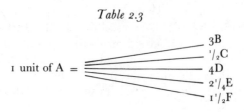

1 unit of A =
$3B$
$^1/_2C$
$4D$
$2^1/_4E$
$1^1/_2F$

2.4.1.4 Standard for deferred payments

A fourth function which is ascribed to money is that of being a standard for deferred payments. This function allows contracts to be made whereby a variety of transactions can take place in the present with payment being made at a later date. The sale and production of goods is made easier by money performing this function since goods can be provided through trade credit, labour and raw materials can be obtained by the producer, and the various parties will know the sums involved and payments to be made at a future date. Clearly this particular function of money is not essential for lending, borrowing, production, and distribution to take place, but it certainly makes such activities easier. During periods of very high inflation, money's performance of this function is inhibited since a deferred payment benefits the debtor and penalizes the creditor as a result of the decline in the purchasing power of money before payment is made. In such circumstances the period of deferred payment is likely to be reduced, or an 'inflation clause' may be introduced so that the deferred payment takes into account the depreciation in the value of money. The introduction of inflation-proofed pensions and savings certificates whose value is linked to changes in the retail price index are examples of such arrangements.

We have now established the four basic functions which money is said to perform: medium of exchange, store of value, unit of account, and standard for deferred payments. However, for something to be defined as money it is not necessary for the money-substance to perform all four functions. The only function which is essential for something to be called money is that of being a medium of exchange. Money may be an unsatisfactory store of value (e.g. in conditions of inflation) and other financial assets may be used to perform this function. Likewise, other commodities could be used as a unit of account. This might arise again under circumstances of high inflation rates where transactions are denominated not in money but in terms of another commodity, money being used only when final payment is made. For example, a sale of machinery could be valued in terms of say, gold, or barrels of oil, with final payment in money being made by establishing the money value of the gold or oil at the time of payment.

2.4.2 MONEY AND MONEY SUBSTITUTES

The approach to money outlined in Section 2.4.1 would seem to indicate that there is no real problem in identifying what money *is* (as opposed to what it does) since *anything* is money which performs a medium of exchange function. However, this is a somewhat debatable contention since it can be argued that in a highly developed economy other media of exchange may arise, for example the use of trade credit. This is used on a very substantial scale [4] between producer, wholesaler, retailer, and customer; the granting of credit from one to the other enables the process of trade and exchange to take place. Clearly, if one identifies the medium of exchange function as being simply the exchange of goods taking place without barter, so long as there is *confidence* amongst the parties concerned that ultimately payment will be made, many 'things' may act as a medium of exchange. Indeed it may not actually be of a tangible form; for example, if a transaction is arranged between two individuals who have complete trust in each other, then *trust* itself may allow a transaction to occur, final payment taking place later. C. A. E. Goodhart,[5] amongst others, has therefore divided the essential qualities of money into the medium of exchange function, which is not unique to money, and the means of final payment function, which is. To refer back to our trade credit illustration, although trade credit acts as a medium of exchange it nevertheless cannot act as a *final* means of payment; only money can perform this function.

The same kind of argument could be used to describe the use of credit cards. They permit a transaction to take place without the use of barter; they act as a medium of exchange but cannot themselves be used as the means of final payment. Only cash or a suitable bank deposit (e.g. a current account) can be used for this purpose.

The store of value function of money is clearly not unique to money; there are many other assets which can perform this function. Money is, however, special in one respect: it is

[4] In 1987 domestic trade and other credit owed by industrial and commercial companies amounted to £ 79 billion compared with £ 88 billion bank loans received by these firms.

[5] C.A.E. Goodhart, *Money Information and Uncertainty* (Macmillian, 1975), Chapter 1.

absolutely liquid, and this applies especially to cash. Although we might be able to give an exact definition of the concept of liquidity, the extent to which assets have this characteristic is relative and not exact. An asset can be said to be liquid if it can be used or converted for spending immediately and without capital loss or other penalty. Following on from this definition, liquid assets are usually those assets for which there is an accessible market, e.g. a stock market, or where the issuer of the asset agrees to buy back the asset on demand, e.g. a bank or building society deposit. [6]

It is the case, however, that assets vary in their nearness to being instant spending power and in their degree of capital-value certainty, or financial penalty. An ordinary share can be sold quickly by telephone through the stock market but there is no guarantee as to the price at which it can be sold. A time deposit placed with a bank can be redeemed by the owner without capital loss but only at the time specified, i.e. it is a liquid asset but 'not yet'. A seven-day' bank deposit can usually be converted instantly to a spendable current account deposit, but only with the condition of a loss of a week's interest.

It is possible to designate a spectrum of assets based on their liquidity characteristics. Figure 2.1 represents a simplified illustration of such a spectrum. At one end lies cash, the ultimate in liquidity; at the other are land and buildings, which may well be very illiquid. It is important to realize that where one places a particular asset (real or financial) in such a spectrum can be a matter for argument. For example, is a certificate of deposit with three months to maturity more or less liquid than a trade bill with the same maturity? One can identify notes and coin as money and having absolute liquidity, but moving along the spectrum the liquidity characteristics change. In most circumstances, for example, a cheque book and a cheque guarantee card can be used instead of cash, but not in *all* circumstances: the cheque guarantee is limited to £50, and a shopkeeper or garage is under no obligation to accept a cheque. Clearly, a current account is not quite the

---

[6] A current account bank deposit derives from the implicit agreement by the bank to accept 'instant repurchase' from the customer, i.e. cheques cashable on demand at the bank.

same as cash. This same approach can be extended further along the spectrum.

Some assets are very close to being spendable and others less so. By convention, those assets which are very nearly spendable in most circumstances, e.g. current accounts, seven-day accounts, are regarded as money; those assets which are not instantly spendable, yet are fairly easily convertible into cash, have been designated *quasi-money* (i.e. not-quite money). Which assets are quasi-money has been the subject of debate, but such financial assets as National Savings certificates, Treasury bills, and certain building society and bank deposits might well be termed quasi-money.

Because the identification of money is important for purposes of economic policy as well as of theoretical interest, there has been much analysis in the economics literature as to how one might disentangle the problem. One way of doing this is to identify substitutability amongst assets. As we have seen, although money possesses a unique property in being a means of payment, it is not unique as a financial asset since there are clearly many other forms of financial asset available. To illustrate the problem, let us take the analogy of an ordinary commodity, e.g. butter. There are obviously a number of substitutes for butter – margarine and other fats – and we can be sure that these are substitutes for butter because we can observe the response of consumers to change in the price of such substitutes. If the price of margarine rises, then to some extent people will switch their buying away from margarine and towards butter; they will buy less margarine and more butter. Similarly a change in the price of butter will cause a change in the demand for butter substitutes. However, if there are *no* substitutes for butter then a change in the price of butter will not result in a change in the demand for other commodities as a direct consequence of the change in the price of butter. People will either continue to buy the same quantity of butter or buy less if their income is sufficient to cover all other expenditures as well as maintaining their butter purchases. There would be no switching to other commodities. At the other extreme, if margarine and other fats are *very good* substitutes for butter then a relatively small rise in the price of butter will result in a substantial switch of demand away from butter towards the

Notes and coins
Bank current accounts Building society ordinary accounts
Seven-day deposit accounts
Time deposits with banks and other financial institutions
Treasury bills
Commercial bills, certificates of deposit
Government securities
Corporate loan stock
Shares
Buildings, machines Land

Figure 2.1 *Liquidity spectrum of selected assets*

various substitutes. The concept which we are using here is known as the price-elasticity of demand [7] (price-responsiveness of demand), and the greater the price-elasticity (responsiveness) the greater will be the switch of demand in response to a relatively small change in the price of butter. It should now be

---

[7] The demand for different products will respond differently to changes in price, and it is this relationship to which the concept of price-elasticity of demand refers. One simple measure is

$$\text{price-elasticity of demand} = \frac{\text{percentage change in demand}}{\text{percentage change in price}}$$

We can also measure the relationship between the demand for one commodity and the price of another, and this is the relationship that is referred to in the text. It is known as the cross-elasticity of demand:

$$\text{cross-elasticity of demand} = \frac{\text{percentage change in demand for commodity X}}{\text{percentage change in price of commodity Y}}$$

clear that the size of this responsiveness to a price change is one way we can establish the degree of substitutability of butter for other fats. A high degree of responsiveness indicates that butter and other fats are good substitutes and a low degree of responsiveness suggests that they are not good substitutes.

We can use this approach when considering whether money can be uniquely identified or if there are in fact substitutes for money. In this case we shall use the rate of interest as our 'price', i.e. the means by which we shall test the existence of substitutes. Let us suppose we have four assets; cash, current account deposits, deposit accounts, building society deposits. Furthermore we will assume that the rate of interest paid on building society deposits rises substantially and the rate of interest on deposit accounts does not alter. What is likely to happen? It is probable that there will be a switch of funds from deposit accounts to building society accounts. In other words, building society deposits and bank deposits may be substitutes to some degree. Now let us suppose further that the rate on deposit accounts also rises. A possible consequence of this is that there would be some switching back of funds from the building societies; but apart from this possibility, what would be the effect on the size of current accounts? It may well be that individuals decide to prune their current accounts to the very minimum required, or indeed so to adjust the timing of their spending that they are able to reduce their current accounts and transfer funds to deposit accounts. It is also conceivable that individuals may even try to economize on their cash balances in order to take advantage of the higher interest rates. (Of course, if cash and current account balances are already at the absolute minimum then a change in interest rates will produce no effect on such balances.) This type of response by individuals to changes in interest rates, if it did occur in the way we have suggested, would be an indication that the four types of assets are in some degree substitutes. By analogy with our butter example, we can suggest that if the response to change in interest rates is relatively large, i.e. a small change in interest rates results in a large switch in the holding of one form of asset for another, this indicates a high degree of substitutability between the assets. If a large change in interest rates produced only a small change in the holding of one form of asset, then this would suggest a low degree of substitutability.

There is some evidence that substitutability does exist between various types of deposit and it has been suggested therefore that attempting to identify definitively those assets which are unambiguously 'money' is a mistaken approach. Nevertheless one can accept the implications of the 'substitutability argument' and at the same time identify those assets which perform the function of means of payment in the UK. Notes and coins in circulation are clearly means of payment since they are legal tender, and current account deposits (demand deposits) are accepted extensively as a means of payment. Furthermore, current account and deposit accounts can be switched easily, i.e. one can use funds in the deposit account as part of one's current account, in effect, but with the penalty of loss of one week's interest. This facility or convention allows us, therefore, to combine the two types of deposit at least for the purpose of defining money. Whether we can go beyond these assets is, as we have indicated, a debatable question and it is one to which we return in the next section.

2.4.3 MONEY STOCK DATA

Section 2.4.2 has shown that defining what money is within the context of a modern economy is rather difficult; at least, it is difficult to draw a hard-and-fast line which is a totally reliable division. It is therefore not surprising that amongst economists this problem of definition is still a source of debate and controversy. There are some economists who take a 'narrow' view of what money is; they suggest that the means of payment functions is *the* deciding factor, and accordingly only cash and current account deposits fulfil this role. On this view of narrow money the inclusion of various assets within the definition would be related to whether they are closely involved in the *spending* behaviour of individuals. On the other hand, other economists suggest that one is really concerned with that collection of liquid assets which are reasonably close substitutes for each other, some of which would be interest-earning assets and would be regarded by their owners as primarily a form of financial investment. 'Liquidity' rather than 'medium of exchange' would be the criterion used to determine which assets should be included in the definition of broad money. The possibility that such a group of assets may not satisfy in a thorough way some theoretical requirement about the nature of money is therefore regarded as largely irrelevant. However, the debate is not settled, and neither the 'narrow definition' of money, as it is called, nor the 'broad definition', is entirely satisfactory. The Bank of England and other central banks therefore publish in their statistical series different definitions of the money stock.

2.4.3.1 Bank of England experience

The Bank of England first published data on the money stock in September 1970,[8] providing three choices of definition. The first, narrow definition, known as M1, consisted of notes and coin in circulation with the public plus sterling current accounts held by the private sector only. The public sector and the external sector holdings were excluded from this definition. A somewhat broader definition, M2, was also devised, and this included M1 but with the definition of private sector sterling deposit accounts with the deposit banks and the discount houses. Finally, a broad definition, M3, was also provided, which included M2 plus all other deposits (sterling and non-sterling) held with the UK banking sector without distinguishing between public and private sector accounts.

In June 1972 the Bank ceased to calculate M2, producing the series for the narrow definition M1 and the contrasting broad definition M3. As well as those changes the Bank introduced certain differences in definition; for example, 'current accounts' were replaced by 'sight deposits'. One of the reasons for this is that 'sight deposits' is an expression which has greater precision of meaning than simply 'current accounts'; 'sight deposits' refers to funds which are available on demand. This is the notion really underlying the classification and use of 'current accounts', but this particular terminology does exclude funds placed 'at call' and which should really be included. The Bank of England also divided M3 into a gross figure and a calculation for sterling deposits (M3 and £M3).

[8]Bank of England *Quarterly Bulletin*, vol. 10, no. 3. (September 1970), p. 320.

The Bank of England published in September 1979 a new series of financial data. This series, entitled 'components of private sector liquidity', was a much broader concept than the traditional money stock data. In the construction of the data for private sector liquidity (PSL) the Bank's emphasis was on the notion of 'liquidity', and the different groups of assets included in the calculation were clustered on the basis of their substitutability. The Bank accepted that there was inevitably an arbitrary element in the choice and presentation of components of PSL as well as deficiencies in the data used. But it was hoped that with time the PSL series might become a valuable statistical series of relevance to the private sector's economic and financial behaviour.

The four main components of the PSL series were 'money', certain money market assets, savings deposits and securities, and certificates of tax deposit. The Bank calculated two measures of private sector liquidity; the broader measure, PSL2, included building society shares and deposits and similar forms of liquid savings instruments.

It is evident that choosing and calculating an 'appropriate' monetary aggregate is not an easy task for a central bank. In an attempt to improve the information available, the Bank of England began calculating from November 1981 a new monetary series, M2, for transactions balances. As its name implies, this new monetary aggregate was intended to identify those types of deposits which might be most readily used for transactions purposes. The other monetary aggregates, M1 and M3, could not be used as a measure of transactions balances. For example, M1 excluded from its calculation clearing banks' seven-day deposits, and yet these deposits, although nominally requiring notice of withdrawal, in practice are available on demand; and it is likely that some part of these balances might be used for transactions purposes. On the other hand, M3 included *all* sight and time deposits, and it is probable that a substantial part of these deposits were treated as financial investments by their holders and therefore not likely to be used for transactions purposes. Furthermore, highly liquid building society deposits could not be ignored since these constitute transactions balances for a very large number of depositors.

In the March 1981 issue of the Bank of England *Quarterly Bulletin* the Bank discussed the measurement and components of a new monetary aggregate: the wide monetary base. This consists of notes and coin held by the public, banks' holdings of cash (till money), and banks' operational balances at the Bank of England. The operational balances are cash account deposits

Table 2.4

Money and financial data at end 1980 (£b)

M1	£M3	M3	PSL1	PSL2
30.6	68.8	75.4	72.6	122.0

Source : Annual Abstract of Statistics

which are held mainly by the clearing banks in order to facilitate the cheque clearing process. Subsequently, the wide monetary base was published by the Bank of England as Mo. There is some doubt whether this particular calculation of the money stock is useful. Research done by the Bank of England itself implies that Mo might be of limited value as an instrument of monetary policy. Indeed, the Chancellor has been cautious in his remarks about Mo; it might only be used as an *indicator* of the growth of narrow money rather than an instrument of economic policy. *Table 2.4* shows the money and financial data calculated for the end of 1980.

2.4.3.2 Contemporary calculations of the money stock

In May 1987 the Bank of England recast and renamed the monetary aggregates. In the associated article describing the changes, the Bank makes the following point : 'The inescapable conclusion is that there can be no unique definition of broad money. Any choice of dividing line between those financial assets included in, and those excluded from, broad money is to a degree arbitrary, and is likely over time to be invalidated by developments in the financial system.' In other words, the Bank is recognizing the high degree of substitutability between liquid assets, including money, and also emphasizing that financial innovation – such as the introduction of new kinds of deposits and other financial instruments – by banks and others is likely to cause further future changes in definitions and components of the monetary aggregates. *Figure 2.2* provides a striking

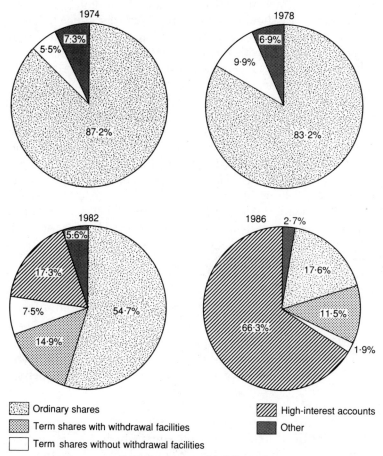

Figure 2.2 *Innovation in types of building society accounts*

Source : Bank of England *Quarterly Bulletin*

example of such financial innovation and change within the building society movement. In particular, the decline in popularity of accounts without withdrawal facilities is evident as well as the decline of the ordinary accounts.

Figure 2.3 and *Table 2.5* give the new monetary definitions and provide numerical illustration of their size. *Figure 2.4* provides a simplified representation of the components of the various aggregates. A number of features are clear from the data. The public's cash requirements grow fairly slowly (2.7

per cent p.a.), and in view of the limited convenience of cash for purchases we should not be surprised at that. Since the bulk of Mo consists of cash held by the public, its similarly low rate of growth (4.9 per cent p.a.) is understandable. However, the other monetary aggregates are different not only in absolute size but also in their growth rates. M1, which is largely sight deposits with the banks (about half of which is overnight money – not just current accounts – placed with banks by firms and financial institutions), has grown on average by 21 per cent each year but is only around one-third as large as the broad money aggregate M4. M2 comprises *non-interest-bearing* sight deposits together with relatively small interest-bearing bank and building society deposits. This calculation is an attempt to capture those small deposits which are probably regarded by their holders as balances largely intended for *transactions* rather than as a financial investment. M2 would be expected perhaps to grow in line with money spending in the economy. From the definition of M4 it is clear that the substantial difference between M3 and M4 is caused by the inclusion of building society shares and deposits within M4.

Although there may well be economic significance in the different rates of growth of the monetary aggregates, it has to be realized that differences can arise simply because of the definitions themselves and not necessarily because there has been a significant change in behaviour. Nevertheless, changes in behaviour can come about because of (a) changes in interest rates yielded by the different financial assets which are the components of the various definitions of money, and (b) changes in the money–income of individuals and companies. For example, a rise in household income would tend to increase the quantity of cash held by the public, and this would increase Mo. However, since cash held by the public is included in the other definitions as well, they too will increase but *proportionately less* than Mo. Changes in relative yields on assets might cause a shift of funds out of, say, non-interest-bearing sight deposits into building society retail (small) shares and deposits. This would cause the M1 calculation to fall, but M2 would remain *unchanged;* M3 would also fall, but M4 would remain unchanged (since M4 includes building society deposits).

Table 2.5

Monetary aggregates (£m)

	Notes and coin in circulation with public	M_0	M_1	M_2	M_3	M_{3c}	M_4	M_5
1984 III [a]	12,167	13,400	50,327	130,682	108,238	125,718	192,761	205,805
1985 III	12,137	14,100	59,045	142,844	123,492	143,190	218,979	233,043
1986 III	12,444	14,700	73,800	164,949	146,977	174,113	253,479	268,114
1987 III	13,179	15,460	89,209	182,109	176,634	207,577	292,556	307,603
Annual % change								
1984 – 87	+ 2.7	+ 4.9	+ 21.0	+ 11.7	+17.7	+ 18.2	+ 14.9	+ 14.3

[a] III indicates that the data is for the third quarter of the year.

Source : various Bank of England Quarterly Bulletins

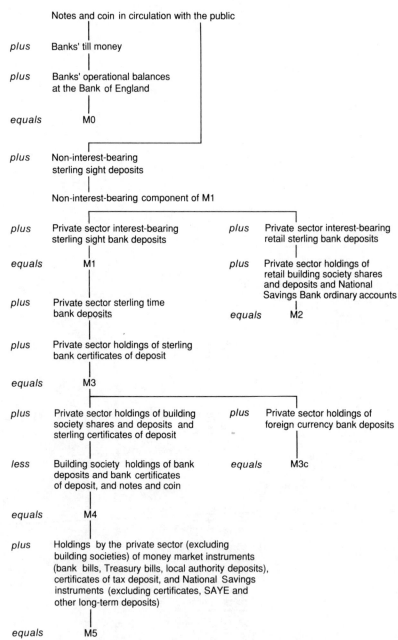

Figure 2.3 *Relationships among monetary aggregates and their components*

In general, as one moves from Mo to M5 the size of the aggregates increases (see *Figure 2.4*) because the monetary definitions include additional liquid assets. These range from the absolutely liquid cash through to time deposits with the banks, and further on include less liquid assets such as Treasury bills and National Savings instruments. We shall be assessing the underlying causes of changes in the monetary aggregates more thoroughly in Chapter 5.

2.5 Summary

(a) The financial system of a modern economy produces a variety of services which cater for the different needs of individuals and firms. This function of financial firms is one with which most people are familiar, but there is another, broader function which the financial system performs and that is the production of financial assets.

(b) Financial assets are part of the total wealth of an individual, the other type of wealth being real (i.e. tangible) assets. However, for the community as a whole financial assets might not really be part of wealth, since such assets have a corresponding liability. Thus the *net* position might be more appropriate: total assets minus total liabilities. If this is so, the net wealth of the community is virtually its physical assets, since financial assets would seem to wash out when offset by financial liabilities.

(c) The growth of financial claims tends to exceed the growth of (physical) capital assets. Two reasons were put forward for this feature. One was that some claims arise because firms, individuals, and governments sometimes go into debt in order to finance current rather than capital expenditure. Additionally, the process of raising funds *indirectly* for use by industrial firms can result in a replication of financial assets/liabilities by virtue of the intermediate operation of financial firms. The balance sheet of the personal sector (*Table 2.1*) was used to illustrate wealth–accumulation behaviour and seemed to show fairly clear preferences as well as changes in behaviour.

(d) Money is the most liquid financial asset in the system. It performs certain functions : medium of exchange and means of final payment; store of value; unit of account; standard for deferred payments. The medium of exchange

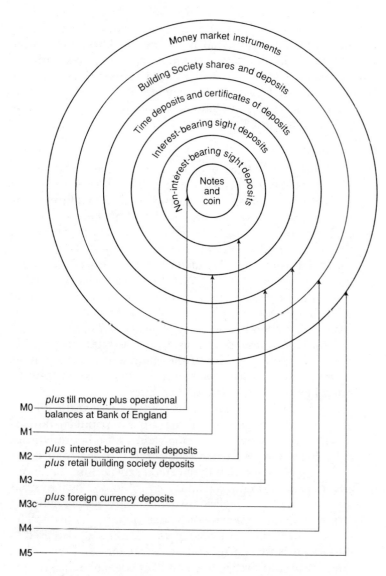

Figure 2.4 *Definitions of the monetary aggregates*

and means of final payment function can be identified as
the most important, since other assets may well perform the

other three functions and, in certain circumstances (e.g. inflationary conditions), do so better than money.

(e) Since money can be designated a financial asset, the possibility of there being substitute financial assets has to be considered. The sensitivity of money holding with respect to changes in the rate of interest on alternative assets was a possible means of detecting the degree or existence of money substitutes.

(f) The problem of identifying money in a modern economy in an unambiguous way has resulted in the production of money stock data, which cover both a narrow approach to money and a broad approach. The narrow approach usually identifies the means of payment function of money and limits the inclusion of assets to those which can be ascribed this role, whereas the broad definition includes other near-money assets, partly on the basis of the substitutability argument.

Postscript

On the 12 July 1989 the Abbey National Building Society became a plc and also a bank. Consequently the balance sheet data for the Abbey National would be included with the retail bank group. Not only would this result in a discontinuity in the statistical series but it would also change the data significantly because of the size of the Abbey National. This event, together with other changes within the financial system has presented the Bank of England with an opportunity to re-think its definitions of the monetary aggregates. Final proposals are likely to emerge towards the end of 1989 but for the present, the Bank has decided to end the publication of the series : M1, M3, and to replace M3c with a new series M4c which will be M4 plus foreign currency deposits placed with UK banks. These changes arise, according to the Bank, because of the large discontinuities created by the re-classification of the Abbey National and the possibility of other building societies becoming plc and applying to change status to that of a bank.

3

Financial intermediation

3.1 Introduction

We have so far considered only in passing the role and operation of financial firms within the economy. It is the purpose of Chapter 3 to delve into the basic operation of such firms and also provide the reader with an overview of their general functioning. Although in reality the range and variety of financial firms is considerable, fortunately it is possible to identify certain features which have general applicability.

3.2 The nature of financial intermediation

3.2.1 FINANCIAL INTERMEDIARIES

In the previous chapter we referred rather loosely to 'financial firms' without specifying the nature of their business which would justify a more precise description or name. Our intention in Chapter 3 is to provide a sharper picture of the sort of firms to which we have referred and the nature of their business operations. If one studies the financial columns of the newspapers or indeed merely looks down the high street of most towns, one would observe an almost bewildering array of competing firms : banks of different kinds, building societies, 'credit agencies', and so on. Fortunately we can simplify the situation by ascribing to these types of business the name and function of 'financial intermediary'. We are able to make this simplification because all these firms have a common function, which is to stand in between those who wish to lend and those who wish to borrow; or, in the terminology used in Chapter 1, to stand in between those with budget surpluses and those who wish to run budget deficits. *Figure 3.1* illustrates in a simple fashion the contrasting possibilities.

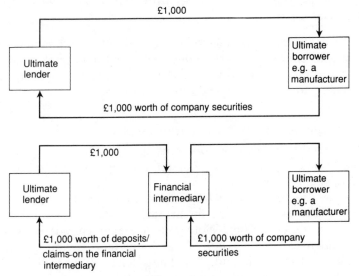

Figure 3.1

The upper section of *Figure 3.1* shows a situation where a financial intermediary does not enter the relationship between the borrower and lender. In this case there is a direct flow of funds between those with surpluses (lenders) and those intending to run deficits (borrowers). An example of this type of relationship might be where a saver decides to buy the new shares of a company which are offered for sale by advertisement in a newspaper. In the lower part of *Figure 3.1* the primary (or ultimate) lender does not provide funds directly to the final (or ultimate) borrower but places funds with a financial intermediary and in return has a deposit or claim on the financial intermediary. (Whether it is a deposit or another type of claim depends on the kind of financial intermediary. For example, if funds are placed with a bank the resulting claim on the bank is in the form of a bank deposit, whereas the payment of a life-insurance premium to an insurance company constitutes simply a claim on the company, which may be 'presented' if death of the insured occurs or, in the case of say an endowment policy, at the maturity date of the policy.) Having received the funds from the ultimate lender the financial intermediary is capable of on-lending such funds to the ultimate borrower, who in turn provides security or securities which are held by the financial intermediary.

The reader at this stage might ask why it is necessary for a financial intermediary to stand in between the ultimate lender and the ultimate borrower. The next section of this chapter attempts to answer this and other questions.

3.2.2 THE NEED FOR FINANCIAL INTERMEDIATION

Perhaps the best way of examining this question is to consider the various circumstances and requirements which apply to lenders and borrowers.

Lenders One might ask what factors influence a lender's selection of the various outlets for his savings, thereby obtaining a claim or financial asset. (Note that we are not considering here the much broader question of why individuals *save*, in contrast with the decision to lend.) Obviously for different individuals there are a number of common elements.

Most potential lenders would probably wish to minimize the risks which attend their lending. In these circumstances risk can take a number of forms : the risk of default, i.e. the borrower is unable to repay; the risk that the market value of the asset held by the lender may fall and thus reduce the wealth of the individual; the risk that the lender may need funds before the loan is due to be repaid, i.e. the term of the loan may in the event prove to have been too long; the risk associated with inadequately diversified assets.

It is likely that a potential lender will consider two other aspects of the transaction : convenience and liquidity (these two are not unrelated to the question of risk). Lenders may have neither the time nor the inclination to examine in sufficient depth the opportunities for different forms of lending which may exist. Many lenders may be disinclined to study the considerable amount of material which is published by companies relating to their commercial and financial status – documentation which is relevant to the decision facing the lender/investor. Thus the existence of assets which eliminate or reduce this type of information gathering and analysis would be of benefit to such individuals.

Perhaps most important of all, the lender is likely to be concerned about the liquidity of his investment. The term *liquidity* can be given a variety of meanings, but in this context we are considering a mix of qualities : the ease with which an asset can be sold and converted into money at the convenience of the holder, and the certainty that the capital value of the asset will be maintained. Many lenders are likely to be very conscious of the uncertainty which attends their own future needs for funds – a chance event may result in an individual's unexpected need for funds – and for many lenders, therefore, the liquidity characteristics of their investment will be very important. One expression of this concern may be a preference by lenders for relatively short-term lending.

Borrowers In some respect the needs of the borrower are rather simpler to express than those of the lender. Fundamentally the borrower requires funds at a particular point in time, for a given period of time, and at the lowest cost. In exchange for such funds the borrower will provide the lender with some form of claim against himself. Such claims may take a variety of forms – shares, bills of exchange, bonds, etc. – but whatever the form, the claim must be acceptable to the lender, otherwise the provision of funds cannot take place. In addition the borrower will require information about the markets for funds in order that successful borrowing takes place. Without such information the borrower may find that either insufficient funds are obtained or they are obtained at higher rates of interest than necessary.

There are at least two major risks which face the potential borrower. One is that the funds required at a particular time may not be available. This may be a result of an overall shortage of funds in the market or imperfect transmission of information within the market, i.e. a potential lender exists but is unaware of the existence of a suitable borrower. The other risk is that the lender may wish to terminate the loan at a time which is inconvenient to the borrower. This in turn may cause the borrower to reborrow, perhaps at higher rates of interest – assuming of course that alternative funds are available. If reborrowing is not possible, then the borrower may be forced to sell assets in order to meet the demand of the lender.

A great deal of borrowing by companies is for the purchase of capital equipment, and much capital equipment (machines, factory buildings, etc.) has a long life. Partly for this reason, a firm which wishes to borrow for the purchase of capital equipment may require the term of the loan to be lengthy so that there is opportunity for the capital equipment to generate sufficient funds to 'pay for itself' over the whole or part of its life.

From what we have discussed so far it is clear that lenders and borrowers are likely to have sets of needs which have to be satisfied before a financial transaction between the two parties can take place. The asset or claim which the borrower provides has to meet the various requirements of the lender – minimum risk, liquidity, etc. – but at the same time the needs or require-ments of the lender must not be too demanding, otherwise the potential borrower will be dissuaded from borrowing and the potential lender will be deprived of an opportunity to make use of his spare funds. An alternative way of expressing the problem in the lender/borrower relationship is that the needs of the lender and borrower may not match. For example, it may be the case that the majority of potential lenders prefer to lend for relatively *short* periods whereas the majority of borrowers prefer to borrow for *long* periods. Clearly if some lending and borrow-ing is to take place there will need to be some means by which the non-matching of needs is resolved. One way this may occur is through the market mechanism itself. Taking the previous example, the problem of short-term/long-term preferences may be resolved by the market if the rate of interest on long-term lending rose sufficiently relatively to short-term lending. Such a change in interest rate would tend to persuade some lenders to 'lend long' and some borrowers to 'borrow short', and thus both groups could be satisfied. However, changes in market interest rates are not the only means by which the incompatibility of requirements of lenders and borrowers can be resolved. Finan-cial intermediation provides an additional way in which the needs of *both* the lender and the borrower can be met.

3.2.3 THE PROCESS OF FINANCIAL INTERMEDIATION

The previous section has shown that in the market for loans there is a problem of reconciling the needs of lenders and borrowers, and it was suggested that the existence of financial intermediaries could help to overcome this problem. This section will examine more closely the operation of a financial intermediary and then show how such operation can help to satisfy both lenders and borrowers.

Figure 3.1 shows the financial intermediary receiving funds from the ultimate lender and then on-lending these funds to the ultimate borrower. At first sight this would seem to be little different to the direct provision of funds from lender to borrower. However, this is not the case since the financial intermediary has provided the ultimate lender with a *different kind* of asset than would have been the case with the direct provision of funds. Furthermore, the financial intermediary has on-lent the funds in exchange for an asset which is less liquid than the corresponding liability in the balance sheet of the financial intermediary.

Broadly speaking, the assets of financial intermediaries are less liquid than the corresponding liabilities. We can make this more clear by the use of a familiar institution – a deposit bank. Such banks, as part of their ordinary course of business, will receive funds which are deposited with them in the form of demand deposits (current account deposits) or savings deposits (deposit accounts). These funds are then used for the purchase of assets, the largest single category being lending to customers. The liabilities of the banks are their deposits, of which a large proportion are repayable on demand, i.e. for the holder of such deposits they are a very liquid asset since they can be converted into cash entirely at the convenience of the holder. However, the bulk of the assets held by the banks are much less liquid than this and cannot be converted into cash at the whim of the bank; many assets, e.g. certain loans to customers, government bond holdings, are for a period of years. A similar situation applies to an insurance company. [1] It has policy-holders who

---

[1] Although these assets may be sold on the stock market by banks and insurance companies they might be reluctant to do so because stock market prices of such securities could be at an unsatisfactorily low level. The decision to sell these assets might thus involve these intermediaries in the risk of capital loss.

may make a claim (the liability of the insurance company) at any moment, whereas its assets (e.g. government bonds, ordinary shares) may not readily be encashed; the assets are less liquid than the liabilities. Whatever the particular type of financial intermediary one is considering, all of them perform the function of creating assets (liabilities against themselves) which are more liquid than the assets which they themselves hold. Their operation is not merely that of being a middleman, i.e. simply passing on funds; they actually generate a new type of asset which is acceptable to the ultimate lender.

Having established this primary operation of financial intermediaries, we can now consider the way this function helps to satisfy the requirements of the ultimate lender *and* ultimate borrower. As before, we shall consider the lender and borrower separately.

Lenders The financial intermediary is able to offer the lender a more liquid asset than the asset obtained from the ultimate borrower by the financial intermediary. This allows the lender to satisfy more easily his need for liquidity and minimum risk associated with his lending. Without the operation of the financial intermediary the lender would either have to buy the less liquid asset offered by the ultimate borrower or not lend at all. By virtue of specialization the financial intermediary is able also to solve the lender's problem of information since the managers of the financial intermediary will accumulate skills associated with the use of funds and the purchase of assets. The lender simply has to decide which sort of financial intermediary suits his needs rather than which type of asset, from a wide range of assets, he wishes to purchase with his funds. Thus the lender has, for example, merely to decide whether to use a building society, deposit bank, Trustee Savings Bank, etc., rather than to choose from a very large range and variety of competing assets. The problem of choice is not eliminated by the existence of financial intermediaries, but for many lenders the problem is made simpler. Furthermore the financial intermediary can act as a diversifying agent for the lender in a way which, say, the small lender would be unable to perform. Possibly the best illustration of this is the unit trust, in which a lender is able to invest relatively small sums by buying units which are based on a spread of companies (see Section 4.13).

Borrowers Some of the problems facing the borrower are also more easily overcome with the aid of financial intermediaries. The specialized nature of financial intermediaries and the scale of their operation does influence the overall provision of funds, since the advantages they offer to potential lenders are likely to encourage the maximum volume of funds flowing from lenders. In addition the scale of operation of financial intermediaries may alleviate the problem of uncertainty of availability of funds for borrowers. This is because there is a greater likelihood that an unexpected reduction in funds flowing to the financial intermediary from one source is offset by additional funds from another. Finally, the existence of financial intermediaries is likely to result in a lower rate of interest paid by the borrower. Lenders will be prepared to accept a lower rate paid to them by the financial intermediary because part of the return lenders obtain is in the form of the liquidity quality of the asset created by the financial intermediary. Thus lenders are content with a lower rate of interest and, in turn, borrowers pay a lower rate. In the absence of financial intermediaries, risks would be greater for the individual lender and accordingly interest rates would have to be higher to compensate for this.

3.2.4 THE ECONOMIC BASIS OF FINANCIAL INTERMEDIATION

So far in this chapter we have described *in general* how all financial intermediaries behave, as well as outlining certain benefits from financial intermediation which may accrue to both the ultimate lender and the ultimate borrower. The purpose of this section is to explain *why* it is possible for financial intermediaries to operate in the way described.

Large-scale operation by financial intermediaries allows them to benefit from a phenomenon which is essentially statistical in nature, and probably the clearest example of this is to be found in the operation of insurance companies. We suggested earlier that the liability of an insurance company is its obligation to pay the policy-holder if the event which is the subject of the insurance agreement actually occurs. For example, the chances that a man aged 20 living in the UK will die within one year are approximately 12 in 10,000, whereas a man aged 75 has almost a 1 in 10 chance that he will die within one year.

This kind of information is calculable for all age groups and is given in considerable detail – likely cause of death, etc. Since population data are also available it is a relatively easy matter to calculate how many people will die within a year, their ages at death, and causes of death. An insurance company will have many policy-holders, and as a group they will probably be representative of the population at large; therefore each insurance company is able to calculate the likely claims which will be made in a given year, and the funds which the company will need to pay the claimants. In order that such claims can be met, the insurance company will need to use the premiums it receives to purchase assets which either mature at the appropriate time or provide sufficient income to meet the likely claims. It is to be noted that the successful operation of the insurance company rests on having a large enough number of policy-holders who are typical of the population at large together with judicious investment of the premiums which flow into the company. If both these conditions are met, the insurance company will be able to operate successfully despite the fact that its assets are less liquid than its liabilities.

A bank also relies on the same kind of statistical phenomenon illustrated for the insurance company. In this instance, however, the problem relates to the likelihood of there being a net withdrawal of funds by depositors resulting in a change in total bank deposits. Observing the day-to-day operation of a bank, we would notice that some depositors are withdrawing funds and at the same time other depositors are placing funds in their accounts. If the bank has a large number of accounts, it is possible that at the same time as one depositor is withdrawing, say, £100 another depositor is depositing £100. The larger the number of accounts the more likely it is that this offsetting phenomenon is taking place. In the same way as the insurance company is able to calculate its liabilities, a bank should be able to make statistical estimates of likely withdrawals and deposits. Provided the bank has a sufficient number of accounts for this offsetting flow of funds to occur, it can purchase profitable earning assets or make loans (with the *net* funds on deposit) which, although less liquid than the banks liabilities, do not result in the bank necessarily risking insolvency.

It is unlikely, however, that the offsetting flow of funds occurs in reality as satisfactorily as in our illustration. One cause of the lack of perfect offsetting is the seasonal variations in the need for cash and the transfer of funds. Nevertheless this problem can be resolved by a bank if it ensures that a proportion of its assets are very liquid, either cash itself or other assets which can be easily converted into cash without risk of capital loss. Experience gained over time will enable a bank to anticipate seasonal and other changes and therefore allow it to adjust its assets accordingly.

It is important to realize that in both our illustrations – the insurance company and the bank – the basic features of financial intermediaries' operations are the same :

(a) The intermediaries rely on a scale of operation sufficiently large to allow them to estimate the probability of changes in their liability position.

(b) The known probabilities associated with their liabilities permit financial intermediaries to purchase assets which are less liquid than their liabilities, and yet to remain solvent.

(c) The intermediaries do not merely pass on funds which have been deposited with them, but in addition create another type of financial asset which constitutes their liabilities. It is this particular factor which differentiates the operation of financial intermediaries from that of middlemen or brokers, whose function is simply to bring the lender and borrower together rather than to operate between them.

A modification of *Figure 3.1* allows it to make point (c) more clearly. *Figure 3.2* shows that the ultimate lender, by lending to the financial intermediary, obtains another kind of financial asset – one which is attractive because it offers interest and yet is highly liquid. The financial intermediary has generated a new kind of asset which did not exist before intermediation. In *Table 3.1* we have summarized the position by aggregating assets and liabilities in the two situations : where lending takes place *directly* to the borrower; and where lending is done *indirectly* via a financial intermediary. In both cases the net asset position is the same (£ 1,000) but the asset total is not; the act of financial intermediation has added to the stock of assets by £ 1,000.

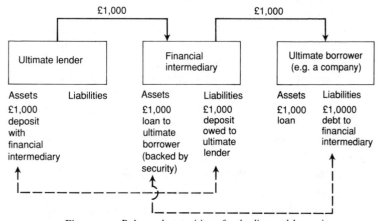

Figure 3.2 *Balance sheet position after lending and borrowing*

Table 3.1 *Aggregate balance sheet position after lending (£)*

Before financial intermediation

Assets		Liabilities	
Money balance held by ultimate borrower (i.e. the company)	1,000	Debt of company to ultimate lender	1,000
Liability of company, held by ultimate lender	1,000	Balancing item : *Net assets*	1,000

After financial intermediation

Assets		Liabilities	
Ultimate lender's deposit with financial intermediary	1,000	Obligation (liability) of financial intermediary to ultimate lender	1,000
Financial intermediary's claim on company (ultimate borrower)	1,000	Obligation (liability) of financial intermediary to ultimate borrower	1,000
Company's money balance held with financial intermediary	1,000	Balancing item : *Net assets*	1,000

There is a further benefit from the large-scale operations of financial intermediaries, which is that the risk of an individual investor (the lender) losing his money is reduced as the size of the intermediaries' operations increase. This reduction in risk for the lender arises for two reasons. One is that the financial intermediary will be able to diversify its assets, i.e. it will hold a *range* of assets of varying degrees of riskiness and return. (The unit trust was an example we used earlier.) The alternative facing an individual small lender may well be to 'put all his eggs in one basket' by placing funds in a single form of investment – a risky proposition. The other reason for the reduction in risk is simply the result of the scale of operations of the intermediary.

To illustrate this point, let us suppose that an individual lender wishes to invest £ 1,000 and chooses to lend the money directly to, say, a friend who wishes to start a business. We will assume that there is a 1 in 20 chance that the borrower will default completely, i.e. at the end of the term of the loan the lender receives the whole of his money back or *nothing at all*. For simplicity we are ignoring the fact that the lender will receive interest on the loan. We need to emphasize the point : the lender faces a 5 per cent chance (1 in 20) that he will lose *all* his investment. Now let us assume that instead of direct lending to the ultimate borrower the lender places his £ 1,000 with a financial intermediary, which is also faced with a 5 per cent chance that the borrower will be unable to repay, and that the financial intermediary has received other deposits so that its total deposits are £ 1,000,000, which it has used to make 1,000 loans of £ 1,000 each. Since 5 per cent of the loans will be bad debts and not repaid to the financial intermediary, the intermediary can *expect* to lose £ 50,000 on those loans. Before considering how the financial intermediary can deal with this, let us return to our individual depositor who has placed £ 1,000 with the intermediary. We can now see that he has exchanged a 5 per cent chance that he will lose all his money if he lends directly to a borrower, for a near certainty that he will lose 5 per cent of his investment as a result of the spreading of a loss of £ 50,000 over all depositors with the financial intermediary.

The opportunity to exchange the risk of losing all one's investment for a near certainty of losing a small fraction of that investment is one which many lenders are willing to take. Furthermore, the rate of interest charged by the financial intermediary can be adjusted so that in the long run the bad debts are covered. Many people cannot risk losing all their savings, and for such individuals a financial intermediary offers considerable benefits.

This section on the economic basis of financial intermediation has highlighted two crucial characteristics of intermediation, which explain why financial intermediaries have developed
and become dominant in the process of saving, lending, and
borrowing. As we have seen, lending involves risk, but financial
intermediaries are able to change the nature of the risk which
lenders experience. This function of *risk transmutation* is one
which intermediaries are able to perform because they operate
on a large scale and as a consequence are able to spread the risk
amongst a large number of lenders (and borrowers). Financial
intermediaries are therefore more than just collecters of funds;
they are not middlemen, but agencies which perform a function
that few individuals are able to do for themselves. Not only do
intermediaries transmute risk, but they also effectively change
the maturity characteristics of the assets which the ultimate
lender might obtain. We demonstrated this phenomenon of
maturity transformation in *Figure 3.2* and, to put it simply, this
function is that of 'borrowing short and lending long' without
necessarily becoming illiquid or insolvent. Again, the performance of this role hinges on the scale of operation of the
intermediary and the accompanying predictions about the
behaviour of the *net* 'deposits' of the intermediary. Together
with the judicious selection of adequate liquid assets, the
economies of scale should ensure that an intermediary not only
meets the needs of both lender and borrower, but also remains
solvent.

3.3 Financial intermediaries and the economy

So far in this chapter we have emphasized the role and value of
financial intermediaries to the individual lender and borrower.
In this section we shall examine briefly the effect of financial
intermediation in connection with the important activity of
saving and investment.

3.3.1 SAVING AND INVESTMENT

We have already suggested that a large proportion of borrowing is needed to finance investment by firms in both the private
and public sectors. The investment in new capital equipment is
a means by which the community maintains and increases its

stock of capital and this, together with technical improvements, permits productivity increase which in turn allows a rise in the community's standard of living. If firms wish to invest, and the productive capacity in the capital goods industries is sufficient to meet the demand, then clearly any means by which purely *financial* impediments are reduced or eliminated is of value.

Financial intermediaries are important agencies which can help to remove two kinds of impediment. One such impediment is the possibility that potential lenders are unprepared to risk direct financing of firms. We have seen earlier in the chapter that a financial intermediary is able to reduce the risk facing the individual lender. By reducing risk to the ultimate lender, the financial intermediaries encourage the potential lender to lend and thus the total of funds available to firms who wish to invest is larger than would otherwise be the case. Another possible impediment to the flow of saving for investment is the lack of suitable assets for ultimate lenders which are issued by ultimate borrowers. For example, a firm may be engaged in a risky business venture – perhaps developing a new product – and therefore the assets which such a firm could offer in exchange for funds to invest in the venture would also be risky. Such assets may be unacceptable to many lenders and the firm may be unable to obtain the necessary funds. However, the intervention of a financial intermediary would allow the borrower to issue the sort of assets which *most suits* the borrower and yet to obtain the funds required, because the financial intermediary is able to create new financial assets (liabilities against itself) which have a liquidity and riskiness which suit the lender. As we have seen, the risk-spreading operations of financial intermediaries allow this to take place.

3.3.2 INTEREST RATES

A valuable service which financial intermediaries perform is that of meeting the liquidity requirements of lenders. For example, several building societies offer a current account facility (with cheque book, cash card, etc.) earning a low rate of interest; an example is the Nationwide Anglia Flex Account. A higher rate of return is available on other kinds of account but without the cheque account facility. Such an arrangement offers the lender the choice of taking his 'yield' from his investment either in greater convenience (liquidity) and less monetary return (interest) or vice versa. Because of this ability of intermediaries to offer greater liquidity, they are able to offer a lower rate of interest to lenders and still retain their custom. In more general terms, applied to the whole economy, financial intermediaries raise the level of liquidity above what it would otherwise be, and, by virtue of that, rates of return to lenders and therefore *rates of interest* charged to borrowers can be lower. If businesses and their investment plans are sensitive to the level of interest rates then presumably financial intermediaries provide a further encouragement to investment as well as saving.

3.3.3 EFFICIENCY

Financial intermediaries tend to become large. One reason for this is that with an increase in the scale of operations, there is a further spreading of risk. This advantage would therefore increase the attractiveness of the intermediary and, if it were profit-making, would enhance both the level and the realiability of its profits. Other advantages of size which might accrue to both individuals and the community is the accumulation of expertise within the financial intermediary. Such expertise would be predominantly in the area of asset choice by the intermediary itself. By exercising such expertise and deploying its funds accordingly, the intermediary may well be allocating investible funds to those projects which are most viable, offering the highest rate of return consistent with risk, and thus ultimately satisfying the requirement of the community for sound investment in real assets as the foundation of future real income.

3.4 Bank and non-bank financial intermediaries

We have so far suggested that *all* financial intermediaries have a common basis for their operation and the same role with respect to the lender/borrower relationship. However, there has developed over the years a controversy which concerns the difference or alleged difference between two groups of financial intermediary. These two groups are often termed 'bank financial intermediaries' and 'non-bank financial intermediaries', commonly abbreviated to BFI and NBFI. In this section we propose to take a brief look at the substance of this controversy.

It is probably accurate to suggest that both parties to the controversy would accept that all kinds of financial intermediary have the characteristics identified in Section 3.2.4. If this is so, where does the controversy lie? An important aspect of the controversy relates to the precise nature and use to which the liabilities of the financial intermediaries can be put. The reader will recall that by virtue of their intermediation all financial intermediaries *create* liabilities against themselves which are the assets held by the ultimate lender. It is suggested by some economists that the key feature which distinguishes BFIs from NBFIs is that the liabilities created by the BFIs are unique in that these liabilities are themselves 'spendable'. In other words, the liabilities of the deposit banks (e.g. Midland Bank) are used as money by the holders of the deposits, whereas the liabilities of most building societies still cannot be used in this way.

An alternative aspect of this controversy emphasizes the *creation* aspect to BFI activities and the *transmission* activity of the NBFIs. BFIs, it is argued, can actually increase the total volume of spending in the economy by their capacity to *add* to the stock of credit in existence, whereas the NBFIs are merely 'honest brokers' transmitting funds which have been created *elsewhere* , i.e. by the banking system. Essentially, therefore, this argument is suggesting that BFIs can add to the stock of credit and NBFIs cannot. How accurate is this assertion? If by 'credit' we mean the availability of funds to an individual or firm which enables the individual or firm to spend in excess of current income, then one can argue that both BFIs and NBFIs are able to perform this function. An illustration should help to make this point clear. Deposit bank liabilities, i.e. bank deposits, are the major component of the UK money stock. This was revealed in *Table 2.5*, where we saw that notes and coin amounted to about 15 per cent of M_1 and only 7 per cent of M_3. This accords with everyday experience, in which the bulk of transactions (by value) are carried out through transfers of bank deposits and not notes and coin; indeed, notes and coin are the small change of the system. This general acceptability of bank deposits as money has the consequence that a very high proportion of the liabilities of the deposit banking system is never presented to the banking system for redemption. It can be argued that this places the deposit banks in a very special position since the bulk of their liabilities is used as money. Thus a deposit bank which makes a loan to a customer can do so simply by crediting the customer's account by the amount of the loan, and the result of this is a matching rise in bank deposits (liabilities) and 'advances' (assets). Since the bank deposit is as spendable as notes and coin, the customer can obviously spend the bank deposit for the purpose the loan was made. The deposit bank (a BFI) has added to the volume of credit and enabled additional spending to take place.

In contrast, it is difficult to conceive of an NBFI behaving in the same way. Take for example the operation of one of the most important NBFIs, the building society. The building society also lends to customers, but in this case the funds which the building society provides the borrower are not the *creation* of the building society since such funds are in the form of either bank deposits or notes and coin. Thus the building society cannot spontaneously add to its liabilities and provide additional funds to borrowers.[2] On the basis of the discussion so far, one could argue that there *is* a basic difference between the BFI and NBFI and the two categories are justified.

However, one can envisage circumstances in which an NBFI is able to add to the volume of credit and enable additional spending to take place. To illustrate this, let us assume for simplicity that we have one deposit bank and one NBFI (a building society), and that the deposit bank liabilities consist of demand deposits and of savings deposits on which interest is paid by the deposit bank. Now let us assume that the building society raises the rate of interest offered to investors and that this results in some customers of the deposit bank transferring part of their savings deposits to the building society. The building society, having received cheques drawn on the deposit bank, redeposits these cheques in its own account with the deposit bank. Total deposit bank deposits remain un-

---

[2] If building societies had been able to do this one would not have observed the periodic appearance of 'mortgage famines' in the 1960s and early 1970s.

changed; it is their character which has altered, there being less savings deposits and more demand deposits. Since the building society has now received additional funds, it is capable of *adding* to its mortgage lending, making such payments by drawing on its larger demand deposit with the deposit bank. In this illustration it would appear that the building society has added to the volume of credit and enabled additional spending (on house purchase) to take place. On the basis of this second argument it would seem that it is not legitimate to distinguish between BFIs and NBFIs, since both the types of intermediary are capable of adding to the flow of credit and enabling additional spending to occur.

A general conclusion might be that BFIs and NBFIs have fundamental characteristics in common, i.e. both types of intermediary perform the basic role and function of financial intermediation, and that the differences are differences of degree rather than kind. In particular the type of financial assets which the BFIs and NBFIs create for the ultimate lender (e.g. bank deposits by the deposits banks, and building society deposits by the building societies) have qualities in common but in different degrees; liquidity, convenience, risk, etc. can be ascribed to any financial asset, but the combination varies depending on the origin of the asset. It must be admitted that the liabilities created by the deposits banks do have the special quality of being used as money – the means of payment and exchange – whereas other financial assets created by other financial intermediaries do not. However, as one economist put it, 'There is nothing unique about being unique.' In other words, a bank deposit has the special quality of being used as the medium of exchange, but nonetheless the asset created by a building society (or other financial intermediary) for its depositors is also 'special' and different from other financial assets.

Summary

(a) Financial intermediaries interpose themselves between the ultimate lender and ultimate borrower.

(b) Financial intermediaries have flourished because the intermediation function allows them to satisfy the needs of *both* the lender and the borrower to their mutual benefit. Lenders obtain a more liquid and less risky asset, and borrowers obtain greater certainty of funds in exchange for the kind of assets which the ultimate borrower would wish to make available to the lender. Without the intermediary it is possible that a lender may not lend because the asset offered by the borrower in exchange for funds has unacceptable qualities, e.g. it may be too risky or illiquid.

(c) All financial intermediaries have balance sheets which reveal that their assets are less liquid than their liabilities. This condition arises because the intermediary is attempting to satisfy the needs of both the lender and the borrower.

(d) The basis for successful financial intermediation is related to the scale of operation of the intermediaries. Large-scale operation allows the risk of default and other risks to be spread over a large number of investors, and also allows the intermediary to hold a more 'balanced' mix of assets than would be possible for the individual investor/lender. This balanced portfolio helps to reduce the risk of losses which might stem from 'putting all one's financial eggs in one basket'.

(e) The existence and growth of financial intermediaries probably aids the process of saving and investment in the economy. If this is so, financial intermediaries contribute to overall economic growth and the growth in the community's standard of living.

(f) Some economists suggest that one can divide financial intermediaries into two kinds: bank financial intermediaries (BFIs) and non-bank financial intermediaries (NBFIs). The basis for this distinction is debatable. Although it is the case that the liabilities (deposits) of the BFIs are used as *money* (medium of exchange and payment) in the economy, whereas the liabilities of the NBFIs are not, it is nevertheless true that NBFIs are capable of adding to the volume of *credit* in the economy. *If* it is correct that changes in the amount of credit available have more effect on spending in the economy than changes in the money stock, then the distinction between BIFs and NBFIs is relatively unimportant. Furthermore, *all* financial assets created by financial intermediaries have special, and possibly unique, qualities, and it may not be legitimate to single out the liabilities of the BFIs for special mention: 'There is nothing unique about being unique.'

4
Main financial intermediaries

4.1 Introduction

The previous chapters have examined both the nature of a rudimentary financial system and the basic functioning of the intermediaries which operate within it. Chapter 4 is intended to look at the main types of intermediaries which have developed and are based within the United Kingdom, and in particular to consider the nature of their business operations.

Britain, and in particular the City of London, has long been known for its expertise in the field of finance, both domestic and international. The large number of financial firms which operate in London is a testimony to the pre-eminence of 'the City' in the whole area of money and trade. Not only do British banks maintain their head offices in London, but around four hundred foreign banks have established branches there. Such banks represent only a part of the whole financial sector in the UK, comprising not only the domestic and international banks but also a whole range of other financial firms – discount houses, finance houses, insurance companies, investment trusts, and so on. The list is extensive and the number of firms operating is considerable. In 1988 around 3,000 investing institutions held assets approaching the astonishing figure of about £1,400,000 million. This very large sum does obscure the fact that some of the financial institutions are very large and some are very small. For example, the main deposit banks have, on average, sterling and other currency assets amounting to around £25,000 million, whereas each building society has, on average, only £800 million in assets. It should be noted, however, that within both groups of financial intermediary the large institutions dominate. The National Westminster Bank

(the largest UK bank), for example, has assets exceeding
£120,000 million, and the top 17 banks operating in the UK
account for more than half of all assets. Similarly, the largest
building society (the Halifax) accounts for assets of over £33
billion, and within the whole industry the largest societies,
representing about 10 per cent of all societies, hold more than
90 per cent of assets.

4.2 Classification

The diversity of business activity and the range of size of these
financial firms does raise the problem of how to classify and
analyse them. Classifying the firms which compose the finance
industry is not merely a manifestation of the economist's urge to
be tidy, but is necessary in order to produce an orderly
framework which makes analysis of the financial sector
possible.

In general, there are several ways in which one may classify
firms: nature of product, number of employees, value of
turnover, capital structure, legal status, method of operation,
etc. All of these approaches have been used to provide a
framework for studying various industries, and one can, of
course, choose several methods of classification and grouping
for the same industry in order to produce a more complete
picture. One question which arises is how one chooses a
particular method of classification. Briefly, one will choose the
approach which is likely to be most useful in the analysis of a
particular industry or problem. For example, if one is concerned about the extent of monopoly in a certain industry,
probably the most useful method of breakdown would be to
classify the firms within that industry on the basis of their share
of total output. But using such a procedure one would be able
to establish whether a small number of firms held a dominant
position (e.g. 2 per cent of firms producing 60 per cent of total
output), and such analysis would be of some assistance in
deciding the extent to which monopoly is present. If one were
applying this approach to the financial world then one would
discover, for example, that within the building society 'industry' there are many firms – almost two hundred – but the
largest three societies account for around 40 per cent of the
industry's assets. In retail banking, on the other hand, there are

only five or so main banks, and within this group one of them, the National Westminster, dominates.

The 'finance industry' consists of many different types of firm producing a wide range of services, and this presents some difficulty in deciding how to classify them. This difficulty is partly the result of imperfect specialization by financial firms, i.e. many firms perform *several* kinds of function for their customers, and the distinguishing features may not be very clear from mere examination of their balance sheets. It may well be necessary to consider also who their customers are and the way in which they operate their businesses in order to differentiate and classify such firms; a good example of this would be the difference between a deposit bank and an accepting house. Our approach will be to use, initially, the BFI and NBFI classification outlined in Section 3.4.

Before November 1981 the Bank of England classification of banking firms for statistical purposes yielded the 'UK banking sector'. This grouping of firms comprised: the clearing banks, the accepting houses, the British and foreign secondary banks, the discount market, the Banking Department of the Bank of England, and a number of finance houses. The inclusion of a firm within the 'UK banking sector' depended partly on an informal appraisal of a firm's size and reputation and also whether there was an obligation for that firm to observe existing credit control arrangements. This classification of financial firms contained certain anomalies, and after the passing of the Banking Act 1979 the Bank of England was obliged to issue lists of 'recognised banks' and 'licensed deposit-takers' (LDTs). After November 1981 these recognised banks and LDTs were classified as part of an extended sector known as the 'UK monetary sector'. The Banking Act 1987 has replaced the earlier Act and has in turn established new criteria for determining whether a financial firm can be called a 'bank'. The distinction between banks and licensed deposit-takers has been abolished, and now an institution which is authorized by the Bank of England and has a paid-up capital of at least £5 million will be able to call itself a bank. The UK monetary sector, for statistical purposes, includes simply the retail banks, the accepting houses, other British banks, the American banks, the Japanese banks, other overseas banks, and the discount market. Significantly, the building societies are not included in the definition of the UK monetary sector.

4.3 Bank and non-bank financial intermediaries

Although we indicated in Chapter 3 that dividing financial intermediaties into 'bank' and 'non-bank' may be debatable, it is initially useful. This is because a major concern of this book is with those private sector financial firms whose liabilities act as a medium of exchange and payment. However, deciding which of the present day financial intermediaries should be classified as BFIs is not an easy matter, and this is because the function of medium of exchange and payment is not performed exclusively by a single group of firms. For example, demand deposit and cheque facilities are offered not only by the major retail banks such as Midland, Lloyds, TSB, and Girobank but also by several of the largest building societies. However, the provision and service is not identical or uniform, and inevitably there is an arbitrary element in our proposed division of the various financial firms.

If one emphasizes the medium of exchange and final payment characteristics of deposits, the financial intermediaries which one identifies as BFIs would be limited to the retail banks, the Banking Department of the Bank of England, and part of the operation of certain building societies. For most other financial firms, this side of their business is very small. The accepting houses and overseas banks in London have few demand deposits of the 'cheque account' kind. If one chooses, however, to lay emphasis on the general business operation of financial intermediaries rather than the nature of their liabilities (i.e. whether they are money or not), then the financial intermediaries eligible for the BFI classification would be extended: the retail banks, the Banking Department of the Bank of England, the accepting houses, other secondary banks (including the overseas banks), and the discount houses. The NBFIs would include the finance houses, the insurance companies, and the majority of the building societies. *Table 4.1* should help to clarify the various categories.

4.3.1 SIZE OF FINANCIAL INTERMEDIARIES

Before considering the various financial intermediaries in more detail, it would be both useful and interesting to examine the relative size of these firms as well as their growth in recent years. *Table 4.1* shows the sterling deposit liabilities of the various intermediaries spanning a period of twenty one years, and *Table 4.2* includes foreign currency deposits for the same period. We must emphasise that the figures quoted are intended

Table 4.1

Sterling deposit liabilities of selected financial intermediaries (UK)

(£ m)

	1966	1976	1979	1982	1987
Bank financial intermediaries					
London clearing banks	8,755	23,785	33,415	56,812 ⎞	Retail
Scottish clearing banks	971	2,513	3,602	6,237 ⎟	banks
Northern Ireland banks	220	850 ᶜ	1,144	1,478 ⎟	
Trustee savings banks	2,149	4,060	5,621	8,674 ⎬ 157,718	
Bank of England Banking Department	515	1,809	1,876	2,478 ⎟	
National Girobank	10	171	417	722 ⎠	
Secondary banks	2,892	19,327	31,419	59,888	129,944
Discount houses	1,156	2,509	4,054	4,836	11,128
Total	16,668	55,024	81,548	141,125	298,790
Non-bank financial intermediaries					
Building societies	5,894	24,790	42,249	66,613	160,380
Finance houses ᵃ	1,026	1,698	2,883	4,895	6,706
Insurance and pension fundsᵇ	16,142	51,352	81,819	144,166	404,900
Investment and unit trustsᵇ	3,586	8,688	9,943	15,423	58,960
Total	26,648	86,528	136,894	231,097	630,946
Overall total	43,316	141,552	218,442	372,222	929,736

ᵃ These figures are approximate.

ᵇ In the case of insurance companies and pension funds, as well as investment and unit trusts, the concept of deposit liabilities is inappropriate and therefore figures for assets have been used.

ᶜ Exact figures are not available because of an industrial dispute in Northern Ireland.

Sources : Bank of England *Statistical Abstract*, Nos 1 and 2; *Annual Abstract of Statistics* 1969, 1977, *Financial Statistics;* various Bank of England *Quarterly Bulletins*.

only to give a broad indication of the changes which have taken place. This is because we have used only five years' figures from the available published data, and the latter are either incomplete or available in a form unsuitable for our purposes, so that we have had to adjust some of the published figures or make estimates. For example, the insurance companies, pension funds, and investment and unit trusts, are financial interme-

Table 4.2

Sterling and foreign currency deposit liabilities of selected financial intermediaries (UK)
(£ m)

	1966	1976	1979	1982	1987
Bank financial intermediaries					
London clearing banks	8,755	28,319	48,846	77,730 ⎫	Retail
Scottish clearing banks	971	3,036	5,780	8,412 ⎪	banks
Northern Ireland banks	220	870 ᶜ	1,397	1,489 ⎪	
Trustee savings banks	2,149	4,060	5,621	8,674 ⎬	241,671
Bank of England Banking Department	515	1,809	1,876	2,478 ⎪	
National Girobank	10	171	417	722 ⎭	
Secondary banks	6,807	115,641	174,548	369,140	657,687
Discount houses	1,156	2,649	4,251	4,944	11,609
Total	20,583	156,555	242,736	473,589	910,967
Non-bank financial intermediaries					
Building societies	5,894	24,790	42,249	66,613	160,380
Finance houses ᵃ	1,026	1,698	2,883	4,895	6,706
Insurance and pension funds ᵇ	16,142	51,352	81,819	144,166	404,900
Investment and unit trusts ᵇ	3,586	8,688	9,943	15,423	58,960
Total	26,648	86,528	136,894	231,097	630,946
Overall total	47,231	243,083	379,630	704,686	1,541,913

ᵃ These figures are approximate.
ᵇ In the case of insurance companies and pension funds, as well as investment and unit trusts, the concept of deposit liabilities is inappropriate and therefore figures for assets have been used.
ᶜ Exact figures are not available because of an industrial dispute in Northern Ireland.

Sources : Bank of England *Statistical Abstract*, Nos 1 and 2; *Annual Abstract of Statistics* 1969, 1977, *Financial Statistics;* various Bank of England *Quarterly Bulletins.*

diaries but are not deposit-receiving institutions. We have therefore had to choose a substitute item for deposits, and in the case of the insurance companies we have used published figures for their funds.

The following remarks may be made about *Table 4.1* and *4.2*.

Sterling liabilities   The overall growth between 1966 and 1987 appears to be very substantial, rising from £43.3 billion to £929.7 billion, which represents an average annual (compound) growth of 15.7 per cent during the whole period. The most rapid growth seems to have been since 1979 at around 20 per cent each year. It is likely, however, that this rapid growth was influenced by the rising and high rates of inflation, which would be associated with the rising *money* value of bank deposits as *money* incomes and spending rose quickly. However, inflation cannot explain the whole of this high rate of growth; part of it would seem to be a reflection of individuals' and companies' preferences to hold particular kinds of deposit.

The relative position of BFIs and NBFIs has changed over the years, the BFI share falling from 38 to 32 per cent. This probably overstates the change, since during this period the building societies were increasingly taking on banking functions – even though they were not classified as banks under the Banking Act. Within the BFI group, however, the retail banks' share of the market has declined significantly – from about 70 per cent to around 50 per cent. This reflects the substantial growth of the sterling business of the secondary banks, most of which are foreign.

The huge growth in the business of the building societies is clearly identifiable. They have grown by over 17 per cent each year, compared with the 13 per cent growth of the traditional retail banks.

Sterling and foreign currency liabilities   By including foreign currency deposits, the data reveal an even more dramatic growth of business; 18 per cent a year. Much of this growth is explained by the secondary banks, since the bulk of their business is denominated in foreign currency. In 1966 only about 8 per cent of business was in foreign currency, whereas by 1987 this had risen to 40 per cent.

retail banks are identifiable by virtue of their branch networks and their important role in operating the payments mechanism (i.e. the economy's money transmission service) through their management of relatively small customer accounts. The wholesale banks have the opposite characteristics: absence of branch network; very limited participation in the payments mechanism; and the servicing of large accounts. Although their asset structure bears some resemblance to that of the primary banking firms, their liabilities are very different in that they are almost entirely term deposits of which the bulk are denominated in foreign currencies. In other words the deposit business of the secondary banks is not part of the UK payments mechanism.

The 'other' deposit-taking institutions' are a diverse group. It might be argued that both the discount houses and the building societies should be included in the primary banking sector, on the grounds that they are both involved to some extent in the payments mechanism of the economy. Whilst accepting this, the differences are at the present time significant and they are thus treated separately from the other banks.

The final category contains institutions which are not strictly deposit-taking but are nontheless very important financial intermediaries. These are the insurance companies, pension funds, investment trusts, and unit trusts.

4.5 Primary banking : retail banks

The retail banks consists of a group of nineteen banks which includes such well-known names as Midland, National Westminster and TSB but also the smaller entities such as Coutts, Girobank, and Co-operative Bank. Altogether they handled most of the money transmission services in the economy and this is clearly reflected in the high proportion of sterling sight deposits which they hold. One can see this in two ways : more than half of their own sterling liabilities are sight deposits; and of the total sterling sight deposits within the banking system, around 80 per cent are deposited with the retail banks.

These banks not only have responsibilities to their customers but also have profit objectives of their own, and it is by this distinction we can examine their operations: their services to customers, and the management of their balance sheets for the benefit of their shareholders.

4.5.1 SERVICES TO CUSTOMERS

An historical function of a bank is a custodial role – taking care of the wealth of its customers. This is a function which the modern bank performs, although in a slightly different way to the early banks. Banks accept cash or deposits from customers, which then represent a liability of the bank in the form of a sight deposit (current account) together with a cheque facility for the customer, or a time deposit (deposit account) which bears interest. These two types of account present for the customer a convenient and virtually risk-free form of holding wealth as well as a safe and useful means of settling debts by means of the cheque. The introduction of cheque cards, bank giro, Visa and Access, together with the relative ease with which seven-day deposits can be converted into sight deposits, as well as the established probity of the primary banks, has meant that the deposits of the primary banks constitute the bulk of the UK money supply and the primary means of payment. The provision of other services such as the standing order and direct debit facilities further enhance the benefits to be derived from using this part of the banking system.

Electronic technology has in recent years permitted an extension of bank services to their customers: automated teller machines, 'home banking', and EFTPOS (electronic funds transfer at the point of sale). The automated teller machines (ATMs) have proved very popular with bank customers and, notwithstanding some problems of reliability, are now very extensively used throughout the UK. Of more limited development has been the introduction of banking services, at a distance, by use of the telephone, so that bank customers with appropriate equipment are able to check their accounts and make payments by using a suitable telephone instrument. Equally uncertain has been the development of EFTPOS which has been delayed by both technical difficulties and some reluctance by the banks to develop this system. EFTPOS is card–based but, in contrast to Access and Visa, is a *debit* card and not a credit card. The customer's account is debited by using a card at the retail outlet. It is likely that the considerable profits stemming from credit cards have created some ambivalence towards EFTPOS from most banks.

An important service which banks provided very early in their development was the granting of loans to customers. Although the details regarding a particular loan facility may vary, one form is that of an overdraft, which allows the customer to draw cheques against his current account up to an agreed limit (interest is charged on the actual amount overdrawn) and is therefore a flexible advance to a customer. Alternatively the bank may provide a loan of a given amount negotiated at an agreed term and interest rate, with repayments of interest and principal being made usually each month. In both cases the bank may require security to cover the amounts involved. Bank preference is usually for relatively short-term lending, although the option or opportunity for a loan to be 'rolled over' – the overdraft facility renegotiated – does mean that much bank lending is in practice for a much longer term. In response to mainly competitive pressures, the banks now provide substantial medium-term lending (usually five to seven years); over 40 per cent of domestic advances other than to the personal sector are medium-term loans.

Apart from private individuals who may require loan finance for the purchase of consumer durables, or a mortgage for house purchase, the major customers of the banks are industry (including the public corporations), the service sector, and the local authorities.

Finally, the banks provide their customers with a range of services which derive from their financial expertise as well as their links with other financial firms, including their own subsidiaries. Services provided include insurance broking, investment services, estate agency, stock broking, leasing, executorship and trusteeship, together with advice on taxation matters.

4.5.2 BANKS AND THEIR BALANCE SHEETS

We have already observed that the primary banks are owned by shareholders who presumably intend their firms' operations to be profitable, even if they do not have the textbook objective of aiming for *maximum* profitability, and it is the aspect of the primary banks' operations that we shall now examine.

A useful approach is to look at the combined balance sheets of these banks and observe their structure and how this has changed over time. For this purpose it is convenient to use the combined balance sheet of the retail banks. *Table 4.4* shows the composition of the assets and the liabilities of the retail banks on four dates within the period 1983 – 88. The percentage share of the total assets or liabilities is also shown for each category.

The following sections consider each of the items in the balance sheet.

4.5.3 RETAIL BANKS' ASSETS

4.5.3.1 Cash

The holdings of this asset by the banks can be divided into the cash balances required by the banks at their branches in the form of till money (the item 'notes and coin' in the balance sheet of *Table 4.4*), and those balances held at the Bank of England, of which part facilitate the clearing operations of the retail banks and the remainder are non-operational deposits. The obligation to hold cash has changed over the years; for example, before September 1971 total cash had to be 8 per cent of gross deposits, and since then the Bank of England has from time to time changed the requirements.

It is evident from the data that the retail banks choose to hold around 1 per cent of their total assets as notes and coin in their branches for the purpose of meeting the cash requirements of their customers, and it is interesting that the retail banking system can be sustained by such a relatively small amount of cash. Clearly cash is the small change of the system, since most transactions are undertaken by either cheque or credit card.

4.5.3.2 Balances with the Bank of England

At the present time, the Bank of England requirement is that institutions with average eligible liabilities (see *Table 4.4* footnote b) of £10 million or more liable to lodge with the Bank *non-operational, non-interest-bearing* deposits of 0.45 per cent of their eligible liabilities. These non-operational deposits constitute most of the cash deposits at the Bank; in March 1988 as

Table 4.4 UK retail banks' balance sheet

	1983 (Sept.) £m	%	1985 (Sept.) £m	%	1987 (Sept.) £m	%	1988 (March) £m	%
Assets								
Sterling assets								
Notes and coin	1,666	1·2	2,001	1·1	2,316	1·0	2,368	1·0
Balance with the Bank of England	431	0·3	463	0·3	532	0·2	477	0·2
Market loans :								
Secured money with LDMA [a]	3,080	2·3	4,132	2·3	4,838	2·0	5,910	2·3
Other UK monetary sector	10,027	7·6	14,883	8·4	21,305	9·0	18,448	7·2
Certificates of deposit	1,221	0·9	2,603	1·5	2,764	1·2	3,832	1·5
UK local authorities	1,844	1·4	1,736	1·0	1,055	0·4	941	0·3
Overseas	288	0·2	1,199	0·7	3,473	1·5	4,073	1·6
Bills :								
Treasury bills	282	0·2	202	0·1	351	0·1	196	0·07
Eligible local authority bills	333	0·2	672	0·3	419	0·2	494	0·2
Eligible bank bills	1,820	1·3	4,555	2·6	4,681	2·0	5,390	2·1
Other bills	74	0·05	95	0·05	234	0·1	601	0·2
Advances :								
UK public sector	1,073	0·8	531	0·3	457	0·2	792	0·3
UK private sector	56,228	42·4	70,697	40·0	101,763	43·1	119,133	46·7
Overseas	4,791	3·6	2,741	1·6	4,331	1·8	4,495	1·8
Banking Department lending to central government	406	0·3	1,495	0·8	717	0·3	477	0·2
Investments :								
British government stocks	5,485	4·1	5,088	2·9	5,578	2·4	6,329	2·5
Other	3,175	2·4	2,640	1·5	3,962	1·7	4,152	1·6
Other currency assets								
Market loans and advances :	27,718	20·9	45,952	25·9	51,892	22·0	47,763	18·74
of which (Advances)	7,747	5·8	13,479	7·6	15,750	6·6	13,964	5·4
UK monetary sector	10,932	8·2	13,422	7·6	11,394	4·8	10,840	4·2
Certificates of deposit	353	0·2	510	0·2	275	0·1	206	0·08
UK public sector	74	0·05	210	0·1	154	0·06	18	0·01
UK private sector	2,444	1·8	4,912	2·8	6,479	2·7	6,189	2·4
Overseas	13,915	10·5	26,898	15·2	33,590	14·2	30,510	12·0
Bills	61	0·04	307	0·1	214	0·1	218	0·08
Investments	1,451	1·1	4,655	2·6	6,160	2·6	6,085	2·4

Miscellaneous assets (sterling and other currencies)	11,016	8·3	13,146	7·4	19,257	8·1	22,655	8·9
Acceptances	1,642	1·2	3,318	1·8	4,548	1·9	7,809	3·0
Eligible liabilities b	69,923	52·8	82,246	46·5	117,117	49·6	134,831	53·0
Liabilities								
Notes issued	753	0·5	929	0·5	1,103	0·5	1,195	0·5
Sterling deposits	86,520	65·3	106,019	60·0	149,176	63·1	167,191	65·6
of which:								
(Sight deposits)	(31,585)	(23·8)	(44,351)	(25·0)	(76,056)	(32·2)	(83,365)	(32·7)
UK monetary sector	10,109	7·6	10,132	5·7	13,539	5·7	17,408	6·8
UK public sector	1,685	1·2	1,958	1·1	3,322	1·4	3,690	1·4
UK private sector	64,672	48·8	78,544	44·4	110,641	46·8	119,431	46·9
Overseas	5,660	4·3	9,737	5·5	12,887	5·4	14,428	5·7
Certificates of deposit and other short-term paper	4,395	3·3	5,646	3·2	8,787	3·7	12,234	4·8
Other currency deposits	27,841	21·0	43,489	24·6	46,177	19·5	43,052	16·9
of which:								
UK monetary sector	5,590	4·2	5,757	3·2	6,710	2·8	6,764	2·6
Other UK	2,781	2·0	4,259	2·4	6,272	2·6	6,228	2·4
Overseas	17,748	13·4	29,078	16·4	28,515	12·1	25,984	10·2
Certificates of deposit and other short-term paper	1,721	1·3	4,394	2·4	4,679	2·0	4,076	1·6
Items in suspense and transmission, capital and other funds (sterling and other currencies)	17,357		26,365		39,845		43,387	
	132,470		176,802		236,302		254,825	

a London Discount Market Association.
b Eligible liabilities comprise sterling deposit liabilities excluding deposits with an original maturity of over two years, plus any sterling resources obtained by switching foreign currencies into sterling. Inter-bank transactions are included on a net basis and adjustments are made for transit items.
Source: Bank of England Quarterly Bulletin

little as £70 million were held for operational purposes. These non-interest-bearing deposits required by the Bank clearly are of considerable value to the Bank, since they provide the Bank with interest-income (perhaps worth as much as £30 million a year at the present time); this can be justified by the benefits gained by the whole banking system from the operations of the central bank.

4.5.3.3 Market loans

The use of the term 'market loans' is to emphasize that this category of lending by the banks is done through the existing markets and not by lending directly to their customers in the form of advances. Such loans are largely short-term lending to the sterling money market (this will be discussed in more detail in Section 4.8.2). Most of these funds are lent to the discount houses as either secured or unsecured money; there is also short-term lending to other banks, domestic and foreign, operating in the money markets. These 'market loans' provide the retail banks with an easy opportunity to on-lend funds for short periods, especially those loans to the discount market which are recoverable 'at call', and with a substantial stock of *liquidity* since these funds are safe and very accessible.

Certain banks are designated 'eligible banks', and this means that bills of exchange which have been accepted by such banks of quality are eligible for rediscount (resale) at the Bank of England. Such eligible banks were obliged from 1981 to maintain with the discount houses funds equal to 2.5 per cent of their eligible liabilities, and with the discount houses and money brokers combined funds to 5 per cent of their eligible liabilities. This arrangement with the discount houses ended in September 1986 and is to be replaced by a broader liquidity requirement; see Section 4.5.5.

Certificates of deposit The certificate of deposit (CD), as its title suggests, is a certificate stating that a deposit of a certain amount has been placed with a particular bank for a given period and at a fixed or floating rate of interest. The certificate of deposit is a negotiable asset, so that depositors who hold this paper can, if they so wish, resell the certificate in a secondary market. The term of such deposits may be from three months to five years, being fixed to suit the needs of both the depositor and the bank issuing the certificate. In principle, there are a number of advantages attached to this type of asset for both the issuing bank and the depositor. The arrangement provides the bank with a deposit for a fixed period and possibly a flexible interest rate; the redemption date is known by the bank, and obviously this can help in the planning of its use of the funds so obtained. Furthermore the bank is able to negotiate a rate on such deposits individually in order to attract these deposits (minimum amount usually £50,000) without incurring the need to raise the *general* level of rates on its deposits. From the depositor's viewpoint the certificate received provides a satisfactory rate of return, but more especially it is a negotiable certificate and thus allows the depositor the possibility of reselling the asset, should the need arise.

The certificate of deposit market in sterling is largely dominated by the banks and acceptance houses, which not only issue CDs but also hold substantial amounts. The reason for this is that CDs provide the banks with a flexible instrument for maintaining their liquidity. *Table 4·5* shows the value of sterling CDs held in March 1988.

Table 4·5

UK monetary sector sterling CDs held within the monetary sector (March 1988)

	£ m	%
Retail banks	3,832	23·5
Discount houses	3,530	21·6
Accepting houses	2,423	14·8
Other British banks	2,422	14·8
American banks	492	3·0
Japanese banks	164	1·0
Other overseas banks	3,481	21·3
Total	16,344	

Source : Bank of England *Quarterly Bulletin*

The retail banks, discount houses, and accepting houses hold 60 per cent of the CDs and other short-term paper. The total value of CDs *held* (£16,344 million) is substantially less than the value of CDs and other short-term paper *issued* by the banks and other institutions in the UK (£33,348 million). One reason for this difference is that since the banks issue and hold CDs there is likely to be double-counting.

UK local authorities   For more than thirty years the UK local authorities have been active in the money markets as both lenders and borrowers. This item shows only funds lent through the local authority money market (see Section 6.12.2) and does not include money lent in the normal course of business, which is included in 'advances'.

Overseas   This item includes all balances with, and funds lent to, banks overseas (except trade and portfolio investments). Bills, CDs, promissory notes and other short-term paper issued by overseas banks and either discounted or held by the retail banks are also included.

4.5.3.4 *Bills*

Under this general heading there a number of different assets which we shall examine in turn.

Treasury bills   These bills, which were first introduced in 1877, are in effect an IOU of the government to the holder of the bill. There is no rate of interest paid on these assets, but rather they are sold initially by tender at a discount by the Bank of England. The bills usually have a life of 91 days, and the method of sale is for the Bank of England to announce the total offer of bills for the following week and invite tenders in large denominations, with a minimum acceptable tender of £50,000. On the Friday of the following week, the tenders are opened and the bills are allocated to the highest bidders. Thus the rate of interest obtained on such bills is the discount on the bill, i.e. an offer for £100 nominal may be, say, £98 which would yield an approximate *annual* rate of interest of 8 per cent. (The banks used not to bid directly for bills on their own account, although they would act on behalf of customers, but purchased such bills as required from the discount houses. Since 1971 the banks formally abandoned this agreement not to bid against the discount houses.) The original purchaser of the bills can specify the day of the following week when the bills are to be purchased and from which the 91 days are to run. This arrangement allows the banks to purchase bills in such a way that there is a steady stream of maturing bills. By this means, the banks are able to ensure a flow of cash, which allows them to meet *foreseeable* cash needs. For recent developments and possible changes see Section 4.8.4.

Eligible local authority bills   Some large local authorities are permitted to issue their equivalent of the Treasury bill. They are eligible for rediscount at the Bank of England. The amounts involved have never been susbtantial.

Eligible bank bills   These comprise all sterling bills which are payable in the UK and have been accepted by an eligible bank, i.e. by one whose bills are eligible for rediscount at the Bank of England. This substantial amount of assets represents a very liquid – of negligible risk and easily cashed – balance sheet item.

Other bills   This item includes local authority and bank bills which are *not* eligible for rediscount at the Bank of England, together with other bills and commercial paper not included elsewhere.

4.5.3.5 Advances

This asset is clearly the largest single item ($£$ 124,897 million in 1988), representing almost half of the total assets and nearly 70 per cent of sterling assets. Advances include all balances with, and lending to, customers not included elsewhere in the balance sheet, and this encompasses lending which is secured or unsecured. It is clear that most of these funds flow to private sector borrowers ($£$ 119,133 million in 1988), and this includes all medium – and long-term lending (i.e. with an original maturity of two years or over) at fixed rates under the Department of Trade and Industry guarantee for shipbuilding in the United Kingdom for UK buyers.

Table 4.6 presents a breakdown of sterling (and foreign currency) lending by the UK monetary sector; the bulk of it (80 per cent) is in sterling. The table demonstrates the spreading of risk by the banks since no one sector is excessively represented. The published data break down banks' lending between a number of sectors: manufacturing, non-manufacturing production, services (non-professional), finance, business and other services. The largest allocation of funds is for finance (i.e. loans to building societies, insurance companies, securities dealers, investment and unit trusts, and others) but even this sector takes only 28 per cent of total lending. Further disaggregation in *Table 4.6* reveals how the banks avoid putting all their eggs in one basket; the spread of lending is considerable. Even the

Table 4.6

Advances in sterling to UK residents from the UK monetary sector (end February)

	1987 £m	1987 £m	1987 %	1988 £m	1988 £m	1988 %
Manufacturing		30,125	14·1		31,248	12·2
of which:						
Engineering	5,665		2·7	5,839		2·3
Textiles, clothing, footwear	1,814		0·8	2,156		0·8
Chemicals	2,081		0·9	2,071		0·8
Other production (non-manufacturing)		16,930			18,256	
of which:						
Agriculture, forestry, fishing	5,959		2·8	6,023		2·3
Construction	6,302		3·0	8,028		3·1
Services (Garages, distribution, hotels and catering)		28,374	13·3		33,485	13·1
of which:						
Transport and communication	3,734		1·7	4,671		1·8
Retailing	7,247		3·4	8,856		3·4
Persons		50,328	23·7		65,987	25·8
of which:						
House purchase	25,518		12·0	35,731		14·0
Other loans	23,845		11·2	28,923		11·3
Financial		60,270	28·4		71,772	28·1
of which:						
Securities dealers etc.	14,431		6·8	13,365		5·2
Leasing	8,341		3·9	9,009		3·5
Business and other services		26,445	12·4		34,949	13·7
of which:						
Property companies	9,987		4·7	15,139		5·9
Business and other services	15,132		7·1	18,548		7·2
Total lending (loans and acceptances)		212,473			225,701	
of which:						
Overdrafts	37,491		17·6	40,944		16·0
Acceptances	14,921		7·0	16,781		6·5

Source : various Bank of England *Quarterly Bulletins*

much publicized incursion of banks into mortgage finance is shown as a rise from 12 per cent in 1987 to 14 per cent in 1988. (The figure for 1984 was 11·3 per cent, which perhaps indicates how cautious the banks have been in developing this side of their business.)

The published data for banks' lending are not available in a consistent form for more than a few years, and this makes comparison difficult. However, even a casual glance at the allocation of loans to the various users in 1987 and 1988 does suggest that the banks are fairly conservative and risk–averse, since the proportion of funds allocated to different borrowers is virtually the same in both years[1]. It might well be urged that the consistent lending pattern over the years reflects the *demand* for funds from creditworthy borrowers rather than a deliberate policy of diversification of their portfolio of loans. In view of the expertise employed by the banks and their need to minimize risk consistent with their profit target, it seems unlikely that the pattern of their lending is chance or simply a reflection of demand; it is more likely to be an indication of the *supply* aspect in the determination of bank lending.

4.5.3.6. Banking Department lending to central government

The Bank of England acts as the government's bank (see Section 4.15.5 for further discussion) and not surprisingly lends to the government. This item comprises holdings by the Banking Department of the Bank of England of all forms of central government debt net of its liabilities to the National Loans Fund and the Paymaster General, i.e. the Banking Department holds assets issued by the central government and hands over funds in exchange.

4.5.3.7 Investments

The retail banks have been reluctant to invest in the private sector of the economy through the take-up of new issues of company shares and stock, or by the purchase of existing company securities through the Stock Exchange. Such pru-

A similar picture emerges if one examines data for 1984. We have not included this in *Table 4.6* because the presentation is not entirely consistent with later years. The correlation coefficient for 1987 and 1988 is 0·99; for 1988 and 1984 (data not presented) it is 0·91.

dence on the part of the banks has meant that the bulk of their investments consists of holdings of gilt-edged securities (such holdings are free of the risk of default since they are either issued by or guaranteed by the government). The banks have preferred to provide finance for industry either directly through the cautious provision of advances to firms, or indirectly through bank subsidiaries and participation in such companies as Finance for Industry Ltd. Thus the item 'investments' consists very largely of stocks issued by the British government and stocks of nationalized industries guaranteed by the British government.

'Other investments' consist of stock and bonds issued by local authorities, probably no more than £ 300 – 400 million; investments in other members of the monetary sector; holdings of securities issued by building societies having an original maturity of one year or more; and deposits with overseas offices which have been invested in fixed assets such as premises and equipment.

Almost three-quarters of the British government securities held by the banking system in the UK are held by the retail banks. Although the maturity composition of such stock is no longer published in detail, one can draw reasonable conclusions based on the aggregate figures published in the November 1987 issue of the Bank of England *Quarterly Bulletin*. The term to maturity of government securities varies from the very short term (say, up to five years) to much longer terms extending over thirty years, and there are even stocks which do not have a redemption date.[2] *Table 4.7* shows the maturity distribution of stocks held by the monetary sector at March 31 in 1984 and 1987.

Although holdings of government securities account for only 3·5 per cent of sterling assets, the banks are faced with the choice of selecting a suitable mixture of such assets. It is clear from *Table 4.7* that banks' preferences can change. Evidently, the monetary sector firms have chosen to hold more longer-dated securities since 1984; over 70 per cent have a maturity

[2] The stock market lists in the *Financial Times* provide a list of most British government securities which are available, together with their prices, yields and redemption dates.

Table 4.7

Monetary sector holdings of British government stocks (31 March)

	1984		1987	
	£m	%	£m	%
Up to five years to maturity	5,114	79·0	2.253	26·0
Five to fifteen years to maturity	1,334	20·5	3,556	41·1
Over fifteen years and undated	37	0·5	2,840	32·9
Total	6,485		8,649	

Source : Bank of England *Quarterly Bulletin*

greater than five years and, of that, 33 per cent have a maturity greater than fifteen years. (In 1982 the banks held around 30 per cent of stocks with a maturity greater than five years.) Government securities are not subject to the risk of default, but they are not immune to market risk, i.e. the market value of the asset may fall, and this – together with the yield on the security – will influence the banks in their decision to hold more or less longer-dated government stock. It would seem that monetary sector institutions since 1984 have taken a more favourable view about government securities and have shifted the balance of their holdings accordingly.

Table 4.4 shows that the retail banks have reduced the weighting of government securities in their asset portfolio (in September 1983 it was 6 per cent of sterling assets, and in March 1988, 3·5 per cent) whilst increasing their total holdings from £5,485 million to £6,329 million. Since the retail banks are the largest holders of government stocks within the monetary sector, it is likely that they have *chosen* to switch to longer-dated securities.

The banks have for many years adopted the policy of purchasing gilt-edged securities (the popular term for British government securities) of varying maturities, not only to spread risk but also to give the banks a steady flow of maturing assets. This provides the banks with flexibility in managing their assets, and also with a flow of cash as their accounts at the Bank of England are credited to the value of maturing stocks. Short-dated government securities can thus provide the banks with a cushion of liquidity as well as yielding interest income.

4.5.3.8. Other currency assets

In October 1979, the UK government abolished foreign exchange controls, and this meant that UK residents could hold foreign currency deposits and invest abroad in real and financial assets quite freely. This change in government policy was not only consistent with the Conservative government's endorsement of 'free markets' but also fitted with the continuing integration of UK money and capital markets with those abroad. The end of foreign exchange controls inevitably meant that banks would be required to extend their services to clients both domestic and foreign. This policy change probably added impetus to a trend already there; at the end of 1978 the London clearing banks held 15 per cent of their assets denominated in foreign currency, whereas in March 1988 the retail banks held 20 per cent of their assets in that form. *Table 4.4* shows that only one-quarter of foreign currency assets are in the form of advances whereas most of these funds are market loans, i.e. they are not directly placed with the ultimate borrower but on-lent to other financial firms, in particular overseas banking firms (£30,510 million flowed in that direction in 1988). This represents the retail banks' involvement in an important money market – the Euro-currency markets (see Section 6.12.2 for further discussion).

'Bills' refers to the banks' holdings of overseas commercial bills (only £218 million in 1988). 'Investments' are those denominated in foreign currency which the banks have made in other financial firms as well as financial assets such as bonds.

4.5.3.9 Miscellaneous assets

These include items in suspense (debit balances awaiting transfer to customers' accounts) and collection (cheques drawn on and in course of collection on banks and other institutions). They also include holdings of physical assets such as equipment leased under operating leases to other firms.

4.5.3.10 Acceptances

This comprises all bills accepted by the retail banks which are still outstanding, excluding those which a bank itself has discounted. It is important to note that these acceptances are not the assets of the banks; they arise from the accepting

function which the banks perform for their customers, and the
bills which have been accepted are owned elsewhere.

4.5.4 RETAIL BANK'S LIABILITIES

The liabilities of the retail banks are shown in the second part of
Table 4.4.

Scottish and Northern Ireland banks which issue their own
private sterling notes are required to hold an equivalent
amount in Bank of England notes. These banks are not in any
way permitted to *add* to the stock of notes in circulation.

It is evident that 70 per cent of the retail banks' sterling
deposits come from the private sector – individuals and firms
using the money transmission services of the banks. However, it
is interesting that of the banks' sterling liabilities, just less than
half are sight deposits: £83,365 million in 1988. But of this
total, about £50,000 million are *interest*-bearing sight deposits;
the remainder, approximately £32,000 million, are the traditional cheque (current) accounts. This represents only 20 per
cent of all sterling accounts. For many years the retail banks
relied on their 'endowment' of funds from customers with
cheque accounts and seven-day accounts. The current accounts
of the retail banks are the main source of the means of payment
in the UK, and in this field the banks – before 1971 and the
emergence of strong competition in retail banking –
could rely on this endowment effect to provide them with up to
half or more or their funds. Vigorous competition amongst
banks and building societies has largely eliminated this easy
source of funds for the clearing banks.[3]

Table 4.8 provides a more detailed breakdown of the source of
sterling funds for the UK monetary sector, and is likely to be
representative of the retail banks since they are dominant in the
sterling markets.

We can make a number of observations about *Tables 4.4* and
4.8 :

(a) *Table 4.8* confirms the view that the personal sector has
    declined in relative importance as a source of funds for the

---

[3] A recent authoritative estimate by one of the major banks suggests that no more than
40 per cent of funds can be obtained from this source.

Table 4.8

Source of domestic sterling deposits (UK monetary sector)

	1988I.		1988I.	
	£m	%	£m	%
Central government	536	0·9	765	0·4
Local authorities	333	0·6	4,512	2·4
Public corporations	562	0·9	1,447	0·7
Other financial institutions	6,723	11·4	50,393	27·1
Industrial and commercial companies	13,146	22·4	46,951	25·2
Personal sector	37,382	63·7	81,877	44·0
of which:				
Persons, households and individual trusts	(29,027)	(49·4)	(58,044)	(31·2)
	58,682		185,945	

Source : Financial Statistics

banks. The contribution of persons, households, and individual trusts has fallen from 49.4 per cent of domestic sterling deposits to 31.2 per cent.

(b) It is the considerable increase in the share of deposits from the other financial institutions which is most striking (from 11.4 per cent to 27.1 per cent). This is likely to reflect the heightened competitiveness amongst financial intermediaries. Financial intermediaries other than banks are attracting a greater share of funds from the personal sector, and these funds are then placed on deposit with the banking system *by* those financial intermediaries. In 1988I the building societies, for example, had almost £7,000 million in bank deposits. Insurance companies and pension funds are also large holders of deposits with the banks – around £12,000 million in 1988I.

(c) *Table 4.4* shows that the overseas sector generated not only foreign currency deposits but also sterling deposits. Although the foreign banks are mainly involved in handling foreign currency bank deposits (see Section 4.6), this item does reveal their importance in sterling banking business. This, too, is a reflection of the greater competitiveness in UK banking since the 1970s; sterling business is not the prerogative of domestic banks.

(d) The retail banks not only buy certificates of deposit, they also issue them to attract deposits. Although this item is not perhaps of great relative importance (4.8 per cent of total liabilities in 1988), it is, as we have seen in Section 4.5.3.3, an important source of *flexibility* for the banks.

(e) Foreign currency deposits represent about 16 per cent of total liabilities (21 per cent in 1983). As we have discussed earlier, this is some measure of the importance of foreign currency business, even for retail banks in the UK. Much of these foreign funds originate from the retail banks' operations in the Euro-currency markets (see Section 6.12.2 for more detailed discussion of these markets.)

(f) The retail banks hold foreign currency deposits, and also foreign currency assets. Although the subject will be discussed below, here we point out that the banks can *choose* the balance of foreign currency liabilities and assets. In March 1988 the banks' foreign currency liabilities (valued in sterling) amounted to £43,052 million, whereas their foreign currency assets were £54,066 million; in September 1983 the position was, respectively, £27,841 million and £29,230 million. The banks had, on both occasions, a balance sheet position where their obligations in foreign currency were less than their foreign currency assets; clearly, in order to achieve this, the banks would have converted sterling into foreign currency via the foreign exchange market. There is some risk attached to this unmatched position; a change in the exchange rate (a rise in the value of the pound sterling in the foreign exchange market) could result in a fall in the banks' asset values if, when their sterling obligations were due, the banks were forced to realize their foreign currency assets at an untimely moment.

4.5.5 BALANCE SHEET STRUCTURE OF THE RETAIL BANKS

4.5.5.1 *Historical overview*

Between 1951 and 1971 the clearing banks were required by the Bank of England to maintain two asset ratios. One was an 8 per cent *cash ratio*, and the other was a *liquid assets ratio* of around 30 per cent (which included cash and other assets such as call money to the discount houses/and bills). Of their remaining assets during this period the banks steadily reduced their holdings of government securities and built up their advances to customers. After 1971 the composition of their assets was subject to a further influence a result of the implementation of proposals contained in a Bank of England policy document, *Competition and Credit Control*. This document marked the beginning of official moves towards deregulation of the banking system, the injection of more competition, and the acceptance that markets not only would play a greater part in the operation of the financial system but also would be the vehicle for monetary policy. *Competition and Credit Control* effectively abolished the cash ratio and liquidity ratio and replaced them with a 12.5 per cent reserve assets ratio (similar to the liquidity ratio). Although this new policy provided some stimulus to competition (but it might be argued that it was the influx of foreign banks to London which was the main factor) it was a failure as a framework for official credit control. In August 1981 the system was again changed, with the abolition of the reserve asset ratio and other devices associated with *Competition and Credit Control*. The period to date is characterized by the considerable emphasis on market forces and application of monetary policy through financial markets.

Up to 1981 the official stance was that the asset structure of the banks was subject to Bank regulation for purposes other than prudential control, i.e. monetary policy. After 1981, official requirements were almost entirely concerned with the banks' management of their balance sheet in relation to their liquidity and capital requirements; regulation for reasons of monetary policy would be applied through the markets. Whatever the reasons, it is clear that over the years the requirements of the Bank of England have had a significant impact on the way the banks have managed their assets and liabilities.

4.5.5.2 Commercial factors

Almost all the UK banks are owned by shareholders, and one of the objectives of such banks is to make satisfactory profits. We shall now consider how this and other objectives have influenced the disposition of bank assets and liabilities.

In banking as in other areas of economic activity, profit is earned for taking risks; the higher the risk incurred, usually the greater the profit which is earned. The risk which banks incur is, as we have seen, closely related to the *liquidity* of their assets. Cash, for example, is absolutely liquid and free of risk but yields no profit for a bank. Certain kinds of bank lending can be very

risky, for example in the setting up of new small businesses, but
such lending can also be very profitable if the business is
successful. Other kinds of bank asset such as government
securities have a *market* value which can fall before maturity. If
such assets need to be sold before maturity then the bank may
experience a capital loss which more than offsets the interest
income generated by the asset in the past. In general, such risk
will increase as the term (life) of the asset increases because the
longer the term the greater the chance of the undesirable event
occurring.

Banks also have obligations to depositors, and a bank must in
no circumstances renege on such obligations. To do so would
mean insolvency and the end of the bank itself. Protection of
depositors' interests is therefore consistent with a bank's objective to earn profits for shareholders and in our earlier discussion
of bank assets we saw that the obligation to depositors can be
satisfied by maintaining an adequate stock of liquid assets.

Consistent with its obligations to shareholders and depositors, as a general principle we would expect a bank to try to
allocate funds amongst its assets in such a way that when the
rate of return on an asset has been discounted for the risk
element, the rates of return on all bank assets are equal. If this
were not so then a bank could increase its overall profits by
reallocating funds in favour of the asset offering the higher
return. The rates of return on selected bank assets for early July
1988 are as follows :

	%
Money with the LDMA	8
Treasury bill	9.71
Sterling CDs (three month)	9.9
British government securities (short – dated)	9.91
Advances to customers	12.5

If we assume that call money with the London Discount
Market Association represents an extremly low-risk asset, then
the difference between that rate of return and the other
categories gives us a rough idea of the risk–premium which may
be present.

Finally, in managing their balance sheet the banks will also consider other general rules which relate to risk :

(a) The banks will require a degree of flexibility in arranging their assets over time so that, for example, there is a steady and predictable stream of maturing assets. Government securities, which are redeemable in cash and have different maturity dates, provide the banks with an asset suited to this need.

(b) The banks will be concerned about the security of their assets, not least from the risk of default. To protect themselves against this, the banks will obtain assets from borrowers as a security. For mortgage lending the security will be the house itself. For company loans the bank might obtain a fixed or floating charge over the assets of the business; for many small companies the security for the bank is likely to be the private home of the owner of the business.

(c) The banks will *diversify* their assets in order to spread risk. We have seen how they do this in the range of advances they make to customers.

(d) The banks will try to match their assets and liabilities term-for-term. For example, if a bank obtains deposits which are repayable in one month and can on-lend such funds for exactly one month, then the bank has reduced risk whilst still earning a profit. Banks can try to do this not only by adjusting the maturity of their assets to the maturity of their liabilities, but also by adjusting their liabilities to their assets through borrowing in the inter-bank market. We examine this more fully in Section 4.6.1. However, essentially it means that if the maturity structure of the bank's assets is out of alignment with the maturity structure of its liabilities, then the bank will try to borrow funds of the appropriate maturity and thus re-establish its liquidity position. The retail banks have been directly involved in the inter-bank market since 1971 – a practice which enabled the banks to move into new markets for lending whilst still retaining their liquidity and solvency.

4.5.5.3 Prudential regulation : liquidity

An overriding constraint on the management of the banks' balance sheet must be the prudential requirements laid down by the Bank of England and contained within the Banking Act 1987. In particular the Bank of England has gradually developed a system of guidance for banks which focuses on their liquidity requirements in relation to the adequacy of their own capital. Such liquidity requirements are intended to govern banks' management policies, and these policies are to be sustained at all times. Until September 1986 all eligible banks were required to maintain balances with the discount houses, gilt-edged jobbers, and Stock Exchange money brokers. These balances (known as 'club money') had two purposes: one was to ensure an adequate supply of funds to institutions which were effectively the main market–makers in important assets (bills and gilt-edged securities) and thus to enable them to perform this function; and the other was that it ensured that eligible banks were holding a minimum stock of secure liquid assets in the form of loans to the discount houses, gilt-edged jobbers, and money brokers. In view of the way this obligation applied to the banks it is clear that the main purpose of the arrangement was to maintain a supply of funds to these market operators. Because of impending changes in financial markets as a result of Big Bang (see Section 4.5.6) this liquidity arrangement would have needed amendment. Instead the Bank formally ended the arrangement in September 1986 and, until an alternative scheme could be devised, the Bank asked the banks not to change their liquidity policies in the interim period.

After discussion with interested parties, the Bank now proposes that banks should hold a stock of highly liquid assets as a proportion of specified liabilities. It is intended that the proportion of highly liquid assets should be in the range of 10 – 20 per cent of those banks' liabilities which fall due 'at sight' and up to eight days. The Bank has established a specification of the relevant liquid assets, which breaks them down into tier 1 (highest–quality liquid assets) and tier 2 (assets with slightly less certain liquidity characteristics). The liability base for the purpose of the calculation will include foreign currency deposits as well as sterling. This novel requirement, not surprisingly, has involved the Bank in consultations with overseas central banks. The Bank intends to consider each bank on a case-by-case basis so that the Bank can judge each bank's cash flow position and deposit obligations and set an appropriate liquid asset ratio. The absence of a *uniform* liquid assets requirement is an interesting condition of the scheme and could, in principle, be discriminatory between the banks such that their usual commercial objectives in relation to their balance sheet are distorted. This will depend partly on the extent to which the liquidity requirement differs from that which a prudent bank would have undertaken as part of normal business practice. Much will depend on how the Bank treats institutions' cash flow position as well as their deposit maturities. The position of the retail banks *before* the introduction of the scheme might well illuminate this matter; a rough estimate is shown in *Table 4.9*. On the basis of this estimate it would seem that the stock of liquidity requirement might well present little or no adjustment problem for the retail banks; it would seem that in July 1987 they were maintaining a ratio which was probably comfortably within range (10–20 per cent) laid down by the Bank. The same calculation for the retail banks for the end of June 1988 also yields a liquid assets ratio of 13 per cent. It could well be that the stock of liquidity ratio is not really onerous – at least not for the retail banks.

4.5.5.4 Prudential regulation : Capital adequacy

The Bank's prudential requirements are more extensive than simply ensuring that the different banks have adequate liquidity. A bank must also maintain adequate *capital*, and this stock of capital must be sufficient to cover the different types of risks

Table 4.9

Cash flow position of the retail banks (31 July 1987) (£m)

Secured money with LDMA	4,566
Eligible bills	6,559
	11,125
Sterling sight deposits	72,978
Foreign currency sight deposits	8,767 [a]
	81,745

'Guestimated' stock of liquidity ratio = 11,125/81,745 = 13.6 per cent

[a] This is a 'guestimate' which is probably too high.

carried on the bank's balance sheet. The capital must be adequate to safeguard the interests of depositors and potential depositors, and must be consistent with that particular bank's commercial operations. In assessing capital adequacy the Bank takes account of the risks of loss to which a bank may be subject. The risks identified are as follow :

Credit risk   The risk of default arising from business on or off the balance sheet. This would cover a bank's direct lending, for example advances, as well as a bank's obligations in the form of acceptances. (At 30 June 1988 banks in the UK had made sterling acceptances amounting to almost £22 billion, 5 per cent of their sterling assets.)

Foreign exchange risk   Banks take deposits and obtain assets in both sterling and foreign currency. One consequence of this is that changes in the exchange rate may alter the size of a bank's commitments when measured in another currency. To the extent that a bank's position is not covered against such an eventuality, it involves that bank in some risk of loss.

Interest rate risk   Changes in interest rates will change the capital value of certain financial assets, e.g. government bonds, certificates of deposit[4]. Banks' balance sheets contain claims which are not capital-certain, and significant and unexpected changes in interest rates can create paper losses if market values of assets fall.

Operational risk   Such risks include the possibility of negligence or incompetence in the management of either the bank's own assets or the assets of others, for example in investment management. As we have seen, one of the consequences of greater competition within banking has been the extension of banking services, including investment management within a bank or banking group.

Contagion risk   A bank might be placed at risk because of risks arising from subsidiaries and other connected companies which might expose the bank to direct financial costs or general loss of confidence.

Concentration risk   The risk which a bank incurs may vary because of the nature of the business and its concentration in

---

[4] A rise in general level of interest rates causes asset values to fall and a fall in interest rates causes asset values to rise. For illustraton of this see Section 6.11.1.

particular areas. Such concentration could be geographical, where a bank is heavily involved in foreign lending; sectoral, such as excessive lending in the property field; or individual, to a particular firm or person. In assessing such risk the Bank would need to look beyond a banks' lending and investment business to activities off the balance sheet, such as the provision of guarantees, underwriting, and acceptance business.

Although it is fairly easy to *describe* the risk which banks might face, it is another matter to *quantify* such risks in order to decide whether a particular bank has adequate capital. Nevertheless the Bank attempts such an exercise based on papers and proposals issued by the Bank in recent years. The essential approach is to weight, as far as possible, the various risks attached to the different assets within a balance sheet. This can be done by multiplying the different assets by their risk factor (for example, an asset with no discernible risk would have a zero weight, with weights increasing as risk increased) and then adding these risk-adjusted assets to form a bank's total weighted assets.

Table 4.10(a) shows the change in weighted assets from 1983 to 1987, rising from £208 billion to £267 billion. The adjusted capital base has also increased from £16.9 billion to £26.3 billion, and in 1987 for example this yielded a risk asset ratio of 9.8 per cent (26.3/267.2 × 100). The information in this table suggests that the capital adequacy of large British banks has increased slightly over these four years when measured by the risk asset ratio. The higher the ratio, the greater the capital adequacy of the banks.

The adjusted capital base (*Table 4.10(a)*) represents mainly the net capital assets of a bank: total capital (paid-up capital and reserves) together with other financial resources which the Bank of England regards as appropriate. The criteria for the inclusion of assets in the capital assests of a bank are that they should be a stable resource which is capable of absorbing any losses which the bank might incur, and that they should also be of a permanent nature. In this respect, a bank's reserves would only be included in the capital base if the likelihood of such reserves being paid away to shareholders was very remote. Nonetheless the Bank does recognize that certain other kinds of capital can provide depositor protection whilst not meeting the above criteria; and this refers to term debt which has a *minimum* maturity of five years and one day.

We can see in *Table 4.10(b)* that in 1987 the primary capital of the large British banks amounted to £24.58 billion (the sum of the five items in the table), and the secondary capital (perpetual debt not included in primary capital together with term subordinated debt[5]) to £5.82 billion. Primary plus secondary capital provides the total capital and, after deducting goodwill, equipment, connected lending of a capital nature, and investments in subsidiaries and associates, this yields the value of the *adjusted capital base*.

The Bank lays down for each bank a minimum risk asset ratio (a 'trigger ratio') calculated mainly on the basis of measuring credit risk and foreign exchange rate risk, and the Bank expects each institution to maintain a target ratio in excess of this minimum trigger ratio. The relevance of such ratios for prudential control of the banks is not only that they ensure that banks are carefully monitoring their own behaviour and policies, but also that they trigger prudent or corrective behaviour by such banks. If, for example, a bank's risk-weighted assets are increasing, then that bank may well have to either adjust its asset position to comply with the Bank of England's requirements, or raise fresh capital by issuing new shares (a useful test of approval by existing and potential shareholders?), or retain more profits than previously in order to build up the capital base of the bank. In each case the bank becomes more secure, to the benefit of its depositors.

Table 4.10(c) shows that in 1986 and 1987 the large British banks made very substantial share issues (£3.4 billion), although part of this was the second call on TSB shareholders. Nonetheless it is clear that with the decline in both retained earnings and raising funds via perpetual debt, without such share issues the large British banks would have been unable to sustain their risk asset ratio at 9.8 per cent in 1987. It is clear too from *Table 4.10(a)* that weighted assets were growing fast compared with the adjusted capital base; balance sheet growth thus required additions to the capital base.

[5] Term subordinated debt is subordinated debt with a fixed maturity which satisfies the Bank of England's conditions for secondary capital.

In December 1987 the Bank published agreed proposals for the international convergence of capital measurement and capital standards (the Basle proposals). These proposals lay down :

(a) A common definition of capital, consisting of tier 1 (or core capital) which is mainly equity capital and disclosed reserves, and tier 2 which would include – at national discretion – supplementary capital (term debt).

Table 4.10

Capital adequacy of large British banks (£ b)

(a) Capital ratios

	1983	1984	1985	1986	1987
Total assets	271·1	315·7	303·1	334·7	345·2
Weighted assets	208·0	245·4	236·0	251·7	267·2
Adjusted capital base	16·9	18·6	23·0	26·5	26·3
Risk asset ratio (%)	8·1	7·6	9·7	10·5	9·8

(b) Capital constituents

	1983	1984	1985	1986	1987
Shareholders' funds	12·95	12·11	13·81	17·54	18·67
Preference shares	0·01	0·01	0·01	0·01	0·01
Primary perpetual debt	—	—	4·05	5·39	4·18
General provisions	1·27	1·79	1·76	1·34	1·29
Minority interests	1·08	0·78	0·40	0·45	0·44
Primary capital	15·31	14·69	20·04	24·73	24·58
Secondary capital	4·03	6·43	5·89	5·62	5·82
Total capital	19·34	21·12	25·93	30·35	30·40

Memorandum item :
Tier 1 capital   16·18
Tier 2 capital   12·77

(c) Sources of new capital[a]

	1983	1984	1985	1986	1987
Retained earnings	0·99	0·77	1·35	1·87	−0.72
Perpetual debt	—	1·20	3·82	1·25	0·09
Term subordinated debt	0·68	1·29	0·05	−0·29	0·50
Share issues	0·25	0·28	0·70	1·42	1·98
	1·92	3·54	5·92	4·25	1·85

[a] Excludes certain items affecting reserves, such as surpluses on property revaluations.

Source : Bank of England *Annual Report under the Banking Act*

(b) A common system of risk weights, applying to all assets on and off the balance sheet to reflect *credit risk*. The basic risk weights to be used in the calculation would be 0, 20, 50, and 100 per cent.

(c) A standard minimum level of capital, which banks would have to hold against their risk–adjusted assets and their business off the balance sheet. The intention is to allow banks to build up to a minimum ratio of 8 per cent by 1992. The Bank's intention is to require all UK banks to meet these minimum standards. The Bank will continue to set individual 'trigger' and 'target' risk asset ratios for each institution or bank, and it is further intended that this ratio will be above the 8 per cent minimum.

4.5.6 RECENT DEVELOPMENTS

In the past fifteen years the domestic banks in the UK have experienced many pressures and changes and these in turn have brought about shifts in the operations of these banks. During the last few years these pressures for change have intensified, and we will now examine the main elements.

4.5.6.1 Financial deregulation

The City revolution   In 1976 the powers of the Office of Fair Trading were extended to include service industries as well as manufacturing. In 1978 the government gave notice that it would, via the Office of Fair Trading, challenge the rule book of the Stock Exchange, contending that it violated the restrictive trade practices legislation. Had the legal process gone its full course, it is likely that it would have been not only slow but also damaging to the international position of the City. In the event, after a change of government in 1979, the Secretary of State for Trade and Industry and the Chairman of the Stock Exchange came to an agreement that court proceedings would cease in exchange for amendments to the rule book. The date for a full change in the rule book was to be 27 October 1986, the Big Bang. The key changes in the rule book were:

(a) For all transactions, commissions would be negotiated; the system of minimum commissions was to end;

(b) The separation of functions in securities trading would cease, in particular the separate functions of broker and jobber. Brokers had previously operated simply as agents for clients who wished to buy or sell securities, and jobbers performed the function of market-maker on the floor of the Stock Exchange but did not deal directly with the buyers or sellers of securities. One reason for the ending of single capacity operation was that with the cushion of minimum commissions taken away, single capacity operation would be unlikely to be sufficiently profitable;

(c) Outside firms would be able to take over firms who were already members of the Stock Exchange.

A number of consequences flowed from these changes which affected the banks. One was that banks could move into stockbroking and market-making by buying existing firms. Thus National Westminster took over the *jobbing* firm of Bisgood, Bishop and also the *broking* firm of Fielding Newson–Smith which, with County Bank, were then formed into the NatWest Investment Bank. Barclays have created a similar structure through their group holding company of Barclays de Zoete Wedd Holdings. Within BZW the group can provide merchant banking services, dealings in securities, and market-making. Other banks have made similar moves but more tentatively, and Midland and Lloyds have withdrawn from some securities business. The major retail banks have spent around £300 million on acquisitions in order to enter a very competitive business where profitability will be hard fought. Foreign banks have also been able to buy jobbing and broking firms, in particular the US and Japanese banks who have had considerable experience already of investment banking and securities trading. Furthermore, these banks are also much more highly capitalized than the UK equivalents and this is significant in view of the intensity of competition.

In addition, as deregulation of the securities industry has opened up London to foreign banks, by the same token the largest UK retail banks have had the choice of remaining largely domestic in their operations or attempting a global presence. So far, National Westminster, Midland, and Barclays have established foreign bases in Europe, New York, and Tokyo.

Building Societies Act 1986   Since the early 1980s the distinction
between the operation of the retail banks and the larger
building societies has become increasingly blurred. In 1982 the
banks moved into the mortgage market in direct competition
with the building societies. Unsurprisingly, the building societies view was that this represented unfair competition since the
existing legislation under which the building societies operated
greatly limited their range of lending as well as their deposit
base. The Act of 1986 has, to some extent, shifted the balance so
that the major building societies represent a substantial competitive threat to the retail banks. (We discuss this more fully in
section 4.9 which examines the building societies.)

Intensification of competition   The retail banks as a consequence
of deregulation have experienced greater competition from the
building societies. *Table 4.1* shows clearly the growth of market
share in sterling since 1966: the building society share rose from
13 to 17 per cent, whereas that of the retail banks fell from 28 to
17 per cent. The data also reveal that the secondary banks
(most of which are foreign) have increased their market share of
sterling business from 6 to 14 per cent. Foreign banks, for
example, now account for more than one quarter of sterling
lending within the UK – a clear indication of their success in
moving into the loan market. It is not surprising that the major
banking groups have begun to diversify their activities and
have moved into estate agency, insurance broking, life assurance, fund management and travel services, as well as broking
and market-making activities associated with the Big Bang.
Although the retail banks have a costly branch network to
maintain, it does provide them with a marketing base which is
almost unrivalled; the banks have over 11,000 branches mainly
controlled by the big five, whereas the building societies have
around 7,000 branches but spread over a larger number of
firms. Such a branch network, together with the computeriza-
tion of customer records, should provide the banks with a
considerable capacity to both target and market the increasing
range of services and products they have to offer.

4.5.6.2 Financial supervision

Following the failures of several small deposit-taking firms in
1973, the prudential supervision of banking firms was subject to

scrutiny and revision. One consequence was legislation in the form of the Banking Act 1979. Broadly, the purpose of the Act was to ensure that banks and other deposit-taking firms would be authorized only after careful vetting of applicants and their experience. The Act also established a deposit protection scheme intended to cushion depositors in the event of bank failure. Unfortunately, in October 1983 Johnson Matthey Bankers (JMB) failed as a result of grossly inadequate lending controls. In response to this, a committee under the chairmanship of the Governor of the Bank of England considered the necessary changes to the supervisory system. From this enquiry emerged the Banking Act 1987 (considered in more detail in Section 4.14).

The banks are required to conform not only to the Banking Act but also to the provisions of the Financial Services Act 1986 in so far as their business activities, in particular their investment services, fall within its scope. This legislation is concerned with investor protection – ensuring that investors obtain the best advice available from authorized individuals. Much of the supervision of those involved in investment business is delegated to self-regulatory bodies, the dominant body being the Securities and Investments Board. In so far as the banks are required to be fit and proper bodies to conduct investment business they are covered by the Financial Services Act, but other aspects of bank supervision are the responsibility of the Bank of England and subject to the Banking Act 1987. A particular difficulty for banks (such as National Westminster) which have moved into investment business, both as market participants and sellers of financial services and products to customers and clients, is ensuring that they comply with the conduct of business rules laid down by the Securities and Investments Board. Rule 5.01, for example, lays down that a firm shall not effect for a customer any transactions which the firm believes to be unsuitable for the customer. One difficulty, for which there is exception to rule 5.01, is that within an investment firm, such as that established by a bank, part of that firm might have information which is relevant to a client dealing with, another part of that firm. Such information may well be relevant to the client but, even though such information could be adverse, the information must not travel through the 'Chinese Walls' within the bank. Since the passing of the Act there have been several cases where these Chinese Walls proved to be no barrier to the improper movement of information. Rule 5.02 highlights further the dilemma of those banks undertaking investment business, since this rule lays down that such firms must offer the customer the best advice on financial products available. Thus a bank should not advise a customer to buy its own insurance products, or unit trusts, if it knows that they are not the best on the market. Clearly this creates a dilemma for those banks operating in this field: *either* a bank intends to offer genuine independent advice, *or* it sells financial products, but it cannot do both.

4.6 Secondary Banking : Wholesale banks

Secondary or wholesale banks are, as their name implies, intermediaries which are mainly dealing in large deposits (compared with retail deposits) and on-lending on a large scale. The minimum sums involved are from £50,000 upwards. It is probably more accurate to conceive of the *function* of wholesale banking rather than a sharply delineated group of financial intermediaries. Nonetheless the banks in London which are primarily involved in wholesale banking are indentified in the published data as the British merchant banks (accepting houses), other British banks, American banks, Japanese banks, and other overseas banks (including consortium banks). A brief description of each of the secondary banking groups is appropriate.

The origin of the merchant banks (accepting houses) is in the nineteenth century; certain merchant venturers gained a high reputation and their bills of exchange could therefore be discounted easily and at low rates. Later these firms moved into the business of accepting bills and eventually developed a range of financial services which include banking, investment management, corporate finance, and underwriting. This group of banks includes such well-known names as Morgan Grenfell, Schroders, and Kleinwort Bensen. The success and survival of this kind of firm rest on their ability to offer specialist services at competitive rates (rather like the small German banks), but the Big Bang has toughened the climate since these firms now have to face large foreign banks keen to move into this kind of business. One response to this threat is to become larger, and this could be by means of, say, the merger of a merchant bank with a larger banking firm. At the end of 1987 there were thirty-four accepting houses.

The traditional business of the accepting houses was the 'accepting' of bills of exchange, a process which effectively meant the addition of the good name and reputation of the accepting house to the bill (for a commission, of course), thus enhancing the marketability of the bill. The sale or 'discounting' of the bill would usually be arranged by the accepting house, and only in the case of default on the bill would the accepting house be liable to use its own resources to cover the bill. However, although the accepting houses are still heavily involved in this and similar business, it is relatively less important than other activities. For example, in 1954 the value of acceptances in relation to total assets amounted to about 60 per cent, whereas this ratio had fallen to around 9 per cent in 1988. Another activity of the accepting houses is to act as agents, mainly for UK companies, in the new issue market, where they advise, arrange, and underwrite new capital issues. They have also extended their advisory activities in the direction of investment management, and especially in connection with pension funds. However, the major change in their activities has been the move towards full banking activity rather than mere agency work. A stimulus to such activity came with the development of the Euro-currency market and with this the application of their expertise to the establishment and operation of the Euro-bond market. The growth of the inter-bank market has also provided additional opportunities.

In the case of the other secondary banks, their establishment and development has been largely the result of response to one particular phenomenon: the growth of the Euro-currency, and in particular, the Euro-dollar market. The central role of London in this field has contributed to the rapid growth in the number of secondary banks. Other British banks consist of the secondary banking subsidiaries of the retail banks (e.g. Barclays de Zoete Wedd Ltd) as well as a substantial number of finance houses (HP companies) which are now classified as banks (e.g. United Dominions Trust Ltd). At the end of 1987 there were around 240 banks in this category.

The American, Japanese, and other overseas banks form a substantial group of over 400 banks. Although the number of foreign banks establishing UK branches has slowed down (partly because the major foreign banks are already established in London), the Big Bang has provided a sustaining interest and several foreign banks have taken over stock market firms; for example, Chase Manhattan bought Simon & Coates, and Union Bank of Switzerland bought Phillips & Drew. Altogether this group of banks holds 75 per cent of the secondary banking business – UK secondary banks having around 23 per cent. Although the foreign banks provide banking services for individuals and companies from their own country, these banks have moved into London because of the opportunities in both the domestic UK banking market and the foreign currency business.

4.6.1 SECONDARY BANKS' BALANCE SHEET

Table 4.11 identifies the main assets and liabilities of the secondary banks in the UK for June 1983 and 1988. Since we have identified the components of the balance sheet in Sections 4.5.3 and 4.5.4, we shall refer the reader to those sections and confine ourselves to several general observations about the secondary banks which highlight the differences between the retail and wholesale banks as well as any changes which have taken place between 1983 and 1988.

(a) It is clear that the bulk (75 per cent) of secondary bank deposits are denominated in foreign currency, mainly US dollars; this compares with 17 per cent for the retail banks. Such a high proportion reflects their international business and their involvement in foreign currency markets.

(b) In 1988 total bank deposits (retail and wholesale) stood at around £985 billion, of which nearly three-quarters were wholesale deposits. Within the wholesale banking group, the foreign banks held over 80 per cent of wholesale deposits.

(c) If one considers only sterling deposits then the wholesale banks account for about half (retail banks also have a half), and the foreign banks hold about 63 per cent of those wholesale deposits.

Table 4.11
UK secondary banks' balance sheet

	1983 (15 June) £m	%	1988 (30 June) £m	%
Assets				
Sterling assets				
Notes and coin	55	0·01	35	0·005
Balances with the Bank of England	203	0·04	447	0·06
Market loans:				
Secured money with LDMA[a]	2,005	0·4	2,567	0·3
Other UK monetary sector	22,416	5·0	50,357	6·9
Certificates of deposit	4,223	0·9	9,063	1·2
UK local authorities	4,247	0·9	791	0·1
Overseas	4,289	0·9	20,352	2·8
Bills:				
Treasury bills	57	0·01	59	0·008
Eligible local authority bills	61	0·01	10	—
Eligible bank bills	632	0·1	712	0·1
Other bills	280	0·06	626	0·08
Advances:				
UK public sector	1,762	0·3	1,248	0·17
UK private sector	29,333	6·5	79,016	10·8
Overseas	5,101	1·1	8,782	1·2
Banking Department lending to central government	—	—	—	—
Investments:				
British government stocks	1,886	0·4	1,805	0·2
Other	1,795	0·4	9,949	1·4
Other currency assets				
Market loans and advances	355,982	79·0	493,820	67·7
of which:				
(Advances)	(93,007)	(26·6)	(111,011)	(15·2)
UK monetary sector	69,011	15·2	65,594	9·0
Certificates of deposit	8,000	1·8	8,570	1·2
UK public sector	1,081	0·2	58	0·008
UK private sector	19,492	4·3	44,176	6·0
Overseas	258,396	57·1	375,423	51·4

Bills	1,062	0.2	2,866	0.4
Investments	9,253	2.0	31,616	4.3
Miscellaneous assets (sterling and other currencies)	7,523	1.7	15,572	2.1
(Acceptances)	(11,603)	(2.6)	(15,349)	(2.1)
(Eligible liabilities) b	(40,792)	(9.0)	(106,812)	(14.6)
Liabilities				
Sterling deposits	68,822	15.2	171,268	23.5
of which:				
(Sight deposits)	(15,141)	(3.3)	(24,433)	(3.3)
UK monetary sector	27,099	6.0	56,545	7.7
UK public sector	919	0.2	3,735	0.5
UK private sector	20,769	4.6	48,193	6.6
Overseas	15,112	3.3	40,312	5.5
Certificates of deposit and other short-term paper	4,913	1.1	22,482	3.0
Other currency deposits	366,810	81.1	524,879	71.9
of which:				
UK monetary sector	79,195	17.5	76,899	10.5
Other UK	10,001	2.2	25,436	3.5
Overseas	217,713	48.1	354,357	48.6
Certificates of deposit and other short-term paper	59,901	13.2	68,189	9.3
Items in suspense and transmission, capital and other funds (sterling and other currencies)	16,537		33,549	
	452,168		729,698	

ª a London Discount Market Association.
b Eligible liabilities comprise sterling deposit liabilities excluding deposits with an original maturity of over two years, plus any sterling resources obtained by switching foreign currencies into sterling. Inter-bank transactions are included on a net basis and adjustments are made for transit items.

Source : Bank of England *Quarterly Bulletin*

(d) Since 1983 the distribution of total deposits between the wholesale and retail groups has changed only slightly, but the holding of *sterling* deposits has changed distinctly. In particular, foreign banks in London now hold just over 30 per cent of sterling deposits compared with 19 per cent in 1983. Of that group the Japanese banks' growth of business has been the fastest, and there has been a relative decline of the US banks in London.

(e) It is clear from the source of funds for the secondary banks that a small amount is in the form of sight deposits (3·3 per cent) with the remainder coming from the inter-bank market as well as the UK private sector. Of their foreign currency deposits, almost 70 per cent originate from overseas, and around 15 per cent from within the UK monetary sector.

(f) About one-quarter of secondary banks' assets are denominated in sterling and the remainder in foreign currency. Of their sterling business, the two important items are market loans to the sterling inter-bank market and advances to the UK private sector. This latter item is especially striking since the total sterling lending was almost £80 billion (of which £47 billion came from *foreign* banks), and this compares with the £119 billion advances by the UK retail banks. In 1983 the comparable figures were £29 billion advances from secondary banks (of which £9 billion originated from foreign banks), and £56 billion from the UK retail banks. The position in 1988 represents a remarkable intrusion of the foreign banks into the domestic market. It is all the more remarkable because the traditional view is that there is to some degree a 'natural' protection of the home market because of the strong local base of the domestic banks. The data show clearly however, that the domestic banks' natural monopoly advantage is no longer substantial.

(g) Although the market for sterling loans has grown, the market share of the UK retail banks has fallen from 66 to 60 per cent whilst that of the foreign banks has increased from 10 to 24 per cent. This change is perhaps not surprising in view of the determined efforts of French, US, Japanese and German banks to penetrate the UK home market in search of corporate customers both large and small. The personal sector may well be secure from the threat of competition from foreign banks since the UK retail banks can rely on their branch network. However, it is interesting to note that there have been some moves into branch banking by foreign banks, e.g. Citibank, and it might be that the expensive branch network of the UK banks is less of an advantage in the longer term as other methods of marketing bank services emerge – particularly with further technological change.

(h) Secondary bank holdings of cash and balances at the Bank of England are small, and this reflects their lack of involvement in the domestic money transmission mechanism.

A crucial feature of secondary bank operation, one which sharply differentiates it from the operation of the primary banks, is that the number of depositors (and borrowers) is very much smaller than that of the retail banks. As a consequence, the secondary banks are unable to manage their balance sheet by relying on the 'law of large numbers'; that is, as one deposit of £1 million is withdrawn there is a lower chance of an offsetting inflow compared with the retail banks' operations and expectations. Accordingly the secondary banks manage their balance sheet and their liquidity by attempting some *matching* of assets and liabilities in respect of their term to maturity.

One reason for this simple objective may be understood if we consider a balance sheet which is perfectly matched. Under such circumstances (ignoring any risk of default) the bank would be operating so that its loans would be repaid at precisely the same time as its own liabilities fell due for repayment. Thus a bank might have borrowed (taken deposits) of, say, £50 million which have to be repaid in six months' time, and is able to find borrowers or buy financial assets which repay or mature (the bank receives funds) in six months' time. In principle, there would be no need for such a bank to operate on the basis of a liquidity rule in respect of the *assets* side of the balance sheet as do the retail banks, because the matching of maturities would guarantee the required cash flow and solvency. We have already noted in this chapter that banks try to manage their assets so that there is a balance of liquidity between the various assets, and that the degree of liquidity varies with the return on such assets; in other words, this 'traditional' approach views the assets vertically in the balance sheet. By contrast, the objective of matching considers the balance sheet horizontally, i.e. relating the maturity of assets acoss the balance sheet in relation to the liabilities. We can observe this technique of matching by examining the secondary banks' foreign currency business. *Table 4·12* presents data (no longer published by the Bank of England) for 1984.

We can see that in August 1984 the secondary banks had taken $ 143,067 million in deposits having a maturity of less than eight days, i.e. they would be liable to repay that amount within eight days, and this accounted for 22 per cent of total liabilities. On the other hand these banks had $ 109,491 million claims against others which were also due to be repaid within eight days, and this represented 17 per cent of total claims (assets). Clearly, these banks' very short-term liabilities exceeded their claims by $ 33,576 million – the net position. At other end of the distribution, liabilities exceeding three years, maturity amounted to $ 18,888 million, whereas the corresponding assets were $ 107,327 million; this represents an excess of claims of $ 88,439 million. Relating the two ends of the maturity distribution, it is evident that these banks are 'borrowing very short and lending long'.

On the face of it the matching of the assets and liabilities is far from perfect although they were, nevertheless, statistically highly correlated. There are three chief reasons for this lack of perfect matching. One is that such a matching is unlikely to be feasible since the demand and supply of funds is, overall, not symmetrical. Roughly speaking, there are likely to be more who wish to borrow long than wish to lend long. *Table 4·12* shows that total claims for one year and over amounted to $ 153,122 million and total liabilities only $ 36,128 million. Another reason for mismatching is that the bank itself might *choose* not to match as closely as is feasible. One explanation for this apparently imprudent attitude is that the bank may have firm expectations of interest rates falling in the future. In this case, it would be appropriate to increase its long-term lending (at current 'high' interests rates) and reduce its long-term borrowing at current rates. When interest rates fall, the bank would then attempt to improve the matching at the long end by increasing its longer-dated liabilities to match its claims at the long end. Since long-term lending yields higher rates of return than short-term lending, the bank may choose to mismatch in order to benefit from higher profit margins, albeit at greater risk. Finally, the bank will rely on the rolling over of its own liabilities, or the ability to borrow in the inter-bank market, or issue certificates of deposit to accommodate any shortfall. It can be seen from *Table 4.12* that 69 per cent of the banks liabilities mature in less than three months, whereas only 56 per cent of the banks' claims mature in the same period. Such an illiquid position could only be maintained by a bank if it expected to be able to obtain accommodating finance when required, or to roll over its own liabilities.

Table 4.12
UK monetary sector : analysis of foreign currency claims and liabilities by maturity (15 August 1984)

Maturity	Liabilities		Claims		Net position
	$m	%	$m	%	
Less than 8 days	143,067	22	109,491	17	− 33,576
8 days to 1 month	130,607	20	102,676	16	− 27,931
1 to 3 months	177,923	27	149,818	23	− 28,105
3 to 6 months	115,518	18	97,193	15	− 18,325
6 months to 1 year	47,613	7	45,002	6	− 2,611
1 to 3 years	17,240	3	45,795	7	+ 28,555
More than 3 years	18,888	3	107,327	16	+ 88,439
	650,856		657,302		+ 6,446

Source : Bank of England *Quarterly Bulletin*, vol. 24, no. 4 (December 1984)

4.7 The Bank of England Banking Department

We have included the Bank of England Banking Department in our discussion of the primary banking sector because this Department is a very important element in the payments mechanism. It provides money transmission services for both the government and the public, including the deposit banks themselves. *Table 4.13* shows the liabilities of the Banking Department as of 29 February 1988. The bulk of the Banking Department's liabilities are deposits, and the two types of deposit to which we shall restrict discussion are public deposits and bankers' deposits.

Table 4·13
Liabilities of the Bank of England Banking Department, 29 February 1988
(£ m)

Capital	15
Reserves	608
Current liabilities:	
Public deposits	360
Bankers' deposits	1,176
Other accounts	1,359
Payable to the Treasury	26
Taxation and other creditors	44
Total	3,588

Source : Bank of England *Report and Accounts* (29 February 1988)

4.7.1 PUBLIC DEPOSITS

The central government is spending and receiving very large sums of money each day; a rough daily average currently would be £600 million. To facilitate such transactions, the government requires a bank, and quite simply the Bank of England is the government's banker. All authorized payments and receipts of the central government must be paid into and come out of the Exchequer, which is the government's central cash account held at the Bank of England. Other deposits which are held at the Bank of England include those of the National Loans Fund, the National Debt Commissioners, the Paymaster General, and the Inland Revenue.

4.7.2 BANKERS' DEPOSITS

The bulk of these deposits are held by the banks operating the clearing system. This includes Midland, Lloyds, Barclays, and NatWest as well as TSB, Co-op Bank, Coutts, Girobank, Citibank, and the Bank of England. The clearing system for money transfers operates in several ways. There is an umbrella organization, the Association for Payment Clearing Services (APACS) which is a separate body from the Committee of London Clearing Bankers, and which is responsible for general oversight of the payments system. Associated with this body are three individual clearing companies which deal with operational clearings. The first covers the general clearing and credit clearing over the whole country of the bulk (by volume) of items – the paper-based part of the system, i.e. cheques. A second company, which operates the largest part of the system by value, is the Town Clearing, which handles big transactions in the City on the same day. Town clearings represent around 90 per cent of all clearings. This company also includes the system known as CHAPS (Clearing House Automated Payments System) set up in February 1984 by the clearing banks. This system enables large transfers to take place speedily – mainly large inter-bank transfers. The third company is responsible for the Bankers' Automated Clearing Services (BACS), which deals with large transfers and regular payments such as salaries, pensions, insurance premiums, and mortgage payments; it is not paper-based but is entirely electronic. Access to these clearing systems can be direct or by associate membership, and this will depend on whether an applicant satisfies the various criteria, in particular that it has an adequate volume of business (0·5 per cent of operational clearings). Membership and access to these systems is available to building societies as well as banks.

Since around 13 million paper transactions are processed through the clearing system *each day*, involving up to 60 per cent of employees in banking, non-paper-based systems would clearly reduce costs. The introduction and extension of EFTPOS (electronic funds transfer at point of sale) would help to complete a computerized non-paper banking system. By 1989 a national EFTPOS system, with 2000 terminals, is to be established in Edinburgh, Leeds, and Southampton; once the technical problems have been dealt with, its national extension is inevitable.

Bankers' deposits serve at least three functions (including their use in the clearing system), and these are examined in turn.

4.7.2.1 Inter-bank indebtedness

We have already seen that the bulk of transactions by value within the UK are undertaken by transferring bank deposits by cheque rather than by the use of notes and coins. The volume of payments by means of cheques is very substantial : for example, during 1987 the average monthly transfers were well over

Table 4.14

Barclays Bank customers	Midland Bank customers	NatWest Bank customers
A £10 m cheques paid to Midland Bank customers	C £6 m cheques paid to Barclays Bank customers	E £4 m cheques paid to Barclays Bank customers
B £12 m cheques paid to NatWest Bank customers	D £3 m cheques paid to NatWest Bank customers	F £15 m cheques paid to Midland Bank customers

Net position between the banks

Barclays Bank 'owes' Midland Bank £4 m (A minus C)
Barclays Bank 'owes' NatWest Bank £8 m (B minus E)
NatWest Bank 'owes' Midland Bank £12 m (F minus D)

£800,000 million. The means by which such vast sums are transferred from one account to another is the operation of the clearing system to which we have already briefly referred. To explain the need for the clearing system and its operation, we shall consider two sets of circumstances. In the first an individual makes payment by means of a cheque drawn on his account with, say, Midland Bank, payable to another individual who also has an account with the Midland Bank but at a different branch. In the second an individual draws a cheque on his account with the Midland Bank, made payable to an individual whose account is with Barclays Bank. How is settlement made in these two cases? In the former case, the debiting on one account and the crediting of the other will be accomplished through inter-branch clearing within Midland Bank, one branch's deposits falling by the amount in question, and the other branch's rising by the same sum. In the second case, however, the indebtedness of the Midland Bank (acting on behalf of its customer) to Barclays Bank may be settled by the transfer of funds from the Midland Bank's account at the Bank of England to Barclays Bank's account at the Bank of England.

In practice, there are millions of cheques and other transfers involved in the daily 'clearings' and it will be the net amount which will be settled by alteration in the banks' balances at the Bank of England. *Table 4.14* should make the position clearer. In the circumstances shown in the table. Barclays Bank's balance at the Bank of England would fall by a total of £12

million, the Midland Bank's balance would rise by £16 million
(of which £4 million would be from Barclays Bank's account at
the Bank of England, and £12 million from the National
Westminister Bank's account at the Bank of England), and the
National Westminister Bank's balance at the Bank of England
would fall by £4 million. Clearly the existence of bankers'
deposits at the Bank of England is a vital facility in settling
inter-bank indebtedness.

4.7.2.2 Notes and coin

A further use to which bankers' deposits are put is the provision
of notes and coin in sufficient quantity, variety, and quality
(e.g. cleanliness of banknotes) to meet the needs of the public.
The public's desire to hold and use notes and coin fluctuates
with seasonal factors, e.g. the demand for notes and coin rises
during the summer holiday period and also at Christmas.
Furthermore it varies according to the public's total holding of
bank deposits; as the volume of bank deposits changes, the
demand for notes and coin also varies in the same direction.
When the public wishes to increase its holdings of notes and
coin, it can do so by drawing cheques for cash against demand
deposits. It is likely that such a change will be spread over all
the clearing banks who will thus find their till money declining.
To offset such a change, the banks can convert some of their
bankers' deposits with the Bank of England as a means of
replenishing their cash holdings.

4.7.2.3 Government transactions

Finally, bankers' deposits are the means by which financial
transactions between the central government and the rest of the
economy (a better expression to use here would be the 'non-
government sector') can take place. When discussing public
deposits we emphasized that the central government is spending and receiving moneys on a very large scale, and since the
central government does not have bank accounts with the
deposit banks of any significant size, the only way in which the
deposit banking system can make payments to the central
government and receive payments from it is by variations in
bankers' deposits. We shall consider this in more details in
Chapters 5 and 6, but it is sufficient to state at this point that *net*

payments by the non-government sector to the central government will result in a fall in bankers' deposits as the banks make payment on behalf of customers, and *net* payments by the government to the non-government sector will result in a rise in bankers' deposits. A simplified illustration will help to make this clear. Let us suppose that an individual is obliged to pay £100 capital gains tax. One method of making payment would be by drawing a cheque on his bank account at, say, Barclays Bank, using the bank giro system, to transfer £100 to the Inland Revenue's collection account at the Bank of England. The final settlement would be made at the Bank of England by *crediting* the Inland Revenue's account (part of the item 'public deposits') with £100, and *debiting* Barclays Bank's account at the Bank of England (part of the item 'bankers' deposits') by £100.

4.8 The discount houses

The discount houses, of which there are eight, are public limited companies and members of the London Discount Market Association (LDMA). Of the eight, four have been taken over by larger institutions (three of them foreign). The discount houses are peculiar to the UK but they are useful and are important elements in the monetary system. Let us first consider the discount houses simply as financial firms in the private sector and examine their business operations. *Table 4.15* provides the balance sheet of the discount market for June 1983 and 1988. The composition of the balance sheet of the discount market is not as stable as other financial firms – and this is illustrated by the two sets of figures – because the discount houses need to be very responsive to changes in the relative profitability of assets and relative cost of borrowed funds[6]. They also need to be very sensitive to *likely* movements in interest rates because their margins are very fine.

The commercial operations of the discount houses are essentially very simple. They seek out loanable funds, mainly from the major banks and the inter-bank market; these funds are usually available on a very short-term basis. Then such funds are used for the purchase of a variety of assets which include

---

[6] Although the two sets of figures seem dissimilar they are in fact highly correlated.

Treasury bills, commercial bills, and gilt-edged securities. This is, of course, the basic operation of any financial intermediary, but the difference here lies in the relationship between the discount market, the banks, and the Bank of England.

Table 4.15 reveals that most of the discount houses' funds are obtained from the banks (in June 1988 the UK monetary sector provided 68.3 per cent of the discount markets' funds) and most of the borrowing from the banks is 'money at call' (86.3 per cent). These funds are lent by the banks to the discount market on a day-to-day basis with the option to call in the loan before noon on a particular day. It is hardly surprising that an important function of the discount houses is to seek out assiduously sources of money which they can use to support the assets in their balance sheet. Without such constant activity, the discount houses would find themselves substantially and frequently short of funds to balance their books. Notwithstanding such activity the discount houses do find themselves short of funds, and we shall examine this in Section 4.8.3.

It is clear from *Table 4.15* that in 1983 and 1988 the discount houses were using 70 per cent or more of their borrowed funds to trade in bills and certificates of deposit. Indeed this fact identifies an important function of the discount houses: they are market-makers [7] in these two kinds of liquid assets – assets which are of importance of the liquidity of the banks. The significance of this role can be gauged by the fact that discount houses hold around 43 per cent of *all* outstanding bills and 30 per cent of sterling CDs which have been issued. Not only do the discount houses help to 'make a market' in these assets, but they also function in this way with respect to local authority bonds and short-dated British government securities. The houses are in the market – buying and selling these various assets – so that it is always possible for others to trade in such assets. This activity provides a stabilizing influence in these markets. In addition the houses are prepared to deal with the banks by supplying them with bills of appropriate maturity to suit the portfolio and liquidity needs of the banks.

[7] This term is being used loosely in the sense of 'making a market' rather than of its interpretation under the Financial Services Act (See Section 4.8.4).

Table 4.15 Discount market balance sheet

	1983 (15 June)		1988 (30 June)	
	£m	%	£m	%
Assets				
Sterling assets				
Cash ratio deposits with the Bank of England	2	0·03	12	0·1
Bills :				
Treasury bills	116	1·9	77	0·7
Local authority bills	232	3·7	–	–
Other public sector bills	–	–	–	–
Other bills	3,269	53·0	3,952	35·6
Funds lent :				
UK monetary sector	20	0·3	1,381	12·4
UK monetary sector CDs	1,792	29·0	3,811	34·4
Building society CDs and time deposits	–	–	675	6·0
UK local authorities	139	2·2	37	0·3
Other UK	88	1·4	337	3·0
Overseas	–	–	132	1·2
Investments :				
British government stocks	401	6·5	24	0·2
Local authorities	152	2·4	–	–
Other	37	0·5	318	2·8
Other sterling assets	26	0·4	65	0·6
Other currency assets	141	2·3	266	2·4
of which :				
CDs	122	2·0	24	0·2
Bills	14	0·2	36	0·3
Other	5	0·8	206	1·8
Liabilities (borrowed funds)				
Sterling	6,031	97·7	10,498	94·7
of which :				
(Call and overnight)	(5,535)	(89·6)	(9,570)	(86·3)
Bank of England	50	0·8	124	1·1
Other UK monetary sector	5,373	87·0	7,576	68·3
Other UK	595	9·6	2,757	24·8
Overseas	13	0·2	41	0·4
Other currencies	142	2·3	274	2·5
of which :				
UK monetary sector	107	1·7	114	1·0
Other UK	25	0·4	144	1·3
Overseas	10	0·1	16	0·1
Total liabilities/assets	6,173		11,089	

Source : Bank of England *Quarterly Bulletin* vol. 23, no. 3; vol. 28, no. 4.

Not only do the discount houses oblige the banks but the houses also have an arrangement with the Bank of England. This arrangement is that the discount houses agree 'to cover the tender'. By this agreement the LDMA members bid for all the Treasury bills on offer each week. Those bills which are not bought by other bidders will be bought by the discount houses. Each house decides its tender price, but collectively the houses guarantee that the Bank of England will be able to sell all the Treasury bills on offer each week. This appears to be a considerable, open-ended commitment by the discount market, but the Bank is always prepared to provide finance, as 'lender of last resort', if the houses do not have sufficient funds to take up the Treasury bills which the houses are obliged to buy.

It is also clear that the discount houses' operations are largely confined to the domestic market, since their foreign currency denominated borrowing and lending is very small. Indeed it is their role in the domestic monetary system which highlights the importance of the discount houses. Because of their importance and because almost all of the discount houses' resources are *borrowed* – their own reserves representing only about 3 per cent of their liabilities – the discount houses have been obliged by the Bank of England to observe certain ratios which relate their trading activities to their capital resources.

4.8.1 DISCOUNT MARKET SUPERVISION

The Bank of England's approach to supervision is that the framework should not be rigid but should evolve in the light of experience [8]. At the present time the Bank requires the discount houses to be separately capitalized in the UK as well as expecting substantial shareholders to accept ultimate responsibility for the liabilities of the discount houses. Supervision is based on close contact with the management of the houses as well as continuous assessment of the discount houses' risk exposure in relation to capital resources. To this end the Bank

[8] This section relies heavily on material contained in the Bank of England *Quarterly Bulletin* for August 1988.

has laid down guidelines (and the Bank emphasizes that these are *guidelines* and are not applied as a simple mechanical formula) which cover measurement and evaluation of capital adequacy, supervision of large exposures, and reporting and monitoring arrangements.

Capital adequacy is assessed by comparing the assets of each discount house – measured in risk-adjusted terms – with its capital base. For measurement purposes, assets are divided into five classes. Four of these classes are treated as giving rise to 'added risk', which is calculated by multiplying the assets in each class by the appropriate weights which reflect the riskiness of each class of asset. The added risk and the actual assets of the discount house together comprise the adjusted total assets of the house, and this total must not exceed 80 times the capital base of the discount house. In addition, added risk alone must not exceed 25 times capital base. The Bank regards these limits as absolute maxima and may well intervene before these limits are reached if it is concerned about an asset portfolio which is 'unbalanced'.

The Bank identified four main types of risk inherent in any assets held :

Credit risk   The risk that the value of the asset might be impaired because of some risk of default.

Position risk   The risk of an unfavourable change in the market value of an asset for other reasons than credit risk, e.g. a change in market interest rates.

Forced sale risk   This is a special case of position risk, in which there is an additional loss of asset value because of the need to sell the asset at short notice at a time when trading is low in that particular asset market.

Settlement risk   The risk that the process of exchanging money for assets will not be completed smoothly and the discount house might suffer further loss of asset value.

The main risks which discount houses experience are probably position and forced sale risks, for example in their holding of gilt-edged securities. *Table 4·16* shows the risk classification of assets provided by the Bank of England. Eligible bills with a maturity of no more than three months, for example, have no added risk factor, whereas gilt-edged securities with a maturity of more than five years are multiplied by an added risk factor of 4. Valuing assets at market value and multiplying them by the risk factor represents a fairly simple exercise to produce a valuation of the added risk assets, which together with the actual value of the assets gives us the adjusted total assets – a total which must not exceed 80 times the capital base.

The capital base is defined in the way which best measures the discount house's ability to absorb losses, and includes the elements shown in *Table 4·17*.

To the extent that a discount house has matched the maturity of assets with liabilities (our discussion in Section 4.6.1 showed that this would reduce risk) then within limits such assets may be netted out of the calculation of the adjusted assets total. Unmatched foreign currency positions (which would create a risk of losses caused by an unfavourable movement in foreign exchange rates) are, however, included in the framework of added risk classes.

Within the terms of the Banking Act 1987, which lays down upper limits of a banks' exposure to an individual borrower, the Bank monitors such exposure by the discount houses and provides fairly detailed guidance as to the extent of such exposure and the circumstances in which Bank of England permission is required prior to a particular commitment by a discount house.

The Bank also expects the discount houses to monitor their positions on a daily basis and to observe the multiplier limits relating to their capital base *continuously*. As well as this, the Bank expects the usual monthly returns from the houses but makes clear that the Bank may ask for additional returns at any time.

As a hypothetical illustration of this system of supervision, we might assume that a discount house has around £300 million capital base and total liabilities/assets of £1,300 million. The added risk calculation might resemble the following :

Table 4.16

Risk classification for discount houses' assets

No added risk	Weight 1	Weight 2	Weight 4	Weight 5
		Added risk classes		
Cash at bankers	Eligible bills 3 – 6 months			
Deposits with Bank of England				
Eligible bills up to 3 months				
Ineligible bank bills up to 3 months	Ineligible bank bills 3–12 months	Ineligible bank bills over 1 year		
Trade bills up to 3 months	Trade bills 3 – 6 months	Trade bills over 6 months		
	Other trade bills up to 3 months	Other trade bills over 3 months		
CDs up to 3 months	CDs 3–12 months	CDs 1–3 years	CDs over 3 years	
Loans to banks and building societies up to 3 months	Loans to banks and building societies 3–12 months	Loans to banks and building societies 1–3 years	Loans to banks and building societies over 3 years	
Other loans to next business day	Other loans longer than to next business day			
Fixed-rate gilts up to 3 months	Fixed-rate gilts 3–18 months (or short positions in such stocks)	Fixed-rate gilts $1\frac{1}{2}$–5 years (or short positions in such stocks)	Fixed-rate gilts over 5 years (or short positions in such stocks)	

Variable-rate assets issued by local authorities or government-guaranteed borrowers, where rate is fixed for up to 3 months	Variable-rate assets issued by local authorities or government-guaranteed borrowers, where rate is fixed for 3–6 months Other variable-rate assets where rate is fixed for up to 3 months (including leases)	Variable-rate assets issued by local authorities or government-guaranteed borrowers, where rate is fixed for more than 6 months Other variable-rate assets where rate is fixed for 3–6 months (including leases)	Other variable-rate assets where rate is fixed for more than 6 months (including leases)	Fixed-rate leases over 18 months
Fixed-rate quoted assets up to 3 months Fixed-rate unquoted assets up to 3 months	Fixed-rate quoted assets 3–12 months Fixed-rate unquoted assets 3–6 months Fixed-rate leases up to 3 months	Fixed-rate quoted assets 1–3 years Fixed-rate unquoted assets 6 – 18 months Fixed-rate leases 3 – 6 months	Fixed-rate quoted assets over 3 years Fixed-rate unquoted assets over 18 months Fixed rate leases 6 – 18 months	
Futures positions and forward commitments in gilts up to 3 months Other forward commitments up to 3 months	Futures positions and forward commitments in gilts 3–18 months Other forward commitments 3–12 months	Futures positions and forward commitments in gilts $1\frac{1}{2}$ – 5 years Other forward commitments 1–3 years Open position in foreign currency	Futures positions and forward commitments in gilts over 5 years Other forward commitments over 3 years Equity investments (including preference shares)	

Source : Bank of England *Quarterly Bulletin* (August 1988).

Table 4·17
Capital base of the discount houses

Amount paid up on ordinary share capital
plus Amount paid up on non-redeemable preference shares
Share premium account
Capital reserves
General reserves
Profit and loss account
Contingency and other reserves (including provision for deferred tax)
Profit/loss in current year to date including unrealized appreciation/depreciation (net of tax payable in respect of current year)
Subordinated loan capital, subject to the Bank's agreement as to amount and terms
minus Net book value of fixed assets (deducting only 20 per cent of the value of freehold and leasehold property)
Goodwill
Book value of interests in subsidiaries and associated companies (share capital and loans)
Unsecured loans to parent company or fellow subsidiaries (secured loans would be treated as adding risk to the book in accordance with the assets against which the loans are secured)

	£m
Discount house assets	1,300
Risk category : 0 × 400 = 0	
1 × 510 = 510	
2 × 250 = 500	
4 × 120 = 480	
5 × 20 = 100	
Added risk 1,590	1,590
Adjusted total book (assets)	2,890

The fictional discount house in the illustration would therefore require a capital base of at least £63·6 million to support the added risk assets (1,590/25) and at least £36·1 million to support the adjusted total book (2,890/80). Since we have assumed that this house has a capital base of £300 million the Bank might well regard its asset and capital base position as comfortably secure (unless some of the components were regarded with special concern).

4.8.2 THE DISCOUNT HOUSES AND THE BANK OF ENGLAND

Not only do the discount houses provide valuable financial services as part of their business operations; they are also an important element in the relationship between the banking system and the Bank of England. However, this relationship will no longer be unique after October 1988 (see Section 4.8.4).

It is perhaps helpful to look first at what was the traditional role of the discount houses : the smoothing out of the ebb and flow of funds between the banks which resulted from transactions *within* the non-government sector, i.e. transactions between the banks necessitated by transactions between banks' customers in the private sector of the economy. We may use the example contained in *Table 4.14* as a means of making this clear. However, before we do so it is necessary to provide an additional assumption (albeit in a somewhat simplified form) which is that the clearing banks maintain a desired level of *cash* reserves at the Bank of England. If a particular banks' level falls, we assumer that the bank will attempt to rebuild such reserves, and if the level rises we assume that the bank will attempt to reduce such reserves since they yield no return. Such reserves are needed, not least because of the clearing banks' obligations towards' their customers in respect of the drawing of cash. The cash must always be available, should customers wish to convert their bank deposits into cash.

We can now trace the consequences of the inter-bank indebtedness which was to be found in the illustration in *Table 4.14*. The net position we established was that Barclays' reserves would fall by £12 million, Midland Bank reserves would rise by £16 million, and National Westminster reserves would fall by £4 million. Barclays and National Westminster need to replenish their reserves by a total of £16 million, and this could be achieved by *calling in* £16 million of their loans to the discount market. However, the Midland Bank would have surplus reserves of £16 million which it would dispose of by *increasing* its lending to the discount market by £16 million. Thus the only change would be a change in the bankers' deposits at the Bank of England, and the accounts of the discount houses would remain the same, by virtue of repaying and borrowing £16 million simultaneously. By this means the settlement of inter-bank indebtedness, arising from the operation of the payments mechanism, could be undertaken in a smooth fashion by the preparedness of the discount market to absorb additional funds as well as repay on demand. This particular role in the discount houses has been taken over by the inter-bank market, in which banks lend and borrow substantial sums for periods ranging from overnight to the typical three month transaction. The amounts involved might range from £500,000 to several million pounds (see Section 6.12.2). Although such inter-bank indebtedness is not longer accommodated by the discount houses, the settlement of such indebtedness, is still undertaken by using the bankers' deposits at the Bank of England.

It is important to point out, however, that if the *whole system* is short of cash then the inter-bank market will not be able to satisfy banks' requirements, and under these circumstances the traditional function of the discount houses would operate. This function would arise, in general, as a result of transactions which take place between the *non-government* sector and the *government* sector. To refer again to the illustration in *Table 4.14*, we saw that there was simply a redistribution of bankers' deposits between the various clearing banks, and the arithmetic of the example was such that the *total* of bankers' deposits remained unchanged. In practice it is unlikely that transfers between banks would cancel out. One reason for this is that individual persons and firms are not only making payments to each other within the non-governmental sector, but also making payments *to* the government sector and receiving payments *from* the government sector (see Section 4.7.2.3). It is conceivable, therefore, that at a particular time the net payments between the non-government and the government sector may be such that bankers' deposits rise (government sector paying out more than it is receiving from the non-government sector in taxes, etc.) or bankers' deposits fall (government sector receiving more than it is paying out to the non-government sector). In the first situation the clearing banks will tend to have surplus funds which they will *lend to* the discount houses, and in the second instance the clearing banks will be *calling in* their loans to the discount houses. By this mechanism the discount houses smooth out the ebb and flow of funds between the government and the non-government sector, preventing unnecessary shortages or surpluses of reserves at the clearing banks. After October 1988 other firms which qualify to operate in the sterling money market alongside the discount houses will also be performing this function; indeed, as we have seen, this is one of the obligations and conditions which such firms will have to accept.

The mechanism by which the Bank of England provides cash as lender of last resort (and also absorbs surplus funds) is an important part of the operation of monetary policy in the UK. It would be useful, therefore, to turn to Section 4.8.3 for further discussion of this topic.

4.8.3 OPERATIONS IN THE STERLING MONEY MARKET

As we have already noted, government transactions with the rest of the economy are very large, amounting to an average of £600 million flowing into and out of the government's accounts at the Bank of England each day.[9] These large daily flows would – if the Bank did not intervene – produce correspondingly large changes in the balances of the banks at the Bank of England. Net government spending would raise these balances and net receipts to the government would reduce the balances. The Bank's money market operations aim to offset these net flows. Under the October 1988 arrangements the Bank will undertake these operations only with the discount houses and others having an authorized money market dealing relationship with the Bank of England. The essentials of the system which connects banks, money market, and Bank of England is that the banks will hold assets in the form of call money to the discount

[9] This section relies heavily on an excellent article 'Bank of England dealings in the sterling money market: operational arrangements', Bank of England *Quarterly Bulletin* (August 1988).

houses which they can use to increase their cash holdings, and they also hold money market assets such as Treasury bills and high-quality bank bills which they can sell to the houses. The discount houses and other operators can in turn either sell bills to the Bank or borrow cash.

In order to operate smoothly the Bank makes forecasts of the movement of funds between the government and non-government sector, and this involves estimating tax receipts, government department spending, changes in the note circulation, National Savings, and gilt-edged purchases and redemptions. Once the position is known on a particular day, for example a cash shortage, the Bank would invite discount houses to offer eligible bills for sale to the Bank. The Bank may specify the kinds of bills which are acceptable on that occasion and might also specify certain maturities. These maturity bands refer to the remaining term of the assets, and comprise :

Band 1	1 – 14 days
Band 2	15 – 33 days
Band 3	34 – 63 days
Band 4	64 – 91 days

Money market operators may at their own initiative offer bills to the bank (but this is rarely necessary), as may the banks at specific times. Another technique available is for the Bank to invite an offer to sell bills but with an agreement to repurchase them later. In all these operations the Bank is able to choose both the quantity and the term of bills it is prepared to accept. If the discount rate at which bills are offered is unsatisfactory (i.e. the selling price) then the Bank is not obliged to buy but usually takes the best available rates on suitable bills of acceptable maturities. If the money market experiences a surplus of funds the Bank would, at its discretion, invite money market operators and banks to bid for Treasury bills. Most of the Bank's operations in the money market will be through purchases and sale of bills, but market operators do have borrowing facilities at the Bank which they may use to balance their books when the day's operations in bills happens to be finished. Collateral is required for such arrangements and the interest charge is, of course, at the discretion of the Bank. *Table 4.18* illustrates the Bank's dealings from 1 to 11 July 1988. It is interesting to note that on 1, 5, and 11 July there was a surplus of funds; the Bank *sold* Treasury bills on those days (indicated by the minus sign). The 'late assistance' refers to situations where a market operator finds itself short of funds after the main bill business with the Bank has been concluded and a personal representation is made at the Bank to borrow funds. Any underlying economic policy motives which might be behind money market operations are discussed in Section 11.3.

Table 4.18

Bank of England operations in the money markets, July 1988

(amount and discount rate p.a.)

Date	Band	Treasury bills		Local authority bills		Bank bills		Late assistance
		£m	%	£m	%	£m	%	£m
1	1	− 75	$8^1/_4$–$8^5/_{16}$					
5	1	−250	9–$9^1/_8$					
7	1	20	$9^7/_8$					190
8	4	5	$9^7/_8$			350	$9^7/_8$	70
11	1	−286	$8^7/_8$–9					

Source : Bank of England *Qurterly Bulletin*, vol. 28, no. 3

4.8.4 RECENT DEVELOPMENTS

In recent years the discount houses have experienced considerable competition and change which has threatened their profitability and even their long–term existence – at least in their present form. One of their difficulties has been the very small capital base which has inhibited an expansion into the deregulated securities markets. Even after the mergers and takeovers of the 1980s, the houses are still fairly small operators. Nevertheless they have attempted to diversify their activities, having accepted the limits to profitability from their traditional activities; discounting bills and trading in short-dated gilt-edged securities takes place on the basis of fine profit margins, and this means that unexpected movements in interest rates can easily upset their profits. Union Discount, for example, one of the four remaining independent houses, has moved into leasing, asset management, invoice financing, and operating in the unlisted securities market, as well as continuing with its traditional discount market business. The strategy of Union Discount seems to recognize that it is a relatively small company and needs therefore to find a niche in the market where the competition from the larger financial firms is not so great. Other houses, for example, have diversified by moving into insurance underwriting and commodity broking as well as fund management.

However, it has been clear for some time that the pivotal position of the discount houses in the money market would not be sustained indefinitely by the Bank of England. This has been confirmed by the announcement by the Bank that from October 1988 the sterling money market will be open to other firms, so long as they are separately capitilized and are prepared to accept certain obligations (presently undertaken by the discount houses). These obligations include (a) offering callable deposit facilities to other financial firms including banks, (b) market-making in eligible bills, i.e. commitment to dealing on the basis of offering continuous and effective two-way prices and same day settlement, (c) participating in the Bank of England's operations in the money market, and (d) underwriting the weekly Treasury bill tender. Along with such changes has now gone the privileged access to the funds from those banks which wished to attain the status of eligible bank. Under monetary control provisions established in 1981, such banks were obligated to keep a minimum proportion of their funds with the discount houses – in effect guaranteeing the houses a certain proportion of their funds.

All these changes recognize that separating the dealing in bills (by providing the discount houses with a unique relationship with the Bank of England) from other asset markets and operators is inconsistent with the ethos of deregulation and competition. Further changes would seem to be inevitable; one which is frequently predicted is the elimination of the distinction between the bill and the gilt-edged markets for trading purposes. The present structure of the discount market is interesting because two houses (Union Discount Ltd and Gerrard & National Ltd) account for around half the capacity of the market, with the other six houses sharing the remainder. Whether this is sustainable, in view of the economies of scale which can be enjoyed [10] is debateable, and further concentration might occur if the October 1988 innovation increases competition significantly.

4.9 Building societies

The building societies are very important deposit–taking institutions. Total sterling deposits are substantially larger than those of the retail banks, and are second only to the insurance and pensions funds within the category of non-bank financial intermediaries. Not only are the building societies important in terms of their total share of financial activity, but they are also highly specialized. Furthermore, their activity is of importance to a large proportion of the population since there are over 36 million accounts with the societies (which includes about 25 million adults) and over $5^1/2$ million borrowers.

Table 4.19

Balance sheet of building societies, 1986

Liabilities	£m	%	Assets	£m	%
Shares and deposits	117,554	83·5	Cash and bank balances	7,058	5·0
Interest accrued but not credited	1,965	1·3	Local authority investments	1,223	0·7
Time deposits	3,470	2·5	British government securities	9,521	6·7
Certificates of deposit	1,521	1·1			
Bonds	5,439	3·9	Mortgages	116,938	82·9
Bank borrowing	2,137	1·5	Certificates of deposit	2,440	1·5
Reserves and other liabilities	8,654	6·2	Other	3,560	2·5
	140,740			140,740	

Source : Financial Statistics (July 1988)

Table 4.19 provides the main items on the aggregate balance sheet. The difference between depositors and shareholders is largely a technical one in that depositors are creditors of the society whereas the shareholders are 'members'; but since the societies are non-profit-making organizations, the shareholders

---

[10] The marginal cost of a transaction worth £20 million may be little different from that of a transaction for £0.5 million.

are not shareholders in the commercial sense. The building societies are well established and trusted, so that it is not surprising that the value of deposits is small in relation to the value of shares, which earn higher rates of interest than those on deposits. Further, the societies offer several kinds of savings opportunities to investors as a means of increasing the stability of funds deposited. Some shares are either for fixed terms or are in the form of contractual savings, and of course such shares offer higher rates of interest than the bulk of shares which are effectively withdrawable on demand (although technically the societies may demand notice of withdrawal, usually of one month). Many building societies now offer a very wide range of assets in order to attract both lump-sum and regular savings, the nature and terms of the contract varying in order to meet the different needs of investors.

On the assets side of the balance sheet the rather surprising feature is that 83 per cent of all assets takes the form of a single asset – mortgages. These are loans to borrowers for house purchase and commercial assets, but commercial mortgage finance is, at the present time, negligible. Mortgages are nominally long-term, usually between 15 and 25 years. However, people change houses once every seven years on average, and this means that on the sale of a house the mortgage is, albeit temporarily, repaid. This means that on present figures the societies receive repayments each year of around £16,705 million – about 12 per cent of their assets – and this is clearly a substantial *cash* flow; the societies are not as illiquid as they might seem. Nevertheless the term of the societies' lending is in sharp contrast to the bulk of their liabilities which, though technically not repayable on demand, are regarded by their holders as very liquid. Almost 95 per cent of societies' shares and deposits come from individuals. It is the liquid nature of the bulk of the societies' liabilities which is part of their attractiveness and thus a crucial element in ensuring an adequate flow of funds into the societies.

However, clearly the societies are in no way matching their assets and liabilities with respect to term. Rather they appear to be borrowing very short to lend long – a policy which, on the face of it, could lead to insolvency. How do the societies

survive? There are a number of explanations, but the following
are the chief ones :

(a) House prices tend to keep pace with the rate of inflation,
and this ensures that the security for a mortgage (the house) is a
very sound one.

(b) The interest on shares and deposits is paid twice yearly,
and almost invariably it is merely credited to the existing
holding. This effectively provides additional funds for the
societies since most depositors are prepared to leave the accrued
interest in their accounts. In 1986 this amounted to £4,000
million.

(c) Existing mortgages as we have seen, are being repaid
continuously in the form of principal, together with the interest
payments. The societies are careful to check that potential
borrowers are likely to be able to make regular payments to the
societies out of income, with a minimum risk of default, and
there is therefore a regular flow of funds from this source.

(d) As the balance sheet reveals, almost 10 per cent of liabilities
are in the form of time deposits, certificates of deposit, bonds,
and bank borrowing, and this reflects the societies' ability to
tap other sources of funds to provide flexibility. Similarly, the
societies hold very substantial amounts of very liquid assets
(mainly deposits placed with the rest of the banking system –
almost £7,000 million in 1986). The societies' ability to issue
and hold certificates of deposits provides additional liquidity.
The societies' holdings of British government securities also
provide liquidity since almost the entire stock held matures in
less than five years.

4.9.1 RECENT DEVELOPMENTS

In recent years the building societies have been subject to
considerable scrutiny and subsequent legislative changes. One
of the most important reports was published by the Building
Societies Association in January 1983 : *The Future Constitution
and Powers of Building Societies*. In this report the Association
mapped out the history and present position of the building
society movement and suggested the need for change. Many of
the proposals were concerned with the legal position of the
societies and control of the societies, but certain proposals

related to the financial operation of the societies. The report pointed out that the Building Societies Act of 1962 which controlled their activities was an excessive constraint on the societies and prevented their meeting new needs and competing with other institutions. In 1982 there were just over 200 independent building societies, but of this number the largest ten societies accounted for over 60 per cent of assets. (By 1987 the number of societies had fallen further to around 150 and the largest six societies accounted for almost two-thirds of total assets.)

The movement towards general deregulation in financial markets has included the building societies. Thus, for example, in the Finance Act of 1985 societies were permitted to borrow some of their funds from the wholesale money markets (as were the banks, of course). But the most important changes were incorporated in the Building Societies Act 1986 and which became operative on 1 January 1987. Since then there have been further changes within the Act which has extended the societies' range of activities. The Act itself is important because it lays down how the societies are to be supervised and the kinds of commercial activities which they can undertake, as well as establishing financial safeguards within their balance sheets. The Act set up the Building Societies Commission, which has the functions of ensuring that societies protect their investments on behalf of their shareholders and depositors; of promoting the financial stability of the societies; and of ensuring that the societies' principal purpose was the provision of mortgages. The Commission was given the 'power to do anything which is calculated to facilitate the discharge of its functions'. The Act also established a Building Societies Investor Protection Board, and the main purpose of this body is to protect investors' funds in the event of insolvency of one of the societies. To fund the Board's activities the societies would be obliged to contribute a levy to the Board. Money from the Board could then be used to compensate investors up to 90 per cent of their deposits subject to a maximum of £10,000. But perhaps the most dramatic aspect of the legislation and subsequent orders laid before Parliament under the Act relates to the broad range of functions and services which the societies are now able to provide. The Act also gives the societies the opportunity to change their status; under section 97 of the Act a society is enabled to transfer its business to a commercial company, i.e. to become a PLC instead of a mutual body. Before a society is able to make such a profound change it requires, in effect, a 75 per cent majority of its present investors in favour as well as approval from the Bank of England.

The functions and range of services which the building societies are now permitted to provide include full banking services, namely money transmission, credit cards, and foreign exchange, and the provision of loans for purposes other than house purchase up to certain limits. Part III of the Building Societies Act lays down not only the kinds of lending that are permitted but also the proportions of different kinds of lending (secured or unsecured) permitted within the asset structure of a building society. Clearly, the statutory obligations have the liquidity and solvency of the societies very much in mind. The societies may also provide a range of investment services within the provisions of the Financial Services Act (see Section 4.5.6.2); of especial significance is that they are, from August 1988, permitted to enter the arena of personal pension plans. They are also permitted to provide a full range of housing services.

The response of the societies to their new freedoms has been impressive. All the major societies – the bulk of the industry – provide customers with cheque accounts. Moreover, and of acute concern to the banks, the move seems to be towards providing current account services which include the payment of interest. The Nationwide Anglia Building Society provides just such an account in its FlexAccount services. It seems inevitable that the major banks will have to move towards this provision; Lloyds Bank is the first major bank to announce this intention. Property development and estate agency, natural developments for the building societies, have become routine services for about half of the major societies. Several of the societies have direct contact or holdings in stockbroking firms; for example, the Cheltenham and Gloucester Society has a share-dealing service with Barclays de Zoete Wedd, and the Bradford and Bingley Society has launched its own personal equity plan. As for changing status and becoming a commercial company, the Abbey National (second largest society to the

Halifax, with about £26 billion of assets) has announced its intention to seek approval to change to a PLC. It is likely, however, that even the largest societies may choose to consolidate their positions under the recent legislation before considering further strategic changes.

4.10 National Savings Bank

Although the National Savings Bank, formerly the Post Office Savings Bank, is not a trustee savings bank (trustees are redundant, since the National Savings Bank is organized by the government which is presumably trustworthy), it is nevertheless an organization very similar in character to the TSBs prior to their emergence as proper banks in 1976. Of the total funds administered by the Department for National Savings (about £35 billion), the ordinary accounts and the investment accounts of the National Savings Bank account for only £8 billion – roughly 22 per cent. The turnover of these two kinds of account provided by the NSB reflects the use to which depositors intend to put such funds. The turnover of the ordinary accounts is approximately 44 per cent p.a., indicating a transactions use for these balances; the turnover of the investment accounts is only 20 per cent p.a., indicating that such balances are regarded as a financial asset and investment rather than for transactions. In contrast, the average turnover of building society accounts is around 40 per cent p.a., and this reflects the changing function of the building societies as they have adopted the practices and services of a bank.

4.11 Finance houses

This group of financial firms is now fairly small. In 1965 there were twenty-six listed finance houses but by 1980 this had shrunk to eight. The main reason for this apparent decline was the introduction of a new classification system for the financial sector of the economy, as well as the legal opportunity for finance houses to be reclassified as part of the banking sector. The published data reveal this change; in 1981, before the changes, the total assets of the finance houses amounted to £6.3 billion, whereas immediately after the reclassification and transfer of some of these firms to the new 'monetary sector' their total assets 'declined' to £2.2 billion.

Table 4.20

Non-monetary sector credit companies, 1986 (£m)

Liabilities		Assets	
Commercial bills	739	Cash and balances with monetary sector	60
Short-term borrowing from monetary sector	1,578	Certificates of deposit	6
Longer-term borrowing from monetary sector	1,853	Other current assets	255
Borrowing from other financial institutions	36	Loans and advances :	
Other UK and overseas borrowing	120	Block discounts	1
Other liabilities (including Capital issues and reserves)	1,380	Industrial and commercial companies	897
		Persons	3,758
		Other assets	729
	5,706		5,706

Source : Financial Statistics (July 1988)

Table 4.20 shows the balance sheet of the finance houses in 1986. It is clear from the main asset items that well over 60 per cent of the finance houses' business is the provision of funds to individuals for the hire purchase of various kinds of goods. This form of instalment credit is used by individuals and firms who wish to buy consumer durables, machinery, and other equipment. In recent years the proportion of the funds going to individuals has increased (in 1982 it was 45 per cent) and this probably reflects the change in personal spending behaviour as economic activity in Britain has accelerated. Personal saving preferences have declined and households seem more prepared to incur debt in order to buy consumer durables.

In the motor trade especially, retailers obtain finance (block discounts) to enable them to hold stocks, and this in turn provides a business outlet for the finance house when motor cars are sold at the retail end. Finance houses also place funds with subsidiaries which are involved in banking, leasing, and factoring. Factoring involves a specialist company (the factor) taking over the debts of a company. One form of factoring, for example, involves the factor providing up to 80 per cent of the value of invoices, and clearly this could be of considerable advantage to a company since, for one thing, its cash situation would be eased. The leasing business of finance houses has grown substantially. In 1967 it amounted to £64 million, and by 1981 this had increased to £890 million; between 1981 and 1986 it continued to expand by over 8 per cent a year, although the total – because of the reclassification in 1981 – amounted only to £601 million in 1986. The leasing of assets such as ships, computers, aircraft and other costly pieces of equipment is an alternative to hire purchase (which involves the option to purchase at the end of the hire period for a nominal figure) and other forms of credit, e.g. a term loan. Leasing, which lasts the length of life of the asset, may be advantageous to firms, and especially those which are not making profits, since the finance house can take advantage of the various tax allowances and incorporate this benefit in the rental charge. Leasing may also benefit a firm in time of credit shortage since the firm, in effect, is guaranteed the finance for the purpose intended, and for the period required.

The items on the liabilities side of the balance sheet give some indication of the reliance which the finance houses place on the banking system as a source of funds; in 1986 £3,467 million was borrowed directly from the monetary sector and other financial institutions. A high proportion of deposits are obtained from the secondary banking sector, as well as borrowing, by use of overdraft facilities. The finance houses compete for funds from the non-bank sector and, as far as the personal and company sector is concerned, such competition would have to be very strong indeed to attract depositors. This is because the alternatives, such as building society shares and other less risky forms of asset, are more attractive to many potential lenders, even though such assets may not offer as keen a set of interest rates as those offered by the more flexible finance houses.

4.12 Insurance companies and pension funds

Insurance companies and pension funds are linked in this section for two reasons. One is that a significant proportion of the pension fund business is done by the insurance companies, and the other is that the operation of a pension fund involves the same sort of approach as that of organizing life assurance. As *Table 4.1* reveals, the volume of funds accounted for by the

pension funds and the insurance companies in the form of life
assurance funds (usually known as long-term funds) is very
substantial.

Broadly speaking the business of insurance, as the term
implies, is with risks and, in particular, the spread of risks. In
the case of life assurance, the insurance company is able to
calculate a spread of the risk of death over time on the basis of
the mortality figures available to the companies, and it is in this
area of life assurance that about one-half of the insurance
companies' business is concerned. The other forms of insurance
which provide the companies' general funds are associated with
contingency risks such as fire and theft. The probability of such
events occurring may be estimated and the risks spread over all
those firms and individuals subject to such risks and wishing to
obtain insurance cover.

The provision of pensions clearly is associated with the
question of mortality and life expectancy, and by virtue of their
life assurance business the insurance companies are experts in
this particular area. They operate two principal services; one is
a combination of an endowment policy, plus an annuity[11]
purchasable on maturity of the policy; the other is the simple
accumulation of funds sufficient to purchase an adequate
annuity on retirement.

In order to meet such future obligations, the insurance
companies and the pension funds need to make use of their
existing funds, together with available new funds, in such a way
as to ensure that when policies mature, or when retirement
occurs, the companies have sufficient funds to meet these
commitments. A fundamental problem facing insurance companies and pension funds is that the future financial obligation
of the companies is calculated on the basis of a process of
continual investment of received funds (premiums, etc.) which
will yield a known dividend or rate of interest. The final
obligation of the companies will be greater, therefore, than the
funds received from policy-holders or potential pensioners.
Thus the companies' current operations in the form of investment policy must take account of this, and accordingly the need

[11] An annuity is a series of payments in the future which are 'bought' by a payment of a
lump-sum in the present.

to maximize current and future profits from investments will be of paramount importance. This objective must be consistent, however, with financial prudence, which in this case will require the firms to acknowledge two factors : (a) the need to adjust the maturity structure of their assets to take into account the long-term nature of their liabilities, and (b) the need to adjust the composition of their assets so as to benefit (from the point of view of reducing risk) from asset diversification.

The different asset structures of the insurance companies and the pension funds do reflect the fact that pension funds are specialist institutions whose requirements are not precisely those of the insurance companies. In particular, the pension funds' obligations are related to the salaries of contributors at retirement. The implication here is that the pension funds need to ensure that their investments will rise, in both capital value and yield, in line with the general rise in incomes of the contributors to the pension schemes. Until recently, the purchase of ordinary shares was one way of ensuring that the value of an investment kept pace with the inflationary growth of incomes. Traditionally the pension funds hold a much higher proportion of their assets in the company sector (in particular, ordinary shares) than the insurance companies do. There are some similarities, however, between the insurance companies and the pension funds in that the bulk of their assets comprises a mixture of government and local authority securities, as well as company securities. The remainder is composed largely of loans, mortgages, and investment in property, and only a small amount is invested in short-term assets (in view of the long-term nature of their commitments). The recent behaviour of insurance companies and pension funds, however, reveals their preparedness to adapt their investment of new funds to changing opportunities. The published figures for the assets of the insurance companies, for example, show that the asset mix changes quite markedly over time. If one takes as an example the mix of British government securities, UK equities, and foreign securities held by insurance companies between 1982 and 1985, the ratio of these assets to each other changed from 4.6 : 5.4 : 1 in 1982 to 2.6 : 4.7 : 1 in 1985. In part this change in the ratio reflects the movements in stock market prices, but it also reflects the willingness of the companies to accept a change in the balance of their asset portfolio.[12]

The insurance companies and the pension funds dominate the provision of long-term capital for the company sector. For example, net issues of new ordinary shares by public companies in 1986 amounted to £7,648 million, whereas the insurance companies and pension funds added to their holding of ordinary shares by almost £6,000 million. These two kinds of financial institution are clearly very important in absorbing new securities coming onto the capital market.

4.13 Investment trusts and unit trusts

The grouping of these two types of financial organization is founded on a major common element in their operation, and that is their capacity to spread risks on behalf of the individual investor. Furthermore, one aspect of their balance sheet suggests another common factor, and that is that the type of claims they hold are of the same kind as the claims which they create. Both points will become more apparent in the following account of the two types of organization. Unit trusts are now quantitatively more important than investment trusts, the market value of assets held by unit trusts amounting to £30,344 million as against £20,474 million held by the investment trusts in 1986.

4.13.1 INVESTMENT TRUSTS

Although commonly designated as trusts, these firms are not proper trusts but are public companies whose funds are obtained in the normal way, i.e. by the issue of ordinary shares, etc. Funds thus obtained are then used to purchase other financial assets, and in 1986 almost 98 per cent were other companies' securities. The remaining investments were in short-term assets such as sterling certificates of deposits, local authority temporary debt, and British government securities. The share of this latter group of assets was only 1 per cent of total assets; £261 million out of a total £20,474 million.

---

[12] In fact this change in the ratio probably disguises a change in preference *towards* British government securities once one discounts for the relative change in asset prices. Nonetheless, the point is still made by observing the change in ratios.

The benefit of an investment trust company to the individual investor is that by the purchase of the assets issued by the company, he can obtain a 'share' in a *wide spread* of assets which are owned by the company. In other words, it allows the investor to avoid putting all his eggs in one basket. Furthermore, if the company is managed by experienced directors, then the individual benefits additionally from the investment skills embodied in the company. In order to divest oneself of a holding in such a company, it is necessary only to sell the asset, be it share or loan stock, through the normal channels. The price obtained will be that quoted on the Stock Exchange.

4.13.2 UNIT TRUSTS

These intermediaries offer similar benefits to the investor, but operate rather differently. In particular, the unit trusts are operated as trusts in that there is a company acting as trustee for the owners of units of the trust as well as another company which manages the trust and decides on its investment policy.

The purchase and sale of units in the trust is relatively simple. It does not involve the purchase or sale of *existing* securities (as with the investment trusts); instead it involves the *creation* of new units or the *elimination* of units in response to demand. Units are bought and sold from the trust itself, and not through the Stock Exchange as are the shares of investment trusts. When units are purchased they are bought at a price which is geared to the total value of the trust, and when units are sold they too are repurchased by the trust at a price which ensures that the total value of units corresponds directly with the value of the fund. This means that if the market value of the assets owned by the trust declines, then the buying and selling price of units also will decline. Accordingly, the value of units will vary as the market valuation of the assets of the fund varies. The calculation of the buying and selling price of units by the trust is determined by a formula laid down by the Department of Trade and Industry, which sets a maximum offer price (the price of a unit when sold by the management company) and a minimum bid price (the price of a unit when bought by the management company). The difference between the two is partly accounted for by various expenses involved in buying and selling, e.g. brokerage charges and contract stamp, and also the profit or 'turn' of the management company. Since the management company's profit from the unit trust depends on the number of units which are traded, it is in the interest of the management company to ensure that the trust is a successful, attractive, and expanding one. In this way, there is a built-in inducement for the managers of the fund to be as effective as possible on behalf of the unit holders.

The distribution of unit trust investments in 1986 was heavily in favour of equities and other company securities. £17,389 million (57 per cent) was invested in UK company assets, £12,243 million (40 per cent) in overseas companies, and only £539 million (less than 2 per cent) in British government securities.

Before the passing of the Financial Services Act the responsibility for supervision of the unit trusts lay entirely with a single body, the Department of Trade and Industry. With the passing of the Act and the setting up of the Life Assurance and Unit Trust Regulatory Organization (LAUTRO), one of the self-regulatory bodies established by the Act, it is likely that unit trust schemes will be supervised partly by LAUTRO and partly by Investment Management Regulatory Organization (IMRO). LAUTRO has the job of supervising the sale of life assurance and unit trust investments by life offices, friendly societies, and unit trust managers. Thus the investment managers will be regulated by IMRO and the marketing by LAUTRO.

4.14 Financial supervision

The rapid internationalization of both money and capital markets which has been taking place in the past ten years or so has produced profound changes in these markets within the UK. Earlier in this chapter we have seen how a number of pressures combined to produce radical change in the London Stock Exchange (the Big Bang): the relatively high cost of securities dealing in London compared with abroad; the developments in computer and information technology; the government's concern about the invisible earnings of the City; and the aspirations and expectations of the older institutional investors as well as those of the renascent institutions such as the building societies. These, and other factors, combined to produced major and fairly rapid change. Alterations of the constitutions of the Stock Exchange yielded, as we have already seen, significant change in the ownership of broking firms and in particular the entry of foreign banks. Changes in practices have occurred, notably the ending of fixed commissions on transactions (a condition demanded by the government in exchange for exemption of the Stock Exchange rule book from the Restrictive Trade Practices Act of 1976), which enhanced competition. Associated with all these changes was a growing concern for the protection of investors; greater commercial freedom for those operating in capital markets implied perhaps greater risk for those less knowledgeable about investment matters. Allegations of fraud and malpractice in the insurance markets as well as anxiety about the adequacy of banking supervision generated further pressure for action.

The Financial Services Act of 1986 was one response to these concerns. In the legislation were laid down general principles, and the objectives of maintaining efficiency, competitiveness, flexibility, and confidence in the financial system, within this framework the Secretary of State for Trade and Industry was to be given powers to authorize and regulate investment business. Most of the powers of the Secretary of State under the Act and the detailed working of the legislation would be operated and devised by the Securities and Investment Board (SIB) which in turn would lay down rules for behaviour. Self-regulatory organizations (SROs) would receive delegated authority from the SIB once such SROs had worked out their own rules and codes of behaviour which satisfied the SIB. *Figure 4.1* is a simplified version of the regulatory structure. Even within this simple diagram it can be seen that there is some overlap in the supervisory functions, and of particular interest and importance is the role of the Bank of England.

Following a major banking collapse (Johnson Matthey Bankers) in October 1984, which revealed inadequacies of supervision under the existing Banking Act 1979, a committee of enquiry recommended a number of changes. One such change was the setting up of a Board of Banking Supervision in May 1986 within the Bank of England, which would have on it, from *outside* the Bank, representatives of appropriate professions who

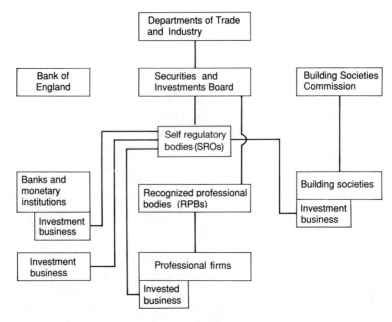

Figure 4.1

would supplement the Bank's own responsibility for banking supervision. Other recommendations have also been incorporated in the Banking Act 1987. The Act formally incorported the Board of Banking Supervision within the statutory framework. The main provisions of the Act and the significant changes are as follows:

(a) The Act lays down certain restrictions on the acceptance of deposits, in particular that it is an offence to undertake deposit-taking business without authorization by the Bank. But the Act also permits the Treasury to amend the meaning of deposit or deposit-taking business. The intention here is to enable bank supervisors to maintain adequate supervision of firms even though institutional and market developments might alter the nature of banking business.

(b) Financial firms which wish to gain authorization under the Act must meet minimum uniform prudential requirements: directors and managers must be fit and proper persons to hold such positions; the business must be run prudently, i.e. adequate capital and liquidity, provisions for bad debts, proper records and internal controls; and the firm must have net assets of not less than £1 million. But the Bank is able to set such prudential standards on an *individual* basis; there is no automatic authorization based on the minimum prudential requirements.

(c) All authorized institutions will be able to use banking descriptions, and a UK–based firm may use a banking name so long as it has at least £5 million of paid-up share capital or undistributable reserves.

(d) Changes of directors and managers must be notified to the Bank, and any person who becomes a significant shareholder (control of 5 – 15 per cent of an institution's voting power) must be notified to the Bank.

(e) Prior notification must be made to the bank if the purchases of shares of a firm result in shareholder control of a UK incorporated institution. The Bank would be able to object and block such changes if it considers the shareholder controller not to be a fit and proper person. This change to the legislation would permit the blocking of foreign acquisition of a UK bank.

(f) Partly as a direct response to the Johnson Matthey Bank failure, Part I of the Act also lays down that if a bank ('authorized institution') has entered into (i.e. already made) a transaction relating to any person as a result of which it is exposed to the risk of incurring losses in excess of 10 per cent of its available capital resources, then it shall make a report to the Bank. If a bank 'proposes' (i.e. intends) to enter into a transaction relating to any one person which either alone or with previous transactions with that person would result in its being exposed to the risk of incurring losses in excess of 25 per cent of its capital resources, then it must make a report to the Bank.

(g) Section 39 of the Act greatly extends and indentifies the powers of gaining information from banks as to their operations – even to the extent of rights of entry of premises on authorization under the Act. Providing false information or failing to provide relevant information to the Bank in its supervisory role becomes a criminal offence.

(h) Auditors and accountants would be able to disclose infor-
    mation to the Bank, if made in good faith, which is relevant to
    the Bank's supervisory role. This is an uneasy provision because
    auditors and accountants have a responsibility to the firms they
    serve. On the other hand, it can be argued that it is unaccept-
    able for an accounting firm which believes that its client is in
    some way acting improperly to feel constrained and unable to
    disclose such information. This part of the Act now permits
    such disclosure.

(i) In respect of the management of banks, the Bank of
    England is empowered to issue quite detailed directions to a
    bank if necessary in the interests of existing or future deposi-
    tors. Such directions might relate to the quality of its assets, the
    source of deposits, or even the removal of a director – in effect,
    very extensive powers. Authorization of a bank may be revoked
    or restricted and thus made conditional on the bank's proper
    conduct of its affairs.

(j) The Deposit Protection Scheme covers all authorized insti-
    tutions, and cover is increased to 75 per cent of the first
    £20,000.

Although Bank of England supervisory powers are more
explicit, extensive and thorough than previously, there are
problems of overlap with other supervisors of the financial
system empowered under the Financial Services Act. This arises
partly because the major financial firms constitute 'groups'
within which a variety of function applies. One way round this
problem has been to establish a 'lead regulator' or supervisor
for such groups who will coordinate activity with other supervisors. In the matter of banking, the foreign exchange market,
and money markets the Bank of England would emerge as the
natural lead regulator, but the detailed application of this
approach will nonetheless reveal problems. The difficulty is
essentially one of establishing supervision of financial firms
which generates no, or minimal, overlap without creating gaps
in supervision. Notwithstanding the considerable extension of
formal statutory supervision under the Banking Act and the
Financial Services Act, it is clear that non-statutory and
informal cooperation and supervision (much favoured by the
Bank in the past) will still have an important part in the
regulatory structures.

4.15 The operation of the Bank of England

So far in this chapter we have regarded some of the operations of the Bank of England as part of the background to a particular financial institution, for example, the discount houses' business operations. In this section we shall try to pull together the various responsibilities of the Bank of England into a more coherent picture.

4.15.1 FUNCTIONS OF THE BANK

The Bank of England is the central bank of the UK and in that respect it is similar in function to that of any other central bank. However, other central banks will differ in respect of their legal and constitutional position. For example, the central bank of the USA, the Federal Reserve, has a considerable degree of independence of action from the government of the USA. Once the head of the Federal Reserve and its other board members have been appointed then, in effect, the management of monetary policy in the USA becomes their responsibility and not that of the President of the USA. On the other hand, the West German central bank, the Bundesbank, is more constrained in its actions by virtue of legislative and constitutional requirements which lay down its responsibilities. The Bank of England also has responsibilities which are laid down in legislation (for example, in the Banking Act), but in the key areas of monetary and financial policy the Bank is not independent. It is the government through the Chancellor of the Exchequer and the Treasury which has the final responsibility and judgement as to what shall be done. Nevertheless, the Bank does have a range of functions in common with other central banks which we shall now examine.

Domestic banking and financial functions

(a) The Bank has familiar banking responsibilities which apply to three groups of customers: the other banks, the government, and overseas central banks and individuals. The banking service to the other banks involves the provision of accounts which the banks can use for settlement after the clearing mechanism has operated each day (see Section 4.7). The government accounts held by the Bank are those which permit the government departments to receive and make payments as well as the handling of monies which flow from the borrowing and repayments which government undertakes. The official accounts are the Exchequer, the National Loans Funds, the National Debt Commissioners, and the Paymaster General. The Bank also handles transactions on behalf of other central banks, e.g. provision of sterling in exchange for foreign currency deposits, and also private customers – mainly its own employees.

(b) The Bank has the important role of being 'lender of last resort' to the banking system, and indeed the whole financial system in extreme conditions. It is through the Bank's operations in the money market that it can do this job (see Section 4.8.3).

(c) As part of its services to the government, the Bank deals with issues of government securities to raise funds for the government and arranges for debt redemptions (paying back lenders to the government) and interest payments.

(d) Although most transactions in the economy are made by the use of bank deposits (cheque accounts), individuals and companies also require banknotes (and coins) which are of the right denomination and quality. *Table 4.21* reveals the way the public's preferences have changed – largely as a result of inflation and the rise in money incomes, as well as the spread of cash dispensing machines. The Bank 'sells' banknotes to the banks (the banks pay by using their accounts with the Bank of England) and replaces those notes which are in poor condition.

(e) The Bank collects, processes, and interprets data of which some are published and others are used as part of the advisory process between the Bank and the government.

Domestic financial policy

(a) Because of the Bank's direct involvement in and experience of financial markets and financial institutions, there is inevitably a body of knowledge and insight within the Bank of considerable value and relevance to the formation of economic and financial policy in the UK. Although the ultimate authority for policy is the Treasury, the Bank will have, nevertheless, a considerable influence on the formation of policy, especially

Table 4.21 *The note issue*

Value of notes in circulation (end February) (£m)

	1985	1986	1987	1988
£1 [a]	528	142	117	108
£5	2,426	2,225	2,029	1,896
£10	5,232	5,459	5.633	5,810
£20	2,137	2,310	2,608	2,932
£50	1,089	1,233	1,475	1,755
Other notes[b]	618	941	984	800
Total	12,030	12,310	12,846	13,301

[a] In December 1987 the Bank announced that after 11 March 1988, Series D Bank of England £1 notes would cease to be legal tender.
[b] Includes higher-value notes used internally in the Bank, e.g. as cover for the note issues of banks of issue in Scotland and Northern Ireland in excess of their permitted fiduciary issues.

Number of new notes issued each year, by denomination (end February) (millions)

	1985	1986	1987	1988
£1	678	—	—	—
£5	515	522	457	449
£10	456	526	469	515
£20	86	122	78	113
£50	10	17	18	21
Total	1,745	1,187	1,022	1,098

Source : Bank of England *Annual Report*

    that which relates to the regulation of markets and institutions.
(b) The Bank is the executive instrument for monetary and financial policy. This derives from its own operations in financial markets, especially the money markets and the gilt-edged market.
(c) The supervision of the banking system is, as we have already discussed, a prime responsibility of the Bank; it ensures the proper management of banks under the terms of the Banking Act as well as through the Bank's informal network of regulation and advice.

External policy

(a) Economic policy within the UK cannot be formulated without considering the external implications, particularly the

impact on the foreign exchange market and the exchange rate
itself. Whatever the policy decision about the exchange rate
(see Section 9.5), the Bank will have the task of implementation through its direct involvement in the foreign exchange
market – the Bank's dealing room. Along with its operations in
the foreign exchange market goes the Bank's management of
the Exchange Equilization Account which represents the UK's
reserves of gold and foreign currency deposits.

(b) The Bank has a considerable responsibility through the
Governor and other senior staff at the Bank of maintaining
relationships with other central banks for the purpose of
cooperation, especially in the area of monetary policy but also
in the field of international banking supervision. In January
1987, for example, the Bank of England along with the USA
central bank issued a proposal for the harmonization and
convergence of supervisory policies on capital adequacy assess-
ments for banks among countries with major banking centres.
It is likely that the Bank's contribution to this difficult area of
regulation will prove to be substantial (see Section 4.5.5.4).

4.15.2 ORGANIZATION OF THE BANK

The Bank employs about 5,000 full-time staff in various
sections. Almost 1,300 people are employed at the printing
works and around 900 people are directly employed in a
banking capacity. Just over 600 people work in the Financial
Markets and Banking Supervision Divisions, and the remainder
are employed in support services such as Corporate Services
and the Registrar's Department. In May 1988 the Bank was
reorganized (mainly as a consequence of the Financial Services
Act), and *Figure 4.2* shows the present structure.

The General Division and Industrial Finance Division are
responsible for supervision in the field of institutional development, techniques in banking, developments in industrial finance
and the coordination of the industrial liaison work of the Bank.
The Banking Department provides normal banking facilities
for customers including the government, overseas central
banks, UK primary banks, discount houses, accepting houses, a
number of overseas banks, and a few private customers together
with Bank employees. Other functions include the acceptance

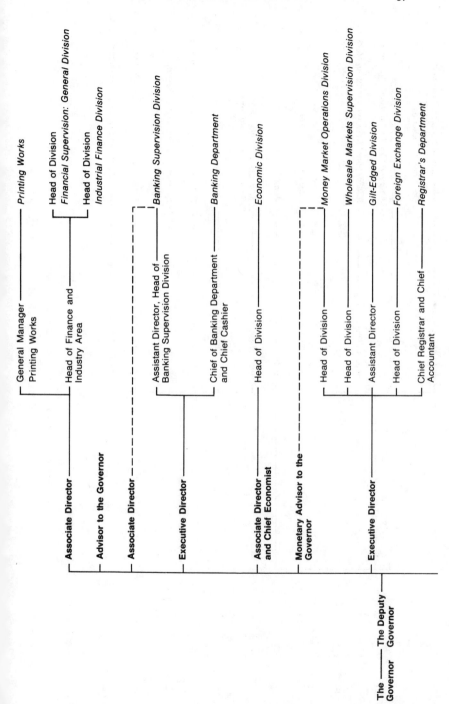

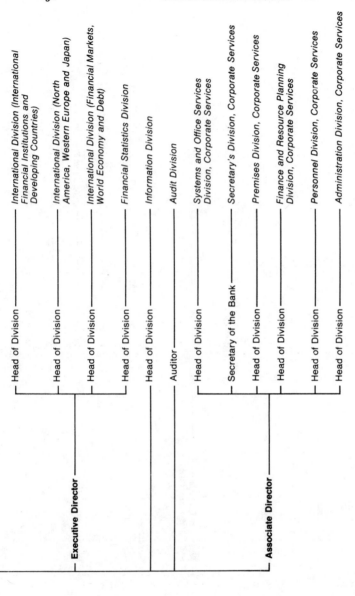

Figure 4.2 *Organization of the Bank of England*

Source : Bank of England *Annual Report*, 1988

or delivery of stocks or bills resulting from Bank market operations and the supply and withdrawal of notes from the main retail banks. The Banking Supervision Division has a crucial role under the Banking Act 1987 and is responsible for supervising banks (but not the discount houses, which are dealt with by the Wholesale Markets Supervision Division) within the terms of the Act. It is perhaps not surprising that this division has experienced substantial increases in staffing, rising from 75 in 1983 to 199 in 1988–89; almost all these employees are managers, analysts, and their assistants. This group of staff is responsible for the supervision of about 550 authorized institutions. The Economics Division is responsible for the collection of data as well as economic modelling and forecasting. This division also issues the Bank's *Quarterly Bulletin*.

The Bank has always had as one of its responsibilities the supervision of financial markets which impinge on monetary policy and the monetary system – the foreign exchange market, the sterling money markets and bill markets, and the gilt-edged market – and with the passing of the Financial Services Act the Bank's involvement has had to become more formal. This is partly because the market participants would, because of the nature of their business, come under the responsibility of a particular self-regulatory organization. In order to prevent duplication of supervisory function and to minimize the costs of supervision to the banks, the Financial Services Act permits certain exemptions to the Act so long as such firms are listed and regulated by the Bank of England. The new division, Wholesale Markets Supervision Division, has been set up to bring together the Bank's supervisory responsibility for wholesale markets in sterling, foreign exchange, and bullion. This division is also responsible for the discount houses. The institutions to be assessed by the new division must pass the 'fit and proper' test, and this includes a test for capital adequacy.

The Foreign Exchange Division is responsible for the foreign exchange market, in particular the operation of the Exchange Equalization Account and the management of the UK's reserves of foreign currency and gold as well as the implementation of foreign exchange rate policy. This division also handles transactions in foreign exchange on behalf of government departments as well as other of the Bank's customers including nationalized bodies and other central banks. The Registrar's Department maintains registers of government and other stocks, making interest and dividend payments and repaying stocks at maturity. The printing works produces new banknotes and is responsible for the destruction of soiled notes. The Several International Divisions under an executive director of the Bank monitor developments overseas and maintain close contact with other central banks and international institutions abroad. The Corporate Services Divisions provide a range of general management services which include computer services, property management, staffing, and the production of the Bank's accounts.

In the Gilt-Edged Division and the Money Market Operations Division there have been substantial and significant changes which require more detailed study; this is done in the following two sections.

4.15.3 GILT-EDGED DIVISION

The various changes within financial markets associated with Big Bang (see Section 4.14) impinged on the way the Bank operated in the gilt-edged market and handled the sales and redemption of government securities. Under the previous system the Bank sold gilt-edged stock through the Government Broker, the broking firm of Mullens and Co., which then sold on to the two key gilt-edged jobbers, [13] Akroyd and Smithers, and Wedd Durlacher. Clearly this restrictive arrangement could not continue after Big Bang; it would have been highly anomalous.

The reformed gilt-edged market which began operations on 27 October 1986 (Big Bang) consisted of two groups of operators. In January 1985, well before Big Bang, the Bank had invited applications from companies which wish to become market-makers. These market-makers undertake to make on demand and in any trading conditions, continuous and effec-

---

[13] Before Big Bang jobbers were single-capacity operators in the Stock Exchange who dealt in government securities only with other operators in the Stock Exchange who wished to buy or sell government securities; they did not deal directly with buyers or sellers outside, but only with other brokers buying or selling for their clients. They were in effect the market-makers in gilt-edged securities.

tive two-way prices (buying and selling prices) at which they stand committed to deal. This function is intended to provide a continuous opportunity to buy and sell government stock and therefore enhance the liquidity of the stock and the public and institutions who buy such stock. The gilt-edged market-makers (GEMMs) would be expected to operate widely and not with a narrow group of operators (as under the previous system), i.e. the gilt-edged market was to become a very widely based market. Because of the necessary changes in the holdings of stock and the commitment of GEMMs as an inevitable consequence of continuous marketmaking, access to additional funds (and disposal of temporarily surplus funds) would be provided by the operation of Stock Exchange money brokers. As a further supplement to the overall liquidity of the gilt-edged market, inter-dealer brokers (IDBs) would be permitted to operate; these IDBs would have the function of enabling GEMMs to unwind the stock positions that arise from their market-making activities. The GEMMs would thus be able to obtain stock from or dispose of stock to other GEMMs via an IDB.

In order that the GEMMs can fulfil their obligations, the Bank provides a dealing relationship with the market-makers such that, effectively, the GEMMs can not only bid for and obtain stock directly from the Bank but can also offer stock back to the Bank as well as switch stocks with the assistance of the Bank. The approach of the Bank in its dealings with market-makers is to try to bring sufficient stock to the market in sufficient quantity, taking one month with another, so that the funding objective of the government is achieved; this objective has been to ensure that the public sector's borrowing during a financial year is covered by stock sales. In order to do this, the Bank issues stock either by offers for sale by tender – in effect an auction – or by supplying relatively small additional supplies ('tranchettes') of existing stocks to the market. The 'offer for sale' method involves the Bank establishing a minimum price for stock, and if offers are made at higher prices then these bids are given priority in the allotment of stock; remaining stock are allotted at the minimum price. If there are insufficient tenders at the minimum acceptable price for stock then, as in the past, the Bank acts as underwriter and would buy up the remainder which would then be sold later 'on tap'. The tender method of selling is used for large (around £ 750 to £ 1000 million) issues of stock. Further consideration is given to operations in the gilt-edged market in Section 6.11.1.

These facilities are at the discretion of the Bank, but clearly a close relationship between the Bank's Gilt-Edged Division and the GEMMs is essential to obtain a smooth market in gilt-edged securities. In 1987 the average *daily* turnover in gilt-edged stocks was £ 6,759 million (65 per cent of total Stock Exchange turnover); this huge turnover requires financing, and it is the GEMMs which require such funds to enable them to fulfil their function of 'continuous' buying. In addition to the facility of the money brokers, the Bank has created two sources of funds for the GEMMs. The Bank itself will make available to GEMMs secured borrowing facilities at the Bank when normal market financing is not available, subject to a limit related to the borrower's capital. In effect the Bank is offering a 'lender of last resort' facility to the market-makers, and because of this the Bank regards secured lending to the GEMMs by banks as high-quality liquidity. Additionally the Bank requires, as part of the liquidity requirements of banks (see Section 4.5.5.3) that they place funds with money brokers and market-makers as well as money market operators.

By the time of Big Bang there were twenty seven such GEMMs, nine money brokers, and six IDBs for which the Bank of England had supervisory responsibility. Matching technological changes elsewhere, the Bank has reformed its own methods and introduced a modern dealing room and a centralized and computerized settlement system. This is the Central Gilts Office Service, which permits faster movement of stocks between participants in the market who are members of the CGO service without waiting for the changes of ownership to be recorded in the main register at the Bank. The Bank has also established along with this a payments system for members of the service which would provide assurance of payment and would clearly assist the movements of stocks between members.

At the time of Big Bang it was suggested that the gilt-edged market contained too many participants. By comparison with the much larger USA market for government securities (and indeed the old system in the UK) it seemed as though the UK market was over-subscribed with GEMMs. By mid 1987 it was clear that the gilt-edged business had become highly concentrated, with the largest ten GEMMs having almost 70 per cent of the market and the smallest ten GEMMs having less than 2 per cent. Profitability in market-making existed for only a few GEMMs. Subsequently Lloyds Bank, Orion Bank, and Hill Samuel have left gilt-edged market-making, but significantly Nomura Securities and Daiwa Securities have applied to become GEMMs. The implication here is that success in the gilt-edged market will be heavily based on long-term strategic planning backed by substantial capital rather than an expectation that market share will naturally accrue to any one participant.

4.15.4 MONEY MARKET OPERATIONS DIVISION

The responsibility of this division is for the Bank's daily operations in the sterling money market, for day-to-day liaison with the discount houses and other money market participants and the treasurers of the clearing banks, as well as for general oversight of the short-term money markets in sterling. Money market operations relate to the relationship between the major banks, the money market operators and the Bank of England itself. The system of public sector accounts in the UK means that the Bank acts as banker to the government, and does so by maintaining a major group of official accounts. Since the government does not hold balances with other banks (other than small working balances), the system of central bank accounts enables the Bank to minimize the amount of money retained in non-interest-bearing accounts, and any surplus cash – albeit temporary – can be used to reduce the amount of government indebtedness or acquire short-term assets. It is a very economical system. This centralized system, however, does mean that transactions between the government and the rest of the economy result in movements of cash between the Bank (its public sector accounts) and the accounts of a few major banks (those banks which are members of the Town Clearing; see Section 4.7.2) which are held at the Bank of England. Forecasting and regulating such movements of cash by money market

intervention is the responsibility of the money market operations division.

Transactions *between* the banks are, of course, taking place on
a daily basis as a result of the transactions between banks'
customers in turn causing inter-bank indebtedness which is
revealed at the end of the day's clearing of cheques and other
transfers. Settlement is achieved by drawing on the banks'
accounts at the Bank of England, and any shortfall of funds
may be offset by the banks themselves borrowing in the sterling
wholesale money market. The Bank's involvement in the
money market arises because of the shortfalls (or surpluses) of
funds in the banking system caused by transactions between the
banks and the government sector. The essence of the Bank's
transactions in the sterling money market is that a shortfall of
funds in the banking system can be remedied by the Bank
providing cash through its purchases of assets from the banks,
or more usually from the discount houses and other operators in
the money market. Any surplus of funds accruing to the
banking system can be absorbed by selling short-term assets to
the market operators. The terms (interest rates) on which such
transactions take place will set the prevailing daily short-term
interest rates and also influence the formation of interest rate
expectation by participants in all the financial markets. The
sterling money market represents an important point of contact
between the Bank (as agent for monetary and financial policy)
and the rest of the private sector financial system. The other
important point of contact is the Bank's operations in the
gilt-edged market. For further details of operations in the
sterling money market refer to Section 4.8.3.

It might seem that the Bank's intervention in the money
market is unnecessarily elaborate since one day's surplus of
funds is likely to be offset by another day's shortages. But
without such intervention the authorities' control over short-
term interest rates would not be possible. If we refer to the two
basic situations we have identified – cash shortage and cash
surplus in the money market – we need to ask what would be
the consequences if the Bank neither alleviated a cash shortage
nor absorbed a cash surplus. In the case of an unrelieved cash
shortage we would find the market operators keenly seeking
funds to repay the banks who are calling in their short loans.

Since the shortage is one of cash, ultimate relief can only be provided by obtaining cash. If the whole banking system is unable to provide cash loans to the discount houses, the result of the discount houses' quest for funds would be fast rising short-term interest rates. Conversely, in circumstances where there is a cash surplus, the discount houses would attempt to utilize such funds by buying bills and/or bonds from the market. The excess demand for bills/bonds would push up their prices, or – in other words – lower their yields (rates of interest). Only when interest rates had fallen sufficiently to induce the holding of the (*zero*-earning) additional cash in the system would interest rates cease to fall. We pointed out earlier that government disbursements and receipts vary from day to day and by substantial amounts, and therefore if the Bank chose neither to alleviate cash shortages nor to absorb cash surpluses, the result would be considerable oscillations of short-term interest rates from day to day. Since such occurrences would have consequences for the movement of short-term funds across the foreign exchanges, as well as feeding through into other financial markets, the Bank undertakes the smoothing operations we have just described : supplying cash or bills.

It should be noted, however, that although the Bank smooths the ebb and flow of funds, this does not prevent it from raising or lowering short-term interest rates as part of monetary policy. A deliberate and persistent shortage of cash in the market, alleviated by the Bank at increasingly penal rates of interest, would result in rising discount rates and other rates on a wide variety of short-term assets such as commercial bills, Treasury bills, [14] certificates of deposit, and time deposit rates. As the rates on these assets rise, so will the rates of interest on other forms of lending, particularly on bank loans and overdrafts. On the other hand, the Bank might push rates to a lower level by, in effect, creating a cash surplus. One means by which this could occur would be for the Bank to purchase Treasury bills from the market (thus putting out cash) in quantities which exceeded the amounts required for a simple smoothing opera-

---

[14] Note that the policy of raising short-term interest rates has the disadvantage for the government of raising its own borrowing costs. A small rise in interest rates will make a considerable difference to the interest payments made by the government.

tion. In practice, the Bank also makes use of 'a nod and a wink' to the market in order to move interest rates in a desired direction. The close contact maintained by the Money Market Division of the Bank of England with the discount market and other major financial firms is often a strong enough link to produce the required change. The appropriate response from the discount houses to the 'nod and wink' would be to alter their bid price for the next issue of Treasury bills. If the market's response was inadequate, the Bank would be quite capable, as we have seen, of making a desired change in rates effective.

The arrangements which operate at the present time in the money market were first introduced in 1981, and few changes have been made since then. The extension of money market participation to other than the discount houses does not not alter the arrangements. One important objective of the changes introduced in 1981 was to make market forces much more pertinent to the determination of short-term interest rates (i.e. the rates at which the Bank would transact with money market participants). The Bank's intervention would place greater emphasis on open market operations (buying or selling bills) and less on discount window lending (lender of last resort) as a means of alleviating cash shortages or surpluses. Furthermore the terms on which the Bank would deal with the market operators would not be fixed from day to day. The Bank's intention, as part of the stance of monetary policy, would be to keep short-term interest rates within an *unpublished* band, and thus preset dealing rates would not be a feature of its market dealings. As we have described above, any desire by the Bank to shift short-term rates can fairly easily be accomplished by changing the terms on which it is prepared to deal with market operators. [15]

[15] For further detail on the Bank's operations in both the money market and the gilt-edged market, the reader should refer to the Bank of England *Quarterly Bulletin*, in particular December 1986 and August 1988. Of considerable interest are the annual Bank of England *Report and Accounts*, published in May, and also the *Annual Report under the Banking Act*. The Bank also published in May 1988 a *Statement of Principles* which it is obliged to do under Section 16 of the Banking Act. This document outlines the basis on which the Bank approves and supervises banking institutions.

4.15.5 THE ISSUE DEPARTMENT AND THE BANKING DEPARTMENT

To complete our description of the Bank of England it is
appropriate to identify the elements in the Bank's balance
sheet. Section 4.7 outlines the main elements of Banking
Department liabilities in the context of the whole banking
system. For convenience these are included in the following
discussion.

The Bank Charter Act of 1844 laid down that the issue of
notes was to be kept separate from the Bank's banking business.
Accordingly, the accounts of the Bank – the Bank return – are
broken down into those of the Issue Department and those of
the Banking Department. This division is purely one of accounting since the Bank is organized as a single entity. *Table 4.22*
gives details of both accounts. The following notes describe the
items in the balance sheet :

Table 4.22

Bank of England balance sheet, 29th February 1988

(£m)

Issue Department
Liabilities

		Assets	
Notes in circulation	13,302	Government securities	1,666
Notes in Banking Dept.	8	Other securities	11,644
	13,310		13,310

Banking Department

Liabilities

		Assets	
Public deposits	360	Government securities	458
Bankers' deposits	1,177	Advances and other	
Reserves and other		accounts	1,283
accounts	2,035	Premises, equipment, and	
Capital	15	other securities	1,837
		Notes and coin	9
	3,587		3,587

Source : Bank of England *Report and Accounts* (1988)

Issue Department
Liabilities

(a) Notes in circulation : this refers to the notes held by the
    public and in the tills of the banks.

(b) Notes in the Banking Department : these are notes held by
the Banking Department to meet the needs of the banks and
indirectly the public. If the public required additional notes
and the Banking Department experiences a drain of notes, it
can obtain more from the Issue Department in return for
securities.

Assets
(a) Government securities : we have referred already to this
item, which consists of unsold government stock used by the
Bank for its operation in the gilt-edged market.
(b) Other securities : this item includes commercial bills and
local authority bills obtained through money market operations.

Banking Department
Liabilities
(a) Public deposits : these deposits are the government's various accounts, in particular the Exchequer and National Loans
Fund accounts as well as those of other departments.
(b) Bankers' deposits : clearing banks, discount houses, and
other banks hold deposits with the Bank which are used mainly
for clearing purposes.
(c) Reserves and other accounts : apart from reserves, this item
consists of the accounts of a small number of private customers
as well as accounts held by overseas money institutions, e.g.
central banks.
(d) Capital : this is the original share capital of the Bank.

Assets
(a) Government securities : these consist of gilt-edged and
Treasury bills as well as loans to the National Loans Fund (in
effect an overdraft facility known as 'Ways and Means Advances').
(b) Advances and other accounts : this item consists of loans to
the discount houses, discounted bills for the Bank's customers,
and advances to the Bank's own customers.
(c) Premises, equipment, and other securities : apart from the
value of tangible assets, this item includes other securities held
by the Bank by virtue of its commercial activities.

4.16 Summary

(a) The diversity of financial intermediaries within the UK provides the economist with a problem of classification. One basis for classification was that used in Chapter 3; the division into bank and non-bank financal intermediaries.

(b) The available data suggest that the non-bank financial intermediaries have grown more rapidly than bank financial intermediaries – particularly the building societies, insurance companies, and pension funds. The major building societies have adopted the basic functions of the retail banks, so that the growth of the non-bank sector might be overstated.

(c) The secondary banking sector has grown very rapidly compared with the primary banks (retail banks); this is largely because of the considerable growth in foreign currency business, most of which is undertaken by the secondary banks.

(d) Deregulation within banking and the Big Bang in the major financial markets have meant that banks – domestic and foreign – operating in the UK have had to reassess their longer-term strategy, in particular extending into the capital market.

(e) Deregulation has required refinements in bank regulation by the Bank of England, and this is incorporated in the Banking Act 1987. The Act provides an institutional framework for prudential regulation of the banks, partly by extending the powers of the Bank of England. Non-statutory regulation of the Banks through the imposition of capital adequacy and liquidity requirements has also been refined further by the Bank. This aspect of bank regulation has been given an international dimension by the Basle agreement of 1987.

Postscript

As a consequence of the changes which permit building societies to become plc and classified as banks, the Bank of England has decided that the term 'UK monetary sector' is inappropriate. In future the term 'banks' will be used instead of UK monetary sector and for statistical purposes, the UK monetary sector data will be renamed 'Banks in the United Kingdom : consolidated balance sheet'.

5

The Stock of Money

5.1 Introduction

In Section 2.4.3 we restated the problem of finding an adequate *definition* of the money stock from a theoretical point of view. The object of this chapter is to consider the components of the money stock and to deal with the question of how and why the money stock might *change*. Finally, we shall consider some basic ideas underlying the problem of regulating the money stock, and the nature of conditions necessary for this to be achieved. Since it is arguable that changes in the quantity of money in the economy affect the level of economic activity and therefore the standard of living of the community, one can understand why the last question is of considerable importance to economists and government policy-makers.

5.2 The banks and the stock of money

5.2.1 DEPOSIT CREATION : the individual bank and the banking system

Whichever definition of money one chooses (see *Table 2.5*) it is clear that the dominant component is bank deposits – regardless of whether one considers M_1 or M_3. Notes and coin in circulation with the public are a relatively small part of the total stock of money. It is crucially important, therefore, that we are able to explain the changes which take place in the volume of bank deposits, and it is the purpose of this section to provide a preliminary explanation. The type of banks with which we are mainly concerned are those banks whose liabilities are treated as a medium of exchange and payment.

It was pointed out in Section 4.5.3 that the primary banks (in particular the London clearing banks) voluntarily had adopted certain safe asset ratios in order to maintain the confidence of the public and to ensure banks solvency. Section 3.2.4 was concerned with the economic basis for financial intermediation and used a deposit bank as an example. We suggested that a bank need not maintain a 100 per cent cash reserve ratio in order to remain solvent so long as it maintained a sufficient quantity of liquid assets (in our example, 'cash') to meet expected and unexpected net withdrawals (loss of deposits). This approach represents our starting-point in the more comprehensive discussion about changes in the volume of bank deposits. It is instructive to examine this topic from the viewpoint of the *individual* bank and also in terms of the banking system *as a whole*.

Let us assume for simplicity that a new bank is established and that this bank is the only bank operating in the financial system. Had we chosen to assume that there are several banks operating, this would not alter our conclusions but it would complicate the description unnecessarily. At the beginning, the bank's only assets are likely to be the funds provided by shareholders which are in part converted into bank premises. This source of funds is not, however, the prime source of profit for such a bank : its main task is to attract deposits from other sectors of the economy. Let us further assume that long banking experience has established that the bank requires a safe minimum cash ratio of 10 per cent of its deposit liabilities. In other words for every £100 deposited with the bank, the bank will need to hold £10 in cash (notes and coin) in order to meet the day-to-day needs of its customers. A cash holding of less than 10 per cent would result, we presume, in the bank being unable to meet the daily *net* demand for cash brought about by customers converting their bank deposits into cash. (Remember that both cash withdrawals and cash deposits will be occurring each day and that it will be the net position which is of concern to the bank.) Since the bank will not need to hold cash in excess of 10 per cent of deposit liabilities, we may assume that the funds deposited in excess of the cash ratio requirement will be used eventually to purchase earning assets for the bank's own balance sheet. The balance sheet we have used in our first illustration displays a cash ratio in excess of 10 per cent (it is, in fact, 12.62 per cent) and we may presume for convenience that this bank has yet to exploit all the opportunities open to it. A

simplified balance sheet might resemble, therefore, bank balance
sheet 1.

Bank balance sheet 1

Assets		*Liabilities*	
Cash	£1,300,000	Customers' deposits	£10,300,000
Other earning assets :			
Very liquid assets	3,000,000		
Less liquid assets	6,000,000		
	£10,300,000		£10,300,000

This approach to changes in the volume of bank deposits
suggests that the bank's role is a passive one – merely to await
customers placing deposits with the bank and then to choose an
array of assets which meet its own liquidity requirements. In
terms of our discussion in Chapter 3, it would be difficult to
distinguish such a bank from any other sort of financial
intermediary, such as a building society or an investment trust,
since the bank appears to be merely transmitting funds (deposits) which have appeared from elsewhere.

Such a view would be erroneous, at least in part, since the
primary banks' deposit liabilities have a special property : they
are generally acceptable as a means of payments and exchange,[1]
i.e. such deposits are *money*. The implications of this are that the
expansion of a bank's business is only partly dependent on
attracting deposits since such a bank is capable of *creating* deposit
liabilities against itself by virtue of the fact that its deposits are
held and used as money. (Indeed, for many purposes the
transfer of a bank deposit rather than cash as a means of
payment is preferable, particularly where large sums of money
are concerned, and for many it is simply more convenient than
using cash.) This phenomenon allows such a bank to purchase
earning assets by creating a corresponding liability against itself
in the form of a bank deposit. Let us consider three
examples.

[1] More precisely, sight deposits and that fraction of time deposits which, by convention, are treated as convertible into sight deposits by the holder of such deposits.

5.2.1.1 Renovation of premises

The bank decides to renovate its premises. Assuming that the firm which undertakes the work has its account with the bank, on completion of the work payment can be made by the bank quite simply by crediting the account of the firm with the appropriate sum.[2] Bank balance sheet 2 might represent such a transaction.

Bank balance sheet 2

Assets		Liabilities	
Cash	£1,300,000	Customers' deposits	£10,300,000
Other earning assets :		Additional customer's	
Very liquid assets	3,000,000	deposit	10,000
Less liquid assets	6,000,000		
Premises	10,000		
	£10,310,000		£10,310,000

5.2.1.2 Lending

An alternative situation could occur where the bank receives a request for a loan or overdraft facility. The majority of firms or individuals who request this facility are unlikely to require the funds in the form of cash but would prefer to have their account credited with the loan (or to utilize their overdraft facility) in the form of a bank deposit. Bank balance sheet 3 illustrates the effect of granting a loan in the form of a bank deposit.

Bank balance sheet 3

Assets		Liabilities	
Cash	£1,300,000	Customers' deposits	£10,300,000
Other earning assets :			
Very liquid assets	3,000,000		
Less liquid assets	6,000,000		
Advances :		Additional customer's	
Loan	10,000	deposit	10,000
	£10,310,000		£10,310,000

It should be noted that in these two illustrations the bank remains solvent despite the increase in its liabilities. The crucial

[2] It should be noted that this represents a simplification for illustrative purposes. The bank would in fact draw the funds from its own accounts. In principle, however, a bank could behave in this way with. the consequences outlined.

factor here is whether the bank's cash ratio is still adequate. Prior to the change in bank liabilities the cash ratio was 12.62 per cent (£1,300,000/£10,300,000, i.e. the bank was maintaining a cash ratio in excess of the safe minimum), and after the change in bank liabilities the cash ratio fell to 12.6 per cent (£1,300,000/£10,310,000).

We have assumed that the safe cash ratio is 10 per cent, and therefore in our examples the bank is sustaining an excessively high ratio. This leads us to consider the extent to which bank business may be expanded safely within the limits of this ratio. In other words, what is the maximum level of deposit liabilities which the bank can sustain with its existing holdings of cash? Since we know that bank cash must be no less than 10 per cent of deposit liabilities, we can express the problem symbolically as

$$C_b = \frac{10}{100} D$$

where C_b represents th amount of bank cash and D represents deposit liabilities. We wish to know the maximum level of deposit liabilities D sustainable by a given volume of cash C_b. By rearranging the terms in the above expression we have

$$D = \frac{100}{10} C_b$$

The volume of bank cash is £1,300,000, and by substituting this in the above expression we can calculate the maximum level of D. In this case it is, of course, £13,000,000. Let us cross-check the answer. If deposits were at that level of £13,000,000, and bank cash holding was £1,300,000, what would be the size of the cash ratio? Obviously it would be 10 per cent, and we can conclude that at that level of deposit liabilities the bank would remain liquid. The numerical value which measures the volume of bank deposits sustainable by, in this case, a given volume of cash (or any other assets used as reserves by the bank) is sometimes referred to as the *deposit multiplier*. Any further increase in the volume of bank deposits, however, would result in the banks' inability to meet day-to-day demands for cash by customers. For example, if deposits were £14,000,000 and bank cash was still £1,300,000, the cash ratio would have fallen to about 9 per cent; the implication of this – given our initial assumptions about the origin of the cash ratio – would be that for every £10 claims to cash (e.g. customers cashing cheques) the bank would have only £9 cash in its tills. Clearly the bank could not sustain such a situation, and it would have either to increase its holding of cash by some means or to reduce its liabilities. (These problems will be considered later.) The important point to realize at this stage is that the bank in our example could expand its deposits further – beyond £10,310,000 – through additional bank lending until the upper limit of £13,000,000 was reached. Thus the expansion of deposits may arise because the bank itself is *creating* deposits through its business activity and not merely as the result of customers placing deposits with the bank.

It is sometimes argued that an individual bank does not create money (i.e. deposits) by its activities since it can only lend what it has got; in other words, the suggestion is that banks merely transmit funds from depositor to borrower and do not *add* to the volume of bank money (deposits). Even if this proposition were accurate, we can show that a bank which only lends what it has got will nonetheless be part of a process of deposit creation. To illustrate this, let us assume that a bank receives deposits of *cash* and only lends *cash*; it does not lend by creating a deposit liability against itself. Let us assume also that the borrower of cash spends the money and that the recipient, e.g. a shopkeeper, deposits the cash in the bank. We will also maintain the assumption of a 10 per cent cash ratio. The sequence of balance sheets 4 and 5 could represent the process

Bank balance sheet 4

Assets		Liabilities	
Cash	£1,000,000	Deposit	£1,000,000
	£1,000,000		£1,000,000

Bank balance sheet 5

Assets		Liabilities	
Cash	£100,000	Deposit	£1,000,000
Cash loan 1	900,000		
	£1,000,000		£1,000,000

of deposit creation. Having made the loan of £900,000 in cash (i.e. the bank is only lending what it has got) the money is spent and received by others, e.g. shopkeepers, who eventually *deposit* such receipts in their bank account. The next stage may be seen in bank balance sheet 6. It should be noted that total bank deposits have risen, and also that position 6 is one of excess cash

Bank balance sheet 6

Assets		Liabilities	
Cash	£100,000	Deposit	£1,000,000
New cash receipt	900,000	New deposit	900,000
Cash loan 1	900,000		
	£1,900,000		£1,900,000

holdings by the bank since its cash ratio is 52.6 per cent (£1,000,000/£1,900,000).

The bank is now in a position to make further loans if the demand exists. Let us assume that there are customers who wish to borrow to the limit that the bank is capable of lending. Balance sheets 7, 8, and 9 illustrate what would be the result.

Bank balance sheet 7

Assets		Liabilities	
Cash	£190,000	Deposits	£1,900,000
Cash loan 1	900,000		
Cash loan 2	810,000		
	£1,900,000		£1,900,000

Bank balance sheet 8

Assets		Liabilities	
Cash	£190,000	Deposits	£1,900,000
New cash receipt	810,000	New deposit	810,000
Cash loan 1	900,000		
Cash loan 2	810,000		
	£2,710,000		£2,710,000

Bank balance sheet 9

Assets		Liabilities	
Cash	£271,000	Deposits	£2,710,000
Cash loan 1	900,000		
Cash loan 2	810,000		
Cash loan 3	729,000		
	£2,710,000		£2,710,000

Presuming that the second loan is spent and then later redeposited with the bank, we would find the situation in balance sheet 8. Under these circumstances, not only have total deposits risen again but the bank's cash ratio is once more in excess of the safe minimum, i.e. the cash ratio is 36.9 per cent (£1,000,000/£2,710,000). Thus the bank is still capable of making further cash loans without experiencing a shortage of cash. We will assume one further round of lending as set out in balance sheet 9,[3] and then attempt to draw certain conclusions.

(a) Although the bank is only lending what it has got, the volume of bank deposits is rising. This occurs because we have assumed that the recipients of the spent bank loans choose to place them in their own bank accounts.

(b) The capacity of the bank to make loans is diminishing. This is because the fixed amount of cash in the system (£1,000,000) is becoming a smaller and smaller fraction of the rising volume of deposits (which are always potential claims on cash). The bank therefore has to make additions to its cash reserve before it considers further lending.

(c) The process of deposit expansion can continue so long as the cash loaned does *not* remain outside the bank, in the hands of the public.

(d) The process of lending can continue (so long as there is a demand for bank loans) until the bank's liabilities are related to bank cash holdings in the ratio of 1 : 10, i.e. the process of expansion of loans and deposits will cease only when the cash ratio has become 10 per cent. This will occur when total deposits are £10,000,000 and cash holdings are £1,000,000. Total lending by the bank will amount to £9,000,000 and yet the whole banking system will have adhered to the maxim of 'only lending what it has got'.

5.2.1.3 Purchase of financial assets

Finally, we should identify another means by which the volume of bank deposits may rise. This can come about through the bank's purchase of financial assets, either from its own custo-

---

[3]The reader should be able to repeat the sequences, showing that a substantial amount of additional lending is possible.

mers or through existing financial markets. In the latter
instance we must add the proviso that the financial assets sold
to the bank are from the non-government sector. (We shall be
dealing with this more fully in Section 5.2.2). If a bank does
purchase financial assets from the non-government sector (e.g.
persons, industrial and financial companies, charities, etc.) the
means of payment is most likely to be the creation and transfer
of a bank deposit to the sellers and, as with the previous
examples, the process of deposit expansion may take place in
that way. Balance sheets 10 and 11 illustrate the point.

Bank balance sheet 10

Assets		Liabilities	
Cash	£1,000,000	Deposits	£1,000,000
	£1,000,000		£1,000,000

Bank balance sheet 11

Assets		Liabilities	
Cash	£1,000,000	Deposits	£1,000,000
Purchase of securities	9,000,000	New deposits	9,000,000
	£10,000,000		£10,000,000

Although the above illustrations of deposit creation may seem
rather artificial, they show nevertheless that the bank(s), by
virtue of the special nature of their liabilities, can increase such
liabilities without becoming illiquid. In the following section
we shall be considering whether there are further limits to the
process of deposit creation by the primary banks.

It would appear that there are two crucial factors which
affect the volume of deposits, regardless of the approach we
take to the mechanism of deposit creation. One is the volume of
cash which the banks hold or to which they have easy access. If
the total amount of cash available is fixed, then this acts as a
constraint on bank activity. The other factor is the size of the
cash ratio. In our examples we have assumed, for convenience,
that the cash ratio is 10 per cent. This has implied that with a
given quantity of cash as a reserve asset, the banks are able to
support deposit liabilities by ten times the quantity of cash they

hold. If the safe minimum cash ratio were 20 per cent, the capacity to support a given volume of deposit liabilities would halve, i.e. the deposit-multiplier would be 5 and not 10. On the other hand, a safe minimum cash ratio of 1 per cent would allow a given cash base to support deposit liabilities up to 100 times the volume of cash held by the bank.

5.2.2 CONSTRAINTS ON THE GROWTH OF BANK DEPOSITS

In the simple illustrations used so far we have seen that if the bank's cash reserves are fixed and if the safe minimum cash ratio is maintained, then our hypothetical bank would be able to expand the volume of deposits by a multiple of 10. This hypothetical deposit multiplier would seem to be very powerful: £1 cash supporting £10 deposit money. (*Table 4.4* contained reference to a cash ratio of 1.0 per cent in 1988. During 1988 the *operational* deposits of cash held by the retail banks amounted to about 1 per cent of liabilities. On the face of it, it would seem that retail the banks are able to generate and support £100 deposit money for every £1 cash held in tills and as operational deposits held at the Bank of England.) There are, however, a number of reasons why such a deposit multiplier is unlikely to be so powerful in a realistic banking system. We shall identify three reasons.

5.2.2.1 Leakages

A particularly important weakness of the preceding account is our assumption that the quantity of cash providing the cash base of the bank will remain unchanged as its deposits expand in the various ways described. There are several reasons why the cash base is unlikely to remain so conveniently stable.

First, the non-government sector is likely to want to hold *cash* as well as bank deposits, and so far we have ignored this phenomenon. It appears that the public's demand for cash is fairly closely related to the volume of bank deposits the public holds (the relationship appears to be closer and more stable than say, the relationship between cash holdings and domestic expenditure). In other words, as additional bank deposits are held by the public, they will wish to convert part of that bank deposit into cash, either by reducing the flow of cash deposits into the banks or by cashing cheques. We must accept therefore that if banks expand their deposits and these deposits are held by the non-government sector, then the banks must expect a drain of cash as the public meets its desired ratio of cash to bank deposits. Thus the process of deposit expansion contains within itself the seeds of its own cessation: the rise in bank deposits steadily reduces the cash ratio, and the additional deposits created generate a demand for cash by the public which in turn reduces further the size of the cash ratio as cash is drawn from the banking system by the public. Our earlier illustrations of deposit creation ignored this probability. The bank's cash ratio and cash holdings were for encashment purposes for the bank's customers. As one customer withdrew cash, another customer would be depositing cash. The point we are making here is that the public is likely to have a *demand to hold cash*.

Our second point directs attention to a constraint which affects the individual bank. Let us alter our assumptions slightly and assume that the total cash held by the banking system is fixed, but that there are several banks in the system – not just one – which maintain the same cash ratio. If we now assume that *one* of the banks decides to expand deposits at a faster rate than the other banks, then this bank will experience the constraint of a cash shortage – a consequence of a movement of cash from its own reserves to the other banks. The reason for this is that deposits expansion through, say, an increase in bank advances will be associated with a transfer of some deposits to the *other banks*. The reason for such transfers is simply that some of the final recipients of the loaned funds (i.e. after the funds have been spent by the borrowers) are likely to have bank accounts with the other banks. Inter-bank indebtedness which will arise after cheque clearings will reveal a *net* indebtedness of the expansionary bank with the rest of the banking system. Settlement of such indebtedness is possible by cash transfers through the agency of the central bank (or in practice by borrowing in the inter-bank market). If the expansionary bank persists in deposit expansion which is out of line with the other banks, the decline in its cash base will put a brake ultimately on such independent expansion.

Thirdly, earlier in this section we emphasized that banks may add to the volume of deposits by the purchase of securities which are sold to them by the *non-government* sector. The reason for this stipulation is that if banks buy securities from the *government* sector, this will tend to reduce the volume of bank deposits. This surprising conclusion is based on the assumption that the government sector uses the central bank as its bank rather than the other banks which operate in the private sector. In other words, the British government uses the Bank of England as its bank rather than, say, Barclays Bank. The following illustration should make the point clear.

Let us assume a bank buys securities which are being sold by the Bank of England (via the Stock Exchange) on behalf of the government, and then examine the consequences. The crucial factor is that the method by which the banks make payment to the government is through their accounts held at the Bank of England (see Section 4.7). If a bank is a net purchaser of government securities from the Bank of England, the result will be a fall in bankers' deposits at the Bank of England, i.e. a fall in the cash holdings of the bank. Since bank liabilities will remain unchanged initially, the effect of the fall in the bank's cash base is to reduce the size of the cash ratio. If the bank was operating at a level of deposits whereby the minimum cash ratio was achieved, the fall in the volume of cash at the Bank of England clearly would push the cash ratio below the safe minimum. If this occurred and the bank was unable to obtain cash from alternative sources, the bank would have to take action to reduce its deposit liabilities until the required cash ratio was re-established. Hence our suggestion above that the consequence of banks buying securities from the government could be a reduction in the volume of deposits. Thus, to the extent that banks buy government securities from the government sector, this represents a leakage of cash from the banks. A further question which will be considered in Section 5.3 is whether the government spends the money raised through the sale of securities or allows it to lie idle as a balance at the Bank of England.

The fourth point concerning leakage is that individual banks are sensitive to the transfer of funds (deposits) by their customers to other financial intermediaries. They are sensitive because this represents a loss of funds which may well be in the form of seven-day deposits – deposits which provide the banks with fairly cheap and profitable funds. A good example of such transfers is the movement of funds by customers from their seven-day deposits into a share account with a building society. Such accounts offer the investor the advantages of a seven-day deposit with a bank – very liquid and very safe – with the additional benefit, usually, of a higher rate of interest. Although this switching of funds is a phenomenon which the banks do not like, it is possible to argue that this 'leakage' is not quite of the same kind as the three we have identified so far. The reason is that the building societies hold working balances with the banks, i.e. a building society will have a sight deposit with a bank or several banks. The other working balance required by the building society will be cash in their branches to meet the cash withdrawals of their depositors and shareholders (see Section 4.9 which deals with building society accounts). Initially the funds transferred to the building society will be redeposited by the building society with a bank and there would therefore be no loss of deposits by the banking system as a whole. The main qualification we need to make at this stage is that to the extent that the building societies will raise their cash holdings (they will need to do this since their own liabilities will have increased as a result of the transfer of funds to them), there will be a loss of cash from the banking system and a depressant effect on the cash ratio of the banking system.

Although such transfers may represent a large leakage to an individual bank, the net leakage to the whole banking system is likely to be much smaller; the actual size will depend on the reserve ratios of the building societies and the cash component of that ratio, i.e. how much cash the building societies drain from the banks. In reality the cash ratio of the building societies is very small – around 1 per cent, smaller than the primary banks' ratio in the UK. It is likely that the policy of the building societies towards the purchase of government securities is of greater significance to the banking system in respect of the potential cash drain. If the building societies used the additional funds deposited with them from the banks to purchase large amounts of government securities from the government sector *itself*, this would cause a more serious cash drain from the banking system than building society adjustments of their own cash ratio and cash holdings. Note that if the building societies – or any other type of financial intermediary – held all their working balances with the banks, the transfer of funds from the banks to such intermediaries would not result, of itself, in a reduction in the volume of bank deposits.

5.2.2.2 Demand for loans

In our earlier account of the expansion of deposits through increased bank lending, we made no reference to the *demand* side for such loans. Implicitly we were assuming that if the banks were able to offer loans and overdrafts, the demand would be there. This assumption is not acceptable, however, since there is no reason to suppose that the demand for bank loans would match the supply at prevailing rates of interest on such loans.

What then determines the demand for loans from the banks? This is a very broad question, so we shall limit our discussion to the business sector. In Chapter 4 we saw, for example, that the primary banks in the UK lend to a wide range of business activity: industry of all kinds, commerce, and finance. The reasons behind such lending are likely to be varied and probably quite complex. We can suggest, nevertheless, that all the borrowers will have in mind the cost of such borrowing in relation to their expected return on the use of such funds and the risks associated with the intended use of the funds. For example, medium-term borrowing by manufacturing firms used for the purchase of capital equipment will be linked closely with the expected return on such investment which, in turn, will be geared to the current and expected demand for the products of that firm. If we generalize this, we can suggest that the borrowing by manufacturing firms is likely to be related to the state of the economy or, slightly more precisely, to the stage of the business cycle which the economy has reached and the course which it is likely to take. During periods when business activity is increasing it is probable that the demand for loans will rise (not least because firms will require additional working capital), and in times of contraction or business stagnation the opposite will be the case. It is possible that the banks might have the capacity and inclination to expand their lending, but the demand for loans might be less than the potential supply. One factor may be that the demand for loans will be less than that which the banks wish to offer because the interest rate charged on such borrowing may be too high. (It will be remembered that we have suggested already that the demand and supply may not match at prevailing rates of interest.) If this is the case, the banks will be induced to lower their interest rates on loans in order to stimulate demand.

5.2.2.3 Banks' lending policy

We have emphasized repeatedly that the primary banks' obligations to depositors are such that the banks must be prudent in the management of their own assets. Since the largest single item is 'advances to customers' (of which only about one-quarter represents personal borrowing) it is important that the banks are careful in the handling of this item. Part of the art of banking is the capacity to evaluate the risk of a potential loan and to judge the appropriate rate of interest and the term of the advance. A misjudgement in respect of these two features of the loan in periods when banks are eager to expand such business – when they are 'under-lent' – could result in the potential borrower changing his bank or requesting a loan from another bank. One problem which arises is that the risk factor of a particular project for which a loan is required is likely to vary with the course of the business cycle. In periods of low business activity many firms will be less profitable and this could be a factor influencing the bank's decision with regard to a loan, i.e. in times of business recession, banks will be less inclined to lend to firms which in past circumstances might have been regarded as a good risk. When a recession ends and there are clear indications that an upturn is beginning, the banks may change their view of the riskiness of loans and allow their lending to expand to certain types of business. The implication here is that the banks might tend to be fair-weather friends and are unlikely to be of assistance to firms at the very times when such assistance is desperately needed (for example, with the continuation or increase of overdraft facilities). Although our remarks so far suggest that bank preference may well be in favour of a high degree of caution, in practice a bank is likely to behave differently. If a bank takes the long-term view, it might realize that the ultra-safe lending strategy could result in the loss of custom: borrowers who have been refused or restricted in their borrowing, yet survive a business recession, are unlikely to maintain their custom with the bank which has been very limited in its assistance. Furthermore, a bank might be unable to extricate itself from commitments to borrowers if by withdrawing further support the result is bankruptcy of a business firm. A bank might be faced with the prospect either of providing additional funds to enable a firm to ride a rough period, or of withdrawing support and losing most of the funds that have already been lent.

For many years the banks have been subject to the criticism that their lending to industry has been far too cautious, in particular their lending to the small and medium firm, so that there has been a shortage of funds facing many firms. New and fast-growing firms have found the problem of adequate supplies of working capital particularly acute (these firms are prone to insolvency or brankruptcy partly as a result of their need for adequate and growing supplies of working capital), and firms which are hoping to invest in the production of high-techno-logy products, or firms using high-technology equipment, often find finance a problem since the risk element may be relatively high for such ventures. However, it is probable that this argument against the banks is less valid than it used to be.

It should be clear that bank lending policy, influenced by the bank's evaluation of risk and uncertainty in general as well as in particular cases, will influence the preparedness of the bank to expand advances and, therefore, its deposits. Our simple model used earlier in this chapter does not take these various elements into consideration.

5.3 The government and the stock of money

5.3.1 THE CASH NEXUS

We observed earlier that financial dealings between the govern-ment and the non-government sector are ultimately transac-tions of a *cash* nature. Chapter 6 deals with the government's finances quite extensively and certainly in much more detail than is intended in this chapter. Our object here is to identify two aspects of the cash nexus between the government and the non-government sector and to consider the possible effects of this relationship on the stock of money.

5.3.1.1 Government spending

The reader is recommended to turn to section 6.3 for details of government spending and receipts. *Table 6.2* shows the items of spending for the financial year 1987 – 88, but it is important to realize that spending is taking place continuously throughout the financial year and is subject to variations during the year; it is not an even rate of spending. The government departments, not all of which are big spenders, have their accounts at the Bank of England (this is the item 'public deposits' in the balance sheet of the Bank of England).

We can choose an item of government spending and trace its possible course from the government sector to the non-government sector, in particular to the banking sector. For simplicity, let us consider the payment of £1 million by the Ministry of Defence on completion of a military contract placed with a UK firm. The Ministry of Defence, having an account at the Bank of England, will draw a cheque on that account for £1 million, made payable to the supplying company. The firm receives the cheque for £1 million and deposits it with its bank – say, Barclays Bank. Barclays Bank, acting on behalf of the firm, will (a) credit the firm's account with £1 million so that Barclays Bank's deposits rise by £1 million, and (b) present the cheque for payment at the Bank of England (for simplicity we shall ignore any other financial transactions involving the Bank of England and Barclays Bank). The Bank of England, will then make payment to Barclays bank by crediting Barclays Bank's account at the Bank with £1 million (bankers' deposits rise by £1 million) and by debiting the Ministry of Defence's account by £1 million (public deposits fall by £1 million). This is not the end of the story, however, since Barclays Bank will find itself holding excess cash. If we assume,[4] again for simplicity, that the cash ratio is 10 per cent, then Barclays Bank is holding excess cash to the tune of £900,000. It is £900,000 and not £1 million because Barclays Bank will need to retain 10 per cent of the extra deposits of £1 million as part of the extra cash needed to sustain the extra deposits. The cash is available to Barclays Bank since its total cash includes accounts at the Bank of

---

[4] Note that this is an assumption for arithmetic convenience and is *not* the case in practice.

England and these, as we have just seen, have risen by £1 million. It is clear that Barclays Bank is now in a position to expand its business on the basis of the inflated cash reserve. If we assume that Barclays Bank *retains* the additional £1 million cash as part of its reserve, it may be able to expand its deposits by increasing its assets up to a maximum level which will be determined by the size of the deposit multiplier.

This simple illustration allows us to draw certain conclusions.

(a) Government spending can add to the volume of bank deposits directly (the firm in our example had increased its bank deposits by £1 million).

(b) Government spending can add to the cash base of a bank and the banking system.

(c) As a consequence of the addition to the cash base, the bank(s) are able to expand their business by virtue of their initially higher cash ratio, i.e. government spending provides a stimulus for the deposit multiplier. In this way the banks may increase their advances to customers or buy other financial assets.

5.3.1.2 Government receipts

As with government spending, we shall choose an illustrative receipt and trace its progress. Let us assume that an individual is liable for capital gains tax of £1,000. On receipt of the tax demand the individual will write a cheque for £1,000 payable to the Inland Revenue's account with the Bank of England. When the Inland Revenue receives the cheque, it will deposit it in its account at the Bank of England. The Bank of England will credit the Inland Revenue with £1,000 and present the cheque for payment by, say, Barclays Bank on behalf of its taxpaying customer. Barclays Bank is able to make payment by means of a reduction in its account with the Bank of England (Bankers' balances fall by £1,000) and Barclays Bank will then reduce its customer's deposit by £1,000. After these adjustments have been made it should be clear that Barclays Bank has experienced a drain of £1,000 cash from its cash reserve and a reduction in deposits by £1,000. The reduction in its cash reserve, however, may result in Barclays Bank's cash ratio falling below the required minimum figure since, if we maintain the assumption of a 10 per cent cash ratio, we can see that the loss of £1,000 *cash* reduces the capacity of Barclays Bank to sustain deposit liabilities of £10,000. Of this £10,000, £1,000 has disappeared as a result of reducing the customer's account by £1,000 after the payment of the capital gains tax, but this still leaves £9,000 deposits unsupported by sufficient cash. If we assume Barclays Bank is unable to replenish its cash reserve, the bank must make efforts to reduce its deposit liabilities by selling assets or by reducing advances by £9,000.

Our illustration allows us to draw additional conclusions:

(a) Government receipts can cause a fall in bank deposits directly (i.e. when the bank reduces the customer's deposit after paying the tax).

(b) Government receipts can reduce the cash base of a bank or the banking system.

(c) As a consequence of the reduction of the cash base and the reduced cash ratio, the bank(s) are induced to cut back further their deposit liabilities, i.e. there is a *negative* deposit multiplier. Thus, the banks may have to reduce their advances to customers or sell other financial assets.

5.3.1.3 Net position

Having examined the effects of government spending and receipts on the level of bank deposits, it should be clear that the effect of the government's spending and receipts on the banking system will depend on the *net* position. Each day the government is spending and receiving money : at times spending will exceed receipts, and at other times receipts will exceed spending. The final effect on the banking system will depend, therefore, on the net figure. For example, on a particular day the government may receive £90 million in taxes and other receipts, and spend £110 million, which in this case represents a net flow of £20 million from the government sector to the non-government sector, and as this feeds into the banking system there will tend to be an expansionary stimulus to bank deposit growth. It should be remembered that such a net outflow, when it finally reaches the banking system, will manifest itself as a *cash* flow from the Bank of England to the banking system. Thus :

(a) Government spending in excess of receipts leads to a net outflow of cash from the government sector, a stimulus to bank deposit growth, and therefore an increase in the stock of money in the economy.

(b) Government spending which is less than receipts leads to a net outflow from the non-government sector to the government sector, a contractionary pressure on bank deposit growth, and therefore a reduction of the stock of money in the economy.

(c) Expressing points (a) and (b) in terms of the central government's budgetary situation, we can suggest that a budget deficit will tend to produce monetary expansion in the banking system, and a budget surplus will tend to produce monetary contraction.

5.3.2 GOVERNMENT BORROWING

In Section 5.3.1 we examined the implications for the banking system and stock of money of a change in the net position of government receipts and expenditure. For example, if government spending exceeded receipts, this would tend to be an expansionary factor influencing the banking system. However, we ignored the implications of the net spending (i.e. the deficit) for government borrowing. We shall consider this question now.

If the government is to cover the deficit, it will need to borrow. [5] (See Section 6.9 for further discussion of government borrowing.) It is important to establish the consequences of government borrowing from the different sources within the economy. These sources are as follows :

(a) The non-bank public (i.e. persons, firms, non-bank financial intermediaries, etc.).

(b) The Bank of England (remember that the Bank of England is the government's banker).

(c) The banking system.

We emphasize that the consequences of these three types of

---

[5] Obviously the deficit could be eliminated by raising government receipts or cutting spending. If we assume that these two possibilities are either impracticable in the short run or undesired by the government, then the only alternative is for the government to borrow.

borrowing are not the same, and we shall examine therefore each of the sources.

5.3.2.1 Borrowing from the non-bank public

In order to raise the necessary funds to cover its deficit, the government may attempt to sell a variety of suitable and acceptable securities to the non-bank public. Let us assume that the government's deficit in the period we are considering is £ 10 million and that the whole of this deficit is covered by sales of government bonds to the non-bank public. We can now trace the consequences of this sale. The non-bank public are likely to pay for the stock entirely by means of cheques drawn on their bank deposits made payable to the Bank of England; the Bank is responsible for arranging bond sales for the government. Thus £ 10 million of cheques drawn largely on the deposits of primary banks will be received by the Bank of England. The Bank will collect payment in the usual way by deducting £ 10 million from the primary banks' balances held at the Bank. The results of this sale of government stock will be initially that (a) bankers' balances at the Bank of England (remember that these balances are part of the banks' cash base) will fall by £ 10 million, (b) the banks will deduct £ 10 million from their customers' deposits and therefore total bank deposits will fall by £ 10 million, and (c) the banks' cash base will have fallen and their cash ratio also will have fallen. If there are no alternative sources of cash and the banks are operating at the minimum cash ratio, the banks would be induced to contract their deposit liabilities. Thus in the first instance sales of government bonds to finance a budget deficit will tend to put contractionary pressures on the banks if the stock is bought by the non-bank public. This is not the end of the matter, however, since we must take into account the fact that the government is borrowing in order to *spend* in excess of its receipts from other sources. We must therefore further take into the account the consequences of such 'deficit spending'. In Section 5.3.1.1. we saw that government spending adds to the volume of bank cash and bank deposits by an amount equal to the amount spent. We can conclude, therefore, in this section that the act of spending the borrowed £ 10 million will recycle the cash which was drained from the banking system when settlement was made at the Bank

of England. The cash will return to the banking sector and
bank deposits will rise by £10 million when the recipients of
government spending make deposits with their primary
banks.

It is evident that we need to modify our earlier conclusion
that government borrowing from the non-bank public produces
contractionary pressure on the banking system. This effect does
not occur because the volume of bank cash and bank deposits
remains unchanged so long as the government *spends* the funds
raised through its borrowing. An alternative view of this would
be that budget deficits financed by asset sales to the non-bank
public leave the monetary base and the banking system unaffec
ted in so far as there is no direct pressure on the deposit
component of the money stock to change.

5.3.2.2 *Borrowing from the Bank of England*

If the government is unable to sell sufficient, quantities of
securities to the non-bank public, it may choose to sell securities
to the Bank of England. Since the Bank of England is a
state-owned body, there is no legal or technical problem: the
Bank of England would have no option but to act in accordance with the government's wishes. The operation would
involve the exchange of securities – printed by the government, of course – for deposits at the Bank of England. So if the
government sells £10 million securities to the Bank of England,
the Bank's assets (securities) will increase by £10 million and
its liabilities (public deposits) will rise also by £10 million. If
we assume that the government spends the whole of these
additional funds in the non-government sector, the final effect
will be (a) a rise in non-government sector deposits with the
banks of £10 million, and (b) a rise in the cash base of the
banking system also by £10 million. The banks, therefore,
would be in a more liquid position since their cash ratio would
have risen and they would be able to expand their business
activities through the purchase of other assets and/or the
expansion of advances through deposits creation (we gave an
illustration of this in Section 5.3.1.1). It is clear that borrowing
from the Bank of England produces an expansionary stimulus
to the banking system as well as increasing the money-stock.
Borrowing from the central bank in the manner described is the

modern equivalent of earlier governments' resorting to the printing press to meet their monetary needs. [6]

5.3.2.3 Borrowing from the banking system

We shall consider two means by which borrowing from the banking system occurs and the possible consequences of such forms of borrowing.

First, let us assume that a bank is maintaining a cash reserve in excess of the safe minimum and decides to purchase government securities which are being offered for sale by the Bank of England. [7] A bank which purchases, say, £5 million of such securities will make payment through its account at the Bank of England, i.e. bankers' balances at the Bank of England will fall by £5 million. Since this represents a reduction of the cash reserve of the bank, the purchase of such securities will be revealed in the bank's balance sheet as a switch in the composition of its assets and there will be no change in its liabilities. Balance sheets 12 and 13 indicate the situation before and after the purchase of £5 million government securities by the bank. In this illustration, the banks' cash ratio has fallen

Bank balance sheet 12

Assets		Liabilities	
Cash in tills and at the			
Bank of England	£10,000,000	Deposits	£50,000,000
Other earning assets	40,000,000		
	£50,000,000		£50,000,000

Bank balance sheet 13

Assets		Liabilities	
Cash in tills and at the			
Bank of England	£5,000,000	Deposits	£50,000,000
Other earning assets	40,000,000		
Government securities	5,000,000		
	£50,000,000		£50,000,000

[6] It is likely that additional notes and coin would need to be produced in these circumstances because the volume of bank deposits held by the non-government sector would rise and the cash needs of this sector would rise also. (see Section 5.2.2.1).

[7] If the banks bought securities in exchange for bank deposits from the *non-bank public*, via the stock market, the effect would be to raise deposits and bank assets by the amount of the purchase.

from 20 per cent in position 12 to 10 per cent at position 13 after the purchase of the securities. It would appear that government borrowing from the bank also has had the effect of changing the structure of the bank's assets. Let us continue the description and consider the use of the funds so obtained. First, the public deposits at the Bank of England will rise by £5 million as bankers' deposits fall by £5 million, and secondly, the government presumably has borrowed the money in order to spend it. As with an earlier illustration, the act of spending by the government will recycle the cash back to the non-government sector and eventually back into the banking system. The banking system will once again have a cash ratio in excess of the safe minimum and will have, therefore, the capacity to expand its business. It should be noted that the preceding analysis assumed that the bank was able to purchase government securities with its surplus cash. If the bank had been maintaining the minimum cash ratio, then the bank would *not* have been able to purchase government securities since such purchases would have pushed the bank's cash ratio below the minimum required.

The second method of borrowing from the banking system which we identify occurs in rather a different way from the first. This method is connnected with what is termed the 'residual financing role' of the banking system. Let us consider a situation in which the government wishes to finance a deficit, but in which the non-bank public is not prepared to purchase all the securities which the government wishes to sell. Under such circumstances the government initially will obtain the funds from the Bank of England (the government must never be short of the funds it needs even if this entails borrowing from its own bank) and such funds are then spent. The consequence of borrowing from the Bank is to add to the cash base of the banking system, and this surplus cash in the banking system may well be used to add to banks' lending at call to the discount houses who, in turn, are likely to add to their holdings of government Treasury bills. Sufficient bills will be on offer from the Bank of England, both to finance the original deficit from the market, and to eliminate the direct borrowing of the government from the Bank of England. On receipt of the funds raised by sales of Treasury bills, the government will repay the

Bank of England, thus reducing its direct borrowing from the Bank (see also Section 4.8.3).

This mechanism reveals how the banking system automatically finances a government deficit through the provision of funds to the discount market, followed by the take-up of additional Treasury bills on offer. If the government cannot finance its deficit by the issue of securities (i.e. relatively illiquid government stock, the necessary funds are likely to be raised by the issue of highly liquid Treasury bills.

The descriptive analysis we have used so far has assumed a budget deficit as the example to illustrate the main points. Until 1987 such an assumption would have been correct for the UK, but after June 1987 the accounts of the government and the public sector moved into a surplus position (see Section 6.8 for further discussion). The reader should attempt to describe the consequences of this situation within the framework laid down in this section. Suppose that the government, for example, is not borrowing from the non-bank public but, because of surplus tax receipts, is *repaying* past borrowing. In Section 5.3.2.1. the reverse situation would be where the government is generating a surplus from taxpayers and then recycling the funds back to taxpayers through repayments of past debt. The Bank of England would therefore be *paying* cheques to the non-bank public which would, in turn, be deposited with the banks; ultimately the banks would present such cheques to the Bank of England for payment, and that payment would be made by transfers from public accounts to bankers' deposits at the Bank of England. Government debt repayment would seem to be expansionary since this is adding to bank deposits and cash, but if such debt repayments are financed by rising tax revenues then this neutralizes the expansionary effect of the rise in bank deposits.

5.4 The balance of payments and the stock of money

This section considers the relationship between the balance of payments of a country and the domestic money stock. So far in this chapter it has been an implicit assumption that the monetary system under consideration was in a closed economy, i.e. one with neither international trade nor international capital movements. This is, of course, an unacceptable assumption, particularly for the UK, and we now propose to study the consequences of changing the assumption to that of an 'open economy'. Our discussion centres on Bank of England operations and the foreign currency market.

UK residents and overseas residents are involved in the buying and selling of goods and services (this causes changes in the flow of income and expenditure in both the UK and foreign countries through imports and exports changes) as well as the buying and selling of assets (this causes changes in the composition of the stock of wealth of UK residents and overseas residents). Both types of activity are likely to have consequences for the domestic money stock of the UK. Before continuing with our discussion we need to adopt a definition of the money stock. In Section 2.4.3.1 we saw that the Bank of England calculated several definitions of the money stock. In particular, the calculation of M3c distinguished between UK private sector holdings of foreign currency deposits and UK private sector holdings of sterling deposits. In the first quarter of 1988 M3 stood at £202,212 million (which excluded foreign currency deposits), whereas M3c amounted to £234,714 million, a difference of £32 billion. These deposits of foreign currency are held by such firms as oil companies, insurance companies, and other firms who are involved in international operations and therefore require foreign currency balances. Capital funds for foreign investment and awaiting investment abroad are also included in this figure of £34 billion. The distinction between M3 and M3c recognizes that it is the sterling volume of deposits which is likely to be the more relevant variable when considering the behaviour of the banking system and the economy.

For several decades the Bank of England has operated in the foreign currency market. Since 1932 the Bank's instrument has been the Exchange Equalization Account, although technically control is vested with the Treasury. The major role of the EEA in the foreign exchange markets is to act as a stabilizing influence on the course of exchange rates, checking undue fluctuations. Between 1944 and 1972 the EEA's operations were within an international framework of fixed exchange rates, and the operations of the EEA had to comply with international agreement (via the International Monetary Fund) regarding the extent of permitted variations in exchange rates. After June

1972 the UK (and later, other countries) defected from the system of fixed exchange rates and instead allowed the market forces of supply and demand for currencies to exercise a dominant influence on the broad movement or trend of the sterling exchange rate, but at the same time intervened in order to 'smooth' the path of exchange rates and avoid violent changes. At the present time the UK continues to operate a regime of exchange rate flexibility, although such flexibility may be limited in relation to certain other currencies such as the US dollar and West German mark. The basic mechanics of the EEA are crucial to our consideration of the impact of the balance of payments on the domestic money stock (sterling M3). It is these mechanics which we will now examine, with the assumption that the EEA is intending to maintain fixed exchange rates or is stabilizing rates at a particular level.

5.4.1 BALANCE OF PAYMENTS DEFICIT

Let us assume that UK residents are attempting to buy £100 million of overseas goods, services, and assets during a particular period, and overseas residents are attempting to buy £50 million of UK goods, services, and assets in the same period. Imports are greater than exports, and there is a balance of payments deficit of £50 million in that period.[8] The manifestation of this in the foreign exchange markets is that there is an excess of sterling being supplied by UK residents wishing to spend on overseas goods, services, etc. If the exchange rate between the pound sterling and other currencies was determined entirely by market forces, the effect would be for the pound sterling to depreciate in value in the foreign exchange market as a result of the £50 million excess supply of pounds. If the object of the government and the Bank of England is to stabilize the exchange rate, then the Bank of England via the EEA will have to supply foreign currency to UK residents (£50 million worth of foreign currency) and take up the £50 million sterling being offered by UK residents through their banks. By the Bank

---

[8] Note that there are some theoretical difficulties associated with the precise meanings of 'deficit' and 'surplus' in the context of the overall balance of payments accounts. See chapter 7.

absorbing the excess supply of pounds and by supplying foreign currency at the desired exchange rate, the exchange rate will therefore be stabilized at the rate since demand and supply would be kept in balance. We can offer a few additional facts and conclusions :

(a) The EEA obtains the currency from the official reserves of holdings of gold and foreign currencies. The official reserves will therefore fall.

(b) The EEA has an additional £50 million sterling, and until 1971 this would have been used to buy UK government Treasury bills. The practice now is for this money to be paid directly into the government's Consolidated Fund.

(c) UK residents make payment for the foreign currency by transferring sterling bank deposits. Since these deposits are transferred to the EEA at the Bank of England, the result is a fall in sterling bank deposits by £50 million and also a fall in the cash base and the cash ratio of the banking system as the cheques drawn on the primary banks are settled at the Bank of England.

(d) Unless other financial changes occur (e.g. the government may choose to reduce its borrowing from the non-government sector as a result of the inflow of £50 million from the EEA to the Bank of England), a balance of payments deficit has a *contractionary* effect on the domestic banking system as well as directly reducing the volume of sterling bank deposits and, therefore, the stock of money.

5.4.2 BALANCE OF PAYMENTS SURPLUS

For simplicity, let us assume that the balance of payments surplus arises from UK residents' purchases from overseas totalling £50 million, and overseas residents are buying £100 million goods, services, and assets from the UK. The £50 million surplus will reveal itself as an excess of £50 million of foreign currencies being offered on the foreign exchange market in relation to the sterling being offered by UK residents. The relative shortage of sterling, without intervention, would result in a rise or appreciation in the value of the pound sterling. In order to avoid such an occurrence the EEA will proceed to sell sufficient sterling (£50 million) to prevent the exchange rate changing, and will absorb the foreign currency being offered by overseas residents. As a consequence of the EEA action we can draw the following conclusions :

(a) The EEA obtains foreign currency from the market and EEA holdings of such funds will rise by £50 million; official reserves will rise by £50 million of foreign currency.

(b) The EEA requires £50 million sterling for sale on the foreign exchange market and these funds will be provided out of the Consolidated Fund.

(c) Overseas residents will deposit the sterling received from the EEA within the UK banking system prior to making payment for the goods, services, and assets bought. Such receipts will increase the bankers' balances at the Bank of England (the transfer of funds between the EEA and the non-government sector being a cash transfer) as well as increasing the volume of bank deposits by £50 million. Not only will the cash base of the banking system rise, but so too will the cash ratio.

(d) Assuming that there are no other financial changes taking place (e.g. the government may choose to increase its borrowing from the non-government sector as a result of the outflow of £50 million from the Bank of England to the EEA), the balance of payment surplus will be an *expansionary* stimulus to the domestic banking system as well as directly increasing the volume of bank deposits and, therefore, the stock of money.

Briefly, our analysis of changes in the balance of payments under a system of fixed exchange rates, or where the Bank of England is stabilizing the rate, suggests that initially

(a) A balance of payments deficit will tend to reduce the domestic money stock by roughly the amount of the deficit.

(b) A balance of payments surplus will tend to raise the domestic money stock by roughly the amount of the surplus.

Earlier in this section we stated that after June 1972 the UK abandoned the tight control over the exchange rate which had been a feature of the previous twenty-eight years. In its place the exchange rate for the pound sterling was allowed to be determined by market forces of supply and demand. Under these circumstances we need to consider the effect on the money stock of changes in UK residents' spending abroad and overseas residents' spending in the UK. If one can assume that the monetary authorities are allowing the exchange rate to be established entirely by market forces, and the EEA is not intervening in foreign currency markets, then the changes in the domestic money stock resulting from official (EEA) transactions cannot, by definition, occur. This does not mean that the money stock is entirely unconnected with the behaviour of non-residents: the definition of M3 excludes UK residents' foreign currency deposits and non-residents' *sterling* deposits. If as a result of trade or capital movements, therefore, non-residents accumulate additional sterling bank deposits which were held previously by UK residents, the effect on the money stock statistics is to reduce the size of M3 and vice versa.

Our discussion of fixed and floating exchange rates leads us to the conclusion that under a system of fixed exchange rates the balance of payments will affect the money stock (unless offset by Bank intervention), and that the influence is both direct (caused by the movements in deposits as a direct result of the buying or selling of sterling) and indirect (associated with the secondary effects on bank deposits through changes in the cash base and cash ratio of the banking system). With floating exchange rates, any change in the money stock is brought about by changes in the composition of assets held by non-residents and the banking system.

5.5 The stock of money

Most of this chapter has been concerned with identifying the major factors which exercise an influence on changes in the money stock measure M3 or alternative monetary indicators. Our descriptive analysis has yielded the following general propositions :

(a) The stock of money may change as a result of the business activities of the primary banks. Their capacity to lend may vary in response to the availability of liquid assets, in particular the cash base. Furthermore, their inclination to expand deposits through advances to customers might be dependent on the general state of the economy, which is something over which they have little control and which is likely to change markedly within fairly short periods of time.

(b) The banking system's capacity to change the stock of money in the economy may be influenced by other factors over which it has little influence. We drew attention to the various leakages from the banking system and particularly to the behaviour of the non-bank public – their preferences for holding cash and government securities.

(c) The flow of funds between the government sector and the non-government sector appeared to be of crucial importance in connection with the capacity of the banking system to vary its volume of business and deposit liabilities. Again, the banks have limited influence over these flows.

(d) Finally we examined how the balance of payments and the foreign sector was likely to have a significant influence on the money stock.

We can now incorporate these various elements into an illustrative calculation of the money stock which is less aggregative than the examples used at the end of Chapter 2. Examining the various items in *Table 5.1*, one can see that the four points identified at the beginning of this section are in fact incorporated: bank lending, public sector spending and receipts, sales of public sector securities to the non-bank public, and the external sector influence. Earlier in the chapter we noted that government borrowing (public sector borrowing requirement or PSBR) will, if financed by the banking system, add to the money stock; conversely a surplus will tend to reduce the money stock. As *Table 5.1* shows, in the second quarter of 1988 the government had a surplus and therefore would tend to reduce the money stock. Additionally, the next two items in the table show that the public sector *repaid* £1,020 million, which would tend to add to the money stock. However, the overall position was a contractionary influence (£630 million) on M4 because of the large financial surplus of £1,650 million. Bank and building society lending to the UK private sector, an additional £21,753 million in the second quarter of 1988, clearly had a substantial impact on the growth of M4. However, the banks and the building societies lent to the foreign sector £4,720 million, and this reduced the growth of M4 because sterling deposits held by foreigners are not included, by definition, in the calculation of M4. Both banks and building societies were adding to their own capital funds substantially

(net non-deposit sterling liabilities), and these items are removed from the accounting of M4 since such liabilities are, in
effect, non-usable or spendable items.

Table 5.1

Counterparts to changes in M4 (1988, second quarter) (£m)

Public sector borrowing requirement (−surplus)	− 1,650
Purchases (−) of public sector net debt by UK private sector (other than banks or building societies)	+ 909
External and foreign currency finance of the public sector (− increase)	+ 111
Total	**− 630**
Banks' sterling lending to the UK private sector (excluding building societies) (+ increase)	+ 14,291
Building societies' sterling lending to the UK private sector (+ increase)	+ 7,462
External and foreign currency transactions of banks and building societies (− increase)	− 4,720
Change in net non-deposit sterling liabilities (− increase)	− 3,376
Change in M4	**+ 13,027**

Note : the + or − sign indicates the effect of that item on the change in M4

Source : Bank of England *Quarterly Bulletin,* Vol. 28, no. 4

We must point out, however, that an important omission in
this section is any reference to the *deliberate* manipulation of
the stock of money by the monetary authorities (the Bank of
England and the Treasury) and the means by which such manipulation might take place. The omission was intentional so that
we could identify basic elements affecting the money stock,
abstracted from the complexities of UK institutional arrangements and conventions.

5.6 Regulating the stock of money

5.6.1 CONTROVERSY

In recent years this topic has become highly controversial. We
shall explain briefly the basic reasons for the controversy, since
Chapter 11 will examine this area of debate much more closely,
with its implications for monetary policy.

One aspect of the problem has been touched upon already in Chapter 2, and this relates to the actual definition of money and the appropriate series of financial statistics to match the chosen definition. For our purposes we can polarize the problem by suggesting either (a) that money can be identified uniquely on the basis of its means of payment function, or (b) that money is not only a means of payment in the economy but also a financial asset for which there is a range of substitute assets. This area of economic analysis is somewhat complicated and for illustrative purposes we shall simplify the problem. If one asks the man in the street how much money he has, he is likely to reply with a catalogue of various types of assets: cash, funds in the National Savings Bank and the TSB, funds entrusted with a building society, and possibly deposits with a another retail bank. From the individual's point of view, the inclusion of these various assets under the heading of money is legitimate since to the *individual* all these various assets are very liquid and represent almost instant spending power. Nevertheless, the economist's view might well be that not all these financial assets really represent instant spending power even though the individual *feels* that they do and acts accordingly (see Section 2.4.2). The existence of a number of financial assets which possess, in varying degrees, some of the properties of money does mean that it is difficult to identify a single asset or group of assets which can be identified unambiguously as money. As the Bank of England has expressed it: 'The inescapable conclusion is that there can be no unique definition of broad money. Any choice of dividing line between those financial assets included in, and those excluded from, broad money is to a degree arbitrary, and is likely over time to be invalidated by developments in the financial system.[9]

The monetary authorities are not concerned primarily to establish the definitive classification and definition of money assets in the economy, but rather to indentify those financial assets which are most closly related to changes in aggregate expenditure (and the price level) within the economy, whatever their precise definition. If it is possible to identify such financial aggregates, then arguably it is these assets which the

[9]Bank of England *Quarterly Bulletin* (May 1987), p. 219.

authorities should attempt to control. Unfortunately the problem does not rest there, since one has then to decide whether the control of such financial aggregaes will provide tight and reliable control over the economic aggregates with which one is primarily concerned; incomes, employment, the balance of payments, inflation. Merely to identify a relationship between two variables A and B does not imply that the relationship is stable or useful as an instrument of economic policy.

Finally, many economists have raised the very practical problem of whether control of the money stock (or an alternative monetary aggregate) is actually possible. Our analysis of the influences on the money stock in this chapter has revealed that there are many factors which will bear on changes in the money stock. One fundamental problem is whether control or regulation really is feasible in an economy which has an elaborate financial system. Clearly it is vital to resolve this question since the *technical inability* to control the money stock (however defined) means that any theoretical justification for such activity instantly becomes redundant.

Since the mid 1970s UK governments have incorporated some emphasis on control of the money stock within policy statements, especially at the time of the Budget. With the election of a Conservative governement in 1979 monetary policy had as its focus the control of inflation through the regulation of the money stock, and targets for its growth were set by the Chancellor. The extent to which control was exercised and the policy objectives were achieved is subject to debate, and this is explored more fully Chapter 12.

5.6.2 THE BASIS FOR CONTROL

So far in this chapter we have used simplified examples of banks' operations, but nonetheless the analysis has been sufficient to allow us to draw a conclusion relating to the problem of control. There are three elements; first, the volume of cash within and accessible to the banking system is relevant to the volume of deposits supportable by the system; secondly, the banking system cannot generate *cash* but is dependent on the central bank as the ultimate source, and thirdly, the banks maintain (voluntarily or by instruction from the central bank) a minimum cash ratio. Given these three factors, one can conclude that the supply of cash to the banking system is the ultimate determinant of the volume of bank deposits, regardless of institutional and conventional factors. If the central bank wishes to control the volume of bank deposits (the bulk of the stock of money in the monetary system), all that is required is tight control of the supply of cash; and since the central bank is the source of supply, it would seem that there is little or nothing contentious about this propostion.[10] Indeed, there is nothing particularly remarkable about it at all since it follows from the structure and rules of the system. Deposits can be levered up or down on the fulcrum of the cash ratio, with the quantity of cash acting as a lever. The essential fact is that the lever and the fulcrum can be virtually *anything,* so long as the central bank (a) is capable of imposing on the banking system a ratio to be maintained, and (b) controls the supply to the banking system of the reserve assets which the banking system is required to hold to fulful the ratio requirement. Much of the controversy in the literature on this matter confuses the validity of these propositions with the reality of a particular institutional framework and its idiosyncracies, which sometimes appear to contradict or negate the basic conditions we have laid down.

5.7 Summary

(a) By the use of a series of simplified bank balance sheets, we showed how credit and deposit creation could take place. An essential feature which underpinned the whole process was the acceptability of bank deposits as a medium of exchange, i.e. money.

(b) In our *simple* model of deposit creation we suggested that the upper limit to such activity was provided by the size of the safe cash ratio and the volume of cash in the banking system. If either or both of these changed, then so would the upper limit to the volume of bank deposits.

[10] We would point out that in reality neither the cash base nor a cash ratio are used for this purpose, and that a cash ratio has been used in this chapter for *illustrative purposes.* For further discussion see *Monetary Control,* Cmnd 7858, HMSO, 1980, and the Third Report from the Treasury and Civil Service Committee, Sessions 1979 – 80, *Monetary Control.* The documentation associated with the latter report is of considerable interest and well worth examination.

(c) We established additional factors which influenced the process of deposit creation by the bank (or banks) – in the particular, the existence of leakages of cash from the banking system into the non-bank sector, i.e. the fact that firms and individuals have a *demand to hold cash*. Further limitations were identified as the demand for credit itself (if firms or individuals do not wish to borrow, there is little the banks can do about it), as well as the preparedness of the banks to provide credit to their customers.

(d) Section 5.3 emphasized the importance of the flow of funds between the government and the non-government sector and its effect on changes in bank deposits and the money stock of the community. We also highlighted the relevance of *how* the government may finance a budget deficit and its consequences for changes in the stock of money.

(e) In an open economy, such as the UK, the flows of funds associated with the changes in the balance of payments could affect the domestic money stock. A balance of payments deficit may tend to diminish the money stock and a balance of payments surplus may tend to add to the money stock.

(f) At the end of the chapter we outlined some of the problems associated with regulating the stock of money in the community, and considered whether or not a firm basis for control exists. It seems possible in principle, but it might well be the case that a central bank is unwilling to introduce such control because the consequence of such a policy might conflict with other objectives of economic policy.

6

Government and the markets

In Chapters 4 and 5 we considered in some detail how changes in the financial position of the government sector impinged on the behaviour of the banking system and financial markets. In particular we noted that changes in government spending, taxation, borrowing, and debt repayment all had a potential impact on the volume of bank deposits and bank lending, as well as affecting the flows of funds through financial markets. In this chapter we intend therefore to consider in more detail the accounts of the government sector and the nature of key financial markets.

6.1 The definition of public expenditure

We have made reference in earlier chapters to the division of the economy into various sectors, one of which is the public sector. The principal feature of this part of the economy is that ownership and control are in the hands of government in one form or another. Therefore the public sector consists of central government, local authorities, and public corporations (the latter including the nationalized industries together with other bodies such as the regional water authorities, British Technology Group, and the Bank of England). However, a problem arises when we want to quantify public expenditure because it may be defined, for example, to include *all* expenditure under the control of the public sector, or only that expenditure which has to be financed by taxation or borrowing. A good example here is the current expenditure of the nationalized industries. In most cases receipts from sales of goods or services covers this expenditure, and so much spending would be excluded from any definition of public expenditure which is only concerned with that expenditure financed by taxation or borrowing.

The definition of public expenditure which was used for many years comprised the current and capital expenditure of central government and local authorities, other than expenditure charged to the operating account of trading bodies, together with the capital expenditure of nationalized industries and other public corporations, and including debt interest and net lending.

This definition was designed to give an approximate measure of that public spending which has to be financed by means other than sales, charges, etc., and so it excluded the current expenditure of public corporations and other trading departments. The capital expenditure of the nationalized industries and other public corporations was included as much of this expenditure is traditionally financed by loans and capital grants from central government. But the above definition of public expenditure has now been amended, since it exaggerates the extent to which the activities of the public sector require to be financed by taxation or borrowing. Indeed, only part of the capital expenditure of the nationalized industries is financed by central government, the remainder coming from internal surpluses or from external sources such as market borrowing.

The present approach to public expenditure might refer to three different definitions :

General government expenditure is the expenditure of central and local government excluding transfers between them such as government grants to local authorities. Capital expenditure of the public corporations would be excluded from this definition unless financed by the government sector. This particular definition of 'public expenditure' is one which most closely relates to definitions of public expenditure used for international comparisons.

Public expenditure planning total is the aggregate used by the Government for control purposes. It is important to recognize that this definition of public expenditure is used flexibly because the intention is to construct accounts which enable government to identify use of resources within the public sector (which includes the nationalized industries and other public corporations) and thus to monitor and control such use of resources. Over time, therefore, this particular definition of public expenditure will be changed. The planning total (January 1988) excludes general government gross debt interest on the grounds that it is not susceptible to the same degree of control as other forms of expenditure – if market interest rates rise then so will debt interest on new securities issued – but includes all the external finance of most public corporations, not just the grants and loans they receive from central or local government. This particular definition is contentious because, for example, it includes sales of public sector *assets* (privatization proceeds) as negative expenditure, and by virtue of this reduces the published figure for 'public expenditure'. In the expenditure White Paper, the data for public expenditure are also presented in a form which excludes privatization proceeds.

Supply expenditure is spending which is directly financed by money voted by Parliament in the Supply Estimates. It finances the bulk of central government public expenditure, but the largest exclusion from this total is the expenditure from the National Insurance Fund which accounts for over half of social security spending. This exclusion is based on the notion that this is an *insurance* fund and not a tax. Supply Estimates include, for example, rate support grant to local authorities, whereas this is excluded (because it is simply an internal transfer) from the other definitions of public expenditure.

Clearly, when there is public discussion of public expenditure it is important to be aware of the definitions and calculations being used in such discussion.

6.2 The growth in public expenditure and its importance in the economy

In this section we will examine the extent to which public expenditure has grown in the UK economy and we will look at some of the problems connected with trying to assess the importance of this growth for the economy as a whole. As indicated in Section 6.1, an immediate difficulty arises because of the existence of several definitions of public expenditure, each of which has been used in official statistics. Therefore *Table 6.1* provides details of the growth in public expenditure using the different definitions.

Table 6.1
Growth in public expenditure 1963–89

(a) Measures of public spending, in cash (£b)

	Pre-1977 public expenditure definition	General government expenditure	1985 planning total definition	1985 planning total excluding PCMOB[a]	Supply expenditure
1963–64	11·8	11·3	—	9·9	—
1964–65	12·8	12·2	—	10·8	—
1965–66	14·1	13·6	—	12·0	—
1966–67	15·6	15·0	—	13·3	—
1967–68	17·7	17·4	—	15·5	—
1968–69	18·7	18·2	—	16·1	—
1969–70	19·6	19·3	—	17·0	—
1970–71	22·1	21·6	—	19·1	—
1971–72	24·5	24·3	—	21·4	—
1972–73	28·1	27·6	—	24·8	—
1973–74	33·6	32·0	29·3	28·5	15·5
1974–75	44·9	42·8	39·4	38·6	25·5
1975–76	56·2	53·8	48·9	48·4	34·1
1976–77	63·3	59·6	54·5	53·2	37·0
1977–78	67·2	63·7	56·8	56·0	40·0
1978–79	77·7	74·8	65·8	65·3	45·7
1979–80	92·3	89·8	77·0	77·5	53·8
1980–81	111·7	108·4	92·7	93·3	67·6
1981–82	123·4	120·1	104·7	104·4	74·3
1982–83	136·3	132·6	113·4	114·6	80·6
1983–84	145·5	140·1	120·3	120·4	86·6
1984–85	153·6	149·5	129·7	128·7	93·8
1985–86	—	158·2	—	133·7	—
1986–87	—	164·8	—	139·2	—
1987–88[b]	—	172·6	—	147·3	—
1988–89[b]	—	183·0	—	156·8	—

(b) Measures of public expenditure as a percentage of GDP

1963–64	37·3	35·8	—	33·6	20·4
1964–65	37·0	35·4	—	33·4	20·2
1965–66	38·3	36·8	—	34·5	20·8
1966–67	39·8	38·4	—	35·9	21·7
1967–68	42·7	42·0	—	39·4	22·7
1968–69	41·6	40·6	—	37·7	22·0
1969–70	40·6	40·0	—	36·9	21·5
1970–71	41·3	40·3	—	37·0	22·2
1971–72	41·2	40·8	—	37·4	22·4
1972–73	41·4	40·7	—	37·8	22·3
1973–74	44·6	42·5	40·4	39·4	23·8
1974–75	50·1	47·9	45·5	44·6	25·6
1975–76	50·6	48·5	45·7	45·3	26·5
1976–77	48·8	46·0	43·9	42·9	25·4
1977–78	44·5	42·3	39·7	39·1	23·3
1978–79	45·0	43·3	40·2	40·0	22·6
1979–80	44·6	43·4	39·7	39·9	22·4
1980–81	47·4	46·0	42·2	42·5	24·0
1981–82	47·6	46·3	43·5	43·4	23·5
1982–83	48·0	46·7	43·0	43·5	23·7
1983–84	47·6	45·8	42·6	42·7	23·6
1984–85	47·0	45·8	43·3	43·0	23·8
1985–86	—	43·75	—	—	22·9
1986–87	—	42·75	—	—	22·9
1987–88 [b]	—	41·25	—	—	—
1988–89 [b]	—	40·75	—	—	—

Source : Economic Trends (August 1985, October 1987)

[a] Public corporations market and overseas borrowing.
[b] 1987–88 and 1988–89 are estimates.

Table 6.1 (a) shows the rapid growth of general government expenditure in money terms over the period from the mid 1960s to the mid 1980s. Average annual percentage growth for the whole period was around 13 per cent, but during the 1970s it was especially rapid at around 18 per cent p.a., whereas during the 1980s it had declined to 9 per cent p.a. The table also highlights our earlier observation about the different definitions of public expenditure. The 'planning total definitions' are based on the 1985 White Paper, and compare with, say, the more significant data for 'general government expenditure'. But even though there was almost a fifteenfold increase in general government expenditure over the twenty-four years merely to measure the growth in money terms may not give an accurate indication of the changing importance of the public sector in the UK economy during an inflationary period. Instead it might be more appropriate to measure the ratio of expenditure to the value of goods and services (gross domestic product or GDP) available to the economy as a whole. By any of the measures available in the *Table 6.1 (b)*, it is clear that since the mid 1960s public expenditure seems to have increased in significance. In 1963-64 general government expenditure as a proportion of GDP was 35.8 per cent; in 1982 – 83 it had risen to 46.7 per cent, but it subsequently declined. It is the rapidly growing significance of public expenditure, especially towards the end of the 1970s, which has caused much concern and controversy since that time.

But, as is often the case, the issue is not as clear-cut as the statistics (or arguments) might at first indicate. Indeed, the ratio of 'public expenditure' to GDP does not give a true indication of the extent to which the government sector absorbs resources in the economy, if this is how the ratio is interpreted. In order to appreciate this argument it is necessary to separate goods and services expenditure and transfer payments and loans. *Goods and services expenditure* may represent a real use of resources by the public sector since physical resources are absorbed from the economy and used in the production of goods and services such as roads, education, and defence. These resources are no longer available for the production of goods and services in the private sector of the economy, although such resource-using expenditure will still benefit the community.

Nevertheless the fundamental difference here is that the individual no longer decides how much of the goods and services he buys; instead, allocation is made on the basis of government decision.

Transfer payments and loans include such items as subsidies to the private sector, social security payments, and debt interest. This category differs from goods and services expenditure in that the commodities bought with such transfer payments form part of personal consumption and investment, i.e. such items merely involve a transfer of money income from some members of society (through taxation) to others (through transfers) and do not involve the absorption of resources by the public sector itself, except in administration. Individuals still decide the amount of goods and services they purchase with such transfer payments through their willingness to pay. Thus the major effect of transfer payments and loans is on the distribution of income, i.e. the people who pay the most in taxes do not generally receive the most in transfer payments.

As an example of the significant difference between transfer payments and resource-using expenditure, compare two situations. Imagine an economy in which all incomes, in whatever form, are taxed at 50 per cent and the revenue is immediately returned to the taxpayers as transfer payments. If the transfer payments received by each individual are identical to the taxation paid, then such a policy will have very little effect on the economy; individuals still decide how much of any particular goods they want to buy, and in this case they still have the same funds with which to buy the goods. But public expenditure will account for 50 per cent of the national income. If the transfer payments received by *each* individual are not equal to the amount of taxation paid, then the distribution of income will be affected since some individuals will now have more to spend than before and others will have less. However, the decision as to which items to consume, and in what quantities, will still be taken by the individual.

Contrast this situation with one in which the government taxes all income at 50 per cent but then uses the revenue to produce goods and services for the benefit of the community. The decision as to the amount of these goods available for individual consumption is now taken by the state and not by the individual. [1] As before, public expenditure accounts for 50 per cent of national income, but this type of expenditure has a more profound effect on the economy.

So, if the intention is to establish the extent to which the public sector absorbs resources in the economy, a better measure might be the proportion of resource-using expenditure to GDP. In *Table 6.1 (b)* the last column shows general government expenditure on goods and services as a percentage of GDP, and we can use these data as an indicator of the resource-using expenditure of the government. We can see that resource-using expenditure grew as a proportion of GDP over the period 1965–76, but so did general government expenditure. In fact the rates of expansion were much the same, implying that transfer payments and loans grew at a similar rate. However, more recent developments indicate a slightly different pattern. Between the 1976–77 and 1982–83 financial years, expenditure relative to GDP remained virtually unchanged, whereas for goods and services expenditure the decline was 2 per cent. Clearly, transfer payments and loans became a larger component of public expenditure relative to goods and services. After 1982 – 83 the share of general government expenditure fell substantially, whereas the goods and services component fell only slightly – suggesting that the change in public expenditure was concentrated on a decline in transfers rather than on goods and services. One might even argue strongly that the significance of the resource-using expenditure ratio can be overstated since much of that spending on goods and services would need to be undertaken, even if not made by the public sector on behalf of the community. At first glance what is perhaps surprising is the stability of this ratio, even though the whole period covers terms of office of Conservative and Labour governments of almost equal time. [2] The average for the twenty-four years covered by the data is 22·9 per cent and the variation around this average is fairly small. The explanation

---

[1] Of course the individual does have some influence on the decision via the voting mechanism.

[2] Labour governments 1964–70, 1974–79; Conservative governments 1970–74, 1979 to the present.

for this is, perhaps, beyond the scope of this chapter, but it might suggest a resilient demand by the community for certain kinds of provision by the state. Such demand might be determined by factors over which governments have little immediate control, such as the age structure of the population; for example, spending on health care would be necessary even without the National Health Service. One can also make the case that the public sector might benefit from the economies of scale in the provision of certain services, so that the real cost of provision is lower than if they are undertaken individually and privately. Clearly these are debatable matters and one should be cautious in interpreting the various data.

The lesson to be learned from this discussion is that various categories of public expenditure exist, each of which has different implications for the economy. Figures which merely show the growth in total public expenditure, either on an annual bais or as a ratio of national resources, ignore many important issues. It should also be recognized that international comparisons of public expenditure are complicated by differences in the definition of public expenditure. For instance, many countries exclude from their budget figures that part of social security benefits which is financed by contributions, whereas the UK does not. Also local authorities and public corporations in other countries often borrow directly from the private sector, and the relevant expenditure is not included in public expenditure. Accordingly, international comparisons of public expenditure must be made with care and interpreted with caution.

6.3 Public expenditure by economic category, spending authority, and function

To date we have focused attention on the two principal economic categories of public expenditure, that is goods and services expenditure and transfer payments and loans. Included in the first of these two categories are consumption and investment expenditure, whereas the latter consists of subsidies, grants, debt interest, and net lending. However, public expenditure can also be analysed by spending authority (i.e. central government, local authorities, and some public corporations) and by function or department (defence, education, etc.). In order to give a comprehensive picture, the Public Expenditure

White Paper provides details of expenditure plans under all three headings. This annual document gives information on the government's plans for the financial year ahead, together with those for future years, considered against the background of the forecast for the resources available in the economy as a whole. The reader is recommended to consult the current document on the government's expenditure plans, [3] whilst in the subsequent discussion we seek to provide some observations of a more general nature.

The breakdown of public expenditure by *spending authority* reveals that the largest spender is central government, which accounts for around three-quarters of the total, followed in turn by local authorities and certain public corporations. Our discussion of the definition of public expenditure in Section 6.1 explained that the capital expenditure of the nationalized industries is only included to the extent that it is financed by central government, but even then the lending is counted as central government expenditure. The public corporations considered here as a separate spending authority include such as the water authorities and the new town and housing corporations, representing in total by far the smallest of the three spending units. Other complications exist with the division into spending authorities since, for example, a considerable proportion of local authority expenditure is financed from central government grants. To avoid double-counting, the consolidation of the public sector accounts excludes such grants from the expenditure totals for central government.

The breakdown of public expenditure by *function* currently reveals twelve major categories of expenditure, of which some details for the financial year 1987–88 are given in *Tables 6.2* and *6.3*. It can be seen that social security, health and personal social services, defence and education and science account for 70 per cent of public expenditure (planning total), and within that group social security accounts for almost one-third of all expenditure. Within the social security programme the largest item is the payment of pensions (42 per cent) followed by income support (17 per cent) and unemployment benefit (8 per

3 *The Government's Expenditure 1988 – 89 to 1990 – 91*, vols I and II, Cmnd 288 – I, 288 – II (HMSO, January 1988).

cent), and over half the social security payments are contributory benefits. Receipts from National Insurance amounts to nearly £29 billion, which is 60 per cent of the social security budget. Of the defence budget, about half is spent on equipment and nearly 40 per cent is payments to personnel in wages, salaries, etc. Within education and science spending, almost £11 billion is spent on schools and nearly £5 billion on higher and further education. (Although these seem like substantial items of spending, it is worth noting that more is spent on, say, alcohol in the UK than on education.) *Table 6.3* provides further detail of government expenditure by identifying the main heads of expenditure within the planning total. This detail reinforces earlier comment on the composition of expenditure, and it is of further interest to relate both composition and growth of expenditure with earlier years. In 1978–79 the allocation of funds (measured in real terms) to the various functions was virtually identical to that of 1987–88. [4] The only distinctive changes were a large fall in the share going to housing (from 6·8 to 4·1 per cent) and notable rises in health and social security. With the exception of transport, housing, and environmental services, all functions experienced a *rise* in real spending from 1978–79, and during the period total real expenditure rose by over 10 per cent. Only in 1985–86 was there a fall in real spending, but it is reasonable to point out that this fall is relative to 1984–85 when there was an exceptional rise in spending under the heading of trade, industry, energy, and employment, which was largely due to much higher external borrowing by British Coal and British Rail, in some measure probably a result of the coal industry dispute of that year.

One may note at this point that *Table 6.2* provides further insights into our earlier discussion of the public sector borrowing requirement. At the time of the 1987 Budget general government receipts were expected to be £168.8 billion and general government expenditure to be £173.5 billion; this would have led to a public sector borrowing requirement revealed at the bottom of the table to be £3.9 billion. The latest estimate contained in the *Financial Statement and Budget Report 1988* reveals an anticipated underspending of £1.7

---

[4] The correlation coefficient is 0·98.

Table 6.2

The finances of the public sector, 1987–88 (£ b)

Receipts

	1987–88 1987 Budget	Latest estimate	1988–89 forecast
Income tax	40·0	41·5	42·1
Corporation tax excluding North Sea	13·5	13·7	17·3
Capital taxes	3·3	3·7	4·7
Expenditure taxes :			
VAT	23·3	24·1	26·2
Local authority rates	16·9	16·9	19·0
Petrol, derv, etc.	7·8	7·8	8·4
Cigarettes and other tobacco	4·9	4·8	5·0
Spirits, beer, wine, etc.	4·3	4·4	4·5
Stamp duties	2·1	2·4	2·0
Other	8·5	8·9	9·4
Total expenditure taxes	67·8	69·3	74·4
North Sea revenues :			
North Sea corporation tax	1·4	1·4	1·5
Petroleum revenue tax	1·7	2·3	1·2
Oil royalties	0·8	1·0	0·6
Total North Sea	3·9	4·7	3·3
Other	– 0·8	– 0·6	– 0·7
Total taxes and royalties	**127·8**	**132·3**	**141·2**

Expenditure

	1987–88 1987 Budget	Latest estimate	1988–89 forecast
DHSS : social security	46·0	46·3	48·5
DHSS : health and personal social services	19·1	19·7	20·7
Defence	18·8	18·6	19·2
Education and science	16·6	17·1	18·0
Scotland, Wales and Northern Ireland	16·0	16·3	17·1
Other departments	33·6	33·0	34·9
Privatization proceeds	– 5·0	– 5·0	– 5·0
Reserve	3·5	—	3·5
Public expenditure planning total	**148·6**	**146·0**	**156·8**

National Insurance and other contributions	28·5	28·7	31·6
Interest and dividend receipts	5·7	6·3	5·6
Gross trading surpluses and rent	3·3	3·0	3·5
Other	3·5	3·4	2·9
General government receipts	**168·8**	**173·7**	**184·9**
General government gross debt interest	17·9	17·5	17·5
Other adjustments	7·0	8·3	8·6
General government expenditure	**173·5**	**171·8**	**182·9**

Expenditure, receipts and borrowing

	1987–88 1987 Budget	Latest estimate	1988–89 forecast
General government expenditure	173·5	171·8	182·9
General government receipts	168·8	173·7	184·9
General government borrowing requirement	4·7	– 1·9	– 2·0
Public corporations' market and overseas borrowing	– 0·8	– 1·2	– 1·2
Public sector borrowing requirement	**3·9**	**– 3·1**	**– 3·2**

Source : Financial Statement and Budget Report (1988)

Table 6.3
Functional analysis of public expenditure, 1987 – 88 estimated out-turn

	£m	%
Defence	18,850	12·4
Overseas aid	3,455	2·2
Agriculture, fisheries, food and forestry	2,503	1·6
Trade, industry, energy and employment	6,265	4·1
Arts and libraries	1,032	0·6
Transport	5,806	3·8
Housing	3,682	2·4
Environmental services	5,193	3·4
Law, order, and protection	7,840	5·1
Education and science	20,938	13·7
Health and personal social services	24,310	16·0
Social security	47,850	31·5
Miscellaneous	3,980	2.5
Total spending	151,704	
Privatization proceeds	− 5,000	
Adjustment	600	
Planning Total[a]	147,300	

Source : Public Expenditure White Paper (1988)

[a] The planning total does not match *Table 6.2* because *Table 6.3* contains later estimates.

billion and higher general government receipts of £ 4.9 billion, providing a negative PSBR, i.e. debt repayment of £ 3.1 billion. The change in the estimates seems dramatic, but the data also provide the explanation; on the expenditure side the Treasury has reduced the reserve from £ 3.5 billion to zero since almost all of this sum proved to be unnecessary (one may note that the other heads of expenditure show estimated *increases*). On the receipts side of the accounts, the main contributor to the changed estimates seems to be the higher than anticipated revenue from expenditure taxes caused by the higher level of household spending on goods and services backed by rising incomes.

6.4 Public expenditure planning and control

Because public expenditure is such a large component of total spending, its planning and control form a key element in the macroeconomic management process. Over the years the annual planning routine has become more sophisticated, and nowadays spans a considerable part of the year. During the summer period departmental ministers put forward their bids for resources in the next financial year, and the Treasury coordinates the process against the background of some global figure for total public expenditure agreed within Cabinet. Invariably, the initial bids tend to sum to more than the desired total figure; accordingly it may take several months of negotiation before these bids are turned into more concrete plans for the year ahead. At this stage, the government may decide to reallocate spending between programmes, in the light of circumstances, or may accommodate extra spending in some areas by raising the global planning total. In the latter case either taxation or borrowing will have to be higher than otherwise to make up the difference. Beginning in 1982 the government proposed that towards the end of each calendar year an Autumn Statement would be published which outlined public expenditure plans for the financial year ahead, together with an update of the Treasury's latest economic forecasts and a summary of National Insurance contribution and National Insurance surcharge changes proposed to take effect in the next financial year. Clearly, public expenditure plans have to be considered against the prospects of the resources that will be available in the economy as a whole. Then it can be decided whether public expenditure should grow at a faster or a slower rate than resources generally, leading to an increase or a decrease in the ratio of public expenditure to GDP. Accordingly the Autumn Statement, which is usually published in November, is able to indicate the implications for public borrowing and taxation levels of the Treasury's economic projections and the plans for public expenditure. For example, if the government has a certain public sector borrowing requirement in mind for the next financial year, it is able on the basis of its other plans and projections to calculate at this stage the fiscal adjustment implied. This may take the form of a tax increase or decrease in the next budget, or else an adjustment to the agreed public spending programmes.

Towards the end of the fiscal year – usually in February – documents known as the White Paper are published which give more detailed public expenditure plans for the year ahead together with provisional figures for the following two financial years. Some changes may take place from the outline figures presented in the Autumn Statement, perhaps in response to more up-to-date information on existing public expenditure levels or possibly minor modifications to policies agreed since then. Finally, about a month later, and usually towards the end of the financial year, the Budget is published. Nowadays this is used by the Chancellor of the Exchequer not only to give details of tax changes, but also as an opportunity to review monetary conditions and policies as well as to present the Treasury's latest economic projections for the next eighteen months. Additional public expenditure measures may be announced if appropriate, with these and the other features presented in the *Financial Statement and Budget Report* (the 'Red Book') which summarizes the budget contents.

Precise planning and control of public spending and borrowing is complicated by a number of factors, apart from the political problems of gaining agreement within government on priorities and the appropriate overall role for the public sector in the economy. Some of the factors are as follows :

(a) Pay is a key element in the overall costs of provision of public services, as our earlier commentary on individual programmes and functions indicated. For public expenditure as a whole, pay constitutes around 30 per cent of total costs although this will vary from function to function. At 1987–88 levels this means roughly that a 1 per cent underestimation in forecasting the wages bill would add over £450 million to public spending. The overall impact on the public sector finances would be affected by the higher tax revenues associated with higher pay to the five million employees in the public sector.

(b) About 40 per cent of public expenditure is 'demand determined' in the sense that, once policy and rates of payments have been determined, costs in the short term depend on the number of qualified applicants. A good example here is social security, where those entitled to pensions in the year ahead may be calculated with some accuracy, but the number of unemployed is a much more difficult matter. The latter is very sensitive to the level of economic activity, among other factors, which in turn is difficult to predict accurately. An underestimation of the numbers unemployed impacts on the borrowing requirement even more than on the public spending total because revenue receipts such as income tax and indirect taxes will be adversely affected.

(c) Over the longer term demographic factors can exert significant pressures on public spending, especially with an ageing population. For example, an increase in the number of pensioners in relation to the working population not only increases social security costs such as pensions, but also puts additional strains on the health and personal social services budget. Of course such problems are not insurmountable, especially if economic growth in the long term is sufficiently strong to provide additional resources. Furthermore, governments can always adjust rates of benefit to accommodate such pressures and other programmes may be modified to take some of the strain. Nevertheless, large demographic changes inevitably pose problems for the planning process, not least because of the political barriers that stand in the way of changes to benefit or provisional levels.

Because public expenditure planning is complicated by such uncertainities, the government's plans for the year ahead usually contain a reserves figure which is intended to meet unanticipated expenditures or accommodate future decisions to add to programmes. The planned and budgeted reserve for 1987 – 88 was £3.5 billion, but in the event – mainly because of rising tax revenues – almost the whole of this sum was not needed. By contrast, in 1982 – 83 the reserve was set at £2.4 billion and was almost entirely used to supplement overspending on programmes.

Another feature of the planning process which was introduced in 1976 was the use of *cash limits*. Cash limits set a limit on the amount of cash the government proposes to spend or authorize on certain services or blocks of services during one financial year. About 40 per cent of public expenditure is directly covered by cash limits. A further 20 per cent is local authority current expenditure, and here the Exchequer grant is subject to cash limits as well. Cash limit control also extends to certain capital expenditures of local authorities. The external finance limits of the public corporations also represent a form of cash limit. Associated with the introduction of cash limits as a control device is the present method of planning public expenditure, which is through cash planning rather than in real terms. Cash limits cannot be directly applied to demand-determined expenditure such as social security, but it is clear that the bulk of public expenditure, directly or indirectly, is subject to cash constraints.

In *Table 6.2* gross interest payments are treated separately from other forms of public expenditure. Debt interest is not included in the planning total for public expenditure because it is determined by the general level of interest rates and so is not susceptible to the same controls as other expenditure. Nevertheless it has to be financed, and a gross debt interest rate bill of £17·5 billion in 1987–88 would appear to suggest that outstanding debts present a major problem for the public sector finances. It must be noted, however, that there is a distinction between gross and net debt interest. The latter excludes interest payments matched by general government interest receipts (shown as £6·3 billion in the income column of *Table 6.2*) or by provision for interest in the accounts of public trading bodies. Accordingly, net interest – which broadly represents public sector interest payments financed from taxation or further government borrowing – is considerably less than the gross figure and was of the order of £11·2 billion in 1987–88, although this was still some 6·5 per cent of total public spending.

When taxation and other receipts are deducted from total expenditure, the difference is known as the *public sector borrowing requirement*. This particular aggregate became an integral part of the Conservative government's economic policy from 1979, with its medium-term financial strategy setting targets for the progressive reduction of the public sector borrowing requirement as a proportion of national income. But precise targeting of the PSBR is a difficult exercise because it is the difference between two very large flows, each of which fluctuates according to economic circumstances. Indeed, the average error between the Treasury's forecast figure at the beginning of the financial year and the out-turn at the end is of the order of 1·5 per cent of GDP, equivalent to about £4 billion in 1982–83. Even the estimated out-turn figure can be revised quite substantially after the end of the financial year.

Table 6.4

Public sector borrowing requirement 1970 – 88

Financial year	PSBR £ m	PSBR % of GDP
1970 – 71	800	1·5
1971 – 72	1,026	1·7
1972 – 73	2,532	3·8
1973 – 74	4,442	6·0
1974 – 75	7,940	9·0
1975 – 76	10,586	9·6
1976 – 77	8,520	6·6
1977 – 78	5,591	3·7
1978 – 79	9,206	5·4
1979 – 80	9,892	4·9
1980 – 81	12,519	5·7
1981 – 82	8,621	3·4
1982 – 83	8,927	3·2
1983 – 84	9,706	3·1
1984 – 85	10,092	3·0
1985 – 86	5,654	1·5
1986 – 87	3,436	0·8
1987 – 88	– 3,487	0·75

Source : various *Financial Statement and Budget Reports*

The fluctuations in the PSBR over the last eighteen years are shown in *Table 6.4* above. Despite volatility from year to year, a rising trend is clearly evident from 1970 to 1976. However, from 1977 – 78 the PSBR as a proportion of GDP has been falling, and it would seem that the government's objective has been achieved because in the financial year 1987 – 88 the PSBR was negative, i.e. the public sector was paying back (not a net borrower) £3,487 million. This represents a substantial contrast to the position three years previously, when the borrowing requirement was £10,092 million. This turnround in the PSBR is explained by the very substantial sales of public sector assets (£5,000 million in 1987 – 88) and the surplus on the general government borrowing position. The general borrowing requirement of the government changed from borrowing £4,851 million in 1986 – 87 to a repayment of £1,896 million in 1987 – 88. The general government borrowing requirement was assisted by the fall in the deficit on current and capital account – a fall of £7 billion comparing the two financial years. This in turn can be traced to the fast growth in central government tax revenues relative to expenditure, which generated – very unusually – a current account surplus of £3·4 billion in 1987–88.

6.5 The central government accounts

In the previous sections our discussion focussed on the public sector accounts and the derivation of the PSBR using one particular financial year as an example. Central government transactions represent by far the biggest contribution to these overall figures, and it is to these that we turn our attention in this section. As before, we will take one particular financial year as an example, but the reader is again recommended to collect current information from the sources indicated at the bottom of the tables.

Central government transactions are classified under two headings, the Consolidated Fund and the National Loans Fund, for which separate accounts are held at the Bank of England. The Consolidated Fund is the central government's cash account and includes revenue and expenditure items, whereas the National Loans Fund deals with changes in financial assets and liabilities, i.e. with all transactions relating to the national debt and most transactions connected with central government lending. In the top part of *Table 6.5* a summary of Consolidated Fund transactions (estimates) in 1987–88 is presented. Under the revenue column are included the major receipts from taxation collected by the Inland Revenue and Customs and Excise departments, vehicle excise duties, and various miscellaneous receipts, including North Sea oil royalties. All the items were identified earlier in *Table 6.2*. The expenditure column of the Consolidated Fund is divided into Supply Issues and Standing Services, this distinction being partly one of procedure; the former has to be approved by parliamentary vote, whilst the latter needs no such authority. Supply Issues expenditure is by far the most significant in money terms, covering the central government's spending on major departmental programmes such as social security and defence. The Consolidated Fund deficit or surplus is simply the difference between expenditure and revenue, and is carried forward to the National Loans Fund where it either reduces or increases the extent to which central government has to borrow.

In the year covered by *Table 6.5* there was a surplus on the Consolidated Fund which was therefore carried over as a receipts item in the final part of the table.

National Loan Fund payments include the interest and the management expenses on the national debt and loans made mainly to the rest of the public sector. A negative item with respect to the latter indicates that the body concerned was a net repayer of loans in that year. Interest paid to central government on these loans, together with the profits of the Issue Department of the Bank of England, contribute to the receipts of the National Loans Fund. The other item here is a provision made in the Consolidated Fund account for the difference between the costs of servicing the national debt and these receipts, the transfer being shown as the balance met from the Consolidated Fund.

In the final part of the table, the balancing item in the accounts is shown as 'net borrowing', which is equivalent to total loans plus the Consolidated Fund surplus. To calculate the central government borrowing requirement, other funds and accounts not included in the National Loans Fund have also to be taken into consideration notably the surplus or deficit from the National Insurance Fund. This is the statutory fund into which all National Insurance contributions made by employers, employees, and the self-employed are paid, and from which expenditure on most contributory social security benefits is met. Thus with a borrowing requirement in the National Loans Fund of £2·8 billion (taking into account the surplus on the Consolidated Fund, and receipts and payments from the National Loans Fund), and a surplus on other funds and accounts of £1·1 billion, the central government borrowing requirement overall was £1·7 billion.

6.6 Methods of taxation

Table 6.2 identifies individual taxes and itemizes their relative contribution to public sector receipts. Another way of examining taxation is according to the broad methods by which it is constructed, that is on income, capital, and expenditure. This is particularly useful when the theory of taxation is considered because the question of what forms the best base for levying taxation lies at the heart of the controversy about the 'fairness'

Table 6.5

Central government Consolidated Fund and National Loans Fund, estimates
1987–88 (£m)

Consolidated Fund

Revenue

Inland Revenue :

Income tax	41,400
Corporation tax	15,600
Petroleum revenue tax	2,330
Capital gains tax	1,350
Development land tax	25
Inheritance tax	1,070
Stamp duties	2,440
Total Inland Revenue	**64,200**

Customs and Excise :

Value added tax	24,100
Petrol, derv, etc.	7,800
Cigarettes and other tobacco	4,800
Spirits, beer, wine, cider, and perry	4,400
Betting and gaming	810
Car tax	1,150
Other excise duties	20
EC own resources :	
Customs duties, etc.	1,470
Agricultural levies	190
Total Customs and Excise	**44,700**
Vehicle excise duties	2,700
Gas levy	500
Broadcasting receiving licences	1,030
Interest and dividends	1,080
Other	9,100
Total Consolidated Fund revenue	**123,200**

Expenditure

Supply Issues	105,100
Standing services :	
Payment to the National Loans Fund in respect of service of the national debt	9,800
Northern Ireland : share of taxes etc.	2,220
Payments to the European Communities	3,770
Other services	100
Total standing services	15,900
Total Consolidated Fund expenditure	**121,000**

National Loans Fund
Receipts

Interest on loans, profits of the Issue Department of the Bank of England, etc.	6,800
Service of the national debt : balance met from the Consolidated Fund	9,800
Total receipts	16,700

Payments
Service of the national debt :

Interest	16,500
Management and expenses	170
Total service of the national debt	16,700

Loans to :

Nationalized industries	– 180
Other public corporations	– 170
Local authorities	5,200
Private sector and within central government	180
Total National Loans Fund lending	5,000
Total payments	21,700

Central government borrowing requirement
Consolidated Fund :

Revenue	123,200
Expenditure	121,000
Surplus	2,200

National Loans Fund :

Receipts	16,700
Payments	21,700
Surplus from Consolidated Fund	2,200
Net borrowing by National Loans Fund	2,800
Surplus on other funds and accounts (net)	1,100
Central government borrowing requirement	1,700

Sources : Financial Statement and Budget Report (1988); Public Expenditure
White Paper (1988)

of the tax system and its effects on the economy. This section intends to examine the methods by which taxation can be raised, and to classify the major UK taxes accordingly.

Taxes on income   Taxes under this heading are those assessed on income from employment and other sources, and on the profits of business and corporations (profits are income to the firm). Therefore income tax and corporation tax are the two major UK taxes which come under this heading. In both cases, certain allowances are deducted from gross income or profits before tax is levied, but the rate at which tax is charged is rather different. The UK income tax rate varies accordingly to taxable income, that is income after deduction of allowances; so the higher the taxable income, the higher the marginal rate of tax. In fact the rate rises currently from a minimum of 25 per cent to a maximum of 40 per cent on earned income. Corporation tax, on the other hand, is levied at only two rates, a standard rate and a reduced rate for smaller companies.

Taxes on capital   It is possible either to tax the value of capital on a regular basis, as with an annual wealth tax, [5] or to tax the transfer of capital. To date the latter has been preferred in the UK with capital being taxed when inherited at death or given away during life through the capital transfer tax, and certain types of capital transfer being taxed at sale through the capital gains tax. Capital transfer tax is progressive by structure whereas capital gains tax is levied at a fixed percentage rate, but in both cases certain allowances or exempt amounts are granted. Stamp duties are also a form of taxation on the transfer of capital, but are officially described as taxes on expenditure because they are levied on the *purchase* of assets such as property, land, and shares. This last example illustrates the difficulty which sometimes arises when attempting to put individual taxes into the three categories.

Taxes on expenditure   Taxes on income and capital are directed at individuals or firms and are assessed according to personal circumstances, whereas taxes on expenditure are levied on goods and services. This difference is the basis of the distinction between direct and indirect taxation : indirect taxes can be avoided to some extent by the consumer depriving himself of

---

[5] See *The Wealth Tax* (HMSO, August 1974).

the goods upon which taxation is levied, whereas direct taxes
cannot. All the revenues collected by the Customs and Excise
are taxes on expenditure, as are local authority rates, stamp
duties, vehicle excise duty, and oil royalties. Value added tax
(VAT) has been the principal indirect tax raised in the UK
since 1973 and is levied on a wide range of commodities,
currently at a fixed rate of 15 per cent. The other major taxes
on expenditure include the excises on oil, tobacco, and alcohol;
these are *specific* in nature – fixed in money terms – in contrast
to VAT which is on an *ad valorem* basis. Because the tax is a
fixed nominal amount per unit of volume or size, the excise rate
has to be raised periodically if tax revenue is to keep pace with
inflation. Local authority rates rank third behind income tax
and VAT in terms of yield. They are classified as an expenditure tax because they relate to the use of a particular good –
property – and the rate charged is not linked directly to
personal circumstances. The new community charge (a poll
tax) would be classified in the same way.
On this basis the ratio of taxes on income : capital : expenditure was of the order of 45:3:52 in 1978–88, whereas the
same ratio calculated for 1982 – 83 was 58 : 3 : 39. This reveals,
 for example, the extent to which there has been a switch away
from income taxation towards taxes on expenditure as the basis
for public revenue.

National Insurance contributions from employees and employers are excluded from these definitions even though they
are similar in character to income tax; National Insurance is
insurance rather than a tax.

6.7 Principles of taxation

In raising revenue through taxation, governments must take
into account the effects of the structure of taxation they adopt
on the operation of the economy. Accordingly there are certain
criteria[6] which need to be considered, the most important
being the following.

Equity The word 'equity' means 'fairness'. The tax mechanism
is often used to try to achieve this, since any system of expendi-

---

[6] Adam Smith's canons of taxation are a similar set of criteria.

ture and taxation is bound to affect the distribution of income and wealth in the community, especially in developed countries such as the UK with their high levels of government expenditure and taxation. Indeed, the question of the most appropriate distribution of income and wealth is one of the most contentious issues in modern society, and consequently political parties tend to have different views on the most desirable distributions to be established.

The first problem is what might be called *horizontal equity*, i.e. the construction of a taxation system which taxes equally people who are in *identical* economic positions. This objective requires the establishment of an appropriate tax base which can be used as a yardstick for measuring people's ability to pay taxes. But income, wealth, or expenditure may be insufficiently precise indicators on their own of relative economic positions. To use an extreme example, a gold hoarder and a beggar may each have zero income but few people would argue that they have the same taxable capacity. In this example it may not be considered equitable in the horizontal sense to tax only income in that ownership of wealth also confers control over economic resources. Therefore the achievement of horizontal equity may require taxation of income and wealth and expenditure if each of these methods of taxation is inappropritate on its own as a yardstick for measuring people's ability to pay taxes.

Even if the problem of horizontal equity and a suitable tax base could be resolved, there would still be the question of *vertical equity*, i.e. the establishment of an equitable system of taxation for treating people in *different* economic positions. In this context we have to consider whether the tax system should be progressive, proportional, or regressive. Taking income as the tax base – even though this might be inappropriate as far as horizontal equity is concerned – we can define proportional taxation as the case when taxation takes the same proportion of income irrespective of the size of income; progressive taxation as the case when taxation takes a larger proportion of income as income increases; and regressive taxation as the case when taxation takes a smaller proportion of income as income increases. To achieve vertical equity the government has to decide not only whether the tax system should be progressive, proportional, or regressive, but also to what extent the system should have these characteristics. Our description of the UK income tax in Section 6.6 indicates that it is broadly progressive, whereas the indirect tax framework is generally regressive with respect to income. Nevertheless, our calculation in Section 6.6 of the ratio of taxes on income, expenditure, and capital does reveal that the balance can shift, and shift quite markedly. It is probably the case that the taxation system in the UK has become less progressive, and the estimates made of the burden of taxation borne by the different income groups suggest that the burden on the higher–income groups has shifted, relatively, towards the lower–income groups.

Incidence   The term 'incidence' refers to the location of the ultimate resting point of the tax burden. With direct taxation the incidence is on the person who pays the tax, as with income tax, but with indirect this may not be the case. For example the *formal* incidence of purchase tax (replaced by VAT in 1973) was upon wholesalers, who paid the tax, whereas the *effective* incidence was mainly upon consumers, who paid higher retail prices as a result of the tax being passed on. This would represent forward shifting of the tax burden; backward shifting might occur if wholesalers negotiated lower prices for the goods they bought from producers.

The incidence of an indirect tax can be upon producer or consumer, the burden of each party being determind by the conditions of demand and supply under which the good is produced. For example an increase in the tax on a commodity in inelastic demand, of which beer has been a good example in the past, will result in most of the tax being passed on to consumers, as producers expect the volume of sales to be fairly insensitive to moderate price rises.

Incidence will therefore be an important consideration to take into account, since indirect taxes may have their major impact on individuals other than those who actually pay the tax.

Incentives to work effort   It is desirable that work effort in the economy should be encouraged if more goods and services are to be produced to satisfy wants. In this respect the government should take into account the effect of the level and types of taxes it adopts on the willingness to work within the community. However, it is often claimed that the progressive nature of the UK income tax has a disincentive effect on work effort because of the high marginal rates of tax it imposes on extra earnings. If this claim is correct, the incentives criterion may be better satisfied by indirect taxes than by direct taxes such as income tax.

The present Conservative government in the UK has made the claim strongly that the disincentive effects of income taxation are substantial, although it has published no evidence for this even though it commissioned and completed a study of this matter. Academic research available at the present time does not produce a clear result. Nevertheless, government policy has been geared to the assumption that disincentive effects are powerful and that in order to encourage the 'supply side' of the economy the rate of income tax should be reduced. Since 1979 the standard rate of tax has been reduced from 40 to 25 per cent, and the highest rate from 60 to 40 per cent.

Resource allocation   The taxation system may also influence the allocation of resources within the economy by disturbing the pattern of consumption and production. It is argued that taxation should not interfere with consumer preferences, but should just raise the revenue required. However, when taxes fall upon certain items and not on others then consumer choice becomes distorted, as some goods become relatively more expensive and therefore, fewer of them are bought. As a result, the output levels of certain commodities will differ from those which would have prevailed in the absence of taxation, and so the allocation of resources in the economy will become distorted. In contrast, direct taxes such as income tax do not affect the choice between goods; the consumer simply has less to spend on all commodities. Furthermore, a general sales tax which imposes the same rate of tax on all goods is preferable in terms of resource allocation to a discriminatory tax such as purchase tax. In fact the present VAT is more akin to a general sales tax than was purchase tax because VAT taxes a wider range of commodities at one basic rate.

Costs of collection/compliance   The choice between different taxes needs to take account of the administrative costs to both the government and the taxpayer. The actual assessment and collection of tax may absorb resources, such as skilled labour, which would otherwise be used to produce goods and services. The present capital gains tax is a good example because of the complicated and therefore administratively expensive arrangements relating to the assessment of the tax. The government also needs to consider the hidden costs to the taxpayer which are associated with tax assessment and collection. Such costs of compliance are quite high under the income tax system because of the need for employers to provide staff and facilities for deducting tax from employees. VAT has also been criticized on similar grounds because of the administrative expense for the taxpayer in the collection of the tax. A similar claim has been made about the community charge.

Buoyancy of yield   An additional consideration is that the system of taxes should produce a sufficient yield to meet current expenditures and at the same time provide the opportunity for larger future yields if such requirements arise. The UK income tax meets this requirement well since incomes tend to rise along with prices over time and so generate increased revenue automatically. VAT also produces a buoyant yield since it is levied at a fixed percentage of the price of goods and services.

Finally, it should be noted that the above criteria often conflict in the case of particular taxes. For example, the UK income tax may be considered superior in terms of equity and resource allocation but indirect taxes may perform better in terms of incentives. Thus the UK government, along with others, relies upon a wide range of taxes for raising revenue.

6.8 The financing of the public sector borrowing requirement

In previous sections we have examined various aspects of public sector finances, and one of the difficulties has been the range of definitions used to describe rather similar receipts, payments, and financial transactions. If one considers the financial deficit or surplus of the public sector, we find that for 1987 – 88 the public sector is likely to be in *deficit* by £2.8 billion. When other financial transactions are taken into account, however, this financial deficit is transformed into public sector borrowing requirement which is in *surplus,* i.e. net repayment of debt, by £3.1 billion. This change is almost entirely the result of including privatization proceeds of £5.4 billion. Because of this kind of adjustment, there is the view that the more significant datum for our interpretation of the public sector accounts is not the well-known public sector borrowing requirement but the public sector financial deficit (or surplus). Although sales of state assets are intended to continue (for example, water authorities and electricity) there is clearly a limit to such sales when further assets are not available, and at that point any deficit on the overall current and capital account of the public sector will re-emerge in the PSBR figure.

Whether the PSBR is positive or negative, it has to be financed either by net sales of assets or by net redemption of assets. In this section we shall look at cases of positive and negative PSBRs and consider how they are financed. *Table 6.6* provides the data for this assessment, using the contrasting financial years of 1984 – 85 and 1987 – 88.

Table 6.6

Financing of the public sector borrowing requirement (PSBR)
(£ m)

	PSBR	Non-bank private sector	Monetary sector	Overseas sector
1984 – 85	10,000	14,433	– 4,515	182
1987 – 88	– 3,543	5,699	– 2,423	– 6,819

Source : Financial Statistics

In the financial year 1984 – 85 there was a substantial borrowing requirement, and 140 per cent of the requirement was met by the non-bank private sector (see Section 12.4.3.1 for discussion of 'overfunding'). The bulk of this sum of £14.4 billion was provided almost equally by the personal sector and the non-bank financial institutions, e.g. insurance companies. The non-bank private sector flow of finance to the public sector would be by the holding of British government securities, Treasury bills, and National Savings, as well as the holding of additional notes and coin. In fact, most of the finance was by means of holding more government securities and National Savings. Although parts of the public sector borrowed from the banks (mainly the local authorities), almost £5 billion of bank indebtedness to the Bank of England Banking Department was reduced during this financial year, so that overall there was 'negative borrowing' from the banking system. Net overseas borrowing was small; although there was substantial repayment of government securities to overseas holders, this was more than offset by the Issue Department transactions in bills, i.e. selling bills.

For the financial year 1987 – 88 the PSBR was negative, i.e. overall the public sector was repaying debt rather than indulging in net borrowing. Nevertheless the public sector raised £5.7 billion from the non-bank private sector, although it repaid substantially to the banking system. In addition there was a substantial rise in the Bank of England's holdings of foreign currency bank deposits, which are part of the UK's Official Reserves, as well as considerable borrowing from overseas by the sale of government securities. The net position, however, was for there to be net repayment to the overseas sector.

6.9 Government accounts and debt

Our discussion so far of the structure of the government accounts and public sector finances has drawn attention to the consequences of the government and public sector moving into surplus or into deficit. Apart from some years in the late 1980s the public sector has been in deficit, and this has entailed, overall, the issue of assets (debt) to finance the shortfall. We have seen that because of rapid growth in tax revenues as well as asset sales, the finances of the public sector have moved to surplus in the 1980s and this has permitted the net repayment of debt. The significance of analysis in Chapter 2 and Chapter 5 can be understood more fully now that we have explored in more detail the nature of the government's accounts. An important consequence of changes in the financial position of the central government is the change in the size of the national debt. We shall now consider this in more detail. (The reader may move to Section 6.11 for consideration of the market implications.)

The national debt is the consequence of accumulated central government deficits from the past. As such it does not represent the outstanding debt of the whole public sector, but covers the liabilities of the central government National Loans Fund. A positive central government borrowing requirement (CGBR) will therefore add to the debt, whereas a budget surplus (or more precisely a negative CGBR) enables the debt to be reduced.

Apart from recent years, the national debt grew most quickly at those times in which war was being waged, since it was then that taxation receipts were insufficient to meet the increased expenditures. Indeed the national debt is commonly assumed to have been inaugurated in 1694 when William III arranged a loan of £1 million through the newly-created Bank of England to finance a war against France. This pattern of wartime borrowing has continued over the years; indeed, the debt increased elevenfold during the First World War to stand at £7,800 million by 1918. In the inter-war period the debt remained fairly stable, but it then rose to over £23,000 million by 1946.[7] During the late 1940s central government provided most of the finance for the substantial housing programmes of local authorities and also provided funds for the nationalization of such industries as fuel and transport. Loans by central government to local authorities and public corporations have continued since then and are still important components of the central government borrowing requirement, as we indicated in Section 6.5. This recent pattern of borrowing represents a marked contrast to previous periods in that the post-war years have been associated with borrowing for the acquisition of capital assets : government infrastructure such as roads as well as assets bought by the nationalized industries.

During the last decade the debt has almost quadrupled in size as a result of a series of large budget deficits. This debt is now equivalent to about £3,500 per head of population and interest payments alone amounted to almost £17 billion by 1987. These crude statistics can give a false impression because it should be remembered that during inflationary periods nominal values are poor indicators on their own. If we measure the size of the national debt as a proportion of national income, and debt interest in a similar fashion, then a different picture emerges (see *Table 6.7*). The figures in the table give a more accurate impression of the impact of the national debt and debt interest than the crude details cited earlier. Over the last thirty years or so the debt has *decreased* substantially when measured as a proportion of GDP, from around 1.6 (1955) to 0.5 (1987).

[7] Most of this detail is taken from *Treasury Broadsheets* (new series), no. 5 (November 1974).

Debt interest has remained a fairly constant proportion of GDP over the same period, fluctuating around 4 per cent. This stability is probably explained by the fact that nominal interest rates on the debt have increased even though the size of the debt in real terms (i.e. as a proportion of GDP) has fallen. The question of whether the debt represents some kind of burden will be dealt with in Section 6.10, but our discussion so far casts doubt on the value of crude figures which merely show its growth in money terms over time.

Table 6.7

The growth of the sterling national debt

Year	Sterling national debt		Debt interest	
	£m	Proportion of GDP[a]	£m	Proportion of GDP[a]
1955	27,761	1·65	708	0·04
1960	28,979	1·28	867	0·04
1965	30,461	0·97	968	0·03
1970	32,366	0·74	1,298	0·03
1975	44,495	0·47	2,761	0·03
1980	91,900	0·47	8,735	0·04
1982	116,254	0·50	11,672	0·05
1984	142,885	0·52	12,789	0·05
1985	155,218	0·51	13,909	0·05
1986	167,595	0·52	15,006	0·05
1987	179,816	0·51	16,284	0·05

[a] Measured at factor cost.

Sources: various issues of Bank of England *Quarterly Bulletin; National Income and Expenditure*

6.9.1 TYPES OF DEBT

Given the size of the national debt, it is essential that a large and stable market for it exists so that the government can continue to finance any excess of expenditure over revenue by borrowing. This consideration will require the issue of different types of debt in order that the various tastes and preferences of the potential market may be met. Accordingly this section examines the types of debt that are issued by the UK central government.

A fundamental distinction is that between marketable and non-marketable debt. Marketable debt is that portion which can be bought and sold on organized markets before the final maturity date. Government stocks (gilt-edged) can be traded on the Stock Exchange and Treasury bills can be sold in the discount market at any time, and so the original buyer does not have to hold these assets for the rest of the period to final redemption. This feature adds to the liquidity of such assets as far as the market is concerned, and so adds to their attraction. However, the price at which these assets can be sold will depend upon market conditions, especially the current rate of interest. Non-marketable debt must be held and redeemed by the original buyer, and therefore organized markets do not exist for the resale and purchase of these assets, such as National Savings certificates. Because of the comparative illiquidity of non-marketable debt, it is not attractive to the financial institutions, but it may be to the private individual for whom its particular characteristics are designed.

The relative importance of marketable and non-marketable debt can be seen from the figures for the total national debt on 31 March 1987 (*Table 6.8;* see also *Table 6.10*). The total national

Table 6.8

Classification of the national debt by type, end March 1987 (£ m nominal)

	£m	£m	%
Official holdings		17,494	9·5
Market holdings			
Sterling marketable debt:			
Government and government-			
guaranteed stock: index-linked	14,376		7·8
other	112,553		60·0
Treasury bills	2,035		1·0
Sterling non-marketable debt			
National Savings: index-linked	2,663		1·4
other	23,915		13·0
Interest-free notes due to the IMF	3,572		1·9
Certificates of tax deposit	2,930		1·5
Other	309		0·2
Total market holdings		162,353	
Sterling national debt		179,847	
Foreign currency debt		5,914	3·2
Total		185,761	

Source : Bank of England *Quarterly Bulletin*, vol. 27, no. 4 (November 1987).

debt consists of the sterling debt and that part of the total debt which is payable in foreign currency.

Marketable debt now represents about 70 per cent of the total, and within this category government stocks are the predominant form of debt. These gild-edged securities are issued with various dates to final maturity and are classified as follows :

Short-dated   The government pays back the borrowed sum to the holder of the security at some specified date within five years.

Medium-dated   The government pays back the borrowed sum to the holder of the security at some specified date within five to fifteen years.

Long-dated   The government pays back the borrowed sum to the holder of the security at some specified date over fifteen years.

Undated   The government is not obliged to pay back the borrowed sum at any future date, unless it so wishes, so there is no fixed redemption date.

Before the Second World War the government relied principally on undated stock as a source of borrowing, but with the subsequent increase in the scale of borrowing and the volatility in interest rates it became more difficult to employ this method, so dated stock became the major component of the national debt. For example, in 1939 nearly half the nominal amount of total debt oustanding consisted of government stocks with no fixed redemption date, whilst long-dated stocks made up another 20 per cent. But by March 1987 undated stock outstanding had diminished to only 2 per cent of all marketable securities, counterbalanced by a greatly increased share taken by short-and medium-dated stock and some rise in long-dated.

The reader may be inquisitive as to why any individual or institution would want to hold an undated security if the government does not pay back the borrowed sum. The reason is that the government is obliged to pay interest on all stocks regardless of maturity; consequently there is a market for the sale and purchase of such securities. As an example of an undated stock, let us take $3^1/_2$ per cent War Loan. When this security was issued, a nominal amount of £100 worth (i.e. the value printed on the bond) carried a coupon rate of $3^1/_2$ per cent p.a.; each year the government would pay £3.50 to the holder of the bond. Such a bond carries no redemption date and therefore holders of these bonds do not know when the bond will be repaid. Nevertheless the bond carries the absolute commitment to a stream of income per year and there is no risk of default. Clearly if the *market price* of the bond is low enough then such an asset could be attractive. If the market price were, say, £50 then the coupon rate of interest of $3^1/_2$ per cent would yield the buyer of this bond an annual rate of return of 7 per cent (£3.50/£50 × 100) (see Section 6.11.1 for further discussion).

Dated stocks provide their holder with a latest date at which the government will redeem the bond and pay back to the holder the nominal price of the bond. The market prices of such stocks can and do vary, and this means that the investor in such stocks must take into account any capital gains (or loss) together with the coupon rate of return in calculating the total yield on the asset. The *gross redemption yield* is calculated as the relevant yield (or true rate of interest) for the investor to consider, and is defined as the gross flat yield together with the apportionment of the capital gain or loss on such dated securities held to redemption.

Changes in yields on other assets which are substitutes for government securities (or changes in the general level of interest rates in the economy) will alter the attractiveness of *fixed interest* stocks which constitute the bulk of government securities which are issued. This in turn will alter the demand for them and therefore their market price. *Table 6.9* illustrates how changes in the yields on assets are in the opposite direction to their market price. Part of the table shows the relationship between the average net price of $2^1/_2$ per cent consols and the average flat yield derived from the average daily price during the year. One can see clearly that when the yield goes up the average net price falls. [8] From the beginning of 1982 to the end of the 1983 the level of market interest rates fell (three months inter-bank rate average fell from 12.25 to 10.13 per cent in the two years) and the yield on consols fell from 11.9 to 10.24 per cent. An investor holding $2^1/_2$ per cent consols would have found the value of his holding rise by almost 15 per cent – quite

[8] The correlation coefficient is – 0.99.

a substantial nominal capital gain, which was better than holding industrial debentures. The capital gain on holding ordinary shares would have been 26 per cent, but the price of ordinary shares was almost six times as volatile as the price of government securities. During the 1970s there were expectations that interest rates would be rising and these expectations continued for uncomfortably long period of time, mainly because a rising inflationary trend was pushing up interest rates in general. Against such a background the real return – the nominal return adjusted for inflation – on conventional gilts was negative, with the result that potential purchasers of stock became disillusioned.

These problems led the UK authorities to consider issuing indexed marketable debt instruments which could be purchased by institutional investors, although the general principle of indexing had been established earlier with the issue of National Savings instruments for which the return was linked to the retail price index. The first issue of *index-linked gilts* was made in March 1981. This and subsequent issues have had the following features:

(a) The value of the principal *on repayment* is linked to the movement in the retail prices index over the life of the stock.
(b) A low nominal coupon is paid, typically around $2^1/2$ per cent, which in turn is related to movements in the retail price index. As with conventional stocks, the coupon is paid in two six-monthly instalments.
(c) A real return is guaranteed only if held to maturity because the market value at any particular time will vary in line with fluctuating expectations about what is considered to be an appropriate real yield.

The merits and demerits of indexed debt instruments were debated for some time before the UK authorities finally decided to issue such securities. Critics of the move pointed out that indexation institutionalizes inflation within the economic system: as more people have their financial assets protected against inflation, both the incentive and the ability to contain inflationary pressures is reduced. Furthermore, because a greater part of the cost of servicing index-linked securities is delayed until repayment, certainly compared with high-coupon conventional

Table 6.9
Security yields and prices

	2¹/₂ per cent consols		Debentures		Ordinary shares	
	Average net price (£)	Average flat yield	Price index	Average yield	Price index	Average dividend yields
1974	16·80	14·95	45·3	16·44	108·8	8·0
1975	17·10	14·25	46·3	15·95	136·0	6·7
1976	17·60	14·25	48·7	15·19	162·9	6·16
1977	20·43	12·31	55·6	13·41	208·8	5·5
1978	21·00	11·93	58·3	12·75	235·3	5·48
1979	22·10	11·39	56·27	13·23	267·31	5·78
1980	21·10	11·88	52·42	14·16	285·68	6·59
1981	19·30	13·01	77·33	15·44	322·16	5·96
1982	21·40	11·90	92·25	13·95	373·31	5·47
1983	24·50	10·24	103·37	12·14	471·23	4·6
1984	24·70	10·16	107·13	11·83	560·52	4·46
1985	24·80	10·11	110·25	11·50	692·02	4·38
1986	26·40	9·47	116·34	10·82	858·57	3·93

Source: Various issues of *Financial Statistics*

stocks, there is less discipline on a profligate government which could be encouraged to borrow excessively and let future generations cope with the consequences.

An argument in favour is that any government committed to a long-term reduction in inflation would not continue to issue high-coupon, long-dated gilts at the yields prevailing in the late 1970s and early 1980s because these would prove expensive in real terms to the taxpayer if inflation did actually turn out considerably lower in the years ahead. Therefore, the issue of index-linked securities might be taken as confirmation of the government's determination to reduce inflation. Although the return on conventional gilts had been negative in the 1970s, this was in contrast with the long-run historical experience, and was largely the result of inflation being much higher than expected. Cheap borrowing of this kind would be sustainable in the future only if inflation continued to exceed expectations, with disastrous consequences for the functioning of the economic and financial system. Apart from this more general argument, the Conservative government elected in 1979 was persuaded to issue index-linked gilts because of the advantages it might provide for controlling the money supply in the short term, which was one of its prime objectives. At times of uncertainty, especially about inflation prospects, selling gilt-edged stocks would prove difficult, and so the money supply might be boosted because of underfunding of the public sector borrowing requirement. If the gilt market was sensitive to money supply numbers – as it was at the time because of the adoption of monetary targets – an acceleration in monetary growth could reinforce uncertainties in the market and make the selling of conventional stock even more difficult. A new debt instrument of the index-linked type would hopefully prove attractive in such circumstances, give the authorities more flexibility in their debt market operations, and therefore avoid the underfunding problem. For these reasons the government decided to make further issues of index-linked gilts in subsequent years, although by March 1988 the amount outstanding was only £15 billion, which is about 11 per cent of total government stocks.

The remainder of the marketable debt in *Table 6.8* consists of *Treasury bills*, accounting for only 1.5 per cent of the total debt at the end of March 1987. This component is sometimes called the floating debt because such very short-term borrowing has to be continually refinanced, whereas dated securities, although requiring to be refinanced at maturity, pose periodic rather than continual refinancing problems. Treasury bills are issued to the market by tender each week and they mature 91 days from original purchase. On Friday of each week a certain amount of Treasury bills is offered to the market, the amount available being announced the previous Friday; if the amount applied for exceeds the amount offered then the allocation goes to the highest bidder. The central government has issued Treasury bills even when it has not had a borrowing requirement for the year as a whole. This practice results from the fact that expenditure flows tend to be more regular than taxation receipts; the bunching of the latter at particular times in the year necessitates borrowing for short periods via Treasury bills. In general, however, the role of Treasury bills in funding the debt has diminished considerably over the years.

Besides issuing Treasury bills by weekly tender, the government through the Bank of England also issues them on 'tap', i.e. government departments with temporary surpluses of funds purchase Treasury bills. This distinction between tap and tender bills will be discussed further when we examine the holders of the debt in the next section.

Table 6.8 indicates that the largest category of non-marketable debt is *National Savings,* which in recent years have become relatively more important. Between 1961 and 1980 the share of National Savings in total market holdings declined from 18 per cent to just over 10 per cent, but by March 1987 this ratio had risen to almost 15 per cent. Since 1975 index-linked instruments of various types have been available, as well as those offering a fixed, guaranteed initial return. National Savings certificates and Save As You Earn contracts are issued in both forms, with the former making up over half of the total National Savings contribution. Other products include premium savings bonds, income bonds and the investment account of the National Savings Bank.

Finally, in *Table 6.8* the item *interest-free notes due to the IMF* relates to the UK's obligations to the International Monetary Fund. This, together with *foreign currency debt,* constitutes total external indebtedness. This component has been a diminishing proportion of total debt over the last twenty years, declining from about 10 per cent in 1960 to less than 4 per cent.

6.9.2 THE HOLDERS OF THE STERLING NATIONAL DEBT

The range of holders of the sterling national debt indicates the success that the central government has in providing types of debt which appeal to both financial institutions and private individuals. The main holders (March 1987) are summarized in *Table 6.10*. (Readers are encouraged to consult the December issue of the Bank of England *Quarterly Bulletin* for current statistics on the size and distribution of the national debt.) In this section we will identify these holders and examine their motives for holding the debt.

Official holdings These represented around 9 per cent of the total sterling debt in 1987 – a figure which has reduced in recent years. Because the national debt is the debt of the central government, and not that of the whole public sector, official holders include only the central government sector and those bodies which have a role in the management of the debt (i.e. the Bank of England). Local authorities and public corporations, the other components of the public sector, are considered to be part of the market. Official holdings may therefore be considered as borrowing by central government from itself; consequently this is a form of double-counting which inflates the size of the debt.

Approximately £12,580 million of the official holdings were held by the Issue Department of the Bank of England as backing for the note issue. This large holding of government securities facilitates the intervention of the Bank in the gilt-edged market for the purpose of debt management, with new issues of government securities being taken up by the Issue Department at first and then fed into the market as conditions permit (see Section 4.15). The Banking Department of the Bank of England held about £458 million, also in marketable debt. Thus the Bank of England holds marketable debt largely in the form of government stocks.

The other large official holders are the National Debt Commissioners, who are responsible for investing the National Insurance Fund and the deposits of the National Savings Bank

Table 6.10

Estimated distribution of the sterling national debt 31 March 1987 (£m nominal, except market value of stocks)

	Total debt	Percentage of market holdings	Treasury bills	Total	Market value	Up to 5 years to maturity	Over 5 years and up to 15 years	Over 15 years and undated	Non-marketable debt
Market holdings									
Other public sector:									
Public corporations	475		3	99		50	50		373
Local authorities	9		–	4		1	1	2	5
Total	484	1	3	103	111	51	51	2	378
Monetary sector:									
Discount market	413		313	11		35	36	28	–
Other	9,355		408	8,649		2,253	3,556	2,840	298
Total	9,767	6	721	8,748	9,397	2,288	3,592	2,868	298
Other financial institutions:									
Insurance companies	37,727		26	37,701	40,795	3,927	18,144	15,630	–
Building societies	8,867		42	8,507	8,833	7,824	683	–	318
Local authority pension funds	3,596		–	3,596	3,874	113	1,449	2,034	–
Other public sector pension funds	6,432		–	6,432	6,959	615	3,076	2,740	–
Private sector pension funds	19,000		–	18,957	20,476	979	8,435	9,543	43
Investment trusts	573			573	624	117	340	116	–
Unit trusts	514			514	566	30	373	111	–
Other	55			55	58	10	7	38	–
Total	76,764	47	68	76,335	82,185	13,616	32,507	30,212	361

Overseas holders:									
International organizations	4,272	50		650	608	354	210	86	3,572
Central monetary institutions	5,393	643		4,750	5,059	2,287	1,608	855	–
Other	9,172	194		8,977	9,764	3,057	5,414	506	1
Total	18,837	887	11	14,377	15,431	5,698	7,232	1,447	3,573
Other holders:									
Public trustee and various non-corporate bodies	713	134		579	629	127	330	122	
Individuals and private trusts	38,574			14,529	15,514	6,600	5,351	2,578	24,045
Industrial and commercial companies	3,445	221(e)		1,140	11,731	8,318	3,867	73	2,084
Other (residual)	13,768			11,118					2,651
Total	56,501	355	35	27,366	27,874	15,046	9,548	2,773	28,779
Total market holdings	162,352	2,034		126,929	134,998	36,699	52,929	37,301	33,389
Official holdings	17,495	534		9,590	9,031	3,979	3,360	2,251	7,371
Total sterling debt	179,847	2,568		136,519	144,029	40,678	56,289	39,552	40,760

Source : Bank of England *Quarterly Bulletin*, vol. 7, no. 4 (November 1987)

ordinary department. Until recently all these funds were automatically invested in central government debt, but since 1973 the National Debt Commissioners have been granted wider investment powers which permit them to direct their balances into other investments, such as local authority debt. The rest of the official holdings are held by other government departments in the form of tap Treasury bills or by the Bank of England in exchange for 'ways and means' advances.

Monetary sector   In 1987 the monetary sector held around 6 per cent of the debt exclusively in the form of marketable debt; this holding has remained fairly stable in recent years. Like all other financial institutions, the banks are concerned with the balance between liquidity and yield as far as their asset structure is concerned. These two qualities of liquidity and yield are usually inversely related, as we pointed out in Chapter 4. However, the banks are inclined more towards liquidity than some other financial institutions, primarily because their liabilities are mostly short-term and subject to instant withdrawl. Therefore Treasury bills and shorter-dated gilts are attractive investments for the monetary sector because of their easy marketability and relatively attractive yields. Nonetheless it is interesting to note that the monetary sector's holdings of government securities has changed between March 1986 and March 1987: in 1986 the preference was clearly for stocks of less than five years to maturity, whereas in March 1987 the holdings were more evenly spread across maturities. Banks' holdings of stocks with a maturity in excess of fifteen years amounted to £222 million in March 1986, whereas this has increased to £2,868 million by March 1987. One factor here might well have been the change in the structure of yields on these assets during that period, since the yields on short-dated stock fell and yields on longer-dated stocks rose.

Other financial institutions   These held approximately 47 per cent of the total debt in 1987, and like the banking sector they are concerned only with the marketable portion. As most people have some form of connection with building societies, insurance companies, pension funds, etc., almost everyone in our society is at least indirectly involved in holding the national debt. Again, like the monetary sector, all financial institutions are concerned with the balance between liquidity and yield but, unlike banks, other financial institutions tend to have longer-term liabilities and are more inclined towards high yield rather than liquidity. For example, pension funds deal in contractual savings which are withdrawn at retirement, and therefore they need to ensure a secure but reasonably profitable rate of return so that these future obligations can be met. As long-dated securities can be more closely matched with the term of their liabilities, then such institutions tend to hold this type of marketable debt rather than, say, Treasury bills. Another consideration in favour of gilts is their favourable tax treatment compared with other investments, in particular their exemption in respect of capital gains tax. Institutions which have their investment returns subject to taxation – basically all except pension funds and that part of insurance company business covering pension contracts – have an incentive to hold these assets rather than, say, money market deposits. But the increasing amount of debt in the hands of non-bank financial institutions over the last few years is not due just to such considerations, but is more a consequence of the rapid growth in insurance companies, pension funds, and building societies.

Overseas holders Overseas holders owned 10 per cent of the total debt in March 1987 in the form of marketable and non-marketable debt. Although this part of the debt is repayable in *sterling* and not foreign currency, this external debt can nevertheless have implications for the balance of payments because the overseas residents are able to sell their holdings for sterling and then convert such sterling into appropriate foreign currency via the foreign exchange market. The International Monetary Fund (an international organization) holds interest-free notes which are classed as non-marketable debt. Central monetary institutions consist of central banks which prefer to keep their sterling balances in Treasury bills or short-dated stocks. These holdings can be fairly volatile because oil-exporting countries, for example, might balance the advantages of interest rate differentials between the UK and elsewhere against the possiblity of appreciation or depreciation of sterling assets. 'Other' overseas holdings are estimated from various sources of information, and include individuals and institutions not included in the other two categories of overseas holders.

Other holders Individuals and private trusts held about 22 per cent of the debt in 1987, but the figures in *Table 6.10* should be treated as estimates because of the large number of accounts which are not in the beneficiaries' names, making identification of the actual owners difficult. A significant proportion of the total holdings in this category is non-marketable debt designed to appeal to the individual because of the special characteristics it possesses. Government securities are also held by private funds and trusts because these investments traditionally give safe yields which may compare favourably with other financial assets. Moreover, 'low-coupon' gilts give relatively little income but a greater capital appreciation, making them particularly attractive to higher-rate taxpayers in view of the lower rate of tax on capital gains than on top incomes and the favourable treatment of gilts for capital gains tax purposes.

Industrial and commercial companies hold only around 2 per cent of the debt, but the figures are only estimates based on the quarterly returns to the Department of Industry of 250 large companies. The holdings are estimated at book value (purchase values) and not nominal or market values.

The classification 'other (residual)' balances the aggregate figures for the debt, which are known, against the data for distribution of the debt. Debt which cannot be allocated elsewhere will be accommodated in this category. Holdings of debt by unincorporated businesses, charities and individuals will be grouped here. In 1987 this category represented almost 8 per cent of the total debt, a proportion which has fallen slightly: for example, the comparable figure in 1982 was 8.2 per cent. One of the problems faced by government statisticians is that in compiling national debt data they are using sources which might not be wholly reliable or which have been supplied for other purposes, and this requires adjustments or estimates to be made. The national debt statistics therefore reveal only broad orders of magnitude and are not precise.

6.10 Is the national debt a burden ?

It is a popular claim that the national debt, either now or in the future, imposes some sort of burden on the community. There are several different arguments put forward in support of this claim and we will examine some of them in this section.

However, almost every commentator who argues that the debt is a burden points out that interest payments, together with the principal on maturing debt, have ultimately to be met out of taxation receipts from future generations. Maturing debt can be refinanced but this will give rise to more interest payments thereafter. It is also claimed that the increasing size of the debt, especially in recent years, has made the situation worse. The latter point has already been discussed in some detail in Section 6.9, where it was argued that a distinction should be made between nominal amounts and real amounts. Although the debt has increased in money terms it represents a smaller percentage of GDP and interest payments associated with it have not increased when measured in similar terms.

Any addition to the national debt is criticized because it is supposed to impose a tax burden on future generations merely to pay for profligacy in the present. This apparently leads to the passing on of the burden of the debt to our children and so should be condemned as immoral. Although this reasoning seems quite persuasive, it can easily be shown to be fallacious. Certainly future generations will face tax payments to meet interest payments on the debt, and also possibly to meet repayment of maturing debt, *but* these payments will be transferred to other people in the same generation who receive those interest payments. This process will simply involve transfer payments between members of the same generation and at worst will affect the distribution of income. [9] So, the real burden of the debt is incurred at the time when the borrowed funds are raised because it is then that people forgo current consumption to lend to the government.

The conditions of the preceding argument seem to be that the imposition of tax burdens on future generations is by itself insufficient ground for claiming that the national debt is a burden. Accordingly, we may say that the welfare of future generations depends not on whether they inherit tax payments or government securities but on whether they inherit additions to the real stock of capital. This gives rise to the distinction between 'productive' and 'deadweight' debt. Deadweight debt

---

[9] This ignores the possibility that some of the interest payments may go abroad, thereby affecting the balance of payments.

relates to previous borrowing which has not been used to add to the existing stock of capital assets, and therefore does not assist the production of goods and services. A typical example of this would be old war debts. The debt may also be increased as a result of borrowed funds being channelled into capital assets, and this is the productive component of the debt. Such investment occurred when several industries were nationalized after the end of the Second World War, and also when public corporations and local authorities borrowed from the National Loans Fund to finance capital formation. We have already established that a significant part of the debt comes under the title of productive debt, and therefore it cannot be regarded as a burden on present or future generations because it facilitates and increases the production of goods and services. Indeed it is analogous to company debt in that both involve a reduction in current consumption in order that capital goods can be produced which will supply more consumption goods in the future. However, we cannot claim that all expenditure on capital assets financed by borrowing is productive since the public sector, as well as the private sector, sometimes makes poor investment decisions. Nevertheless, this distinction between productive and deadweight debt is an important consideration in answering the question of whether or not the national debt represents some form of burden to the community.

A further argument for claiming that the debt is a burden on the community arises from the distinction between the external and the internal debt. Internal debt is that debt which is held within the community, whereas the external debt is held abroad. An external loan enables a country to consume more than it is currently producing, but at the expense of consuming less than future production when the debt is repaid. Internal borrowing does not enable a nation to consume more than it produces, although it does allow it to divert consumption from the present to the future if internal borrowing finances capital expenditure, and its main effect is, as we have argued above, to bring about an internal transfer of purchasing power in the future when debt interest is paid.

The external debt is, however, claimed to be a burden because of its effect on the balance of payments. As of March

1988, the debt which is repayable in foreign currencies [10] amounted to £4,725 million or about 2 per cent of the total debt (internally and externally held). In the first instance, the purchase of part of the UK national debt by overseas residents will assist initially the UK balance of payments on capital account because of foreign currency inflows. However, the resale of this debt to UK residents by foreigners or repayment to foreigners on maturity of the debt result in capital outflows. But the periodic interest payments to foreign holders of debt are recorded as outflows in the invisibles section of the balance of payments current account. Thus it necessarily follows that outflows of currency will exceed inflows, and therefore the outcome will be detrimental in aggregate for the balance of payments. [11] This is a burden in the sense that debt interest paid abroad represents a charge on the balance of payments which has to be met by increased exports, reduced imports, or other net capital inflows, if the external position is to remain unaltered. It should be noted that even the external debt may not impose a burden on the community. If such borrowing is used for productive investment, then the goods and services produced may be sold abroad or may replace imports and so could offset the interest payments that arise in the balance of payments accounts.

6.11 The financial markets

Our substantial discussion in this chapter of the government (and public sector) financial accounts has described and explained how changes in expenditure and receipts of the central government occur. Recall that there is a substantial flow of funds from central government to the other parts of the public sector, i.e. local authorities and the public corporations and nationalized industries. Such changes in expenditure and receipts in turn lead to financial adjustments within the government sector because the net result of such changes will mean

[10] Table 6.10 is concerned with *sterling* debt, not debt which has to be repaid in foreign currency; this element is therefore not included and is identified separately in the published statistics.

[11] It should be noted that foreign holdings of *other* UK public sector debt also give rise to interest payments abroad, but that UK holdings of foreign government debt produce inflows of interest payments to the UK.

that the government needs to borrow or, as recently, is able to repay debt. In either case the sale of government assets to cover a deficit or the purchase of its assets in the event of a surplus has other consequences, in particular for the growth of the money stock in the economy and also the level and structure of interest rates. An early report on the workings of the monetary system published in 1958 went so far as to suggest that the management of the government's debt was at the very core of monetary policy and monetary management in the UK. This proposition can still be justified today. In this part of the chapter we intend to look at the links between debt management and these monetary variables and consider in further detail the financial markets in which the government operates or in which it exercises influence. To some extent we have considered these links before, and it might be useful to refer back to Sections 5.3 and 5.4 before continuing.

6.11.1 Debt Management and the Gilt-Edged Market

Debt management is necessary when existing debt matures and is either refinanced, perhaps by issuing more stock, or permanently redeemed if the public sector finances are in surplus. Debt management is also required if the public sector is running a deficit and the shortfall has to be made up by sales of debt. The size of annual redemptions is also an important element in managing the debt because for the UK gross redemptions are very substantial. In March 1988 the nominal value of market holdings of dated [12] government stocks was approximately £130 billion and the Bank of England estimated that the average life of dated stocks in market hands (as opposed to official holdings) was 10·6 years. This means that *on average* the annual gross redemptions of stock are around £12 billion. The net position will be less than this but nevertheless it does give some indication of the financial management required. Buoyant tax revenues may, for a time, provide some latitude and an easing of debt management, but such revenues could change if, for example, a recession occurred and income and spending growth in the economy slackened, feeding through to

[12] For example, 13·5 per cent Exchequer stock 1994, of which there is £1,100 million outstanding, must be redeemed no later than a specified date in 1994.

lower growth of income tax and VAT receipts. However, the redemptions of dated stocks have to take place, otherwise confidence in such stocks would fade, and therefore the funds to repay must somehow be acquired.

Since the mid 1970s UK monetary policy has focused on monetary aggregates such as sterling M3 and at the present time M4. Emphasis has been placed by both the Treasury and the Bank of England on the effect changes in public sector debt holdings on these monetary aggregates. We explained the basis for this view in Section 5.3, and in, particular how sales of government debt to the non-bank private sector can help contain the growth in bank deposits and consequently the money supply. Therefore one important function of debt management policies is to achieve sufficient sales of gilt-edged securities and other government debt instruments in such a way as to be consistent with the attainment of specified money supply targets. The main purchasers of debt in the non-bank private sector are financial institutions such as insurance companies and pension funds which prefer marketable debt such as bonds. However, the authorities at times may have difficulty in selling sufficient stock to ensure steady growth in monetary aggregates and this can lead to undesirable increases in monthly money supply figures. Thus problems in selling sufficient quantities of government debt at the appropriate time can complicate the business of short-term monetary control.

Accordingly the elevation of monetary targets to a central role in economic policy necessitated innovation in the techniques and instruments used by the Bank for debt management. The traditional means of issuing bonds was for a specified stock with a fixed coupon to be offered to the market at a fixed price. [13] If demand was weak the Issue Department of the Bank would take up the unsold stock and feed it onto the market at a later date at a 'tap' price in line with current prices of similar government bonds. It has suggested, however, that sales of stock could be more easily facilitated if the Bank adopted greater flexibility in the price at which stocks are marketed. One possibility would be *not* to set prices for new stock but instead to invite tenders for the amount alloted in a similar way

[13] The coupon refers to the nominal rate of interest on the bond.

to the procedure for Treasury bills. This would enable the authorities to sell the amount of stock necessary for monetary control but only at a price (i.e. rate of interest) determined by market demand. An objection put forward to this idea by the Bank was that it might lead to instability in the gilt-edged market in periods of uncertainty and consequently result in greater volatility in interest rates. Instead, the Bank has introduced a minimum tender price method for issuing new stock, but this has the more limited purpose of allowing the government to benefit from an improvement in market senti-ment and price between the announcement of terms of the new stock and the date for payment. Tenders for conventional stock now normally have a minimum price which is set in line with market prices at the time the new stock is announced. All successful bidders pay a common striking price, which is the lowest price at which tenders are accepted, but higher bidders have priority in the allotment of stock. Tender offers usually involve a relatively sizeable amount of stock – around £ 1,000 million – and to spread the impact on cash flows (see Section 4.8.3) the stock is often offered for subscription on a partly paid basis. This allows the authorities to take advantage of favour-able sentiment in the gilt-edged market and yet lock in some funding (purchase) for later periods, effectively smoothing the profile of gilts sales with the intention of a similar effect on monetary growth.

By far the more radical innovation to have taken place is the introduction of *index-linked* government securities. As was ex-plained in Section 6.9.1, they may be particularly attractive when investors are worried about the future course of inflation and are, therefore, reluctant to purchase conventional secu-rities. As such they may be a useful 'bear' instrument which could help the Bank maintain the momentum of its funding programme and so contain short-term volatility in the mone-tary aggregates. Tenders for index-linked stock normally have no minimum price, but in practice, as with tenders for conven-tional stocks, the Bank would not normally allot at a price below the market position at the time the stock was announced. The allotment method is the same as with conventional stocks already outlined. At March 1988 there were fourteen index-linked stocks with a redemption value at that time of £ 15 billion (since they are index-linked their redemption value will change with the rate of inflation). The total of index-linked stocks outstanding – the bulk of which are redeemable after the year 2000 – represents only 10 per cent of all marketable stocks.

It has been implicit in the discussion so far that the government (i.e. the Bank of England as manager of the national debt) is concerned to ensure that government debt is bought in the right quantity and at the right time. Indeed, the Bank has made clear [14] that its fundamental long-term objective in the gilt-edged market is to encourage the development of a broad and liquid market for stocks, which it is hoped will enable the government to meet its funding policy aims at least cost. Because of the size of the national debt and, until recently, the need to add to it as a result of a positive government borrowing requirement, it is essential that the government should be able to maintain a stable and growing demand for the securities it produces. Indeed, throughout the 1960s this was the prime aim of debt management. The argument was that holders of debt would be discouraged if the market prices of bonds (and therefore their yields, or rates of interest) were subject to undue fluctuation. The policy of 'leaning into the wind' was adopted whereby the authorities intervened in the gilt-edged market to moderate fluctuations in market prices and therefore yields. This did not mean that market prices were stabilized at a particular level, only that fluctuations in rates were ironed out. The adoption of this policy meant that money supply control was relinquished since the authorities would always buy back any large amount of bonds that were offered to the market, thereby automatically providing the market with money. In other words, control of the money supply was sacrificed in order that interest rates (i.e. yields on government stocks) could be stabilized. This objective of ensuring a stable market for the national debt is still supported by the methods which the Bank of England uses to operate the business of debt management.

The Bank has expressed it thus :

> If the market is to function effectively and develop successfully the issuing authorities [i.e. the Bank of England] need to adopt

[14] Bank of England *Quarterly Bulletin*, vol. 26, No. 4 (December 1986), p. 569

a broadly consistent pattern of behaviour.... . In the case of a system such as our own, involving a more or less continuous official presence in the secondary market [for gilt-edged securities]... the constraint relates to the prices at which the Bank deals. Final investors and market intermediaries would be unable to operate with any confidence unless they have reasonable assurance that we will not arbitrarily change the prices at which we deal day to day; we must work with the price trends set by the market itself. This constraint can mean that we fall behind in our funding objective (though we have not in practice done so to any significant degree for many years) and this too can cause short-run disturbance. [15]

The Bank is also concerned to provide an adequate variety of stocks for the needs of the market in order to meet the funding requirement of the government, as well as to maintain a reasonably smooth maturity pattern of the debt and ensure that the average life (maturity) of the debt does not become unduly short. We noted earlier that in March 1988 the average maturity of dated stocks in market hands was 10·6 years compared with 10·9 years in March 1987; this represents a small decline in average maturity and, correspondingly, a slight rise in the overall liquidity of government stocks.

The issuing of stocks to meet these requirements of debt management is undertaken with the least possible disturbance to market conditions; any downwards effect on prices is limited by the knowledge in the market that the Bank does not sell stock on a falling market. The same principle applies to the operations by the Bank in the secondary market, i.e. dealing in stocks which have already been issued but where the Issue Department of the Bank bought up the unsold balance to be sold 'on tap' on later occasions. Again the Bank makes clear that the guiding principle is that stock is not sold on a falling market but only when it is stable or rising. Typically the Bank sells successive blocks of stock at progressively higher prices, the steepness of the progression depending on the underlying strength of demand. If market prices fall in an erratic or disorderly way then the Bank may provide a measure of market *support* by buying stock which is offered to the Bank outright, usually at prices somewhat below the prevailing market price. Stock sales only resume if the market prices resume their initial level or, if the fall in prices has ceased and the market appears to have stabilized.

Clearly, handling supply (and also demand) in the gilt-edged market is a sensitive operation. The Bank recognizes that it is unable to sell more stock at *lower* prices; the demand relationship is evidently not the same as that for, say, fresh fruit where a lower price would encourage sales. The difference is that if the Bank lowered the price of tap stocks substantially in order to sell more, this would lower the price of other stocks already in the hands of investors and create capital losses for them. In turn such investors would either sell those stocks quickly before further capital losses took place, thereby putting further downward pressure on prices, or hold and resolve to buy no more gilt-edged in the future. The Bank might thus in the short run achieve greater sales of stocks, only to find in the long term that confidence and demand for gilt-edged stocks have been reduced. But the implications are that a 'vigorous funding operation' as a means of draining cash and liquidity from the banking system, and thus of impinging firmly on the growth of bank deposits and the money stock, is only a 'textbook possibility' and not a real one.

We should recall that the price level for gilt-edged stock will be inversely related to the yield (or true rate of return/interest) on the stock. To take a simple example, assume a stock is offered for £100 and bears a nominal rate of interest of 10 per cent p.a. until redemption. If the price of that stock falls in the secondary market to, say, £95 then new buyers of that stock will still obtain £10 p.a. from the government even though they may well have paid only £95 for it. However, their rate of return or true rate of interest on that stock has risen to £10/£95 × 100 = 10·53 per cent; the fall in the stocks price has pushed up its yield. A rise in the price of such stock to £105 would lower yields to £10/£105 × 100 = 9·52 per cent. If you doubt this, return to *Table 6.9* and observe this relationship obtaining between the average net price of 2 1/2 per cent consols and the average flat yield. The holder of 2 1/2 per cent consols will receive £2·50 p.a. from the government for each £100 worth of nominal stock held. What matters to the investor is the *market* price of this stock, which at present levels of interest rates would have to be well below the nominal value of £ 100. Indeed we can work it out from the relationship already outlined. We have seen that

$$\text{yield } \% = \frac{\text{nominal rate of return}}{\text{market price}} \times 100$$

This relationship can be rearranged as

$$\text{market price} = \frac{\text{nominal rate of return}}{\text{yield}} \times 100$$

So if in 1986 the average flat yield on 2 1/2 per cent consols was 9·47 per cent and we know the nominal rate of return is 2 1/2 per cent, then the market price must be around 2·5/9·47 × 100 , which equals £ 26·40. Check *Table 6.9* and you can see that this is precisely the average price for 1986. In other words, if the market prices of government stock fall/rise then the general level of rates of return (true interest rates) rise/fall. A decision by the government and Bank of England to raise interest rates is tantamount to a decision to allow the level of prices of gilt-edged to fall. Since 65 – 70 per cent of the turnover of the stock market is in government securities – they constitute the bulk of the market for financial assets – it is not surprising that changes in the prices and yields on government stock influence the prices and yields on all other financial assets. It is possible, of course, that changes in prices of government securities are triggered and influenced by changes elsewhere, i.e. the Bank of England is *following* the market in setting the prices of gilt-edged, but the reverse influence must also be a very important factor. In *Table 6.9* the changes in average flat yield on consols, average yield on debentures, and average dividend yield on ordinary shares move very closely together; they are highly correlated. All parts of the market for financial assets are related to each other because in some degree the various assets are substitutes for each other, and it is hardly surprising that changes in yields in one part are transmitted to the other parts of the market. [16] This relationship gives the Bank of England in its management of the national debt considerable influence

---

[16] The mechanism whereby this occurs is through buying and selling of assets in response to profitable opportunities and is known as *arbitrage*.

over the level of interest rates (true yields) in the economy. It must be said, however, that if the Bank of England were required to change interest rates in the economy very firmly then this could be done. The Issue Department holds, as we have seen, substantial tap stocks and this, together with the dominance of government stocks in the trading in the stock market, does mean that the authorities may, if they wish, exercise considerable influence over the price and therefore the yields on their own securities and ultimately other asset yields and prices. This must be so since the Bank could, in the last resort, buy in vast quantities of gilt-edged stock by printing the necessary money to purchase the securities (which would push prices up and yields down); conversely, it could print and sell unlimited quantities of gilt-edged at whatever market price necessary (which would push prices down and yields up). Although it is highly unlikely that the Bank of England would approach such a situation, nonetheless the market is aware of the considerable power which lies within the Bank, and therefore, the instrument does not have to be used in order to be effective (see Section 6.12).

In recent years the financing of public sector deficits has relied largely on the sale of gilt-edged securities of varying maturities and on National Savings. The personal sector has been an important supplier of funds. An examination of the national debt (see *Table 6.10*) reveals that the bulk of the debt consists of government securities spread between the four categories of maturities; upto five years, five to fifteen years, over fifteen years, and undated. The percentage distribution at March 1988 was as follows :

Up to five years	28
Five to fifteen years	45
Over fifteen years	25
Undated	2

The distribution of holdings will reflect the preferences of particular holders. For example, the pensions funds and insurance companies hold well over half the longer-dated stocks, and this is not surprising in view of the nature of their business which requires long-term investments. The banks and building socieities on the other hand lie predominantly at the shorter end of the market for stocks, again reflecting their preference for liquidity which matches their business operations. Individual holdings show a more balanced ownership of debt. The distribution of holdings will also reflect the *expectations* of investors, and particularly their expectations of future movements in interest rates. For example, if one expects the rate of interest on long-term securities to fall then it might be rational to switch from holding short-dated securities to holding long-dated securities *before* the fall in rates occurs. If one's expectations are correct and acted on, then when rates fall the market value of the long-dated assets will rise, thus providing a capital gain. In principle, the authorities should be able to exercise some influence over the rates of return (yields) on the assets of different maturities through their own decisions about debt management.

In summary, we can now see that the public sector finances have an impact on the debt position of the government and therefore on the sale and redemption of government securities. Such sales and redemptions are likely to cause the volume of bank deposits to change and ultimately the money stock. These changes in debt management also have an effect on the level of yields (interest rates) in the economy. However, the impact on the volume of bank deposits, and the changes in yields, are two sides of the same coin. It is therefore likely to be very difficult indeed to have one monetary policy objective directed towards the growth of bank deposits and the money stock, and a separate policy objective towards the level of interest rates which is *independent* of the effect on the money stock. Furthermore, the Bank has made clear its objective of debt management policy, which is to sustain and foster the market for debt. This in turn means that dramatic and vigorous changes in the handling of government debt and the terms on which it is sold (and bought) are unlikely. In view of these possible inconsistencies of policy and tactics, it is arguable that if the authorities wished to emphasize control of interest rates as the main element of monetary policy then tight and predictable control of the growth of the money stock would be more difficult or impossible. Conversely, any sustained attempt to control the growth of the money stock would imply a loss of control of the level of interest rates in the economy.

6.11.2 DEBT MANAGEMENT AND THE MONEY MARKETS

In Sections 4.8.3 and 4.15 we examined in some detail the functioning of and operations in the sterling money market. We saw that a money market becomes necessary in a developing financial system for three main reasons :

(a) Banks in the retail banking business are likely to have periodically and frequently the need to utilize funds for a short period by on-lending but in a highly liquid form.

(b) As operators of the payments mechanism, the banks will incur inter-bank indebtedness with each otther. In a sealed system the sum of the credits and debits will balance, i.e. bank A's indebtedness at the end of a day's clearing will be matched somewhere in the system by a surplus of funds with bank B or C. There will be a need for some device for bringing the parties together so that short-term borrowing and lending between them can take place.

(c) Government spending and taxation causes an ebb and flow of cash between the government sector and the whole of the non-government sector. This daily movement of funds is likely to result in negative and positive movements of cash into and out of the banking system on a daily basis. Such a change in the liquidity position of the banking system requires some kind of corrective mechanism, otherwise the banks will be forced into substantial adjustment of their liabilities and asset structure to accommodate these changes in order to remain solvent. Since such changes are quite likely to be offset one day by another, it could be argued that such sharp repercussions would really be an unnecessary disturbance. Again there needs to be some system by which the ebb and flow of cash can be neutralized.

It is the role of a money market to provide the mechanism whereby these two kinds of imbalances (inter-bank imbalances and those between the banks and the government sector) can be offset smoothly. The inter-bank imbalances are, in the UK, offset in a variety of ways which we discuss below. Imbalances between the government and non-government sectors are remedied through the sterling money market which, at the present time, is effectively the discount market (see Section 4.15).

The ebb and flow of funds between the government and non-government sectors arise not only because of the flow of tax payments, government spending (including transfers to the public corporations and the local authorities), National Savings and certificate of tax deposit receipts, but also because of debt management operations. Sales of government debt cause a flow of receipts to the central government, and debt redemption causes an outflow (debt redemptions account on average for around 5 per cent of the daily cash flow between the two sectors). Both redemptions and new issues are to some extent uncertain in their effect on cash flows, but nevertheless can be predicted by the Bank with reasonable accuracy. These latter flows not only have some influence on the level and the structure of interest rates in the economy (i.e. a longer-term effect; see the previous section), but also have a very short-run consequence because of their impact on the cash flows between the government and non-government sectors and eventually in the money market.

Our earlier accounts in Chapter 4 of the discount houses and the Bank of England's operations in the sterling money market provide a description of how the Bank smooths the cash flows. The point we would emphasize there is that the Bank can influence short-term interest rates through its money market operations because it can establish the terms on which it is prepared to alleviate cash shortages which may emerge each working day. Although this is technically possible, the Bank takes the view that the extent to which it is able to *dictate* the general level of interest rates can be exaggerated. [17] The Bank's assessment appears to be that the financial markets themselves are immensely powerful, and that if the Bank attempted to change the level or the structure of interest rates against market sentiment then the Bank would ultimately be forced to change its stance. As the Bank expresses it, 'We need always to try to work with the grain of the markets to achieve the required effects.' Consistent with this view perhaps is the use of technical devices for intervention in, say, the money market as a means of changing market *expectations*, in addition to their direct impact

[17] See 'The instruments of monetary policy', Bank of England *Quarterly Bulletin*, vol. 27, No. 3.

on flows of funds or interest rates. Or the Bank's aim may be to slow the momentum of a particular interest rate movement generated by the market rather than to obstruct or change it altogether. In this instance the Bank's decision-making would be focused on the timing of its own manoeuvre as much as anything else. Pressure in the money market may be achieved through the usual procedure of inviting the discount houses to offer bills if there is a cash shortage, with the limitation that the Bank may not purchase sufficient bills to cover the shortage if the rates at which the bills are offered is too low. This must represent a severe discipline on the market and ensure that the bills are offered at rates of discount which will be known to be acceptable to the Bank. Ultimately the discount houses would require funds from the Bank even if this were by using their borrowing rights at the Bank, with the interest rate determined, of course, by the Bank. If the Bank wishes to send a strong signal to the markets then it may do so by operating with a higher profile through publicized lending to the sterling money market. The Bank may publish an announcement that discount houses wishing to use their borrowing facilities are invited to do so at 2.30 p.m. and on such occasions the interest rate at which the loans are made is usually published. This is the equivalent of a change in Bank rate in the 1950s or a change in minimum lending rate (MLR) adopted after 1972.

Additional control is exercised because of the commitment by the discount houses and other operators in the sterling money market that they will bid for all Treasury bills which the Bank offers for sale at the regular weekly tender, and conversely by the Bank's preparedness to invite bids for bills if the banks and discount houses have surplus cash. The Bank holds a large quantity of high-quality commercial bills and local authority bills, which it is able to sell to the discount houses. These assets have been acquired by the Bank in the course of previous money market operations. As of mid 1988 this stock of marketable bills stood at £6 billion. The Bank is of course prepared to deal in Treasury bills, but debt management policy has resulted in a sustained decline of the volume of Treasury bills held within the banking system. In March 1988, total market holdings of Treasury bills amounted to £2,809 million, of which only £431 million was held within the banking system. [18] By contrast in 1977, for example, the banking system held nearly £3,000 million of such bills. The government's financial needs have, for many years, required only limited recourse to the issue of Treasury bills, and between 1983 and 1987 Treasury bills have contributed at the most about £3 million of the central government's borrowing requirement. The present weekly issue of Treasury bills is primarily for the purpose of maintaining an active market in such bills rather than because of a financial requirement of the government. [19]

Intervention by the Bank in the manner described allows the Bank not only to exercise influence over short-term interest rates but also to prevent unnecessary and disruptive oscillations of short-term interest rates which would occur without such intervention (see Section 4.15.4).

6.12 Parallel money markets

6.12.1 INTRODUCTION

So far we have discussed the operation of the money market and described the important relationship between the Bank of England, the discount houses, and the primary banks. Indeed, twenty years ago it would have been possible to refer to 'the money market' with little or no ambiguity. Such a reference would have conjured up the picture of the discount houses being involved in the utilization of a primary bank's surplus funds (via 'money at call'), and the transmission of such funds to other banks who were temporarily short of funds, and who were therefore calling in their loans to the discount houses. The

---

[18] In August 1988 the Chancellor of the Exchequer announced that there would be an issue of Treasury bills denominated in ECUs (see Chapter 9). The first monthly issue of ECU900 million took place in October 1988 and was heavily overbid. Since the Treasury bills are denominated in ECUs this provides some hedge against exchange rate movements for foreign holders, especially within the European Community, and is intended to add flexibility in the management of the UK's foreign exchange reserves as well as to assist in the development of the use of the ECU in international financial markets. The programme of monthly Treasury bill issues is intended to enhance London's role as a major centre for ECU transactions.

[19] It can be argued that for the purpose of influencing short-term interest rates what matters is not the *total* of bills outstanding in the market but the *marginal* quantities which the Bank is prepared to deal in. It is demand and supply at the margin which is important, and not the stock which already exists.

Table 6.9
Security yields and prices

	2½ per cent consols		Debentures		Ordinary shares	
	Average net price (£)	Average flat yield	Price index	Average yield	Price index	Average dividend yields
1974	16·80	14·95	45·3	16·44	108·8	8·0
1975	17·10	14·25	46·3	15·95	136·0	6·7
1976	17·60	14·25	48·7	15·19	162·9	6·16
1977	20·43	12·31	55·6	13·41	208·8	5·5
1978	21·00	11·93	58·3	12·75	235·3	5·48
1979	22·10	11·39	56·27	13·23	267·31	5·78
1980	21·10	11·88	52·42	14·16	285·68	6·59
1981	19·30	13·01	77·33	15·44	322·16	5·96
1982	21·40	11·90	92·25	13·95	373·31	5·47
1983	24·50	10·24	103·37	12·14	471·23	4·6
1984	24·70	10·16	107·13	11·83	560·52	4·46
1985	24·80	10·11	110·25	11·50	692·02	4·38
1986	26·40	9·47	116·34	10·82	858·57	3·93

Source : Various issues of Financial Statistics

discount houses were performing the function of smoothing the temporary surpluses and deficits due to inter-primary-bank indebtedness. In addition to this function, the discount houses were active at the short end of the market through the discounting of both Treasury bills and various qualities of commercial bill as well as short-dated government bonds. The bulk of funds – in 1952, for example, the total funds were £1,028 million – was derived from domestic sources and especially from the London clearing banks, and most of these funds were used to purchase public sector assets, either Treasury bills or short-dated bonds. The business activity of the discount market at that time contrasts strikingly with the activity of accepting houses and other secondary banks in the UK, since total deposits of this latter group were only £835 million, and half of these funds were placed with the discount market or other UK banks.

From around the middle of the 1950s, and especially in the latter part of the 1960s, the activities of the various other banks – the secondary banks – expanded substantially. In addition, two other factors became important : the financial needs of the local authorities, which after 1955 had to meet a greater proportion of their borrowing requirement from the market; and the growth in business activity of the finance houses (hire purchase companies), who were increasingly providing credit for firms and individuals whose needs were not met by the primary banking system. Until credit controls became more extensive, the unavailability of bank finance usually resulted in a simple switch to the hire purchase companies.

Clearly the need of local authorities for funds would have to be satisfied somehow, otherwise they would not be able to perform their functions; and the available evidence also suggests that the demand for funds by firms and individuals for equipment and consumer durables is influenced much more by the availability of funds than by their cost. Therefore the local authorities and hire purchase companies could and would demand funds very actively, with the result that interest rates on their borrowings would tend to be higher than rates prevailing in the traditional markets. Not surprisingly, the secondary banks took advantage of this demand by undertaking the provision of funds of large amounts for varying terms – the sort of business for which they were well suited. Coincidentally, the easier movement of short-term funds internationally after the end of the 1950s meant that the secondary banks (remember that this category includes the overseas banks in the UK) could usefully attract foreign currency deposits (mainly Euro-dollars) which could be converted into sterling or, as we have seen in earlier chapters, on-lent as a foreign currency deposit. The introduction of dollar certificates of deposit (CDs) and later sterling CDs (see Section 4.5.3.3) at the end of the 1960s provided a further fillip to the growth of the secondary banking sector.

Such massive banking expansion could not take place, however, without the parallel development of a money-market arrangement whereby the operators in these markets for funds could alleviate their cash and liquidity position from day to day or, indeed, during the day. For an individual bank, the main financial instruments which provide such flexibility are inter-bank deposits (sterling and foreign currency) and CDs (sterling and dollar). The illustrative bank balance sheet used in Chapter 4 have shown the banks hold CDs as a liability and an asset, i.e. banks issue CDs as well as buying CDs. The variability of terms on such assets, as well as their high degree of market-ability, has meant that these assets have become much more a means of inter-bank borrowing and lending than financial instruments to attract funds into the banking system. We have also seen that the primary banks hold substantial deposits – both sterling and foreign currency – from other UK banks, and the borrowing and lending of these balances between the participant banks are a further source of financial flexibility, though mainly for the secondary banks. Since 1971 and the beginning of the process of banking deregulation there has been a very considerable growth in the use of sterling CDs and also inter-bank deposits. The substantial ebbs and flows of funds, occurring daily, are largely between the various banks rather than between the banks and the government sector, and the use of sterling CDs and inter-bank deposits as a means of offsetting such flows would seem to be the natural development. The accommodating role of the discount market, as we have seen, is of importance primarily when the banks are collectively experiencing movements of funds between the government and the non-government sector.

6.12.2 THE MARKETS

Although it is convenient to divide the money markets into distinct components, it is important to realize that in practice there is no rigid separation between the parallel markets or indeed the parallel markets and the discount market. The markets do not have a physical existence but are simply a communications network of telephone and electronics between the financial institutions operating in these markets. The markets are highly integrated, with the result that, for example, funds raised in the local authority market may ultimately flow to one of the other parallel markets. The funds that flow in the markets are usually placed by brokers rather than directly, and in contrast to the discount market the lending in the parallel markets is unsecured and does not benefit from the lender of last resort provision of the Bank of England.

Local authority market We have seen in the previous section that the local authority market developed as a consequence of the greater financial independence thrust on the authorities in the 1950s. Local authorities raise funds either by issuing bills and bonds or by obtaining market loans. About 12 per cent of local authority borrowing is temporary debt, of which about one-fifth are bills, and the remainder consists of 'very short-term deposits with the authorities, most of which mature within three months. Well over £30 billion of local authority debt is long term in the form of bonds or mortgages. Market loans by the banks to local authorities approached £2 billion in mid 1988, with similar sums from other financial institutions.

Finance house market With the reclassification of a number of finance houses as part of the monetary sector (i.e. within the framework of the Banking Act 1987) this sector has become less important as an indentifiable group. About 60 per cent of funds flow from the rest of the banking sector to the finance houses. The remaining funds are derived from issuing bills and certificates of deposit, and taking deposits from industrial and commercial companies as well as from the personal sector.

Inter-bank market This is a very large and important money market which involves both primary and secondary banks. A considerable proportion of the lending and borrowing is over-night and within three months, although loans can extend upwards to five years. Borrowed amounts come mainly within a range of £5 million to £20 million, with a minimum of £0.5 million. The loans are also unsecured, in contrast to the loans to the discount houses. In mid 1988 the market loans amounted to £70,000 million, with most of this coming from overseas banks operating in London; this compares with loans to the discount market of about £7,500 million. It is clearly a very large market, and is used by the banks for adjusting their liquidity position each day as a consequence of either gains or losses of deposits between other banks. This market can also be a source of marginal funds for banks wishing to extend their lending, but its main function is that of relieving surpluses or shortages of funds by banks lending to or borrowing from each other. This market has assumed an importance not only for its smoothing role but also because the rates of interest determined in this market are in turn used by banks for setting their base rates; the rates also affect discount rates elsewhere, including the discount market itself. The three-month London inter-bank offered rate (LIBOR) is the key rate, and also quoted is the London inter-bank bid rate for funds (LIBID). It is useful to refer back to Section 4.5.5.2.

Certificate of deposit market We discussed in Section 4.5.3.3 the origin and nature of certificates of deposit. The sterling CD market is about half the size of the inter-bank market at around £30 billion. It is an important market for the banks who, as we have noted, issue as well as buy CDs. The prime advantages to be gained in using CDs, compared with say an inter-bank deposit, are that the asset is marketable and the funds are certain for a set period of time and at a known interest rate. CDs are thus a very flexible and liquid asset with which the banks can adjust their balance sheets. Banks' holdings of CDs amount to about £12 billion, which indicates that a substantial proportion of CDs are held outside the banking system. This is hardly surprising in view of their advantages to, say, a company treasurer, who would find the marketability of CDs and their variable maturities a convenient way of using company funds for relatively short periods. There are risks of capital losses (as well as capital gains) on CDs because, as fixed-interest-bearing assets their market price will be subject to change as the general level of interest rates varies. However, the short-term nature of CDs probably means that the risk of realized capital losses (i.e. forced-sale risk) is small. The marketability of CDs is sustained because of the dealings in this market by the discount houses, who are large holders as well as dealers.

Commercial paper market Commercial paper (CP) – until recently, denominated only in foreign currency – is a short-term instrument consisting of unsecured promissory notes with a fixed maturity, typically between seven days and three months, issued in bearer form and on a discount basis; in other words, they are IOUs to whoever happens to hold them. Although they do not bear interest they are issued (sold) in the first instance at less than their repayment value, i.e. sold at a discount, in the same way as which Treasury bills are sold. This kind of asset may be issued by industrial and commercial companies, bank holding companies and subsidiaries of foreign-owned companies. CP can be sold directly by the issuer to investors, who are mainly institutional investors such as money market funds, insurance companies, pension funds, and bank trust departments, or the CP can be placed by an intermediary such as a bank or a securities dealer. CP is not usually 'accepted'; it is 'one-name paper' by being the obligation of the issuer only, CP can be issued for purposes other than trade. The development of the CP market represents an illustration of the process of 'securitization' whereby borrowers issue their own debt directly rather than borrowing from the banking system. The role of the bank in this process is reduced to simply advising and placing the securities. Securitization has emerged for a number of reasons, which include the relative cheapness of this kind of borrowing for a company with a good name (bank borrowing rates must on average include a margin to cover bad debts, which can be avoided by good name companies that issue their own short-term assets). For lenders, who are increasingly used to purchasing securities, they represent a higher rate of return than that obtained on bank deposits yet with little risk attached. The issue of various kinds of promissory notes and other CP has been a feature of the foreign currency short-term markets for some years, and London has become the centre for Euro-notes and Euro-commercial paper. Recent estimates by the Bank of England indicate that foreign currency denominated notes and CP amount to well over $50 billion.

In April 1986 the Bank announced that sterling CP issues of up to one year would be permitted by certain companies. The first issues were made by overseas companies which were mainly the overseas financing subsidiaries of UK companies. This latter device was used by UK companies because of some legal uncertainities about sterling CP (SCP). By August 1987 a total of £11·2 billion SCP had been issued, but taking into account redemptions the total paper outstanding by that date was £2 billion. Most of the SCP issued had original maturities of between fifteen and forty-five days and the number of issuers was seventy-nine firms. For many companies the Euro-commercial paper market might still represent a cheaper source of finance if they are major names, and this might be a limiting factor on the growth of the SCP market; the outstanding issue of £2 billion is relatively small compared with the other money markets.

There is no secondary market of any significance in SCP, and this is probably due to the very short-term maturities which are typical of SCP as well as the inclination of investors to hold to maturity. A precondition of a developing secondary market would be a lengthening of typical maturities (which would tend to generate sellers of SCP who had unforeseen liquidity requirements). The experience in the USA, where the CP market dates back to the nineteenth century, is that of a vigorous primary market but little secondary activity.

Inter-company market   This market originated in 1969, mainly as a consequence of difficulties in obtaining credit from the banking system. The market involves lending by firms with surpluses to those with deficits through the agency of a broker. The terms of lending range from a few months up to three years. The total amounts involved are probably only a few hundred million pounds; the total will depend on the cost and availability of credit from other financial intermediaries, especially the banks.

Euro-currency market   Our examination of the money markets has related largely to dealings in sterling. It is appropriate, however, to consider in more detail the foreign currency business of the money markets, i.e. dealings in Euro-currencies. What, then, are Euro-currencies? Euro-currencies usually refer to deposits denominated in foreign currency which are placed with banking institutions in countries not associated with that particular currency. For example, a US dollar bank deposit placed with a US or UK bank in the United Kingdom would be a Euro-dollar deposit. Similarly, a sterling deposit placed with a bank in Frankfurt would be a Euro-sterling deposit. The Euro-currency business of banks in the UK therefore comprises deposits and lending in currencies other than sterling. In practice, most of the business – about 70 per cent – is in US dollars, and participation in the Euro-currency markets is not limited to European countries but is world-wide.

The origins of the Euro-currency markets are varied. An important development dates from 1958 with the convertibility of sterling and most European currencies, and the greater freedom of movement of funds across national boundaries. Ironically, another influence was the preference of the USSR and other communist countries for holding dollar balances outside the USA. One very important stimulus to the Euro-currency market, however, has been the differences in interest rates prevailing in the major financial centres. In particular, higher interest rates outside the USA have encouraged the transfer of dollars to banks outside the USA and on-lent at a profit. Paradoxically, US banks on occasion in the past have used the Euro-dollar market as a source of funds to be transferred back to the USA as a means of meeting credit demand from within the USA.

During the 1960s the growth of the Euro-dollar market was aided by restrictions imposed on capital exports from the USA, since this forced the banks to look outside the USA for the dollar balances their customers needed to finance their external trade and investment. In the late 1960s and 1970s the growth of international trade and the use of US dollars for its financing, as well as the expansion of multinational companies having transnational investment needs, caused further growth in the market for US dollar bank deposits. The emergence of OPEC's balance of payments surpluses (largely in US dollars), and the associated demand for dollars by deficit countries to finance their balance of payments deficits, triggered a large recycling of dollar bank deposits mainly through London.

London is the largest centre for Euro-dollar business, followed by New York and Frankfurt, although offshore centres have grown rapidly in the Caribbean and the Far East. The precise size of the market in foreign currency bank deposits is uncertain, but it is likely that the Euro-dollar part of the market, by far the largest, amounts to over $1,500 billion, with the total market around $2,000 billion. One of the reasons for doubt about the exact size of the markets is that much of the lending and on-lending is between banks and not between banks and the ultimate borrower. This results in some double-counting in the data.

Currency deposits have three main sources : governments and official bodies such as central banks; the commercial banks; and international trading companies, especially large US companies. The main ultimate borrowers of these foreign currency deposits are non-bank users such as multinational companies. However, the main *users* of Euro-currencies are the banks themselves, who use this telephone market as an international inter-bank market; about half the deposits are used in this way. For the users of the Euro-currency market there are a number of advantages : to the supplier of funds it offers attractive rates of interest and is anonymous; it is a very flexible market in terms of maturity of loans; and the security of loans is high where the large international banks are involved. To the ultimate borrower, the attractions are that rates of interest are very competitive compared with domestic rates; with the relaxation of exchange controls in most countries, especially the UK, this means that Euro-currencies can be easily converted into any other currency through the foreign exchange markets. For countries with balance of payments problems (particularly the fifteen heavily indebted nations; see Section 8.2.2 and 9.6.2), borrowing through the Euro-currency markets via international banks has been advantageous because to some extent the stringent conditions typical of loans from the IMF can be avoided. Where there have been signs that a particular sovereign borrower has not been prepared to adopt domestic policies which would enable foreign debt repayment to take place smoothly, international banks have aimed to tie further lending or rescheduling of debts to the adoption of IMF conditions. This has not always proved possible and some rescheduling has taken place without conditions. [20] One consequence of the international debt problem has been a marked slow-down in the growth of the Euro-currency markets since 1982.

As with the sterling inter-bank market, so with the Euro-currency market : the banks in London borrow and lend on an unsecured basis for periods as short as overnight or as long as five years, although most of the borrowing is for six months or less. The amounts involved can be $ 1 million upwards. We noted in our examination of secondary banking, however, that most of the borrowing and lending is for a few months only (see *Table 4.12*). In addition to inter-bank lending activity, dollar CDs issued by London banks are also traded on a substantial scale in the currency deposit market.

The Euro-currency markets have usually been regarded as a largely unregulated money market. In view of the recent international agreement on capital adequacy (see Section 4.5.5) it now seems likely that the banks' Euro-currency operations will be subject to some degree of supervision and regulation.

6.12.3 THE PARALLEL MARKETS AND MONETARY MANAGEMENT

The regulation of the parallel markets can be viewed in two ways; prudential control and monetary control. In November 1986 the Bank of England established its Wholesale Markets Supervision Division in compliance with the new Financial Services Act. Operators in the various parallel markets may apply for exemption from the Financial Services Act for certain kinds of transactions, i.e. wholesale transactions, but exemption is granted only if they are listed by the Bank of England and come under the non-statutory supervision of the Wholesale Markets Division. This supervision relates to the *quality* of the

---

[20] One has to remember the old adage; if I owe the bank £1,000 *I* have problems; if I owe the bank £1 million, *the bank* has problems. Borrowers are not necessarily always at the mercy of the lender.

participants and the claims in which they deal. The significance of these markets in relation to monetary policy regulation is rather different :

(a) The Bank of England exercises influence over short-term interest rates through its operations in the sterling money market (the discount market) but there is no such direct contact with the parallel markets. This may not matter because changes in short-term interest rates engineered in the discount market will be transmitted to the parallel markets, and there will be no slippage in this effect, i.e. higher short-term rates in the discount market cannot be frustrated by lower rates in the parallel market(s). It can be argued that as long as the authorities are prepared to see the demand for credit regulated by the markets then the parallel markets can be left to themselves. But if an alternative control regime were required then the parallel markets' flexibility might well be a source of slippage – a means of avoiding monetary control.

(b) The close relationship between the domestic parallel markets and the market in foreign currency deposits (the Euro-currency markets) may well relate to the question of slippage. The Euro-currency markets, and especially the Euro-dollar market, are very large. In the absence of exchange controls there is the potential for a movement of funds out of US dollars and into sterling. Such funds flowing into the UK and converted into sterling could be used to purchase short-term assets, e.g. short loans to local authorities, CDs. If rates of interest in the parallel markets were more competitive than in the markets for government assets, then such an inflow of funds could add to domestic bank deposits and the money stock.

(c) The ease with which funds can flow in the Euro-currency markets does raise the possibility of an effect on the foreign exchange rate if the absence of exchange controls enables switching from one currency to another. This is also linked with the question of how far interest rate changes in one country can be independent of interest rate levels in another if there is the possibility of shifts in foreign currency bank deposits to take advantage of interest rate differentials.

6.13 Interest rates

The borrowing and lending taking place in the money markets, the buying and selling of gilt-edged securities, Treasury bills, commercial bills, and other financial assets, involves the calculation of a *rate of interest* on the borrowing, i.e. the calculation of *yields* on assets. The interesting question for economists as well as those who deal in the markets for these various assets is: 'What factors' affect and determine interest rates?' An obvious beginning is based on the observation that buying and selling is taking place, i.e. there is *demand* and *supply*. This suggests that we are really talking about prices, and that perhaps basic demand and supply analysis can help to answer our questions. For the practitioner who has to deal daily with such matters, the demand and supply approach is a useful one. For the economist, however, it is important to try to provide a clear and consistent body of theory. It is not our intention to approach this topic from a wholly theoretical standpoint, but we would point out that the economist takes the view that there are two parts of the problem which require explanation: (a) what determines the general *level* of interest rates in an economy, and (b) what determines the *structure* of interest rates, i.e. the relationship between different interest rates.

Table 6.11 and *Figure 6.1* illustrate the point we are making. It can be seen that during 1987 the path of interest rates was broadly downward, i.e. the level of interest rates was falling, although there was a temporary reversal from July to September. However, there were differences *between* interest rates even though they were falling. It is clear from *Figure 6.1* that from January to May the yield on twenty-year gilt-edged (long-term lending) was well below the rate of interest on seven-day and three-month borrowing, whereas after May and particularly after September the relationship was reversed. It is striking too that the yield differential between the three assets was not constant during the year; from January to May the yield differentials narrowed and then after May widened. Furthermore, if we take a simple average for the year we find that the yield on twenty-year gilt-edged was 9.475 per cent, the three-month inter-bank rate was 9.674 per cent, and the seven-day inter-bank rate was 9.592 per cent. The *variability* of rates, however, was highest for seven-day funds and least

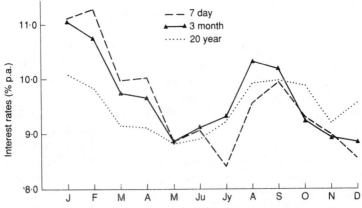

Figure 6.1 *Interest rates : inter-bank market seven-day and three-month, and twenty-year gilt-edged, 1987*

variable – by half as much – for the gilt-edged stock. Curiously, had one had perfect foresight it would have been possible to have gained a higher rate of return by very short-term (very liquid) lending than by tying up funds in long-term gilts; this is the reverse of what one might expect, and interest rate theory has to be able to explain such a phenomenon. Not only can we observe the movement of rates over a relatively long period of time, such as a year, but we can also study the daily movement of rates by reference to, say, the *Financial Times*. *Table 6.14* provides a selection of rates which applied on 5 December 1988.

6.13.1 LEVEL OF INTEREST RATES

The determination of the level and structure of interest rates is a controversial topic in economics. We can, however, make some headway by referring back to Chapter 1. In that chapter we noted that some sectors of the economy might be in deficit and others in surplus. The surplus sector(s) can be regarded as the suppliers of funds and the deficit sector(s) as the demanders of funds. Interest rates which borrowers are prepared to offer are likely to have some relevance to the *direction* of the flow of funds and the *volume* of funds which are flowing. The figures which we used in Chapter 1 for illustrative purposes, revealed that in 1985 the personal sector and the company sector were in

Table 6.11

Yields and interest rates, 1987 (per cent per annum)

	Retail bank deposit account (7 days notice)	Inter-bank market			Treasury bills 3 month	Trade bills 3 month	Gilt-edged 5 year	Gilt-edged 20 year
		7 day	1 month	3 month				
Jan	6·92	11·125	11·09	11·06	10·85	11·31	10·36	10·09
Feb	6·92	11·28	10·94	10·75	10·46	10·97	9·89	9·83
March	5·6	9·97	9·90	9·75	9·54	10·13	8·94	9·16
April	5·54	10·01	9·87	9·66	9·39	10·25	8·94	9·12
May	4·69	8·87	9·87	8·87	8·68	8·81	8·44	8·82
June	4·69	9·06	9·03	9·12	8·96	9·44	8·63	8·90
July	4·69	8·41	9·03	9·31	9·14	9·63	9·04	9·23
Aug	4·95	9·57	9·81	10·31	10·12	10·75	10·11	9·92
Sept	4·95	9·94	9·97	10·19	10·02	10·50	10·17	9·98
Oct	4·61	9·31	9·29	9·25	9·07	9·72	9·96	9·88
Nov	4·12	9·00	9·00	8·95	8·67	9·31	8·78	9·20
Dec	3·58	8·56	8·59	8·87	8·38	9·03	9·07	9·57

Source : Financial Statistics

surplus and the public sector and overseas sectors were in deficit. However, the deficit of the overseas sector represented an inflow to the UK (the overseas deficit, of course, represents a surplus to the UK showing up as a favourable balance of payments), and our attention in this chapter is drawn to the position of the public sector. It is not unreasonable to suggest that the financing of the public sector deficit by the personal and company sector would have to be done at rates of interest which were acceptable to these sectors in surplus. Arguably there might well have been competition between the public sector and the overseas sector for the available funds.

The year 1985 provides a contrast with more recent experience. If we take the data for the second quarter of 1988, the financial surplus/deficit position of the sectors is very different, is shown in *Table 6.12*. Although the residual error for these

Table 6.12

Flow of funds, 1988 II (£m)

Public sector	+ 1,439
Industrial and commercial sector	+ 1,345
Personal sector	− 4,381
Financial institutions	+ 1,972
Overseas sector	+ 2,914
Residual error	− 3,289

Source : Bank of England *Quarterly Bulletin*, vol. 28, no. 4

quarterly figures is substantial, we are still able to make fairly reliable observations, consistent with other data on the economy. The public sector is in surplus, which reflects the turn-round in the public finances discussed earlier in the chapter; the overseas sector surplus indicates the deterioration in the UK balance of payments; and the deficit on the personal sector is partly a measure of the substantial decline in the sector's saving. The point that might be made here is that the deficit of the personal sector – indeed, *any* deficit – has to be financed by the surplus sectors at interest rates which ensure an adequate flow of funds and a corresponding movement of debt (assets) to the surplus sectors.

If deficit sectors wish to finance an increase in their deficits then this might be a factor which tends to raise interest rates. It is certainly the view of the present Conservative government that a public sector deficit can drive up interest rates, although it may well be easier to argue theoretically that a rising deficit from any sector will represent an upward pressure on interest rates rather than a particular sector's deficit.

It has also to be remembered that markets for funds are highly international. The absence of official controls on the movement of funds between financial centres means that factors which are relevant to say, interest rates in New York are also relevant to interest rates in London. Thus it has been argued that the large public sector deficit in the USA is not only currently sustaining high rates of interest in the USA but is also responsible for high rates of interest in European financial centres as well – including London. If we compare, say, the interest rate on US government Treasury bills (three-month) with the three-month inter-bank sterling rate in London, we find that they move fairly closely together (even without taking into account the problem of the exchange rate). Not surprisingly we also find that the rate of interest on Euro-currencies seems to influence interest rates within a country; the three-month Euro-dollar rate and the three-month inter-bank sterling rate are, for example, also fairly closely related.

Another factor which has been of considerable importance in affecting interest rates in the UK has been the rate of inflation. As the rate of inflation increases, the effect on the lender is to reduce further the *real* value of both the interest and the capital. It is to be expected therefore that a lender would wish to maintain the real value of his capital and to obtain an interest rate which will vary with the rate of inflation. Thus if the inflation rate rises we would expect the level of interest rates to rise. Changes in the retail price index and yields on long-dated government securities are presented in *Table 6.13* and *Figure 6.2*.

It does seem as though changes in inflation rates are matched by changes in interest rates in the same direction, but it is noticeable that in seven of the years the rate of inflation was higher than the rate of interest. In those years the investor would have experienced a fall in the real value of his capital. This means that the lender or investor would have received a *negative* rate of return in that the value of his wealth – if it had been invested in twenty-year government bonds – would have

Table 6.13

Inflation and interest rates

	Change in the retail price index (%)	Yields on 20-year gilt-edged (% p.a.)
1970	6·4	9·25
1971	9·4	8·90
1972	7·3	8·97
1973	9·2	10·78
1974	16·1	14·77
1975	24·2	14·39
1976	16·5	14·43
1977	15·9	12·73
1978	8·3	12·47
1979	13·4	12·99
1980	18·0	13·79
1981	11·9	14·75
1982	8·6	12·88
1983	4·5	10·80
1984	5·0	10·69
1985	6·1	10·62
1986	3·4	9·87
1987	4·2	9·45

Source : Annual Abstract of Statistics

been less at the end of the year than at the beginning. One interesting implication of this is that perhaps lenders make poor forecasts about future rates of inflation, since a rational investor in each those years would have been better off converting his wealth into assets (or goods) whose price would rise at least in line with inflation. Clearly this would be a strategy which would have other kinds of attendant risks as well as being less convenient than holding financial assets. (There is further consideration of the relationship between inflation and interest rates in Section 12.4.4.) Nevertheless, if one takes the whole period, the real rate of return (the nominal rate discounted by the rate of inflation) for investors in twenty-year gilt-edged was positive – an annual average real rate of return of about 1.2 per cent.

Reference to the current issues of the *Financial Times* will reveal that the general level of interest rates and the spread of interest rates vary from day to day. Of special interest to us in

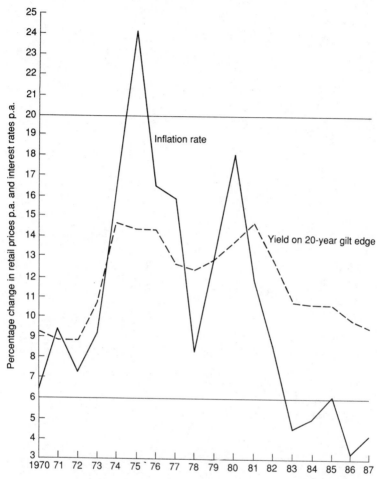

Figure 6.2 *Percentage change in the retail price index and yields on twenty-year gilt-edged securities*

this chapter has been the money markets. *Table 6.14* provides a collection of money market rates. Of particular significance in these markets is the attitude of the Bank of England and its intervention in the bill markets; in other words, whether or not the Bank wishes to see short rates move. The discussion of the Bank's operations in the sterling money market in Chapter 4 revealed the influence which the Bank can exercise over short-term rates. However, the influence of the Bank is concent-

Table 6.14
London money rates, 5 December 1988
(annual rates %)

	Sterling certificate of deposit	Inter-bank	Local authority deposits	Local auth. negotiable bonds	Finance house deposits	Company deposits	Discount market deposits	Treasury bills	Eligible bank bills	Fine trade bills
Overnight	–	$13\frac{1}{2}$	$12\frac{5}{8}$	–	–	–	13	–	–	–
Seven days notice	–	$12\frac{15}{16}$	$12\frac{3}{4}$	–	–	–	$12\frac{3}{4}$	–	–	–
One month	$12\frac{7}{8}$	$13\frac{1}{16}$	$12\frac{7}{8}$	$12\frac{1}{4}$	$13\frac{1}{16}$	13	$12\frac{5}{8}$	$12\frac{11}{16}$	$12\frac{23}{32}$	$12\frac{23}{32}$
Three months	$13\frac{3}{16}$	$13\frac{3}{8}$	$13\frac{1}{4}$	$12\frac{1}{2}$	$13\frac{1}{4}$	$13\frac{9}{32}$	$12\frac{5}{8}$	$12\frac{21}{32}$	$12\frac{23}{32}$	$12\frac{23}{32}$
Six months	$13\frac{3}{16}$	$13\frac{3}{8}$	$13\frac{1}{4}$	$12\frac{5}{8}$	$13\frac{5}{16}$	$13\frac{5}{16}$	–	–	$12\frac{1}{2}$	$12\frac{1}{2}$
One year	$12\frac{15}{16}$	$13\frac{1}{4}$	13	$12\frac{5}{8}$	$13\frac{3}{16}$	$13\frac{1}{4}$	–	–	–	–

Source : Financial Times

Table 6.15
London money rates, 1 August 1980
(annual rates %)

	Sterling certificate of deposit	Inter-bank	Local authority deposits	Finance house deposits	Company deposits	Discount market deposits	Treasury bills	Eligible bank bills	Fine trade bills
Overnight	–	$10-19$	–	–	$16\frac{1}{4}-16\frac{7}{8}$	$15-16$	–	–	–
One month	$17-16\frac{3}{8}$	$17-17\frac{1}{4}$	$16\frac{7}{8}-17\frac{1}{4}$	$17\frac{1}{2}$	$17\frac{3}{8}-17\frac{1}{2}$	$15\frac{5}{8}-15\frac{7}{8}$	$14\frac{17}{32}-14\frac{19}{32}$	$16\frac{7}{16}$	17
Three months	$16\frac{1}{8}-15\frac{7}{8}$	$16\frac{1}{8}-16\frac{1}{4}$	$15\frac{5}{8}-16$	$16\frac{1}{2}$	$16\frac{1}{2}-16\frac{3}{4}$	$14\frac{3}{4}-14\frac{7}{8}$	$14\frac{25}{32}-14\frac{13}{16}$	$15\frac{5}{16}$	16
Six months	$15-14\frac{5}{8}$	$14\frac{15}{16}-15\frac{1}{16}$	$14\frac{1}{2}-14\frac{7}{8}$	$15\frac{3}{8}$	$15\frac{1}{2}$	–	–	$13\frac{1}{8}-13\frac{15}{16}$	$14\frac{1}{2}$
One year	$13\frac{3}{4}-13\frac{1}{2}$	$13\frac{3}{4}-13\frac{7}{8}$	$13\frac{3}{4}$	$14\frac{3}{8}$	$14\frac{1}{4}$	–	–	–	–

Source : Financial Times

rated on very short-term borrowing, e.g. overnight, seven-day borrowing. Nevertheless, the markets for money are very competitive and information is swiftly transmitted between markets. The forces of demand and supply (arbitrage) will ensure that changes in one market or part of a market are quickly felt in other markets. We have already seen that the net flow of funds between the government and the non-government sector is an influential factor since this will affect the cash available in the non-government sector and therefore the financial sector. Changes here can affect short-term rates, depending on whether there is a cash shortage or surplus. The relative demand and supply of the various assets will affect their prices and therefore the yields (interest rates) obtained on such assets.

In *Table 6.15* we have presented money-market rates for 1 August 1980. It is interesting to compare *Table 6.14* and *Table 6.15*. Not only is the general level of interest rates higher in 1980, but the relationship between interest rates *over time* is also different. For example, on 1 August 1980 *one-year* inter-bank deposit rates ranged from $13^3/4$ to $13^7/8$ per cent, whereas *one-month* inter-bank deposit rates ranged from 17 to $17^1/4$ per cent. However, the yields on the same assets on 5 December 1988 were $13^1/4$ per cent and $13^1/16$ per cent respectively. What might this suggest? There is the implication that in August 1980 there was a strongly held market view that in the coming months *interest rates would fall*. Indeed, one year later interest rates in the inter-bank market were around 13 per cent. In this case, the market's expectations were borne out. The information contained in *Table 6.14*, however, suggests that the market's expectation was that interest rates are likely to stay more or less the same, or perhaps rise slightly. This point is developed more fully in Section 6.13.2.

One interest rate of particular relevance to the clearing banks is the London inter-bank offered rate – in particular the three-month rate. This rate (LIBOR) is the market rate which the banks will have to pay in order to obtain marginal funds in the inter-bank market. Since a substantial proportion of the term lending of the banks is financed by wholesale funds obtained through the inter-bank market, LIBOR rather than base rate will be used as the basis for setting interest rates on certain types of bank lending. Margins over LIBOR will be fixed according to the quality of the borrower. Using LIBOR as the basis for setting interest rates on term lending is of benefit to the banks since it gives them the opportunity to match their lending on the basis of similar rates as well as similar term with the wholesale deposits they obtain through the inter-bank market.

In summary, we have noted so far that the level of interest rates in the economy which are necessary to induce an adequate flow of funds from surplus to deficit sectors and groups may well be influenced by the following factors :

(a) The *volume* of funds required to finance the deficit sector(s) may be a relevant factor; for example, large deficits might cause a higher level of interest rates than a small deficit.

(b) Until recently, the public sector was the largest deficit sector.The financing requirement of the public sector could have an impact not only on the level of short-term interest rates established in the money market, but also in the securities (glit-edged) traded at the longer end of the market.

(c) The international nature of money and capital markets may result in the level of interest rates in the UK being influenced by rates of interest prevailing in Euro-currency markets, and such rates might be affected by conditions in the currency's country of origin. Of particular relevance here is the USA.

(d) The rate of inflation and the yield on assets could be closely linked. Our data on the UK inflation rate and the yield on twenty-year government bonds suggested quite a tight relationship.[21] This would be an understandable phenomenon since we would expect lenders to obtain a rate of return higher than the rate of inflation. If they did not, then the real value of their capital asset would decrease.[22]

[21] The correlation coeffcient is 0.78.

[22] If one lent £100 for one year at 10 per cent interest, but during that year the rate of inflation was also 10 per cent, then at the end of the year the interest received would only just be sufficient to compensate one for the 10 per cent decline in the real value of one's capital whilst on loan. There would have been no gain to the lender.

6.13.2 STRUCTURE OF INTEREST RATES

So far we have been concerned mainly with some of the factors which will influence the level of interest rates. What then of the structure of interest rates? As we have already suggested, this is a controversial field in economics. Nevertheless we can identify some of the factors which might be relevant. Indeed we have already mentioned one factor which is regarded as very important, and that is *expectations* of future interest rates – especially future short-term interest rates. For example, if it is expected that the rate of interest on a one-year bond commencing today is 5 per cent and that the rate of interest on a one-year bond in one year's time is likely to be 6 per cent, then the annual rate of interest on a two-year bond commencing today *must* be (about) 5.5 per cent. If this were not the case then it would be easy to buy two, separate, one-year bonds instead of a two-year bond. Arbitrage would then result in the yield over the two years being equalized. In principle, therefore, once we know the expected future short-term interest rates we can calculate the yields on assets of any maturity.

In *Table 6.16* we can see how this might work. Suppose (and this is a large supposition) we know, or have a view which is firmly held, about the likely movement in interest rates on short-term assets such as Treasury bills and high-quality commercial bills. We are assuming that the assets are of such quality that there is virtually no risk of default. Column 1 represents the time periods, each of three months, extending into the future; column 2 reveals the firmly expected rates of return on Treasury bills in each period. If investors are free to move between assets and at little cost, then the rates of return in columns 3 and 4 must follow. For example, if it is expected that rate of return on a Treasury bill in the next six months is going to be 2 per cent in the first three months and 2.5 per cent in the second three months, then the market rate of return on a six-month bill *must* be around 4.5 per cent, i.e. the sum of the two blocks of three months. If that were not the case then investors would hold Treasury bills for the first three months, and on maturity would buy another quantity of Treasury bills for the following three months. The market price of a six-month bill would have to adjust downwards to ensure that investors

Table 6.16

Structure of interest rates

Time period (3-month period)	Expected rate of return on a 3-month Treasury bill (%)	Rate of return on a 6-month bill (%)	Rate of return on a 1 year government bond (%)
t_1	2·0		
		4·5	
t_2	2·5		
		5·3	9·9
t_3	2·8		
		5·4	10·9
t_4	2·6		
		5·6	11·5
t_5	3·0		
		6·1	11·1
t_6	3·1		
		5·5	10·7
t_7	2·4		
		4·6	9·7
t_8	2·2		
		4·2	
t_9	2·0		

would find such bills attractive. The same reasoning applies to a longer-dated asset such as a one-year government bond. Such a bond must offer investors a rate of return on time period t_1 to t_4 of about 9.9 per cent, otherwise a rational investor would simply hold four lots of Treasury bills during that period. In practice the arithmetic required to calculate such yields is more complicated than used here, but the underlying principle is the same.

Of course yields vary on different assets because the assets themselves are different, for example, in such matters as *risk* and *marketability*. But if we were considering assets which were more or less identical in these respects, then we can suggest, as our illustration reveals, that the *period to maturity* of the asset in relation to expected short-term interest rates will be influential in determining the different yields to maturity on such assets. The expectations approach to the structure of interest rates which we have just outlined may seem implausible and on the face of it very difficult to test as a theory. A considerable amount of ingenious economics research has been applied to this problem, and there is evidence that the formation of a yield structure can be explained in terms of expectations theory. One should remember that because it may be difficult to measure investors' expectations, this does not mean that such factors are not important in determining behaviour in financial markets.

The Bank of England calculates yield relationships (a yield curve), and it is usually one which shows the rate of interest (yield) on assets rising as the period to maturity increases, as in *Figure 6.3*. Although the relationship need not be, and is not

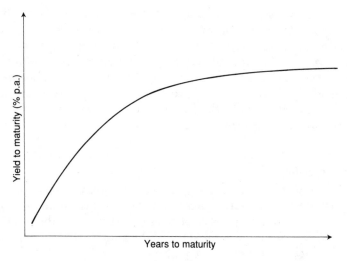

Figure 6.3

always, of this form, we can identify other reasons why it is likely that for much of the time short-term interest rates are likely to be lower than long-term interest rates. The preference of lenders might be for short-term lending because they have short time horizons and are averse to risk, whereas borrowers (who might well be borrowing in order to buy long-lived capital equipment) are likely to want to borrow for relatively long periods. In these circumstances interest rates on long-term lending will have to rise in order to persuade *lenders* to lend long term, and conversely, short-term interest rates would need to fall in order to persuade some *borrowers* to borrow short term rather than long term as they prefer. Clearly, in this situation short-term rates will be lower than long-term rates.

In *Table 6.14* we can observe the risk element because, for example, the yield on one-month and three-month bank bills and trade bills is slightly more than the comparable yield on Treasury bills. Although bank bills and fine trade bills are of similar quality to Treasury bills, they are *not quite* as secure or as marketable. In *Table 6.15* the differences in margins between these assets emerge even more clearly. The same relationship can be observed in *Table 6.11* trade bills offer higher yields than three-month inter-bank deposits, and three-month Treasury bills offer the lowest yields of the three assets.

We can also suggest that risk increases with time. One is able to predict the events of, say, tomorrow with a high degree of certainty, but one's circumstances in a year's time or five years' time are shrouded in doubt. If this is the view taken by many in the markets for funds then we would expect long-term borrowing/lending to carry a risk-premium to compensate for the greater uncertainties of the future compared with the security of the present and near future.

To summarize so far, the structure of interest rates in the economy may well be influenced by :

(a) Investors changing their expectations about the future course of short-term rates of interest. If this explanation of changes in the structure of rates is correct, then the level of yields in the money markets and the anticipated government financial requirements could have an influence.
(b) Inherent differences in the quality of the assets, and especially their riskiness and marketability.
(c) The maturity of the assets being marketed; the longer the maturity, the more likely the yield on that asset will be higher than assets of shorter maturity.
(d) Market expectations about changes in the general level of interest rates. This approach seems to offer a convincing explanation for fairly short-term changes in the yield differential between assets.

Finally, over fairly short periods of time, we can observe movements in the yield relationship between assets which could be caused by investors identifying a turning-point in the movement of the general *level* of interest rates. Let us suppose a substantial proportion of lenders (buyers of assets) take the view that the general level of interest rates is likely to rise in the fairly near future. The rational response to this expectation would be to delay lending long term until interest rates had risen, and to lend short term so that advantage could be taken of the anticipated rise in rates when it actually occurred. (If an investor lent long term at low rates of interest then that investor would be 'locked into' low rates for the term of the loan.) In these circumstances surplus sector(s) would have a strong preference to offer short-term lending and little inclination to offer funds for the long term. There would be an excess supply of funds short term and a shortage of funds long term. From the borrowers' point of view, if they shared the same expectation about interest rates, they would have a preference to borrow long rather than short term and thus to take advantage of the low rates of interest prior to the expected rise. For the same reason, borrowers would be disinclined to borrow short term. There would therefore be a strong demand for funds long term and a deficiency of demand at the short end.

If we now put lenders and borrowers together, we find a substantial supply of short-term funds but little demand, and a substantial demand for long-term funds but relatively little supply. We would therefore predict that if the market expected a rise in the general *level* of interest rates, then the yield *differential* between short-term and long-term borrowing (assets) would widen because short-term rates would tend to fall and long-term rates tend to rise. If we examine *Figure 6.1* we can see that between January and May the yield gap between twenty-year government bonds and the LIBOR rate (three-month inter-bank rate) narrowed because, relatively, long-term rates were rising and short-term rates were falling. In January the yield gap was −0.97 per cent and this had 'widened' to −0.05 per cent in May; this widening of the gap heralded a rise in the general level of interest rates. However, towards September we can see the gap narrowing, which suggested that the market expected the general level of rates to fall, as indeed they did. In November the gap is beginning to widen once again, and this would indicate a growing market expectation that the level of rates was about to rise again; but in fact this did not happen until much later in 1988.

6.14 Summary

(a) Public expenditure can be defined in different ways in the UK, and also the definition can vary between countries. In the past twenty-five years public expenditure has risen in real terms and as a proportion of GDP, but recently it has begun to fall as a proportion of GDP. Resource–using expenditure as a proportion of GDP has remained fairly stable at around 22 per cent.

(b) Much of public spending, around 40 per cent, is demand-determined – for example unemployment benefit and health care – and this is difficult to regulate. Almost three-quarters of central government expenditure is accounted for by only four areas – defence, education, health, and social security – and much of this expenditure will be difficult to cut back in the short term. In an effort to control the rise of public spending, governments have used cash limits.

(c) The balance of public sector spending and taxation yields the public sector borrowing requirement, which until recently has almost always been positive, i.e. the public sector needed to borrow. The existence of a PSBR (negative or positive) gives rise to the creation or destruction of financial claims against the government, and these claims (assets) are – as our examination of the national debts shows – part of the asset portfolios of almost every type of financial institution. Changes in the public sector's borrowing position have an important influence on the operartion of the financial system.

(d) Because of the influence of changes in the national debt on the money supply and the level and structure of interest rates, debt management will be inextricably linked with the operation of monetary policy in the economy. Accordingly, we argue that one of the aims of debt management will be to influence the major monetary variables in line with current monetary policy. Additionally, debt management policies will take account of the need to ensure a stable market for government borrowing, otherwise the option of running future central government borrowing requirement may be restricted. A third aim of debt management is to minimize the cost of servicing the debt, so that the government is not faced with excessive payments of interest in the future. We noted that these three aims of debt management often conflict, so it may become a matter of choice as to which has greatest priority.

(e) The emergence of a public sector surplus (and with it public sector debt repayment), which may last several years, does not invalidate the contention that debt management is linked with monetary policy. Repayment of public sector debt implies a choice of which debt is to be repaid. In principle, the authorities could use surplus public sector funds to redeem (or purchase in the open market) debt across the whole range of maturities, or to select debt from the long end or the short end of the market. Such discriminatory debt redemption could have an effect on the *structure* of interest rates in the economy, as well as the whole operation of debt redemption having some effect on the *level* of interest rates. Thus, for example, heavy redemptions at the long end might well create a relative shortage of longer-dated assets, pushing down their yields and in turn encouraging the issue of this kind of debt by the private sector (the corporate sector). The sterling national debt is nonetheless still considerable (as shown in *Table 6.10*), and at the present rate of net redemption the debt will remain substantial for some time to come. It is arguable that the negative PSBR is largely a result of temporary factors: sustained growth of incomes since 1981; North Sea oil and gas revenues; and privatization proceeds. An economic downturn, the absence of state assets for sale, and the decline in North Sea output could quite conceivably push the public sector finances into deficit once again.

(f) The argument that the creation of the debt imposes a taxation burden on future generations ignores the fact that the future interest payments are paid back to the same generation. What matters for the economic well-being of future generations is the capital stock available for the production of goods and services, and this was the basis of our distinction between productive and deadweight debt. The national debt might represent a burden if held overseas because of the effects on the balance of payments, and this was the basis of our distinction between the external and the internal debt.

(g) The financial markets deal in assets ranging from the very liquid, Treasury bills, to the relatively illiquid undated gilt-edged such as consols. One of the functions of financial markets is to enable funds to move from surplus sectors, to deficit sectors, and this they do by providing either a primary market or a secondary market in various assets. A significant flow of funds in the economy is that which moves between the government and the non-government sectors. These flows take place because of government spending and taxation and also because of the substantial amount of government debt which has to be redeemed each year. The markets affected by these flows are the sterling money markets and, at the longer end of the asset spectrum, the gilt-edged market.

(h) We have suggested that the condition of the government's finances impacts on these markets and may cause changes in the level and the structure of interest rates at the short end as well as the long end. The size of the flows through the markets between the deficit and surplus sector(s) may affect the *level* of interest rates, although we have suggested that the *structure* of interest rates may be dominated more by expectations of future short-term interest rates. Nevertheless it is possible to argue that the size of deficits may well be one of the factors which causes expectations to shift.

(i) Although the authorities (the Treasury and the Bank of England) may wish to exercise tight control over the level and structure of interest rates within the UK, these may well be difficult to attain on a sustained basis because of the open nature of the UK economy, especially since the ending of exchange controls in 1979. For example, variations in domestic interest rates seem to be closely related to changes in foreign currency deposit interest rates in the Euro-currency markets. It may well be the case that international short-term money flows have a significant impact on interest rates within the UK.

7
The balance of payments

7.1 The balance of payments accounts

The balance of payments account of any one country is essentially a record, over a period of time, of all economic transactions between domestic residents and residents of other countries. Residents include not only individuals but also governments and firms, even though the last may be foreign-owned subsidiaries. In the subsequent discussion we will use the UK balance of payments records for 1987 as an illustration, but the reader is again reminded that up-to-date statistics can be collected from the sources indicated in the tables.

7.1.1 THE STRUCTURE OF THE ACCOUNTS

The UK balance of payments account for 1987 is presented in *Table 7.1*. All currency flows are measured in sterling and, where payments are received or made in foreign currencies, they are converted into sterling at the appropriate exchange rate. The structure of the accounts is broadly similar for other countries; therefore most of the following discussion is applicable to them also.

The *current account* consists of all transactions involving goods and services and can be subdivided into the visibles and invisibles sections. The *visible* balance is simply the difference between the value of exports and imports, a positive or negative sign indicating a net inflow or outflow of currency respectively. An analysis of the type of imports reveals that over the years the UK has imported most of its raw materials and foodstuffs, but since the 1950s the proportion of imports made up of manufactured and semi-manufactured goods has increased significantly. Consequently an increasing proportion of UK imports now comes from industrial nations, particularly the European Community (EC) countries. A similar analysis of exports shows that

Table 7.1

The UK balance of payments accounts, 1987 (£m)

Visibles :

Exports	79,422
Imports	89,584
Visibles balance	− 10,162

Invisibles :

Receipts	79,905
Payments	72,430
Invisibles balance	+ 7,475
Current account	− 2,687

Transactions in UK external assets and liabilities

Liabilities (inflow)

Overseas investment in the UK :

Direct	5,954
Portfolio	10,094
Borrowing from overseas by UK residents :	
Banks	52,806
Other than banks and general government	3,445
Other external liabilities of general government	1,570
Total transactions	73,869
Net financial transactions	− 2,317

Summary

Current Account	− 2,687
Net financial transactions	− 2,317
	− 5,004

Assets (outflow)

UK investment overseas :

Direct	− 15,372
Portfolio	6,973
Lending to overseas residents by UK banks	− 50,296
Deposits and lending overseas by UK residents other than banks and general government	− 4,682
Official reserves	− 12,012
Other external assets of central government	− 797
Total transactions	− 76,186
Balancing item	+ 5,004

Source : Economic Trends

the UK traditionally exports manufactured and semi-manufactured goods, and that the proportion of UK exports destined for the EC has increased since the 1950s also. The UK visibles balance has regularly been in deficit in the post-war period, with surpluses recorded in only six years up to 1987. But subsequently the build-up in North Sea oil production conferred a major boost to the trade balance, contributing substantially to surpluses in this section of the accounts in the three years 1979 – 1982. So net trade in oil, which had been a major deficit item up to the end of the 1970s, moved into a surplus of around £300 million in 1980 and expanded dramatically to over £4 billion by 1987. If the contribution of oil is stripped out, the UK visible trade position in 1987 is rather worse. It is pertinent to note that exports and imports constitute a high proportion of GDP – around 25 per cent in each case – and so the UK can be described as an 'open economy'. The UK's dependence on world trade has important implications for the health of her economy in that fluctuations in world trade or in her own trading performance can have potentially significant effects on domestic income and expenditure flows, and therefore on output and employment levels.

The *invisibles* section of the current account records a variety of transactions between one country and another, subdivided into services; transfers; and interest, profits, and dividends. Private sector services make a substantial contribution to the UK invisibles surplus, especially in such areas as banking, insurance, other financial services, shipping, and travel. Governmental services are usually a net deficit item because of overseas grants and aid to the less developed countries of the world. Transfer payments are a large negative item not only because of private transfers of funds abroad (e.g. to relatives in other countries) but also as a result of government transfers in the form of the UK's contribution to the EC. Interest, profits, and dividends have had a positive net contribution over the years, mainly as a consequence of previous long-term investments abroad by the UK private sector. Again the public sector contribution tends to be negative because interest payments on that part of the national debt held abroad constitute an invisible outflow.

The UK invisibles balance is invariably in surplus, despite the deficits incurred by government. Indeed it has been estimated[1] that the UK accounts for around 9 per cent of world invisibles receipts, more than any other country except the United States. But, despite the large surplus on the invisibles account, the *current balance* for the UK has often been in deficit – less frequently since the mid 1970s but increasingly since 1985.

The current account quantifies how well a particular country performs in the buying and selling of goods and services with the rest of the world, whereas 'transactions in external assets and liabilities' records capital transactions. Before discussing individual items, it is useful to make some general comments about the types of flows in this *capital account*.[2] First, there is the distinction between official and private transactions, the former being carried out by government or governmental agencies and the latter by the rest of the community. Secondly, most capital movements can be classified into those which are long-term and therefore more permanent in nature, and those which are short-term and more easily reversible. Long-term transactions are usually carried out after consideration of the general prospects for profitability in other countries, whereas short-term transactions are determined more by interest rate differentials or by the prospect of capital gains or losses from potential exchange rate movements. Finally, a distinction is often made between direct investment and portfolio investment, even though the former is generally long-term and the latter short-term in nature. Direct investment includes capital expenditure abroad on factories, equipment, and the like, but portfolio investment takes the form of stocks, shares, and other financial assets.

With these distinctions in mind we can now examine the types of flows recorded in the capital account using the figures for 1987 as an illustration. *Table 7.1* shows that capital transactions are carried out at an official level (changes in assets and liabilities of both central and general government) and also by

[1] See *Economic Progress Report* (June 1977).

[2] For ease of presentation the 'transactions in external assets and liabilities' section of the balance of payments accounts will be referred to as the capital account.

the private sector. So when a UK firm builds a factory overseas there is a capital outflow (–), but when interest, profits, and dividends arise from such investment there is an inflow of funds (+) in the invisibles section of the current account. The large outflow of private investment overseas – around £22 billion in 1987 but having grown substantially since 1981 – has caused controversy in recent years, particularly since it has far exceeded overseas investment in the UK. Since 1980 the net position on direct and portfolio investment has amounted to over £75 billion investment overseas. This large net outflow of long-term capital has been stimulated by two sets of factors. First, the abolition of exchange controls in 1979 encouraged UK institutions and individuals to increase their holdings of overseas securities and assets; and secondly the large surpluses on the current account arising from North Sea oil revenues gave UK residents the resources to purchase foreign assets. The size of the benefit from North Sea oil can be gauged by the fact that between 1980 and 1987 the surplus on oil alone was over £38 billion.

Also associated with the ending of exchange controls was the freedom given to UK banks to engage in external sterling lending which, in 1987, amounted to almost £4 billion (net). Until 1987 the net position of the banks in respect of foreign currency lending and borrowing was an inflow of around £4 billion, which largely reflected borrowing to finance other types of transactions such as the purchase of overseas bonds. Within this category of transactions are substantial movements in sterling assets and liabilities of a short-term nature, which include money market instruments such as certificates of deposit and commercial bills as well as simply the bank deposits of overseas residents. These funds, because of their short-term nature, can be quite volatile; they come under the general heading of 'sterling balances' which is discussed in more detail in the next section. Assets and liabilities of UK residents *other* than banks and general government include assets with banks abroad, the working balances of UK companies, export credit and trade credit, as well as UK residents' holdings of foreign notes and coin. UK liabilities within this category refers to borrowings from overseas sources, import credits and other trade credit from abroad, the short-term liabilities of building societies and other financial institutions, and the commercial paper liabilities of UK non-financial companies. The UK's official reserves comprise gold and foreign currencies, as well as the UK's reserve position with the IMF (including special drawing rights). The negative figure of $-£12,012$ million represents an *inflow* to the official reserves. The external asset and liability position of general and central government includes the changes in the asset and liability position of official bodies such as the UK Atomic Energy Authority as well as the flow of inter-government loans, and export credits refinanced by the Export Credit Guarantee Department.

To summarize, in 1987 the UK had an overall deficit on the current account and a *net* outflow of funds of a capital nature which totalled £5,004 billion, but this was offset by inflows of funds and receipts of the same amount but which could not be identified individually: this is covered by the balancing item. The balancing item is included to bring the sum of all the balance of payments entries to zero, since outflows must equal inflows even though not all items can be identified and included within the various categories of the balance of payments accounts. This item arises because of errors and omissions in the recording of payments and receipts, and it is simply the difference between the total value of recorded transactions and the actual flow of funds. Although the balancing item might appear large it does in fact represent only about 2 per cent of the total flows in the balance of payments.

It is important to understand that the balance of payments accounts balance, not because of an accounting trick but because of economic reality: what we pay abroad in foreign currency and bank deposits must be matched by inflows of some kind from abroad. If, for example, the UK is spending more abroad on foreign goods than the value of the UK goods it is selling to foreigners, then that shortfall has to be financed in some way; borrowing is one such way. Indeed, as we have seen from the examination of *Table 7.1*, the capital flows are crucial to financing the UK's current account deficit. Within this part of the balance of payments accounts we can see that the change in the official reserves constitutes an important adjustment of the overall accounts. If more funds are flowing into the UK than going out then the official reserves of gold and foreign currency will tend to rise, and if there is an excess of outflows then the official reserves will fall.

The foregoing discussion confirms that an overall balance of payments 'deficit' or 'surplus' cannot exist; indeed, the account must balance. Ultimately this can come about through changes in the official reserves and other forms of 'official financing' such as government borrowing in the Euro-currency market or, conversely, foreign debt repayment. But countries can face a problem if they have a negative balance for official financing, because the extent to which any country can run down its reserves or borrow from abroad is limited in the long term. A requirement for official financing can arise under fixed and floating exchange rate systems, however, but explanation of how the official financing operations of the authorities vary under these different exchanges rate systems will be given in Chapter 8 and 9.

Although the accounts must balance, it is still common practice to talk in terms of balance of payments 'deficits' and 'surpluses'. The usual interpretation is that a deficit and a surplus refer to a negative and a positive balance for official financing respectively. However, the question then arises as to whether official financing (most of which is changes in official reserves) is the best indicator of a country's balance of payments position. Official financing is an important guide since it incorporates all the elements in the balance of payments account. But by itself it can be misleading in that a country may, for example, be able to offset a current and long-term capital account deficit by pushing up domestic interest rates to attract short-term capital inflows. Such a situation would in fact confirm that a country was facing a balance of payments problem, with high domestic interest rates constraining economic activity and so giving rise to increased domestic unemployment. Alternatively, emphasis is often given to the current balance as an important indicator since this section of the account indicates the trading success of a nation. However, it is possible that a current account deficit or surplus is more than offset by capital flows in the opposite direction, so that a current account surplus may not prevent a run-down in the official reserves and/or the need to borrow from abroad. This brief discussion suggests that any *one* particular indicator may not be considered appropriate in all cases, and therefore we need to look at all aspects of a country's balance of payments account before we can attempt to assess its balance of payments position. Indeed it is often preferable to separate the account into two sections, the current and the capital account, and to look at the sort of adjustment problems which countries face in each of these areas.

7.1.2 THE STERLING BALANCES

When we examined the capital account (the transactions in UK external assets and liabilities) in the UK's balance of payments records we noted that the sterling balances are a volatile source of capital movements. These balances have in the past posed serious problems both for the UK's balance of payments policies and for the functioning of the international monetary system. Their influence merits separate treatment in this section.

The sterling balances can be defined as sterling bank deposits, money market liabilities, British government stocks, and Treasury bills held by overseas residents, of which 85 per cent was bank deposits at the end of June 1988. These balances do not consist of all external sterling claims since overseas holdings of equities, for example, are not included. Moreover they focus merely on sterling liabilities of a particular type and ignore financial assets, both long-term and short-term, held by UK residents as claims on foreigners. As such, they give a far from complete picture of the UK's financial position. The key characteristic associated with the liabilities defined as sterling balances is that they are short-term and as such represent a potential source of instability which could affect the capital account of the balance of payments and the sterling exchange rate.

Table 7.2 presents the sterling balances as they stood in mid 1988, but the reader is again reminded that current statistics should be collected from the indicated sources. The table shows that the sterling balances can be subdivided into that part held by overseas monetary institutions (official holdings) and private holdings. The size of the balances at one point in time is subject to wide variation, with some holdings tending to fluctuate

Table 7.2

Sterling balances, end June 1988 (£m)

Type of holder	Official	Private	Total
European Community	755	19,473	20,228
Other developed countries	5,793	16,412	22,205
Oil-exporting countries	5,128	4,857	9,985
Other developing countries	1,597	4,576	6,173
IMF	2,098	—	2,098
Offshore banking centres	—	8,549	8,549
Other	220	1,426	1,646
	15,591	55,293	70,884

Source : Bank of England Quarterly Bulletin, vol. 28, No.4, Table 16

according to anticipated exchange rate movements. Thus when sterling is generally expected to depreciate, holders of sterling balances may liquidate these claims because of the anticipated capital losses which may accrue to them. Of course these holders also have to take into account any interest rate differential which may be obtained if their funds are held in sterling; indeed, a rise in interest rates is one of the traditional weapons used by central banks to contain such speculative outflows.

Thus the potential problem posed by the sterling balances is that a sudden liquidation could put pressure on the sterling exchange rate as a result of the implied deterioration in the capital account. This means a greater need for official financing, which in turn requires that sufficient official reserves are available or that there is the capacity for the UK authorities to borrow externally on reasonable terms. So in the first instance a comparison of the size of the official reserves relative to outstanding sterling balances gives some indication of whether a run-down in the latter poses a serious threat. In June 1988 official reserves were valued at £48·5 billion compared with outstanding sterling balances of almost £71 billion. Even so, the short-term nature of the sterling balances does not necessarily imply that every element is volatile. Interestingly, it seems to be the official component which is the most unstable, as illustrated by the sterling crisis in 1976 when holdings by central banks and government institutions fell sharply but private sector holdings proved to be quite resilient. Accordingly the fact that the ratio of private to official holdings has been rising in recent years – from about 2 : 1 in early 1979 to over 3 : 1 in mid 1988 – it might seem to make the threat posed by the sterling balances to be rather less than suggested by the crude figures.

The sterling balances originally came into existence as a consequence of Britain's dominant role in nineteenth-century international trade. Traders in other countries started to use sterling as a means of settling debts between themselves, as well as with the UK, rather than use a less common means of exchange for which the trading value was uncertain. So sterling became an internationally acceptable means of exchange, in a similar manner to an asset that becomes commonly acceptable as a means of exchange within the domestic economy. The monetary authorities of overseas countries also found it convenient to hold sterling balances because these balances provided a means of support for their own traders and a reserve for their international operations.

During the Second World War, Britain was able to purchase a great deal of her raw materials and imports by simply crediting the sterling accounts of overseas governments, especially the Commonwealth countries, and this meant that there was a substantial increase in the size of the sterling balances. Thus the acceptability of sterling as a reserve currency in international operations was advantageous to Britain because it meant that for a time she was able to finance her current account deficits by generating an increase in the sterling balances. The balances remained more or less stable in size after the war until the mid 1960s, although their ownership did change. During this period the dollar was the dominant key currency in international trade, and so at times in the 1960s the United States was able to finance her payments imbalances by increasing the supply of dollars.

A country's currency will only remain internationally acceptable (i.e. its liabilities will be acceptable as a means of exchange) if its value *vis-a-vis* other currencies remains fairly stable. By the mid 1960s it had become increasingly obvious that the UK's current account was showing signs of chronic imbalance, and this made the holders of sterling balances uneasy about the prospect of capital losses if sterling were devalued. Accordingly some of these holders switched their funds to other currencies, with the result that the overall balance of payments position deteriorated. So a run-down of sterling balances exacerbated the current account problem and led to pressure on the exchange rate which eventually resulted in the devaluation of sterling in 1967. By this time it was widely recognized that the sterling balances were a potentially disturbing force upon the UK balance of payments and exchange rate; therefore measures were introduced to try and nullify the effect of any future liquidation of these balances.

The first attempt to deal with the sterling balances problem on an international basis was made in 1966 under the so-called currency 'swap' arrangements. A group of central banks and the Bank of International Settlements agreed to make available to the UK swap facilities (i.e. foreign exchange in return for sterling) to offset any reduction in the UK reserves caused by a fall in sterling balances, either private or official. After the devaluation in 1967 the countries in the overseas sterling area [3] still continued to diversify their reserves into other currencies, and so a new arrangement was needed to deal with this specific problem. Accordingly the Basle facility of 1968, again arranged through members of the Bank for International Settlements, provided the UK with credit facilities of $ 2,000 million to meet reductions in the official and private sterling balances of the overseas sterling area. Furthermore, the UK made individual agreements with sterling area countries whereby each undertook to hold a certain proportion of its reserves in sterling in return for a dollar guarantee on the bulk of their sterling reserves. However, these arrangements were not extensively utilized, primarily because of an increase in confidence in sterling after a successful period for the UK balance of payments, and by the time the sterling guarantee arrangements terminated in 1974 only £130 million had been paid in compensation.

The early 1970s saw an increase in the sterling balances, largely as a consequence of the substantial rise in the official

[3] The overseas sterling area consisted mainly of Commonwealth or ex-Commonwealth countries which pegged their currencies to the pound and held their reserves in sterling. Since 1972 the number of countries pegging their currencies to the pound has diminished markedly, and they now hold only a proportion of their reserves in sterling.

holdings of the OPEC countries which followed a massive increase in the price of oil. Sterling was an attractive currency for the reserve holdings of these countries because London was one of the few financial centres capable of dealing with such large inflows. But the UK balance of payments had started to deteriorate by 1973 as the result of an increasing current account deficit (due mainly to more expensive oil imports) and a run-down of the official sterling balances. Consequently the sterling exchange rate fell rapidly and the official reserves declined as attempts were made to support the exchange rate. After a series of such crises, in which the run-down of the official sterling balances was a prime factor, there was a further attempt to deal with the sterling balances.

In early 1977 another Basle facility was concluded under which the Bank of International Settlements, with the support of the central banks of eleven countries, agreed to provide the UK with a $3,000 million facility in respect of any net decline in official sterling balances below the amount outstanding in December 1976. The agreement permitted the UK to draw on the facility over a two-year period, with provisions for an extension for a further year. The scheme was supplemented by an offer of foreign currency bonds to official holders of sterling balances, with the intention of promoting an orderly further reduction in the international reserve role of sterling. However, only about £400 million was taken up under the foreign currency bond scheme, and this was no doubt partly a reflection of a widely held optimism in the future benefits of North Sea oil production on the UK balance of payments and exchange rate.

In recent years the sterling balances have become less of a problem for the UK authorities, principally because of a distinct improvement (until recently) in the balance of payments. Current account surpluses were recorded in seven out of the eleven years between 1977 and 1988, aided considerably by the build-up in North Sea oil production towards the end of the period, and this helped to improve confidence in the role of sterling as one of the major non-dollar reserve currencies. It will be of more than passing interest to see whether holders of sterling in 1989 and 1990 remain sanguine in view of the £20 billion trade deficit and overall current account deficit in 1988.

7.2 The adjustment problem

In Section 7.1.1 we explained that it is sometimes difficult to ascertain a country's balance of payments position without looking at several aspects of its balance of payments account. However, some form of adjustment will inevitably be required if a country persistently faces the problem of finding official finance, given that the official reserves are finite and the extent to which a country can borrow abroad may be limited. Therefore adjustment may need to be carried out on the current or capital account, or on both. But adjustment problems may arise for any size of unit for which inflows and outflows are not identical, ranging from an individual to a region or even to a large geographical area such as a country. Later in this chapter we will examine the nature of the adjustment problem according to the size of area under consideration, and we will see that there are some similarities in the problems faced by the regions of the same country and those of different countries.

When investigating the adjustment problem it is useful to make the distinction between automatic and discretionary adjustment. The basic difference is that *automatic adjustment* comes about by itself as a result of prevailing economic forces, whereas *discretionary adjustment* requires policy actions to rectify the disequilibrium. Thus automatic adjustment may come about if a fall in the demand for an area's goods and services leads to a moderation in prices or incomes in that area. The result will be an improvement in the area's balance of payments since its exports are more competitive and yet lower income will give rise to reduced imports from other areas. Discretionary adjustment may come about if the government of the area under consideration reduces demand for the commodities imported from other areas (through increasing taxes or reducing government expenditure, for example), or if it reduces prices in the area relative to its competitors (perhaps by devaluing the value of the area's currency, assuming it has its own currency).

It should be pointed out here that the distinction between automatic and discretionary adjustment is easier to make in theory than in practice. For example an area may suddenly face a reduction in the demand for its goods and services which brings about partial automatic adjustment as a consequence of a moderation of prices and incomes in that area. The government may attempt to assist the adjustment process by reducing the demand for the area's imports, but it is then difficult to establish the extent to which any observed reduction in imports is a result of this discretionary adjustment or of the automatic adjustment.

7.2.1 Determinants of the current account balance

When the adjustment problems facing any size of geographical area are analysed, it is possible to identify those general factors which influence the current and capital account. In this section we intend to concentrate attention on the determinants of the current account, and for the sake of convenience we will direct our discussion at this stage to the adjustment problems facing countries. Also we will treat visibles and invisibles as synonymous since, apart from some governmental services and transfers, there is no economic distinction between selling motor cars (visibles) and selling insurance (invisibles).

The factors which influence a country's current account include the price of exports and imports, the level of demand at home and abroad, the respective quality of products traded in competitive markets, and the length of the delivery period. Of these probably the most significant, and certainly the most easily influenced by government policy, are prices and the level of demand. A relevant observation in the latter case is that the level of imports into the domestic economy is directly related to the level of domestic demand since the consumption of most goods, including imports, tends to increase as economic activity rises. By similar reasoning, the level of imports into other countries (e.g. UK exports) will be related to the level of demand in these countries, and therefore UK exports are a function of overseas demand. From the policy viewpoint the national government cannot directly influence foreign demand, but it is able to use fiscal, monetary, and incomes policies to manipulate the level of domestic demand.

When discussing the impact of prices on the current balance, it is first necessary to recognize that value consists of quantity multiplied by price. Accordingly the effect of a change in the price of exports or imports on their respective values is dependent upon what happens to quantity. In international markets one of the major influences on the relative prices of traded goods and services is exchange rate movements. Now conventional economic theory states that the quantity sold of any good or service tends to vary according to price, other things being equal. Therefore a rise in the domestic price of imports, perhaps because of a decline in the exchange rate, should lead to a fall in the quantity demanded. The relationship between price, quantity, and value is, of course, known as *elasticity*. The elasticity of demand for imports is calculated as the percentage change in quantity demanded divided by the percentage change in price. If this value is greater than 1 (i.e. elastic), then the rise in price will bring about a greater percentage fall in the quantity sold and so the value of imports will decline. If the elasticity of demand for imports is less than 1 (i.e. inelastic), then an increase in the price of imports will bring about an increase in the value of imports.

To take an example, let us assume that the UK's total imports amount to 72 units of a particular good priced at £50 per unit, giving rise to an import bill of £3,600. Suppose now that the price of each unit of the good rises to £60 because of a 20 per cent decline in the exchange value of sterling. The application of the concept of elasticity can be illustrated by taking three examples of what might happen to the quantity sold in response to this rise in the domestic price. In case A in *Table 7.3* the quantity sold falls to 60 units, giving an identical import bill of £3,600. When measuring elasticity, it is essential to recognize that the calculation of the percentage change in quantity and price depends on whether we work from the initial values to the final values, or vice versa. [4] In practice, it is necessary to calculate the change in quantity (12 units in case A) and the change in price (£10 in case A) and divide each by the *average* quantity (66 units in case A) and the *average* price (£55 in case A). The percentage change in quantity is then

[4] If we start from the initial situation, then the percentage change in quantity is 12/72 and the percentage change in price is 10/50, giving an elasticity of 5/6. Starting from case A and working back gives a percentage change in quantity of 12/60 and a percentage change in price of 10/60 – an elasticity of 6/5.

Table 7.3

	Quantity	Price	Value of imports	Elasticity of demand for imports
Initial situation	72	£50	£3,600	
Case A	60	£60	£3,600	$\dfrac{12/66}{10/55} = 1$
Case B	58	£60	£3,480	$\dfrac{14/65}{10/55} = 1\cdot17$
Case C	62	£60	£3,720	$\dfrac{10/67}{10/55} = 0\cdot78$

12 / 66 and the percentage change in price is 10 / 55, giving an elasticity of demand for imports of 1. In cases B and C different assumptions about the change in quantity imported in response to the 20 per cent rise in price give elasticities of greater and less than 1 respectively, indicating a decrease and an increase in the value of imports.

The calculation of elasticities allows us to evaluate the consequences of a depreciation of the domestic currency. What factors determine the elasticity of demand for imports? One consideration is whether or not there are close substitutes at home for the imported products and, assuming there are, if it is relatively easy for demand to be diverted to home-produced substitutes. If the imports consist of items which are difficult or impossible to produce in the domestic economy, such as essential raw materials and foodstuffs, then one would expect the demand for such imports to be inelastic. Furthermore, if substitutes do exist then can domestic industry immediately supply the extra goods and services to replace imports? It usually takes time for specific industries to increase their output of import substitutes, and so the elasticity of demand for these goods and services may be low in the period immediately following a price change. However, the elasticity may be higher when domestic industry has had more time to increase its output. It may also be the case that an increase in demand for the products of some domestic industries gives rise to an increase in price, thereby reducing the price advantage gained through the increase in the price of imports.

When there is a depreciation of the exchange rate, the foreign price of a country's exports should fall but the price charged in terms of the home currency will probably remain the same. The goods and services exported will become more price-competitive in foreign markets and so the quantity sold should increase. Any rise in the quantity sold will increase the value of exports measured in terms of the home currency since the domestic price is unchanged. Accordingly a depreciation of the exchange rate will increase the value of exports as long as the elasticity of demand is greater than zero. However, supply constraints may again exist in the domestic economy when certain industries have to increase their production in order to satisfy an increase in export demand. Consequently the value of exports will rise subject to the length of time it takes to increase domestic output in the export industries.

The above arguments suggest that the influence of a fall in the exchange value of the domestic currency on the current balance will depend upon the elasticity of demand for imports and exports measured in terms of the home currency, acknowledging that supply constraints may reduce the respective elasticities in the period under consideration. The latter qualification gives rise to what is known as the 'J curve' effect, i.e. the current account might at first deteriorate as a result of a fall in the exchange value of the domestic currency but then improve when domestic industry has had sufficient time to increase its output of import substitutes and exports. 5

Our discussion of the factors affecting the current account also needs to take account of the influence of the terms of trade, which is the ratio of export prices to import prices. A change in the exchange value of the home currency will alter the terms of trade and subsequently influence the current account in the manner described earlier. However, factors other than the exchange rate affect the terms of trade and therefore the current account. One example is the oil shocks of 1973 – 74 and 1979 – 80, during which oil-exporting countries experienced a rise in their export price index and oil-importing countries faced a rise in their import price index. Some countries

5 A graph of the current balance over time would presumably show a deterioration at first, followed by a marked improvement to a better current balance than initially, and then the absence of any further improvement. Hence the use of the letter 'J'.

therefore benefited from an improvement in their terms of trade whilst others suffered a deterioration, and this resulted in increased current account surpluses in oil-exporting nations and increased deficits elsewhere. (In the case of oil, demand proved to be inelastic and so the rise in price dramatically improved the current balance of oil exporters.)

7.2.2 ADJUSTMENT BETWEEN REGIONS

Adjustment to a payments imbalance between any size of geographical area can be analysed by considering the nature of adjustments on the current and capital accounts. Adjustment between regions seems to attract much less attention than adjustment between countries, mainly because capital account adjustment is much easier for regions of the same country.

If region A (e.g. Yorkshire) incurs a trading deficit with the rest of the UK as a result of a fall in the demand for its goods and services, then the first indication will be a fall in the monetary balances held by people in region A. However, there is no immediate problem for inhabitants of region A because the branch banking network, which covers the country as a whole, is in a position to make extra loans to region A. So banks in region A will find that they have a higher ratio of loans to deposit liabilities, but branches in other regions will find that they have a lower ratio. Accordingly the existence of a branch banking network facilitates the immediate financing of trading imbalances between regions, although the branch banking network may not be willing to finance such deficits permanently. [6]

A payments imbalance will itself set in motion economic forces which should bring about some adjustment on the current account. For example, a reduction in employment and incomes in region A as a result of a fall in the demand for its goods and services will constrain the demand for imports from other regions. If the payments balance persists, then region A can finance the current account deficit by either trying to borrow more from the branch banking system, selling financial

---

[6] With a unit banking system, in which each area has its own reserves, there may be more immediate problems because payments imbalances will lead to pressure on the reserves of the banks in deficit areas.

assets to other regions, or raising new finance on the national capital and financial markets. This capital account adjustment is generally much easier for a region than for a country since capital inflows are more readily attracted by the existence of a common currency, common capital and financial markets, and the absence of restrictions on capital movements between regions. Financial assets of a similar type from separate regions are generally acceptable in the country as a whole since these assets are not subject to exchange rate movements, different conditions regarding sale and purchase, restrictions on transfer between regions, etc. As a result, the ease with which capital transactions can be conducted between regions ensures that the finance of current account deficits can take place without many of the problems which countries with separate currencies face. These observations suggest that regions with current account imbalances can finance their deficits without a great deal of difficulty and disruption.

Although the finance of current account deficits is much easier on a regional basis, it does not mean that such finance can take place indefinitely without there being some adjustment on the current account. Indeed, the branch banking network is unlikely to continue extending loans to the deficit region without there being some indication of action to reverse the monetary flows. But it is likely that some adjustment will take place automatically on the current account because employment and incomes in region A will be depressed as a result of a fall in demand for its goods and services, and this tendency will be reinforced by the unwillingness of the banks to continue extending loans. Since imports are related to income levels, it may be expected that the current account situation should improve by itself. Such automatic adjustment may be more effective at a regional level because the marginal propensity to import (i.e. the proportion of any additional income spent on imports) will tend to be higher the smaller the area under consideration, owing to the increased dependence on trade with other areas. Thus a given fall in incomes will tend to have a larger effect on the level of imports. Furthermore, automatic adjustment may be reinforced by relative price movements (e.g. unemployment may lead to lower wage costs in the depressed region) which reduce the price of region A's goods in national markets and so possibly improve the trading balance of region A, given the appropriate elasticities. But because region A does not have its own currency, it is not possible for a depreciation to bring about a relative price change.

In summary, adjustment between regions of the same country is greatly assisted by the ease with which capital movements can take place. Capital inflows are smoothly carried out because of the existence of a common currency and common capital and financial markets, and because of the lack of restrictions on capital movements. Thus flow adjustment (current account) is greatly assisted by the ease of stock adjustment (capital account). Nevertheless, current account problems still exist, as is evident from the persistent regional disparities in income, wealth, and employment. In such situations automatic adjustment, via changes in demand and relative prices, may not be very effective in preventing sustained economic decline in particular regions, and therefore regional policies (i.e. discretionary adjustment) may be required.

7.2.3 ADJUSTMENT BETWEEN COUNTRIES

The extent to which capital movements can finance current account deficits between countries is constrained by the existence of separate currencies. The foreign holder of financial assets produced in *country* A now has to take into account such factors as potential exchange rate movements, the effect of country A's financial and monetary policies on their financial market, changes in taxation in country A, and the existence of exchange controls. These considerations imply that capital movements between countries are not as smooth or as easily achieved as capital movements between regions. Furthermore, potential exchange rate movements may also lead to speculation in country A's financial assets, with the result that these financial assets become less attractive because of uncertainty in their international value. [7] Thus the substitutability of financial assets between countries tends to be much lower compared with regions despite the existence of some common financial markets (e.g. the Euro-currency market). Indeed, countries prefer to

---

[7] This happened with the sterling balances in the 1960s and 1970s; see Section 7.1.2.

keep a stock of internationally acceptable reserves to finance their trading imbalances because capital account adjustment is not smooth and immediate.

Some automatic adjustment should take place when a country's current account position deteriorates. Indeed our earlier discussion indicated that a fall in export demand, for instance, will reduce domestic national income and thereby decrease the value of imports (by an amount given by the marginal propensity to import). A contraction in the money supply brought about by a deterioration in the balance of payments may constrain national income also. Additionally, price movements may encourage some automatic adjustment, given the appropriate elasticities, either through the reduction in demand causing the home country's products to be more price-competitive, or through the reduced demand for home currency leading to a decline in its exchange value.

Despite the working of automatic adjustment forces, most governments adopt some form of discretionary adjustment (i.e. policy measures by the authorities) because of the constraints associated with the financing of trading imbalances. In particular, the domestic stock of internationally acceptable reserves is limited and the 'costs' of borrowing abroad may be prohibitive. [8] So the domestic authorities may have insufficient time to wait for automatic adjustment, even if it would work eventually.

The two major types of adjustment policies are known as 'expenditure-reducing' and 'expenditure-switching'. The former policy is based on the observation that the level of imports is related to domestic national income. Fiscal and monetary policies designed to reduce domestic demand should improve the current account by reducing the value of imports. Exports should not be affected as much because they are related more to overseas demand. An expansion in demand could be used to increase the value of imports in a country experiencing a current account surplus, but countries having such surpluses usually attempt to avoid participating in the adjustment process. It is the deficit countries which have borne the main brunt of the adjustment burden. Expenditure-reducing policies in-

---

[8] If borrowing is via the IMF, then the loans raised are often conditional upon certain types of domestic policy being carried out to improve the balance of payments.

clude cuts in government expenditure, increases in taxation, and changes in monetary variables such as interest rates and the money supply (see Chapters 11 and 12 for further discussion). Besides undertaking expenditure-reducing policies, the government can implement policies to change the division of a given volume of expenditure between imports and exports. Expenditure-switching policies include such measures as import controls and devaluations (or managed depreciations) of the domestic currency. Of course a decision to devalue / depreciate the currency must be taken only under conditions in which the relative elasticities are of an appropriate value, otherwise it will be unsuccessful.

These two discretionary forms of adjustment are often used as complements rather than as alternatives. For example, the devaluation of sterling in 1967 (expenditure-switching policy) was supported by an expenditure-reducing policy in the form of an increase in interest rates, cuts in government expenditure, and lending ceilings applied to the commercial banks A rationale for using such a combination of policies is that for a devaluation to be effective UK firms have to produce more goods to replace imports and to supply the extra export demand. At the time, government policies were aimed at restricting domestic demand to create the conditions in which industry could supply the extra requirements. The current balance worsened immediately after the devaluation but then showed a surplus for the years 1970 – 72, only to return to deficit again in 1973. This fluctuation in the current balance after the 1967 devaluation illustrates the 'J curve' effect referred to in Section 7.2.1. A similar 'J curve' effect seems to have occurred after the depreciation of the pound between 1980 and 1983 especially. The value of imports of non-oil goods rose sharply relative to the volume of goods imported.

7.2.4 THE ADJUSTMENT PROBLEM : SOME GLOBAL CONSIDERATIONS

We have seen already that the nature of the adjustment problem tends to vary according to the size of area under consideration, as is indicated by our comparison of the problems faced by regions and countries. If we take a global perspective, we will find that adjustment at the national level has profound implications for the functioning of the world economy as a whole.

If there were only two countries engaged in world trade, then the deficit of one country would be equivalent to the surplus of the other since one country's exports are the imports of the other. By similar reasoning, when we consider trade between many nations we would expect deficits and surpluses to cancel out in the aggregate since it is still the case that one country's exports constitute imports elsewhere. The important point, therefore, is that adjustment between deficit and surplus countries should be carried out in such a way that international trade is encouraged rather than discouraged. Thus individual nations would find it easier to achieve high output and employment in their domestic economies.

Is there a danger, then, that the adjustment policies of trading nations might conflict and so be detrimental to trade, output, and employment on an international scale? If deficit countries adopt expenditure-reducing policies to contain domestic demand for imports, there will be a reduction in world trade unless surplus countries simultaneously undertake policies to expand their economies. Indeed an expansion of demand in surplus countries also would assist the overall adjustment process since imports would be stimulated into their economies and export demand would be encouraged in deficit countries. Our argument suggests that the adjustment process should be seen as applying to surplus as well as to deficit countries, otherwise the world economy could suffer from a deflationary bias if deficit countries undertake expenditure-reducing policies without offsetting policies being carried out elsewhere.

The argument that adjustment policies need to be coordinated to promote the development of world trade can be extended further: governments need to take cognizance of the fact that their domestic policies often influence the operation of the international economy. One positive response to this is for governments to acknowledge that a sustained world economic recession could require common action by the countries concerned to ensure a more speedy recovery in output and employment. A country on its own may be reluctant to stimulate demand through the introduction of the appropriate fiscal and monetary policies because this may lead to increased imports into the domestic economy and associated balance of payments problems. However, agreed and coordinated action by all countries to expand their domestic economies should bring about the desired expansion in demand without imposing balance of payments problems on one particular country. [9] Indeed it is possible that countries' balance of payments positions will remain more or less the same – if that is desired – as long as governments collectively agree on an appropriate degree of expansion in their respective economies.

It seems sensible, therefore, to suggest that the interests of the world community as a whole would be furthered if all trading nations accept that their policies can have an effect on other parties. Coordinated and agreed action would appear to provide the best approach to international economic problems of which the adjustment process is a prime example. In this respect it would seem to be in the interests of trading nations as a whole to devise exchange rate systems and international institutions which facilitate adjustment to payments imbalances without discouraging trade and reducing output and employment. It is against this background of the need for coordinated adjustment policies that we will examine in Chapters 8 and 9 the operation of exchange rate systems and the associated roles and functions of international organizations. Then the advantages and disadvantages of alternative adjustment arrangements can be evaluated.

7.3 Summary

(a) The balance of payments account must balance like any other set of accounts. For example, any net outflow of currency on the current account and the capital account transactions in external assets and liabilities will be offset by official financing in the form of a reduction in the official reserves or borrowing from abroad. However, a nation will face problems if it persistently requires official financing since such sources of finance are limited in supply.

(b) The sterling balances pose a potential problem for the UK balance of payments as they consist of capital balances which

---

[9] It may be the case, however, that a general expansion of demand would stimulate inflation in the world economy. But the argument that policies need to be coordinated would still apply.

could be liquidated at short notice. Indeed the UK balance of payments has been vulnerable over the years to sudden rundowns in the sterling balances, which have subsequently led to pressure on the sterling exchange rate and the need for appropriate policy measures.

(c) Balance of payments adjustment may come about automatically as a result of existing economic forces, or governments may deem it desirable to intervene by undertaking policies to assist the adjustment process (discretionary adjustment).

(d) In terms of the current account, the major avenue through which automatic adjustment operates is via changes in the exchange value of the domestic currency, assuming floating exchange rates are in operation. The effect of a depreciation on the current account depends upon the elasticity of demand for imports in the domestic economy and the elasticity of demand for exports from the domestic economy. Additionally, the time period over which such elasticities are measured is of importance since supply constraints may restrict the extent to which the production of exports and import substitutes can be increased.

(e) Current account adjustment also may come about through governments undertaking expenditure-reducing or expenditure-switching policies. In the former case the government attempts to reduce the demand for imports by operating restrictive fiscal, monetary, and incomes policies. In the latter case a typical policy response is for a government to depreciate the value of its country's currency, thereby giving domestic products a price advantage both at home and in international markets. But again the success of an exchange rate variation on the current account balance depends upon the elasticities of demand for imports and exports.

(f) The nature of the adjustment problem can be highlighted by comparing the problems faced by different sizes of geographical area. A region (e.g. Yorkshire) does not face immediate difficulties if it experiences a current account deficit because capital account adjustment is facilitated by the existence of common currencies. However, countries with their own currencies have a more immediate need for discretionary adjustment in that their financial liabilities are not as readily acceptable as those of regions of the same country.

8
The Bretton Woods system

8.1 Exchange rate systems

In the previous chapter we identified the major variables which influence the current account of the balance of payments and examined how automatic and discretionary adjustments operate to rectify payments imbalances. Although we identified the exchange rate as one of these important variables, we did not examine how different exchange rate systems affect the adjustment process. This section is designed to explain briefly the operation of various exchange rate arrangements, before we analyse in more depth in this and the next chapter how the type of exchange rate system influences the adjustment mechanism.

International trade is complicated by the existence of separate currencies, each used as mediums of exchange within their own national boundaries. Consequently an effective system of international trade requires the adoption of exchange rate arrangements which enable the currency of one country to be exchanged for currencies of other countries. But how is a rate of exchange between two currencies established? Since a rate of exchange measures the price of one currency in terms of another, its determination can be compared with the price of any other item. When market forces are allowed to operate, rates of exchange are determined by the demand and supply of currencies. The *demand* for the domestic currency in foreign exchange markets derives from exports of goods and services plus capital inflows, irrespective of whether payment is made in domestic or foreign currency. For example, if UK exports or capital inflows into the UK are paid for in sterling, then foreigners have to purchase pounds in foreign currency markets with their own currencies, thus giving rise to a demand for pounds. If UK exports or capital inflows into the UK are paid for in foreign currencies, then UK residents will sell these currencies in foreign exchange markets to purchase pounds, since only the latter can be spent in the domestic economy, and so the demand for pounds will rise. Conversely the *supply* of the domestic currency in foreign exchange markets derives from imports and capital outflows, irrespective of whether actual payment is made in domestic or foreign currency. For example, if UK imports and capital outflows from the UK are paid for in sterling, then foreigners receiving these sterling payments will exchange them for their own currencies in the foreign exchange markets, and so the supply of pounds in these markets will rise. If UK imports and capital outflows from the UK are paid for in foreign currency, then domestic residents have to obtain foreign currency with pounds, and so the supply of pounds will increase in foreign exchange markets.

When market forces alone are allowed to determine the exchange value of currencies, a *free-floating* exchange rate system is said to exist. But will a free-floating exchange rate system operate smoothly? If a country faces a current account deficit due to a sudden rise in the value of its imports, there will be an increased supply of the domestic currency in foreign exchange markets which should depreciate the exchange rate. But actual movements in the exchange rate will also depend upon capital transactions. Indeed, capital movements may offset the current account deficit if speculators think that the exchange rate will recover to its former level in the near future, as could be the case if the current account deficit is thought to be temporary. In this situation capital inflows should increase and capital outflows decrease because buying the domestic currency now would provide capital account transactors with a potential capital gain. Alternatively speculators might think that the exchange value of the domestic currency will fall even further in the future, perhaps because they expect the current account deficit to become permanent, and so capital inflows will decrease and capital outflows decrease accordingly. In the latter case the exchange rate will depreciate even further due to net capital outflows at the existing rate of exchange. Therefore an exchange rate will be established at which capital account transactions offset the current account balance, but the demand and supply of currency may be equated (i.e. there should be no need for official financing) only at the expense of large fluctuations in exchange rates.

In practice, governments have usually been reluctant to leave exchange rate determination completely to private market forces because of the danger that large fluctuations in exchange rates might ensue. If large fluctuations in exchange rates are to be expected under free-floating, such a system may be undesirable for international trade and payments since the uncertainty[1] caused by price fluctuations could inhibit world trade, output, and employment.

It is also possible to have a *rigidly fixed* exchange rate system in which the exchange values of currencies are fixed in terms of some common unit such as gold. In fact a gold standard operated in the international economy prior to 1914 and for a period after the First World War. The essential feature of the gold standard was that each country's currency had a fixed value in terms of gold (i.e. gold was the *numeraire*), and therefore exchange rates were effectively fixed. Under a gold standard it is possible for gold to circulate domestically as the legel tender along with banknotes which can be exchanged on demand for gold. An alternative, which operated in the UK from 1925 – 31, is that the central bank is not prepared to convert banknotes into gold for domestic residents but is willing to convert such paper into gold for foreigners. In the latter case the Bank of England would have to hold a gold reserve to meet the demand of foreigners who wanted to convert sterling into gold. One notable feature of the gold standard was that it allowed automatic adjustment to take place via changes in expenditure and output. A country facing a payments imbalance would suffer an outflow of gold which would necessitate a reduction in the domestic money supply since gold was required to back the note issue. Interest rates would then rise as the central bank increased its discount rate to discourage borrowing and the demands for legal tender. The higher cost of borrowing would discourage spending on investment and other goods, and

---

[1] Such uncertainty can be partially offset by dealings in the forward market. This market enables traders to agree a rate of exchange, now, at which foreign currency can be exchanged for domestic currency at an arranged future date, this rate being fixed regardless of what happens to the rate of exchange in the meantime. However, there is a cost to the trader in terms of a premium, and this may be high when large exchange rate fluctuations are experienced.

therefore domestic output and employment would eventually fall. Accordingly adjustment to payments imbalances would come about since deficit countries would experience deflationary pressures which would constrain their demand for imports and make their exports more competitive due to lower wages and prices. Surplus countries would experience inflationary pressures from an inflow of gold which would increase their demand for imports and make their exports less competitive. However, the gold standard did not always work as smoothly or effectively as this description indicates since many countries were unwilling to follow the simple rules of the game. In particular, surplus countries often neutralized an inflow of gold by preventing it from adding to the domestic money supply. The adjustment mechanism did not work very effectively in such circumstances, as the history of the operation of the gold standard in the period after the First World War indicates.

So far we have briefly explained how a free-floating and a rigidly fixed exchange rate system are supposed to operate. Between these two extremes there are various alternatives, two of which have operated since the ending of the gold standard in 1931. A system of *managed floating* enables exchange rates to be determined essentially by private market forces, but governments intervene in the foreign exchange markets to try and moderate any short-term fluctuations which may arise due to destablizing capital flows or other factors. Such official intervention may in theory reduce the degree of exchange rate volatility, and so partially reduce the uncertainty in world trade that might result from a free float. A system of managed floating has existed in the international monetary system since 1973, and its operation will be discussd in Chapter 9. However, managed floating also was adopted in the 1930s when the gold standard was abandoned in the severe economic conditions of the time. The experience then was that floating did not appear to be very successful since individual countries depreciated their currencies so as to gain a competitive advantage over their trading rivals. Consequently a lack of cooperation in the international monetary system only served to intensify the economic problem of the 1930s.

Another alternative is an *adjustable peg* arrangement under which exchange rates are fixed at agreed values, but revaluations and devaluations of currencies can be undertaken under certain conditions. Such a system may provide fairly stable exchange rates for the development of world trade and yet still permit some degree of adjustment via the exchange rate. The remainder of this chapter will investigate this type of system as it operated in the international economy from the Second World War until 1973.

8.2 The adjustable peg system

At the Bretton Woods Conference in 1944 the Allies came together in an attempt to design an international monetary system that would operate in the post-war period. One of the main objectives of the negotiators was to devise a new system which would avoid a return to the economic conditions of the 1930s. Accordingly the Bretton Woods Conference resulted in the formation of the International Monetary Fund (IMF) and its associated articles of agreement, which put into effect the agreed views of the negotiators. In the following discussion we will summarize the features of the Bretton Woods (or adjustable peg) system under the headings of adjustment, liquidity, and cooperation. We then examine the operation of the system.

8.2.1 ADJUSTMENT

One characteristic of the Bretton Woods system was the arrangement for fixed but adjustable exchange rates. This was an attempt to retain some of the advantages of the gold standard, since stable rates of exchange were thought to be beneficial to the conduct of trade and other international transactions, and yet adjustments in the exchange rate were deemed desirable for a country facing a permanent payments imbalance. The articles of agreement stipulated that gold was the official *numeraire* in terms of which each currency's exchange value was to be pegged, but it became common practice for countries to adopted a par value for their currencies expressed in terms of the dollar. Individual monetary authorities were then responsible for maintaining the exchange value of their currencies within a band 1 per cent either side of this agreed par value. From 1949 until 1967, for example, the UK agreed to maintain the exchange value of the pound within a band 1 per cent either side of the agreed central value of £1 = $2·8. If exchange rate pressure arose to force the market rate outside this limit, then the central bank concerned (the Bank of England) was obliged to intervene in the exchange markets. When the pound was approaching the rate £1 = $2·82, the Bank of England would sell pounds and buy dollars; if the rate approached £1 = $2·78, the Bank of England would sell dollars and buy pounds. Additionally, the exchange value of the dollar was pegged in terms of gold at the rate of $35 an ounce. The US authorities were willing to buy and sell gold [2] to other central banks at this price, and therefore currencies were convertible into gold via the dollar.

The dollar was therefore the key currency under the adjustable peg system. Domestic monetary authorities had to hold dollar reserves to support their exchange rates in foreign exchange markets and at the same time currencies were officially convertible into gold via the dollar.

Adjustment to a payments imbalance is restricted under a rigidly fixed exchange rate system since the authorities lose one of their policy tools, that is the ability to vary the exchange rate of their currency. However, the Bretton Woods arrangements allowed countries to change their par values if they experienced a 'fundamental dis-equilibrium' in their balance of payments. The criteria were never carefully defined, but the necessary IMF approval was granted if the country concerned was judged to have a persistent need for accommodating (i.e. official) financing. If the proposed change in parvalues was less than 10 per cent, then prior approval of the IMF was not required. It was envisaged, therefore, that long-term changes in the competitive position of a particular country could be rectified by a change in the par value of its currency.

8.2.2 LIQUIDITY

International liquidity can be defined as those assets which are internationally acceptable in the payment of debts. The supply of international liquidity is of concern since sufficient finance must be available to assist the development of trade, and yet excess liquidity should be avoided since it may stimulate

[2] After the war the USA held approximately 60 per cent of the world reserves of gold.

inflation. Now the need for liquidity derives both from the demands of individuals and private bodies to finance trade and investment flows, and from the operations of central banks. The finance of trade and capital flows can be carried out in various currencies when the latter are freely convertible into each other, although payment may be preferred in currencies which have a more stable exchange value. Central banks require reserves of international liquidity for two reasons: to support the domestic exchange rate in foreign exchange markets; and to meet the possibility that in any given time-period payment to foreigners will exceed receipts.[3] Governments had the obligation to maintain the par values of their currencies under the adjustable peg system, and the arrangements described in Section 8.2.1 indicate that the dollar was used primarily in this capacity. The dollar also became a principal source of liquidity for private transactions (e.g. oil payments) because of the dollar's crucial position in the international monetary system, which made it a safe and acceptable medium of exchange.

Further arrangements were made by the IMF under its general account to organize an additional source of liquidity to meet the temporary needs of deficit countries. The facilities have survived the adjustable peg system and are still in operation today. Each member country[4] has a quota which reflects its economic size and importance as a trading nation. The size of the quota determines the extent to which a country can draw currencies from the pool held by the IMF as well as each country's contribution to the pool. Each member originally contributed 75 per cent of its quota in domestic currency and the remaining 25 per cent in gold, although the latter proportion must now be contributed in other reserve assets such as foreign currencies or SDRs (see Section 8.2.5). If a country requires foreign exchange (e.g. dollars) to a support the par value of the domestic currency, then it purchases foreign exchange with its own currency. Such a drawing results in an increase in the Fund's holdings of the member's currency and a decrease in the IMF holdings of the currencies that are

[3] Both these requirements are met by official financing in the balance of payments accounts.
[4] There were originally 30 members, but by 1988 the number had increased to 151.

borrowed. If the UK for example, purchases foreign currencies when the Fund's holdings of sterling are 75 per cent of the UK quota,[5] then drawings equivalent to 25 per cent of UK quota are available without restriction. This drawing is known as the gold tranche (now called the 'reserve tranche') because it is equivalent to the contribution of gold from the member country under previous quota arrangements. After this tranche has been drawn, the Fund's holdings of sterling will be 100 per cent of the UK's quota.

Under the Fund's ordinary facilities members may purchase additional foreign currencies, but only if they accept increasing restrictions upon their domestic policies. A country can draw by additional tranches, each equivalent to 25 per cent of its quota, until the Fund's holdings of that member's currency are 200 per cent of its quota. Thus four tranches are available after the reserve tranche has been utilized, each known as credit tranches. However, the IMF requires increasingly detailed programmes of how the member concerned will rectify its payments imbalance before access to the higher credit tranches is granted. Often these programmes are expressed in terms of agreed monetary and financial targets to which the member country is expected to adhere. As a result, drawings are phased over a number of years and are granted in accordance with the successful attainment of the agreed programme. A country is required within 3 – 5 years to repurchase its drawings through buying back its own currency with foreign currencies. But countries now have the option of making drawings under a standby arrangement whereby they negotiate access to the credit tranches but only use the facility if and when it is required. In recent years, especially since 1982, a number of countries have developed very serious international debt problems. The IMF identifies fifteen heavily indebted countries including Brazil, Argentina, Chile, and Yugoslavia – most of them are in South and Central America – and their indebtedness is largely to private sector banks through the Euro-currency markets. Rescheduling of such debts has become a necessity for the private banks, and a practice which has emerged is that new agree-

---

[5] If the Fund's holdings of sterling are less than 75 per cent of the UK quota, the UK can purchase, without restriction, foreign currencies up to the point where the Fund's holdings of sterling equal 100 per cent of the UK quota.

ments have been made conditional on such countries accepting the stringent programmes of the IMF which are intended to promote effective adjustment of a country's balance of payments and ensure that the use of Fund resources is temporary. The extension of the IMF's role is discussed further in Chapter 9.

With the increasing value of world trade, it became necessary to periodically adjust the quotas of member countries. Even so, the IMF facility was often insufficient to meet the needs of countries requiring foreign currencies to support their rates of exchange. During the early 1960s a group of ten of the larger and richer members of the IMF agreed to make available to the Fund additional resources which could then be used by any member of this group of ten. These arrangements, known as the general arrangements to borrow (GAB), have been utilized extensively by the UK over the years.

The IMF also introduced supplementary facilities during the 1960s in addition to the ordinary facilities outlined above. The compensatory financing was designed to give temporary support to countries facing short-term fluctuations in export earnings, predominantly primary producing nations. The buffer stock financing facility was designed with the intention of making finance available for schemes to allow the holding of buffer stocks to prevent undue price fluctuation in certain products. In the 1970s a temporary oil facility was established through which oil exporters made finance available, via the Fund, to assist the balance of payments problems caused by the sudden rise in the price of oil.

All the above arrangements were made in order that members of the IMF could finance any short-term balance of payments deficit without variations in their exchange rates. If there was a 'fundamental disequilibrium', then the appropriate action was a devaluation of the currency since temporary finance would delay rather than solve the basic problem.

8.2.3 COOPERATION

The economic recession of the inter-war period had been intensified by the adoption of 'beggar my neighbour' policies, since many countries abandoned the rules of the gold standard and attempted to gain a competitive advantage over their trading partners by introducing tariffs and depreciating the value of their currencies. These sorts of policies were bound to be self-defeating, as we indicated in Section 7.2.4, since the volume of world trade contracted and therefore output and employment stagnated on an international scale. It was against this background that the negotiators at Bretton Woods accepted that more cooperation would be required after the end of the war.

A strong element of participation and cooperation is embodied in the institutional arrangements for the operation of the IMF. Each member of the Fund appoints a governor to the board of Governors, and this body is ultimately responsible for policy decisions. The large number of members involved means that a full meeting of this board would be too cumbersome for the day-to-day administration of the IMF and so it meets only once a year, mainly to ratify any new proposals. Most of the business is carried out under the control of an executive board of twenty-two directors. The five largest members (France, Germany, Japan, the UK and the USA) appoint their own directors, and the remaining directors are elected by groups of other members. Although all members participate in the decision-making process, votes are allotted in proportion to the size of their quotas. Therefore a governor or an executive director exerts influence in accordance with the economic importance of the area he or she represents. Over the years, the IMF has provided a forum for many important discussions affecting the international monetary system, and the process of debate and collective decision-making has encouraged cooperation in this area.

The Bretton Woods arrangements tried to ensure cooperation in the international monetary system, not only through the institutional arrangements for the operation of the IMF but also through the widespread acceptance of certain rules of conduct. International trade was to be encouraged by member countries maintaining par values for their currencies so that stable rates of exchange would prevail. General agreement to minimize trade and currency restrictions, although not possible at first, was also considered to be another essential step in this direction. Of course long-term adjustment must be carried out as countries' competitive positions change, but expenditure-reducing policies seem to be the only option for the authorities under a fixed exchange rate system. The danger, then, is that such a system may suffer from a deflationary bias as a result of the attempts of deficit countries to resolve their payments imbalances by reducing domestic demand. The Bretton Woods arrangements recognized these problems by encouraging long-term adjustment to be carried out through deficit countries devaluing when their balance of payments was in 'fundamental disequilibrium'. Indeed it was hoped that overall adjustment would take place successfully through the cooperation of member countries in accepting such rules of conduct.

8.2.4 OPERATION OF THE SYSTEM IN THE 1940S AND 1950S

Although the IMF began operations almost immediately after the Second World War, the Bretton Woods system did not become fully operational until after 1959. The war caused such widespread damage and disruption to national economies and trading patterns that the system of pegged exchange rates could not be operated without recourse to exchange controls. The effective working of the adjustable peg system required deficit countries to have official reserves at their disposal for supporting their currency at the par value. Since many countries had depleted reserves and weak trading positions, they adopted extensive exchange controls in an attempt to regenerate their economies without being subjected to the full rigours of the adjustable peg system.

The late 1940s witnessed the general operation of a system of bilateral arrangements for trade and payments. In effect, country A fixed its exchange rate against that of country B by closely controlling the amount of country B's foreign exchange available to its residents for trade and other purposes. However, these bilateral arrangements were not universal in that the dollar and sterling areas were each characterized by a system of multilateral trade and payments based on the dollar and sterling respectively. In the sterling area, for example, all inter-country trade was conducted in sterling so that the receipts from any one country in the area could be used to make payments to any other.

The Bretton Woods arrangements were designated to foster a network of multilateral trade and payments in the world as a whole, since this was deemed desirable for the development of world trade. A general system of multilateral trade and payments became more tenable in the 1950s when the European Payments Union was formed to take over payment settlements between European countries (including their colonies and dependencies). The EPU recorded surpluses and deficits of any one of its members with each of the others, and settlement was made via the EPU on the net deficit or surplus of one country with the rest. Accordingly a system of multilateral payments came into operation in the area covered by the EPU; one country's deficit with another member of the EPU was now identical to a deficit with any other in the area. So the non-communist world came to be dominated by two payments systems, the dollar area and the EPU, each involving multilateral payments arrangements.

The moves towards a common system of multilateral payments were concluded with the general acceptance of current account convertibility in December 1958. Individuals from any one country were now able to obtain any other currency for trade purposes simply by *purchasing* it via the foreign exchange markets. However, most countries still retained some degree of control over capital account transactions, mainly because the volatile nature of capital flows was thought to present potential problems for the stability of their exchange rates.

8.2.5 THE STRAINS OF THE 1960s

Our previous discussion has explained that the Bretton Woods system did not become fully operational until after the general acceptance of current account convertibility in 1958. However, most of the next decade was a testimony to the wisdom of the Bretton Woods arrangements since international trade grew at an unprecedented rate. As a consequence, almost every economy benefited from rapid growth and high employment. There can be little doubt that the new order in the international monetary system, characterized by its arrangements for adjustment, liquidity, and cooperation, was a major factor in these developments. As the 1960s progressed, however, it became evident that certain strains were developing in the Bretton Woods arrangements.

A major problem arose from the way in which the adjustable peg system was operated. Section 8.2.1 has already indicated that the intention of Bretton Woods was to erect a system of fixed but adjustable exchange rates within which countries experiencing a 'fundamental disequilibrium' in their balance of payments could devalue. However, a devaluation of the domestic currency came to be regarded almost as a sign of failure by countries facing permanent imbalance, and so was avoided for as long as possible. Consequently exchange rate adjustment to long-run changes in a country's competitive position was not carried out in the manner visualized by the founding fathers of the system. The UK's position in the mid 1960s provides a good example since she tried to avoid a change in her par value for as long as possible but in the end was forced to devalue because of increasing capital outflows.

Adjustment also came to be regarded as a problem relevant to deficit and not to surplus countries. Thus the whole burden of adjustment was thrown onto the economies of certain weaker countries who were themselves reluctant to devalue and preferred to adopt expenditure-reducing policies. These developments gave rise to the claim that the system suffered from a deflationary bias since expenditure-reducing was the major policy weapon used. Nations such as Germany and Japan, increasingly recognized as chronic surplus countries, were reluctant to *revalue* their currencies upwards to assist the overall process. The Bretton Woods conference had accepted that adjustment should be borne by surplus as well as deficit countries through including a 'scarce-currency clause' in the articles of agreement. If IMF holdings of a particular currency were depleted to an extent that threatened its ability to provide that currency to other countries, then that currency could be declared 'scarce'. The IMF was then authorized to ration that currency among its member countries, and the latter were allowed to discriminate against the exports of the country in question. Such a clause, if invoked, would obviously encourage a country to reduce its surplus, but it was never called into effect.

Towards the end of the 1960s, however, the adjustable peg system came under increasing pressure from the growth in short-term capital movements. Increased capital mobility was a result of a number of factors. The growth in world trade led to the development of multinational corporations and banks whose increased scope of operation made them more concerned with the placement of funds in a wide range of currencies. Indeed, the development of the Euro-currency market meant that most large organizations became increasingly aware of the possibility of switching funds between currencies in order to make capital gains (or avoid capital losses) and to benefit from interest rate differentials. If a country was facing a payments deficit, then short-term capital outflows would tend to increase because of the potential capital gains accruing to holders if that country devalued its currency. A rate of exchange of £1 = $2·8, for example, would give $2,800 for every £1,000. If the pound was expected to devalue to £1 = $2·4 then the holder of sterling balances could sell his £1,000 now (at £1 = $2·8), buy back pounds at a future date (at £1 = $2·4), and hence make a sterling capital gain of £167. Such speculation was of a 'one-way' nature in terms of risk; the holder of these (sterling) balances would make a capital gain if the currency was devalued but would suffer no losses if the exchange rate remained unchanged. Thus there was every incentive for speculation [6] against the weaker currencies, as the UK found to its cost prior to the 1967 devaluation. These increased capital flows led to mounting pressure on the adjustable peg since an increasing stock of reserve currencies was required to maintain par values in the face of larger capital movements.

Another major problem for the adjustable peg system was the liquidity arrangements discussed in Section 8.2.2. The system was a form of gold exchange standard since all currencies were expressed in terms of the dollar and the latter was officially convertible into gold at the fixed price of $35 an ounce.

[6] Such 'speculation' may have been for basic commercial reasons since, for example, the widespread belief that sterling might be devalued encouraged UK traders buying overseas goods to purchase the required amount of foreign exchange immediately, while it was relatively cheap, whereas overseas traders making payments in sterling would delay buying pounds since sterling was expected to cost less in terms of foreign currency in the future.

Nevertheless the dollar was the principal reserve asset, and was likely to remain so for as long as the rest of the world accepted dollars and the monetary authorities of individual countries did not exert their option of exchanging dollars for gold. Indeed, during the 1950s there had been fears that there might be a liquidity shortage unless the USA took steps to increase the supply of dollars. But by the early 1960s opinions had changed markedly, partly as a result of the arguments put forward by Robert Triffin. He argued that the international monetary system, based largely on the dollar, contained certain inherent contradictions. The demand for reserve currencies was growing more quickly than the supply of gold, so a liquidity shortage could only be avoided if the supply of dollars was increased. But an increase in the supply of dollars implied a persistent US balance of payments deficit (e.g. exporters to the USA accept payments in dollars, or payments overseas by US residents are made in dollars), and this would undermine confidence in the dollar as a reserve currency because dollar claims were growing in relation to US gold reserves. The effect of a loss in confidence would be a desire to convert dollars into gold at the official price, and accordingly the system would collapse since the most widely held reserve asset would cease to be accepted as such. The world would face either a liquidity shortage which constrained the development of trade, or a collapse of the system as confidence in the dollar waned.

Triffin's theoretical analysis gained more credence when the US balance of payments appeared to move into overall deficit. Although America's current account was always in surplus during the 1960s, her net capital outflows, particularly private investments overseas, more than offset the current account surplus in most years. As a result, the USA suffered a net outflow of gold in every year but one during the 1960s as pressure of the kind described by Triffin built up.

A potential solution to the liquidity dilemma was the introduction of some other form of reserve asset. The IMF set about the problem by devising the *special drawing right* (SDR) as a means of settlement among its members. This new form of liquidity, unlike gold, was essentially a book-keeping transaction which created additional reserve assets for member countries. It was introduced in 1970 following an amendment to the articles of agreement of the IMF and the formation of a special drawing account. The nature and purpose of the SDR can be described as follows :

(a) Participating countries were allocated SDRs in proportion to their quotas, these allocations being known as their 'net cumulative allocations'. The SDRs were issued initially over the three-year period 1970 – 72, when SDR 9 billion were issued; a further SDR 12 billion were issued between 1979 and 1981 (valued in pound sterling at roughly £15 billion).

(b) Any participating country is able to use its SDRs as of right. There are two ways in which this can be done. There may be a *transaction by agreement*, which means that a country which wishes to use its SDRs makes a voluntary agreement with a prescribed holder such as a central bank which then exchanges the SDRs for foreign currencies. Funds obtained by this method are not limited in their use to balance of payments difficulties. Alternatively a holder of SDRs having a balance of payments or reserve problem activates its SDRs through the special drawing account, and the Fund designates other participants to whom the SDRs may be transferred in exchange for foreign currency. This use of SDRs is known as a *transaction with designation*.

(c) A participant is not obliged to provide currency for SDRs beyond the point at which its holdings of SDRs in excess of its net cumulative allocation are equal to twice its net cumulative allocation. A participant, if it wishes, may provide currency in excess of the obligatory limit. Transactions by agreement amount to almost twice transactions with designation.

(d) An incentive to creditors to hold the SDR is provided by interest charges on users of SDRs transferred to creditors. The SDR interest rate is determined by reference to a combined market interest rate based on an average of rates on short-term instruments; the rate is set weekly. The interest charge for users of SDRs provides an incentive for correction of balance of payments problems and subsequent *repurchase* of the SDRs used. Once the repurchase has been made, the payment of interest would cease.

(e) The SDR was originally defined in terms of gold at a value of $\frac{1}{35}$ of an ounce (equivalent to $1 at the prevailing official price); hence its former title of 'paper gold'. In 1974 the value of the SDR was linked to a basket of sixteen national currencies, so the link with gold was severed. A subsequent revaluation in 1981 established the SDR in terms of five national currencies – dollar, yen, mark, pound and French franc.

In theory, the SDR possesses several major advantages over gold as a reserve asset. The supply of SDRs can be controlled in line with the demand for reserve assets, and the costs of provision are very low since it is merely a book-keeping transaction. However, the increased payments deficits of the USA during the early 1970s provided the international monetary system with extra liquidity in the form of dollars, and further issues of SDRs were not made until 1979 – 81. Since 1981 there have been no further issues of SDRs because the executive board of the IMF cannot provide a consensus as to the need for a further issue of SDRs. The difference of view seems to be that a deficiency of official reserves and lack of access to funds by some countries is a reflection of their creditworthiness rather than a global lack of reserves. At the present time SDRs constitute only 2 per cent of countries' official reserves – some measure perhaps of the limited contribution of SDRs.

8.2.6. BREAKDOWN IN THE 1970s

The eventual collapse of the adjustable peg system came about as a result of intensification of the pressures that had developed during the 1960s. Exchange rates had only been adjusted as a last resort by deficit and surplus countries, and so were not used speedily enough to prevent prolonged payments imbalances and exchange rate crises. However, the weakness of the adjustment mechanism became critical when the United States, the linchpin of the system, suffered continual balance of payments problems. It appeared difficult for the dollar to be devalued since the exchange values of all other currencies were tied to it and the dollar itself was tied to gold. Furthermore, confidence in the exchange value of the dollar was essential since it provided the bulk of the reserve assets in the system: any devaluation of the dollar would give rise to fears that it might be devalued again, and hence there would be a reluctance to hold dollars as a reserve currency. It was feared that a severe liquidity crisis might ensue and that the world economy would then be plunged into economic recession.

Confidence in the dollar as a safe reserve asset declined markedly from around 1970 onwards when the USA encountered larger balance of payments deficits. The USA wanted surplus countries like Germany and Japan to revalue since it was difficult for payments imbalances to be resolved through a devaluation of the dollar. In contrast, surplus countries argued that the USA should solve her balance of payments problems by introducing expenditure-reducing policies at home, as had other countries. The USA had never needed to undertake such policies previously, since acceptance of the dollar's role as a key reserve asset had meant that she could meet any payments deficit simply by increasing the supply of dollars. Thus there was fundamental disagreement on what steps should be taken to resolve the problem, and cooperation between members of the international monetary system reached a low ebb.

The American administration adopted a policy of 'benign neglect' in the early 1970s in accordance with its view that surplus countries should revalue. This policy meant that the USA did not take any special steps to control her deficit but instead allowed the balance of payments to deteriorate. But the increased mobility of international capital flows was bound to bring added pressure on the system of fixed exchange rates under such conditions. Other countries, especially those in surplus, were facing an inflow of dollars in exchange for their currencies because of the potential capital gains that would accrue to speculators if the dollar was devalued. These speculative pressures encouraged countries to utilize the option of converting their official holdings of dollars into gold at the fixed price of $35 an ounce. The US Treasury began to experience a depletion of its gold stock, so in August 1971 it announced that official convertibility of dollars into gold was temporarily suspended. [7] An essential link in the Bretton Woods arrangements, that of official convertibility into gold via the dollar, had thus been broken.

In response to these events, the monetary authorities of countries other than the USA decided that they would no

[7] The temporary suspension turned out to be permanent.

longer intervene to stabilize their exchange rates against the dollar, since this would have meant their accumulating large quantities of dollars for which (a) the exchange value was uncertain, and (b) the option of convertibility into gold at a fixed price had been terminated. Accordingly individual currencies were allowed to float since there was no other option, although the governments concerned ensured that it was a 'managed' rather than a free float. Then in December 1971 the Smithsonian Conference was convened in Washington in an attempt to reach agreement, on a multilateral basis, for some new arrangement to perpetuate the adjustable peg system. Several steps were taken in this respect :

(a) There was a revaluation of most major currencies against the dollar, notably a 13·5 per cent increase in the value of the Deutschmark and a 17 per cent increase in the value of the yen.
(b) The band of fluctuation either side of the new parities was widened from 1 per cent to 2·25 per cent, thus allowing for a larger margin of exchange rate fluctuation before official intervention was required.
(c) The official price of gold was increased to $38 an ounce, but this move had little significance since the dollar was no longer officially convertible into gold.

Although the conference brought about the first international agreement on a multilateral adjustment in exchange rates, it did not prevent the collapse of the adjustable peg system. Indeed, once the dollar effectively had been devalued it became more likely that the same might happen again in the near future. Consequently lack of confidence in the dollar, combined with the high mobility of capital flows, led to severe pressure on the new parity structure. The UK floated sterling in June 1972, largely because of her own balance of payments difficulties, and most other major economies had followed suit by March 1973. The emergence of new exchange rate arrangements is contained in *Table 8.1*, which shows the exchange rate arrangements now in operation. Just over one-third of IMF countries have exchange rate policies which permit their currency to change in value against others according to market forces. Within the independently floating group are the UK and the USA. Within the

Table 8.1
Exchange rate systems, March 1988

	Number of countries
Flexible systems	
Independent floating	18
Managed floating	26
Flexible against a single currency or group of currencies	12
	56
Pegged systems	
Pegged against US dollar	40
Pegged against French franc	14
Other	5
Pegged against a currency composite :	
SDR	7
Other	29
	95
	151

Source : IMF *Annual Report* (1988)

European Community, member countries (other than the UK) are part of the European Monetary System, which is an arrangement whereby these countries fix their exchange rates against each other but have flexible rates against non-member countries. The countries which have chosen to fix their exchange rates against the US dollar and the French franc are those which continue to have close commercial (and political) links with these two countries. Although the classification of countries in *Table 8.1* suggests that a large majority of countries have opted for stable exchange rates, in fact this is not so; those countries which are pegged to the US dollar will find their exchange rate moving against other currencies, because the US dollar itself is an independently floating currency. However, it is likely that these various arrangements help to reduce the *volatility* of exchange rates and thus reduce uncertainty.

8.3 The World Bank (the International Bank for Reconstruction and Development)

Origin and purpose The World Bank, like the IMF, was designed at Bretton Woods and began operations in 1946. The two institutions have adjoining offices in Washington. One of the initial purposes of the World Bank was to aid post-war reconstruction through the provision of finance, since private capital markets were not expected to be able to cope with the scale of the problem. In practice, the US Marshall Aid programme provided most of the necessary finance and the World Bank came to be responsible for assisting economic development in mainly the poorer countries.

Source of funds Member countries have to make capital subscriptions which reflect their IMF quotas. However, only 10 per cent (originally 20 per cent) of this subscription is paid to the Bank, the remaining 90 per cent acting as a guarantee for the Bank's lending. As at June 1987 the Bank's subscribed capital was over $77 billion. The major source of funds is from its borrowings in world capital markets, but the Bank obtains a substantial flow from its retained earnings and the repayment of loans. The Bank issues bonds in capital markets such as the New York market. Since its inception it has made loans totalling over $140 billion to 110 countries.

Nature of operations The Bank lends on a commercial basis (although loans usually have a grace period of five years before repayments) since the intention is to supplement private finance, not compete with it. Consequently the Bank satisfies itself that the borrower can meet the interest and capital repayments before making the loan. Also the Bank makes a general appraisal of the merits and priority of each proposal in order to allocate its funds effectively. In view of this, the Bank's loans are usually directed towards developing countries which are in a more advanced stage of economic development.

The Bank lends to governments and governmental agencies, although private organizations can borrow if the national government guarantees the loan. The length of the loan is dependent upon the character of the project and the debt position of the borrower, but twenty years is a typical period. Lending is normally limited to the financing of the foreign exchange costs of the imported goods and services to be used in the project.

The Bank also provides its members with technical assistance and advice on projects, since the less developed countries often lack the required technical expertise.

Recipients of loans Loans go mainly to the Asian, African, South American and Central American countries with low levels of GNP per head. The Bank's outstanding lending has increased from $250 million in 1947 on one project to a total of $29.7 billion by June 1980. Loans made during the 1950s were mainly for the development of infrastructure, such as transport and electric power schemes. Loans have more recently been extended to finance education and other socially oriented projects.

Many of the less developed countries have found it difficult to meet the service charges on their loans to the World Bank. To accomodate this, the World Bank was expanded into the World Bank Group which now includes the International Development Association (1960) and the International Finance Corporation (1956). The purpose of the International Development Association is to provide capital funds for poorer developing member countries on more flexible terms. The countries which qualify for assistance are those with a per capita GNP of less than US $791 (valued at 1983 dollars). Term of loans from the IDA are more favourable than those demanded by the IBRD and can be up to fifty years with repayments deferred for the first ten years, with no interest charges. For the period 1984 – 87 the usable resources of the IDA had been expanded to over $39 billion, with funds provided by subscriptions and contributions from the more advanced and prosperous members.

The objective of the International Finance Corporation is, on the other hand, intended to encourage the growth of productive *private* enterprise in less developed countries, particularly where sufficient private capital is not available on reasonable terms. The IFC borrows most of its funds from the World Bank but it also raises money from private capital markets. By 1987 the IFC had approved investment projects over $9 billion. Most of the projects are in Asia and about 40 per cent of the funds went to projects in very poor countries;

investment in fertilizers, chemicals and petrochemicals was the largest single group.

8.4 Summary

(a) Various exchange rate arrangements can be adopted, ranging from free-floating at one extreme to a rigidly fixed system at the other. The extent to which the exchange rate can contribute to the adjustment mechanism, in either an automatic or a discretionary manner, is influenced by the type of exchange rate system in operation.

(b) The adjustable peg system was characterized by its arrangements for adjustment, liquidity, and cooperation. With adjustment, the essential feature was the fixed but adjustable exchange rate structure in which the dollar held a central position. All currencies came to be expressed in terms of the dollar, and the dollar was officially convertible into gold at a fixed price. Consequently world trade was encouraged since all currencies were exchangeable for each other and for gold at stable rates of exchange.

(c) The liquidity arrangements came to be based on both the IMF quota schemes and the supply of dollars. However, there was an intrinsic weakness in such a system, as was pointed out by Triffin. He argued that the system was bound to collapse, either because a liquidity shortage would ensue if the supply of dollars failed to keep pace with the growing world demand, or because the persistent balance of payments deficits of the USA (which provided dollars to the world) would reduce confidence in the dollar and so lead to the conversion of official dollar balances into gold.

(d) Cooperation in the international monetary system was enhanced by the institutional arrangements made at Bretton Woods. Through the creation of institutions such as the IMF and the World Bank, a forum was provided for discussion and decision-making on an international scale. At the same time rules of conduct were established for the behaviour of member nations.

(e) The causes of the breakdown of the adjustable peg system are related to its three major features described above. The adjustment mechanism in the 1960s was characterized by the reluctance of all countries to adjust their exchange rates, especially those countries in surplus. Accordingly, adjustment via the exchange rate was not able to compensate adequately for long-term changes in competitive conditions. The deterioration in the US balance of payments in the early 1970s caused particular concern since the dollar was the linchpin of the international monetary system. When the US authorities failed to undertake domestic policies to remedy the external situation, some countries started to exercise their option of converting their dollar balances into gold. These moves brought about the suspension of the official convertibility of the dollar into gold and the eventual adoption of floating exchange rates.

9
Managed floating

9.1 The general operation of the system, 1973 to date

9.1.1 HISTORICAL BACKGROUND

Chapter 8 has already examined the reasons why the adjustable peg system collapsed. In summary, an exchange rate system needs to be sufficiently flexible to cope with long-run changes in countries' competitive positions. But the adjustable peg system did not adequately specify if and when countries in surplus or deficit were to undertake exchange rate adjustment. Such a shortcoming is illustrated by the imprecise meaning of the term 'fundamental disequilibrium', the required condition for a devaluation by a deficit country. This deficiency proved fatal when the dollar faced a prolonged confidence crisis in the early 1970s. It was extremely difficult for the USA to devalue since all currencies were expressed in terms of the dollar, and yet surplus countries were not very keen to revalue their currencies. However, speculative pressure, stimulated by the increasing size and mobility of capital flows, eventually brought about the suspension of official dollar convertibility into gold and the subsequent abandonment by individual monetary authorities of their obligation to maintain fixed exchange rates.

The adoption of floating exchange rates was thus a consequence of the collapse of the adjustable peg rather than the result of a collectively planned decision. Once the system of fixed exchange rates had been abandoned there was no alternative but for currencies to float. However, the system of floating exchange rates was thought at the time to be a temporary feature of the international monetary system : it was hoped that a new framework would be found for a return to some kind of adjustable peg in which the burden of adjustment was clearly defined, both for deficit and surplus countries, and in which reserve assets were not based primarily on one currency.

Accordingly, many negotiations took place within the IMF (especially through the so-called committee of twenty) in an attempt to find some generally acceptable basis for a return to such a system. But these extensive discussions failed to provide a common area of agreement, mainly because of divergent national interests and unfavourable economic developments such as inflation, recession, and the oil crisis. *Table 8.1* revealed the extent to which flexible exchange rates have been adopted.

The first few years of floating proved to be fairly successful, especially in the light of the prevailing economic conditions. Consequently floating came to be accepted as a permanent feature of the international monetary system, even though the Bretton Woods Conference had disapproved of such arrangements. Therefore at the Jamaica Conference of the IMF in January 1976 a second amendment to the articles of agreement (the first amendment being the introduction of SDRs) was made by which the system of floating exchange rates was legalized. In fact the rules were changed so that now an 85 per cent affirmative vote was required before the IMF could sanction a return to an adjustable peg arrangement.

A floating exchange rate should, in theory, 'solve' the balance of payments problem automatically. In practice, however, the elasticity of demand for imports and exports may not be of an appropriate value or else it may take considerable time before such automatic forces become effective. Under such circumstances speculative capital movements cannot be relied upon to offset any temporary deficit on the current account because capital flows may prove to be volatile in an uncertain world. Accordingly *managed* floating was generally adopted when the adjustable peg was abandoned. Under managed floating, the domestic monetary authorities intervene in the foreign exchange markets to smooth out excessive short-term fluctuations in the exchange rate. But it can be difficult to ascertain whether exchange rate pressure is temporary or permanent in nature; consequently the decision when and to what degree the central monetary authority should intervene is largely a matter of judgement. If a country's exchange rate is generally thought to be overvalued, however, then the central bank concerned would face heavy losses of foreign currency if it attempted to maintain the exchange rate at its current value. Large reserves of foreign currencies would then be required to buy the domestic currency in support operations, but the growth and mobility of capital flows has made most countries accept that such a defence is impractical.

With floating, a potential complication arises because of the difficulty in establishing whether the domestic currency's exchange value is increasing or decreasing. The home currency may appreciate in terms of one currency and yet depreciate in terms of another. To take an example, sterling appreciated against the dollar in late 1987 but depreciated against most of the EC currencies. If we want an overall measure of the value of the domestic currency then some weighted average of changes in its exchange value against all other currencies is required. The weights should indicate the relative importance of each of these currencies, perhaps in terms of the volume of trade which the respective countries conduct with the domestic economy. For sterling and the other major currencies the 'effective exchange rate' is a general measure of the exchange value of the domestic currency, and it is calculated on such a basis.[1] However, it is still common to see exchange rates expressed in terms of the dollar, partly because this had long been the accepted practice under the adjustable peg, and also because of the USA's continuing dominance in the world economy and financial system.

To facilitate comparison with the adjustable peg, the major features of managed floating can be described under the headings of adjustment, liquidity, and cooperation.

9.1.2 ADJUSTMENT

Under floating, the exchange rate can operate as a form of automatic adjustment to payments imbalances, although such adjustment may not be full or immediate. Floating exchange rates have the added advantage that responsibility for the burden of adjustment does not have to be assigned to particular countries: with floating, the exchange rate mechanism itself

---

[1] Appendix 1 to this chapter illustrates the calculation of a weighted exchange rate index and also describes the new index (sterling exchange rate index or sterling ERI) to be used from December 1988.

should lead to an appreciation of strong currencies and a depreciation of weak currencies. In contrast, the operation of the adjustable peg was characterized by disputes as to whether the burden of adjustment should be borne by deficit or surplus countries.

Discretionary adjustment via the exchange rate is not easy under managed floating. The existence of large and mobile capital flows makes it extremely difficult for national governments to overcome market pressure and maintain an exchange rate which is not compatible with general market sentiment. Nevertheless some form of discretionary adjustment may still be required, especially for deficit countries, since there is no guarantee that the exchange rate will adjust smoothly in such a manner as to ensure an equilibrium in the balance of payments. Countries with balance of payments problems – in the sense of having requirements for official financing which put a strain on official reserves or on the capacity to borrow abroad on reasonable terms – have had to resort to traditional defensive measures in such circumstances. Thus expenditure-reducing policies are most appropriate when the problem is identified as a deteriorating current account balance, whereas tighter monetary policies may be preferable if capital outflows are the source of undesirable pressure on the exchange rate.

An additional consideration is that the adjustment process prior to floating was influenced by the one-way nature of speculative flows. Since countries were obliged to maintain par values, it was possible for speculation to be carried out against the stronger and weaker currencies in the knowledge that the currencies concerned might be revalued or devalued respectively, but there was no danger of the strong currencies being devalued or the weak currency being revalued. With managed floating there is a risk that speculators will suffer capital losses since the monetary authority is no longer attempting to defend a rigid par value, and so the exchange rate can move in either direction in response to market pressures. This reasoning suggests that capital flows are potentially more stabilizing under floating. However, both the weaker and stronger currencies have experienced bouts of speculative pressure, thus indicating that capital flows have not been a particularly stabilizing force under managed floating.

The competence of the adjustment mechanism under managed floating was given a thorough testing by the oil shocks of 1973 – 74 and 1979 – 80. In both instances a massive disruption to trade and capital flows took place. For example the combined current account surplus of the OPEC countries expanded from $8 billion in 1973 to $60 billion the next year before subsiding back to only $5 billion by 1978; and in the aftermath of the second oil shock the surplus rose to $65 billion in 1979, $110 billion in 1980, but was then eliminated by 1983 as oil prices came under some downwards pressure. At first glance the size of the surpluses, their volatility, and the corresponding deficits in oil importing countries would appear to pose an overwhelming problem for any type of exchange rate system. Indeed it is difficult to envisage how the adjustable peg system could have coped with the scale of this problem, whereas the system of floating exchange rates did.

The impact of the oil shocks on financial flows and the foreign exchange markets has been affected by the means of payment for oil and the asset preferences of OPEC countries. Practically all payments to OPEC countries are made in dollars, because this is the traditional means of payment. So in the first instance a sharp rise in oil prices necessitates an increased demand for dollars, but whether this is maintained depends very much on the decisions of OPEC countries. After accepting payment in dollars, oil-exporting countries can decide to keep their enlarged surpluses in this form, either in deposits or in longer-term investments, or they can switch into other currency assets. If they choose the former, the dollar can be expected to strengthen relative to other currencies. After the second oil shock, for example, there was a tendency for reserves to be kept in dollars, primarily because of the relatively high interest rates being offered on dollar deposits at the time, and so during the early 1980s the dollar was a strong currency. In the aftermath of the first oil shock, however, there was a greater tendency for OPEC countries to diversify their assets into traditionally strong currencies such as the Deutschmark and Swiss franc, a move which effectively boosted the international value of these currencies.

Another dimension to the trading imbalances caused by the two oil shocks is not so much the currency consequences but the recycling problem. This relates to the need for the international financial system to reconcile the financing needs created by deficits in some countries with the extra resources available to others. The first oil crisis created particular concern in this respect, but the development of the Euro-currency market greatly facilitated the process. A large proportion of the oil surpluses was kept in a fairly liquid form and redeposited in the Euro-currency market, where it was on-lent to the monetary authorities of deficit countries, thus enabling them to finance their deficits. The smoothness with which the financial system dealt with the first oil shock surprised most people and suggested that the new floating exchange rate regime might cope better with large shocks of this type than the adjustable peg system would have.

9.1.3 LIQUIDITY

The abandonment of a fixed exchange rate in favour of floating means that there is potentially less need for government intervention in foreign exchange markets, and therefore a reduced need for international liquidity to meet this purpose. Governments, however, have on occasions intervened in foreign exchange markets to influence their respective rates of exchange, although a greater variety of currencies has been used now that exchange rates are no longer pegged exclusively to the dollar. On the other hand, the growth in the Euro-currency market has provided an enlarged source of borrowing for monetary authorities who wish either to support their exchange rates or to meet the needs of official financing. This was particularly the case after the first oil crisis when the Euro-currency market may have responded too easily to the financing needs of some countries, effectively building up problems for the future. It has been suggested that lending to finance trade imbalances may have been too lax, and as such contributed to the inflationary resurgence in the late 1970s. By the early 1980s problems for some Central and South American countries in meeting interest and principal repayments on outstanding loans gave rise to fears of an international debt crisis. This led to a reappraisal by the Euro-currency markets and banks of their exposure to borrowers in the non-industrialized world, carrying with it the danger that attitudes could swing too far in the opposite direction and that too restrictive a stance might jeopardize international trade and economic growth.

Some nations have continued to use the IMF facilities, despite the success of the Euro-currency market in providing large-scale finance. Indeed in December 1976 the UK negotiated a standby facility of SDR 3,360 million ($ 3,900 million), the maximum amount available under the British credit tranches. Other IMF facilities have also been utilized extensively, especially by the less developed countries. All these countries have been willing to borrow from IMF – even though there are conditional policy restrictions – because the Euro-currency markets have become more concerned with the creditworthiness of their customers. In fact there have been various instances where the banks in the Euro-currency market have been willing to extend credit only if the country in question has already obtained IMF credit and its associated conditionality.

What, then, has happened to the dollar and gold, the two key reserve assets under the adjustable peg? The prolonged speculative pressure against the dollar in the final stages of the adjustable peg system indicated there was an oversupply of this currency. The first oil crisis gave rise to renewed demand for dollars, since payments to oil exporting countries are made in this form, but in the late 1970s this was followed by another dollar crisis which undermined its integrity as the key international reserve asset. Reforms in US monetary policy from 1979 – which led to much tighter monetary conditions and higher interest rates – paved the way for a resurgence in the dollar in the early 1980s, supported by the increased demands arising from the second oil crisis. Thus to date the era since Bretton Woods has seen several major changes in the fortunes of the dollar, which is still by far the most important reserve currency in the international monetary system. Not only has this led to a high degree of volatility in the foreign exchange markets, but at the same time trade and capital flows have been undertaken against a greater background of uncertainty than was customary in the 1960s.

The role of gold has always been a controversial issue in the international monetary system, but with the advent of floating its importance as a source of international liquidity has been reduced in several ways. When currencies were allowed to float, gold was no longer the ultimate *numéraire* in which exchange values were expressed; indeed, discussions at the time accepted that the SDR (based on the value of national currencies from 1974) would be the *numéraire* in any future return to an adjustable peg system. Moves towards the demonetization of gold went further when, under the second amendment to the articles of agreement in Jamaica in 1976, it was agreed that the IMF should dispose of one-third of its gold holdings. One-half of this was to be sold by auction, and the profits above the official price of $42·2 an ounce were then to be used to promote aid to the less developed countries, whereas the other half was to be sold back to members at the prevailing official price. The notion of an official gold price at which inter-central-bank transactions were to be conducted was also abandoned. Finally, countries were no longer required to pay a quarter of their IMF quotas (or quota increases) in gold; in future they were allowed to use foreign currencies or SDRs, assuming further allocations of the latter were to be made. Advocates of a return to gold still remain, and at times there have been proposals to consider reinstating it as the key reserve asset in the international monetary system. Such views have not received widespread acceptance, however, and as time goes by the chances of a reinstatement of some form of gold standard look more and more remote.

9.1.4 COOPERATION

The replacement of the adjustable peg by floating implies that fewer rules of conduct are necessary for coordinating the system of exchange rates. Countries no longer have to decide the rate of exchange at which currencies should be pegged, or the responsibility for ensuring that par values are maintained at agreed values. Indeed, advocates of floating have frequently argued that the need for fewer rules, and reduced formal cooperation, confers an important advantage on the present system over its predecessor.

It must be remembered, however, that the Bretton Woods arrangements and the associated rules of conduct were designed with the intention of avoiding the conflicts of national interest which had been associated with the previous period of floating. At that time, the adoption of floating exchange rates was also thought to be advantageous since the constraints of the gold standard could be abandoned. Nevertheless the pursuit of policies based on national self-interest led to competitive depreciation and the introduction of tariffs and other trade restrictions. Trade, output, and employment suffered as a consequence on an international scale. The present system of managed floating does contain the possibility of direct conflict if official intervention is carried out at cross-purposes. Thus the central bank of country A might buy currency B in order to keep the domestic exchange rate at a competitive level, whereas country B might simultaneously try to keep the value of its currency down by buying currency A. In this manner a lack of cooperation, fostered by a system of floating exchange rates, can lead to conflict and mutually frustrating policies.

In summary, cooperation is still necessary if trade, output, and employment are to develop to their full potential. This need for cooperation is especially pressing during a period of economic recession, since nations are then more concerned with gaining a competitive advantage over their rivals so that domestic employment levels can be maintained. Accordingly, the danger with floating exchange rates is that the less formal arrangements for cooperation may foster insufficient inter national cooperation of policies for the alleviation of sustained economic recessions or containment of inflationary pressures.

9.2 Exchange rate determination

In Section 8.1 it was explained that the determination of a currency's exchange rate value is in principle broadly the same as the establishment of the price for any other financial instrument, commodity, or good. Essentially it is a matter of identifying the sources of supply and demand. Our discussion in the last two chapters and this one reveals three broad types of transaction which give rise to the demand and supply of currencies :

Current account   flows in the form of exports and imports of goods and services.

Capital account   transactions, either private or official, long-term or short-term.

Government intervention,   usually involving the direct buying or selling of domestic and foreign currencies by central banks.

The relative balance of these factors has changed over time and is influenced by the type of exchange rate system in operation.

Under the Bretton Woods arrangements government intervention at predetermined levels, or parities, was the characteristic feature of the system. Central banks agreed to buy or sell unlimited amounts of currency at points 1 per cent either side of their established par values, although the mere fact that they were prepared and willing to do this was often sufficient to limit the extent to which they had to intervene in practice. In this period capital account transactions were at a much lower level than they are nowadays, partly because many countries still had restrictions or limitations on this type of flow. Accordingly, the regular demand and supply of currencies in the foreign exchange markets tended to be dominated by current account transactions, which were expanding quite rapidly as international trade grew faster than domestic growth rates. If persistently large current account imbalances arose, the anticipation of devaluation or revaluation would give rise to speculative short-term capital flows in the same direction, putting added pressure on the exchange rate in question. Typically the central bank of the country facing downwards pressure on its currency would intervene for a time by running down its official reserves, but eventually might decide to devalue if there was no sign that domestic policies were likely to contain the situation.

With current account performance playing the dominant role in determining the demand for and supply of currencies, attention became focused on the relative competitiveness of each country's goods and services in international markets. Section 7.2.1 examined some of the mechanics involved, in particular the relevance of elasticities in influencing the extent to which price changes impact on the value of exports and imports. Before floating exchange rates were adopted, such price changes were constrained to differences in domestic inflation rates. But because inflation differentials were relatively small during the 1950s and 1960s, it often took some time for marked divergences in competitiveness to emerge. When they did, a change in parity values was often the end result. For example the devaluation of sterling in 1967 was mainly the consequence of higher inflation in the UK over a number of years than that experienced by her major trading partners. By the early 1970s not only had the general inflationary climate changed for the worse, but at the same time the Bretton Woods arrangements were breaking down. In this new environment it was widely believed that exchange rates, freed from restrictive intervention, would adjust reasonably smoothly to divergences in competitiveness, as predicted by the *purchasing power parity theorem.* Simply stated, this asserted that the actual exchange rate between any pair of currencies would fluctuate to offset differences in inflation between the two countries in question. Or expressed another way, real exchange rates – that is nominal exchange rates adjusted for inflation differences – should remain more or less constant over time. A temporary deviation might occur because export and import volumes could react slowly to exchange rate movements, but these lags were thought unlikely to be excessively long, especially if capital account transactions anticipated the process. Thus 'speculators' would buy undervalued currencies and sell overvalued ones, and in so doing would speed up the adjustment process.

Figure 9.1 shows the movements in real exchange rates of the major currencies over the period 1974 – 88. Measurements are made relative to the US dollar, with 1975 as the base year.

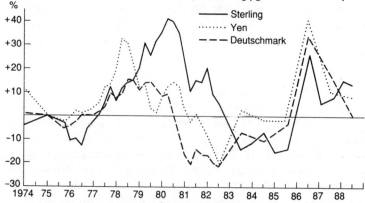

Figure 9.1 *Deviation of real exchange rate from purchasing power parity, using the dollar as base currency*

Source : derived from data in : Bank of England *Quarterly Bulletin;* National Institute *Economic Review*

Wholesale prices are used as an indicator of movement of
domestic costs up to 1983 and retail prices subsequently. [2] Our
attention should be focussed on the direction of movement and
the relative change. What seems clear from the chart is that the
real exchange rates have deviated by much larger amounts over
the period 1978 – 88 than in the early years of floating. For
example, sterling's real exchange rate relative to the dollar rose
by over 40 per cent between late 1977 and late 1980, only to fall
by about 35 per cent in the following two years. In other words,
according to the principle of purchasing power parity, sterling
was overvalued against the dollar and subsequently undervalued against the dollar if one simply compares relative prices
of goods in the two countries. If the explanation offered by
purchasing power parity for exchange rate levels is correct then
these deviations are due to buying and selling of dollars and
sterling which are motivated by factors other than the relative
prices of goods involved in trade. It is interesting to note that
the movements of the real exchange rates do seem to move
around the level appropriate to a purchasing power parity
explanation. Although the evidence presented does not refute
the claim that in the long run exchange rates compensate for
domestic inflation differentials, it does show that over periods of
several years real exchange rate anomalies can and do occur.
Moreover this short-term instability can be very substantial.

One of the reasons why the purchasing power parity theorem
has not worked so well over short periods is that the influence
on currencies of current account flows has diminished, while
capital account transactions have assumed a greater role.
Moreover, these capital transactions have not always been
stabilizing in the manner assumed by some proponents of
floating exchange rates. The tendency for international capital
flows to increase has been evident for some time, and was
causing problems for central bank intervention in the final
years of the Bretton Woods system. But over the last decade
there has been a rapid acceleration in this type of transaction.
A relaxation in restrictions and controls on capital flows was a

[2] The calculations used to adjust the exchange rates are year-on-year movements of
prices. This may be inappropriate and it is arguable which is the most suitable deflator
to use. Similar computations by the IMF suggest that *Figure 9.1* has captured the
direction of change correctly and the relative movements.

key factor, but generally it is the increasing internationalization of business operations and their financing which lies behind the development. Investment institutions, companies, and banks have become much more sophisticated in the operation of their affairs across national boundaries, as witnessed by the spectacular growth in the Euro-currency markets. Furthermore the OPEC countries have accumulated massive portfolios of international financial assets as a consequence of the two oil shocks, and the management of these assets can have a marked impact on the foreign exchange markets. Pension funds, insurance companies, and other investment institutions in the industrial economies have also become large accumulators of financial assets in recent years, with a greater tendency to consider international diversification of their portfolios. Asset portfolio adjustments by these various groups can nowadays have a dominant effect on foreign exchange markets even if this appears to run contrary to what might be suggested by purchasing power parity relationships.

Table 9.1 gives some indication of the size and importance for the UK of these changes in recent years, notwithstanding the particular consequences of North Sea oil investment. It is clear from the table that exports of goods and services have grown from £53 billion in 1977 to £159 billion in 1987 (with a similar growth in imports), i.e. 11 per cent growth each year on average. Transactions in liabilities (capital inflows) have also grown but in a much more irregular fashion. The ratio of the capital inflows to the trade and commerce position has averaged 0.31, although clearly it has also been quite volatile. In other words, capital inflows have averaged 31 per cent of the trade and commerce flows of the UK; in 1979 and 1986 however, they were over 50 per cent. A similar picture emerges when we examine the *net* flows arising from transactions in assets and liabilities. In each of the ten years the UK accumulated net assets (net flows abroad) and the data again show considerable variation during the period, ranging from net outflows of £0.7 billion to £14.3 billion.

A natural consequence of the growth and sophistication in international capital flows is that decision-makers have become more aware of potential short-term gains. This suggests that the foreign exchange markets are now more sensitive to actual and

Table 9.1

UK trade and capital flows (£b)

	Exports and invisibles (credits)	Capital inflows	Capital inflows ÷ exports and invisibles (credits)	Net transactions in assets and liabilities[a]
1977	53·0	9·9	0·19	− 3·9
1978	59·9	1·5	0·02	− 2·9
1979	73·8	39·4	0·53	− 0·7
1980	88·5	39·6	0·44	− 3·9
1981	108·0	43·4	0·40	− 7·4
1982	120·8	29·0	0·24	− 2·3
1983	126·7	25·8	0·20	− 4·4
1984	148·0	24·3	0·16	− 7·7
1985	158·6	44·2	0·28	− 8·9
1986	149·9	80·4	0·54	− 14·3
1987	159·4	73·7	0·46	− 2·3

[a] A negative sign indicates an accumulation of assets by the UK.

Source: derived from issues of *Economic Trends*

prospective interest rate developments, especially as they impact on the key reserve currencies. Also official intervention has
become much less effective in this environment, making it
difficult for governments to oppose trends established by private sector transactions.

One reason for this limited ability of central banks to
intervene in foreign exchange markets is that, generally, official
reserves of gold and foreign currencies have not increased in
line with the size of the flows which can disturb exchange rates.
Although in the case of the UK there have been substantial
additions to the official reserves in recent years (a consequence
of foreign exchange market intervention, even though the
UK has, technically, a floating or market-determined exchange
rate) this growth in the reserves has not matched the increase in
capital flows. In 1986, for example, the UK's reserves (valued
in US dollars) were lower than in 1979. The official reserve
itself is also vulnerable to changes in exchange rate, which
compounds the problem of ensuring adequate reserves. As the
value of the US dollar fell in the mid 1980s, so did the value of
the UK reserves. Since the mid 1970s the monetary authorities
of the UK and other countries have felt a greater concern for
the domestic monetary consequences of intervention in the
foreign exchange market. As we saw in Chapter 5, the buying
and selling of foreign currencies by the Bank of England, using
sterling, can have an effect on the domestic money stock.At
times adherence to money targets might prove incompatible
with heavy intervention in the currency markets. The floating
exchange rate regime has thus become less managed from about
1980 than was the practice in its early days, with the US
authorities in particular more reluctant to engage in foreign
currency transactions. The one exception is the European
Monetary System, where member countries have continued to
operate some form of managed exchange rates, although parity
adjustments here have been much more frequent than in the
Bretton Woods era.

9.3 Monetary union, the snake, and the European Monetary System

Despite the adoption of floating exchange rates, within many
European countries there has been a persistent desire to

maintain some degree of exchange rate stability. Since 1979 this desire has been manifested in the European Monetary System, whereby most of the member countries of the European Community have agreed to limit the fluctuations of their respective currencies. But this scheme should be seen in the context of the longer-term aspirations of some countries for greater economic and monetary union in Europe, and the steps that have been taken to achieve this.

Monetary union has long been seen as a way of bringing about greater economic and political unity within the Community. The Werner Report of October 1970 mapped out a stage-by-stage plan to achieve economic and monetary union (EMU) by 1980, although it concentrated more on monetary union and assumed that economic union would automatically follow. The stage outlined in the Werner Plan were as follows :

(a) A progressive narrowing of the margins within which the exchange rates of member currencies would be permitted to fluctuate *vis-a-vis* each other, with some arrangement for financing of countries in deficit by the countries in surplus.
(b) A pooling of foreign exchange reserves.
(c) Eventually the elimination of exchange rate margins, with the establishment of a common currency recognized as being perhaps the best way of embodying this.
(d) The establishment of a single central bank.

The Report's recommendations were approved in principle by the European Community (EC) in 1971 and, as a prelude to the first stage, central banks were invited to restrict fluctuations in their currencies around the existing par values. Under the then prevailing adjustable peg arrangements, any one currency could fluctuate within a band (or 'tunnel') 1 per cent either side of the dollar par value, so if one EC currency moved from its floor to its ceiling and another moved from its ceiling to its floor there would be a 4 per cent relative fluctuation in the values of the two currencies. The avoidance of such fluctuations was considered desirable not only as a first stage in monetary union but also for the smooth operation of the Common Agricultural Policy, since food prices are calculated according to the exchange value of member currencies.

However, the widening of the margin of fluctuation either side of par to $2^1/4$ per cent at the Smithsonian Conference in December 1971 posed a threat to EC plans for limited exchange rate fluctuations amongst member currencies. If one EC currency rose from its floor to its ceiling against the dollar, whilst another fell from its ceiling to its floor, there would be a 9 per cent change in the relative values of the two currencies. Accordingly the 'snake in the tunnel' scheme was devised as a way of restricting EC exchange rate fluctuations. The basic idea (see *Figure 9.2*) was that members agreed to maintain no more than a $2^1/4$ per cent band around *all* their respective currencies so as to set a limit to the degree to which exchange values could fluctuate (the 'snake'). At the same time, all EC currencies would move together as a bloc within the $4^1/2$ per cent Smithsonian band of fluctuation against the dollar (the 'tunnel').

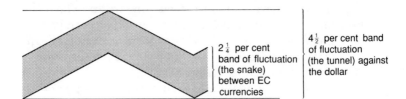

Figure 9.2 *The snake in the tunnel*

Obviously the snake arrangements required intervention by domestic monetary authorities when currencies looked likely to break out of the $2^1/4$ per cent band. Therefore the EC central banks made arrangements to sell the stronger currencies when they threatened to break through the snake ceiling and to buy the weaker currencies when they seemed likely to fall through the snake floor. Furthermore, a settlement arrangement was made whereby the creditor countries could exchange on a monthly basis their accumulations of the weaker currencies (which they had been buying in the EC exchange markets) for some other form of reserve asset. The six original members of the EC commenced operating the 'snake in the tunnel' scheme in 1972, and the UK along with Eire and Denmark also participated in May 1972 while negotiating entry to the

Community. But sterling was soon withdrawn from the scheme when the pound was floated in June 1972.

The advent of generalized floating in early 1973 meant that there was no longer any requirement to keep the snake in the tunnel. The snake was now allowed to float against the other major currencies, but a maximum spread of $2^{1}/_{4}$ per cent was still retained for the currencies in the snake. Also in 1973, the European Monetary Cooperation Fund (EMCF) was established as a body to operate the snake arrangements, its major responsibilities being to record the currency transactions between the central banks of the participating countries and to administer the short-term financing settlements. However, the successful operation of the snake was hindered by the adverse circumstances of the time: exchange rates were no longer pegged against the dollar; there had been a massive increase in oil price which resulted in larger payments imbalances and severe exchange rate pressures; domestic rates of inflation were showing a tendency to diverge markedly; and the world economy was moving into recession. Under such pressures it proved very difficult for monetary authorities to intervene in foreign exchange markets to ensure stable rates of exchange between all EC currencies. Indeed, Italy left the snake in February 1973; France left in January 1974, rejoined, and then left again in March 1976; and the UK and Eire remained outside the scheme after 1972. The EC seemed to have moved further away from the aims of the first stage of the Werner recommendations now that most exchange rates in the Community were floating against each other.

Although the Werner plan failed, the concept of EMU was not abandoned. Indeed it was still argued that determined efforts should be made towards monetary union so that eventually a common currency could be issued by a European central bank. Such a development would aid economic and political union and, like the existence of a common currency between regions of the same country (see Section 7.2.2), would facilitate capital account adjustment between member countries. However, it is now recognized that progress in this direction requires a great deal more cooperation in other fields, such as monetary and budgetary policy, than was originally acknowledged. The Marjolin Report (1975) identified such weaknesses in the previous conception of EMU and suggested that cooperation on a much wider basis was required before EMU would become tenable. The Tindemans Report (1976) recommended a gradual approach towards EMU, and suggested that the countries able to proceed in the direction of monetary union should do so, and others should follow suit later when conditions became more favourable. Neither of these reports, however, has made the previous mistake of trying to set targets or deadlines for the eventual achievement of EMU. At the Bremen summit conference in July 1978 a new impetus was given towards monetary union by the agreement of heads of the nine Common Market governments to press ahead with a detailed study for a new *European Monetary System* (EMS). The main points of the plan, intended to promote closer economic and monetary integration in the EC, are as follows:

(a) The scheme aims to limit fluctuations of member EC currencies against each other. Exchange rate intervention is to be carried out by central banks according two sets of criteria. One is a *parity grid* arrangement, whereby upper and lower intervention rates are established for each currency against every other currency. No member's currency can move by more than $2^{1}/_{4}$ per cent against any other member currency, although initially the Italian lira was allowed to move by up to 6 per cent. The second is the *ECU divergence indicator*. The European currency unit (ECU) is used as a basis for calculating a central rate for each member's currency. The ECU is based on a basket of EC currencies, including sterling, weighted according to their relative importance in EC output. [3] Each currency is allocated a maximum percentage deviation against its ECU central rate, and when it has reached this limit there is the presumption (but not an obligation) that the domestic government concerned will undertake remedial action.

(b) An exchange rate stabilization fund has been created by the pooling of 20 per cent of the gold and dollar reserves of central banks with the European Monetary Cooperation Fund

[3] The ECU, as a composite currency unit, contains specified amounts of the currencies of ten of the member states of the European Community; German mark 0.719; pound sterling 0.0878; French franc 1.31; Italian lira 140; Dutch guilder 0.256; Belgian franc 3.71; Luxembourg franc 0.14; Danish kroner 0.219; Irish pound 0.00871; Greek drachma 1.15.

in return for issues of ECUs. The ECUs are then available for use by central banks, to finance foreign exchange intervention and to settle claims between the Community's central banks. At first the EMCF was to be used merely as a way of recording transactions and as a temporary depository for the pooled reserve funds. At a later stage – initially set for March 1981 – it was to be developed into a full European Monetary Fund. This has not, however, happened and the EMCF continues. The funds deposited with the EMCF can be used for supporting the currency grid of exchange rates between member countries as well as the provision of medium-term credit facilities. The credit facilities are available 'very short term', up to ten weeks; 'short-term', up to nine months; and 'medium term', between two and five years. However, funds provided in the third category would be available only if a country's domestic policies were adjusted to that prescribed by the Community's Council of Ministers.

The new EMS first began operations in March 1979, but without the participation of the UK in the exchange rate mechanism. However, the Bank of England has been party to the arrangements for placing gold and dollar reserves with the EMCF on a three-month temporary basis in exchange for ECUs. The UK continues to remain outside full membership.

The parity grid arrangement is similar in its operation to the snake in that absolute intervention points are set for each member currency against every other at which central banks are obliged to buy or sell their own currencies. But in practice it is the divergence indicator which often triggers intervention because it is designed to serve as an early warning device for when strong or weak currencies look likely to test their parity limits. This is a distinctive feature of the arrangements, both because it identifies pressure at an early stage and also in that it establishes the *source* of disturbance and whether it is a weak or strong currency. Apart from intervention, the other usual response to currency pressure has been a rise or reduction in interest rates. However, interest rate rises on weaker currencies have been more frequent and larger than the reductions which have been effected by countries with strong currencies. But despite intervention and interest rate adjustments, it has been necessary for realignments of exchange rates to take place on a frequent basis.

Since the EMS became operational there have been ten realignments of parities. This has involved the revaluation (upwards) of some currencies whilst others were devalued. The realignment of January 1987, for example, required a 3 per cent revaluation of the Deutschmark and the Netherlands guilder and a 2 per cent revaluation of the Belgian/Luxembourg franc. One of the reasons for the exchange rate adjustments is that inflation rates and trade performances of member countries have failed to converge sufficiently, making exchange rate adjustments necessary in order to maintain a reasonable degree of competitiveness and prevent excessive balance of payments imbalances.

In September 1987 the committee of European Community central bank governors decided to change a number of rules relating to interventions and financing within the EMS and strengthen cooperation among the various central banks. These changes followed the exchange rate realignments of January 1987, and the basis for concern was that individual EC countries' currencies continued to move differently in response to the depreciation of the US dollar. If this situation persisted then it would clearly undermine the cohesion of the EMS. The September changes were intended to make the EMS less vulnerable to external influences, and to this end further agreement on foreign exchange intervention policies and interest rate policies was made with the particular objective of reducing incentives for short-term capital movements. Three measures were agreed:

(a) The duration of the very short-term financing which central banks could draw through the EMCF was increased to three and a half months (an increase of one month). This change applied to the *obligatory* foreign exchange intervention, i.e. when exchange rates moved to their limit. Also, the financial ceiling applied to the renewal of short-term central bank indebtedness, automatically available for exchange rate intervention, was doubled.

(b) Finance from the EMCF for intra-marginal intervention in foreign exchange markets (i.e. interventions within the permitted margins of fluctuation, but not obligatory on a member country) was made easier. Some EC countries had argued that if intra-marginal interventions could be financed through the EMCF then this might prevent the obligatory interventions when a currency had reached the limits of its permitted flexibility.

(c) The use of ECUs for repayment of intervention borrowings by a member country was also made easier as long as the creditor country (i.e. the country providing the currency which was needed for foreign exchange support operations) did not develop an unbalanced composition of reserves. This aspect of the agreement would be subject to review in the light of experience.

These changes were seen as part of a comprehensive strategy to foster exchange rate cohesion. Such cohesion was dependent also on all member countries achieving through their economic and monetary policies further convergence towards internal stability. There was agreement to strengthen the procedure for joint monitoring of economic and monetary policies within each member country.

9.3.1 AN ASSESSMENT OF THE EMS

The more immediate objective of the EMS was to ensure greater stability of exchange rates between member countries. The realignment of exchange rates discussed above might suggest that it has *not* been very successful in promoting greater exchange rate stability. But such matters are relative: the major currencies outside the EMS have been characterized by a high degree of exchange rate volatility, and the proper comparison is to consider the effect on intra-community exchange rates *without* the operation of the EMS. The mere fact that the original members of the EMS have remained within the scheme suggests some degree of success. More recently the relative stability of the EMS currencies (including the more vulnerable Italian lira) has been a result of not only exchange rate intervention by Community central banks but also coordinated interest rate adjustments under the September 1987 agreement, intended to strengthen the operational mechanisms of the system. This latter change is clearly important since foreign exchange intervention by one central bank within the EMS could be undermined by an 'inappropriate' interest rate policy (thus causing changes in capital flows) by another central bank.

Nevertheless, it is widely recognized that exchange rate adjustments within the EMS will only become less frequent if the economic performance and the economic policies of member countries are converging and consistent. This too was recognized in the 1987 agreement. To some extent the commitment to fixed parities by member countries is of itself a discipline and an inducement to pursue policies which will assist in the convergence of economic performance. For example, relatively high rates of inflation in one country will tend to produce balance of payments 'deficits' and a downward pressure on the exchange rate; such a country thus faces the necessity of imposing anti-inflationary policies in order to maintain the exchange rate.

The longer-term aspects of the EMS, however, have not been a success. The European Monetary Fund has not come into existence and the moves towards a common currency and a Community central bank are little nearer reality. Without the full membership of the UK within the EMS and a commitment to the longer-term aims, such developments within the Community seem difficult or unlikely. The reluctance of the UK and other member countries to go further stems from the inherent feature of monetary union: the relinquishing of a high degree of sovereignty in economic policy-making to a supra-national body. One might add, however, that if member countries achieved and sustained fixed parities then this would be the virtual equivalent of a single European currency.[4]

9.4 The European Investment Bank

In this chapter we have examined the impact of floating exchange rates on the hopes for economic and monetary union within the EC. At the same time we explained the role of one EC institution, the European Monetary Cooperation Fund, in administering the snake and then the EMS arrangements. Here

[4] The Scottish pound circulates within England quite freely because the 'exchange rate' between the English pound and the Scottish pound is Scots £1 = English £1 and it is known with absolute certainty that this will always be the case.

we intend to explain the operation of another EC institution, the European Investment Bank, which will probably have an important part to play in future progress towards economic and monetary union within the EC.

Origin and purpose The European Investment Bank (EIB) is a European Community institution set up under the Treaty of Rome in 1958 as a source of long-term finance for investment projects. The board of governors consists of the finance minister from each member state. The routine management of the EIB is carried out by a board of directors, of which there are nineteen nominated by member countries, with France, West Germany, and the UK appointing nine directors. The terms under which the EIB was formed prescribe that the purpose of finance provided shall be to support: projects aiding development of less advanced regions of the Community; modernization and conversion projects in essentially declining areas; and projects, usually large, which are of interest to several member countries or the Community as a whole.

Source of funds Its main source of funds is bonds and loans raised on a commercial basis on the capital markets in the EC and on other international markets also. In addition, it has capital subscribed by member states of the EC. The Bank's statute stipulates that its lending cannot exceed 250 per cent of its subscribed capital. Paid-in capital by member countries amounts to about 10 per cent of subscribed capital and represents only a small part of the total funds obtained by the EIB.

Nature of operations The Bank operates on a non-profit-making basis, and so its interest charges are close to the average rates it has to pay in the EC and international capital markets. These relatively low interest rates make it an attractive source of finance to borrowers, and the fact that it is a non-profit-making organization means that it can involve itself in socially oriented projects which may have long pay-off periods.

Loans are intended to supplement finance obtained from other sources, and so the EIB only lends up to 40 per cent of the cost of fixed investments of a project with a minimum size of around £1 million. The term of the loan is approximately 7 – 12 years for industrial projects but can go up to 20 years for infrastructure investments (these are investments in areas such as energy, transport, and communications which are beneficial to economic expansion in general). It is also intended to help finance small ventures, and the EIB grants 'global loans' to intermediary financial institutions, such as Finance for Industry in the UK, which on-lend the funds for suitable projects after prior approval from the EIB. Finance for major projects is provided by loans negotiated directly with the Bank.

Adequate security for loans is required since the EIB itself borrows at commercial rates. Thus the Bank prefers a guarantee from industrial or financial groups associated with the project, a public authority, or from the government in whose territory the project is being undertaken. EIB loans are usually made in the form of a 'cocktail' of several currencies, depending upon the currencies which the Bank has available at the time of the loan. Loan repayments are due in the currencies in which they are made. Repayments can be delayed for up to four years until the project yields a return, but thereafter they are normally due in six-monthly instalments.

Recipients of loans   Between 1981 and 1985 the EIB undertook loans of ECU28.5 billion,[5] and of this over 90 per cent was within the European Community. Almost half of these funds allocated within the Community were used in Italy, with France and the UK obtaining 15 per cent and 13 per cent respectively. Much of the bank's lending in the UK has gone to major public sector developments such as the Sullom Voe oil terminal in the Shetland Isles, British Rail's advanced passenger train, and various National Water Council projects. The EIB made available ECU1.8 billion to countries outside the Community, mainly Mediterranean and African countries.

9.5 Fixed versus floating exchange rates

The previous chapter and the present one have examined in detail the operation of both a fixed and a floating exchange rate system. This section attempts to identify the major strengths and weaknesses of these two systems. It should be recognized that floating exchange rates have usually been adopted (e.g. in

---

[5] Based on the 1988 value of the ECU this would be approximately equivalent to £ 20 billion.

the 1930s and since 1973) when adverse conditions have caused a breakdown in the prevailing system of fixed exchange rates. Therefore the comparison of the two systems in practice should take account of the unfavourable circumstances in which floating has been introduced.

9.5.1 CASE FOR FLOATING (AGAINST FIXED) EXCHANGE RATES

Simplicity There is no need for countries to decide what constitutes the appropriate exchange rate or for their general agreement on whether deficit or surplus countries are responsible for the adjustment burden. It is simply demand and supply pressures which determine the appropriate exchange rate for each currency.

Continuous adjustment If a country is suffering balance of payments difficulties because of a long-run decline in its competitive position, then a floating exchange rate allows a gradual depreciation of the home currency to come about, thus providing a continuous stimulus to exports and a continuous discouragement to imports. [6] In contrast, the adjustable peg system was characterized by long periods of crisis in deficit countries such as the UK with exchange rate adjustment occurring infrequently and belatedly, e.g. the devaluations of 1949 and 1967. The operation of the adjustable peg required deficit countries to carry out expenditure-reducing policies between exchange rate adjustments, whereas floating permits automatic adjustment to take place via the exchange rate.

Independence of domestic policies Under the adjustable peg system, deficit countries had to direct fiscal and monetary policies at the external situation since expenditure-reducing was the only way in which the balance of payments could be improved without devaluation. In the UK, for example, economic expansions often had to be cut short by restrictive domestic policies as an increased demand for imports led to a deterioration in the balance of payments. Consequently internal policies were often dictated by the external situation. But if exchange rate variations are successful in bringing about automatic adjustment, then governments may have greater independence in the use of

[6] See Appendix 2 at the end of this chapter for an illustration of this process.

domestic policies. In the UK at the present time (1988) the balance of trade deficit has increased from £10.2 billion in 1987 to almost £20 billion in 1988. This is the largest trade deficit (relative to national income) in recent history and has been caused largely because of the sustained growth of domestic incomes and spending since 1981. The growth of imports has been over 11 per cent p.a. whereas export growth has only been 7.7 per cent p.a., and if one considers exports and imports of goods *other than oil products* then the figures are 13 per cent p.a. import growth and 9 per cent p.a. export growth. Ultimately there would be a depreciation of the exchange rate under a free-floating regime, but the policy response of the government has been to prevent this occurring by sustaining a high level of domestic interest rates. This has reduced independence in the use of domestic policies.

Insulation from external inflation With fixed exchange rates, inflation abroad is transmitted directly into higher import prices. Of course the effect on the domestic price level will be influenced by the importance of imports in the home economy and by the ability of domestic industry to provide substitutes for the higher-priced imports. Floating, on the other hand, insulates a country with stable prices from world inflation since its currency would be continually appreciating, thereby offsetting the rise in import prices. [7]

Reduced need for official reserves With floating, there should in theory be no need for official intervention in foreign exchange markets, and therefore no need to accumulate large stocks of official reserves. But in practice, government intervention may be considered desirable to neutralize short-term disturbances in the exchange markets. Nevertheless, as long as floating exchange rates are not too volatile, there should be a reduced need for official reserves.

9.5.2 CASE FOR FIXED (AGAINST FLOATING) EXCHANGE RATES

Effectiveness of current account adjustment under floating A floating exchange rate may not be very effective in eliminating a country's current account deficit (or reducing a current acco-

[7] This is demonstrated in the illustration in Appendix 2 to this chapter.

unt surplus) if the elasticites of demand for imports and exports are of an inappropriate value. Therefore continuous current account adjustment via a floating exchange rate may not always be successful.

Uncertainty Capital flows can be unstable. A country which experienced volatile movements in capital flows, operating under a floating regime, would find that balance of payments equilibrium might be attained only by tolerating very wide swings in the foreign exchange value of its currency. Such experience would prove highly disturbing and create considerable uncertainty for business, especially importers and exporters, in that country. The attainment of fixed exchange rates would prove highly attractive. This uncertainty argument in favour of fixed exchange rates is based upon the apparent instability of capital flows. This is illustrated in *Table 9.1,* which shows the net transactions in assets and liabilities between 1977 and 1987. The final column reveals that there has been a continued accumulation of assets by the UK, but the variability of these net transactions is clearly considerable, ranging from £0.7 billion to £14.3 billion. One writer has expressed the problem very succinctly :

By its very nature, the foreign exchange market is a nervous, high-risk, ultra-sensitive mechanism, primarily geared to short-term developments. Of the tens of billions of dollars in daily transactions cleared through the market, only a fraction derive from such fundamental factors as foreign trade and long-term investment. On a day-to-day basis, the market is instead dominated by short-term capital movements in search of quick profits or a hedge against exchange risks. [8]

If there are considerable fluctuations in exchange rates under floating, world trade may be inhibited since traders will become reluctant to enter into commitments because the price paid on delivery may vary to such an extent that the transaction is no longer profitable to one of the parties. [9] In contrast, exchange rate fluctuations cannot by definition be a source of

[8] Charles A. Coombs, *The Arena of International Finance* (Wiley, 1976).

[9] Note that exchange risks can be covered by dealings in the forward exchange markets, but such transactions can be expensive.

uncertainty in world trade under a fixed exchange rate system.

Effects on domestic inflation If exchange rate fluctuations are fairly large under floating, then economies with depreciating currencies should encounter rising import prices. These rising import prices will tend to feed back into domestic prices, especially if imports are a large proportion of GDP and the elasticity of demand for imports is low. The present policy of the UK government towards the exchange rate, to which we alluded in *Section 9.5.1,* is to prevent depreciation, and one of the reasons for this policy is an anxiety that a depreciating pound would raise costs of imports and thus cause a further deterioration in the inflationary situation. [10]

With fixed exchange rates, an inflationary impulse from the exchange rate can only arise when there is a devaluation of the domestic currency. Furthermore, supporters of fixed exchange rates argue that under their system countries have to take action to control domestic inflation or else they will lose reserves under their commitment to support the exchange rate at the prevailing parity. But with floating, it is argued, no such discipline exists. The domestic authorities can simply allow internal inflation to push down the rate of exchange.

Independence of domestic policies The extent to which floating exchange rates enable governments to have greater independence in their domestic policies may be exaggerated. Although the domestic authorities do not have the immediate problem of defending a fixed exchange rate under the present system, the external situation has still had an overriding influence on most countries' domestic policies, as was indicated by UK experience during most of the 1970s and the late 1980s.

Need for official reserves Because governments have frequently intervened in foreign exchange markets, the operation of floating exchange rates has, like the adjustable peg system before it, required the availability of official reserves. The major reason for this is that exchange markets appear to be

---

[10] To illustrate this point fairly simply; the UK imports about 30 per cent of the goods and materials needed, which means that a 10 per cent depreciation of the pound will add about 10 per cent to costs of imports and add about 3 percentage points to the internal rate of inflation, assuming the higher costs are passed on in higher prices.

fairly volatile, and therefore governments have required large reserves of foreign currencies to moderate unwanted fluctuations in the exchange value of their currencies. Therefore, managed floating does not have the advantage of making redundant the holding of official reserves.

Any judgment on the preferability of fixed or floating exchange rates must take into account these considerations and recognize that it is a matter of balancing advantages against disadvantages. However, it must be acknowledged also that the conditions of the time have an important part to play in determining the feasibility of any particular type of exchange rate system. Under stable conditions some form of fixed exchange rate system may work effectively, but floating may be the only option when the world economy is in a state of instability. Thus floating has often been adopted as a last resort when a system of fixed exchange rates has collapsed, as was the case in 1973.

9.6 Some recent developments in the international monetary system

9.6.1 THE INTERNATIONAL MONETARY FUND

The widespread acceptance of floating exchange rates has been associated with a period of less favourable economic developments, such as massive payments imbalances arising from large but often irregular oil prices increases, declining commodity prices (which seriously affect less developed economies), high interest rates during the 1980s (which worsened the debt position of many countries), and lower average economic growth compared with the Bretton Woods era. Together these factors have put new pressures on the international monetary system and on institutions such as the IMF which were designed to operate in a different economic environment. *Table 9.2* shows the changes in the balance of payments (current account) of industrial and non-industrial countries. Although by 1987 the imbalances had declined significantly, one can see the difficulties which faced the developing countries, especially non-fuel exporters. Amongst the industrial countries the emerging deficit problems for the USA and the UK are very clear. It would seem, however, that from 1986 the overall deficit

Table 9.2

Summary of payments balances on current account, 1980–87[1] including official transfers (US $b)

	1980	1981	1982	1983	1984	1985	1986	1987
Industrial countries	−58·1	−15·9	−19·9	−17·3	−58·4	−48·0	−16·4	−43·3
Canada	−1·0	−5·1	2·3	2·5	2·1	−1·4	−7·6	−8·0
United States	1·9	6·9	−8·7	−46·3	−107·0	−115·1	−138·8	−154·0
Japan	−10·7	4·8	6·9	20·8	35·0	49·2	85·8	87·0
France	−4·2	−4·8	−12·1	−4·7	−0·8	0·6	2·9	−4·4
Germany, Fed. Rep. of	−13·8	−3·6	5·1	5·3	9·7	16·5	39·3	45·0
Italy	−10·0	−9·1	−6·2	1·5	−2·5	−3·7	2·6	−1·0
United Kingdom	7·1	13·7	7·8	5·7	2·7	4·2	0·2	−2·6
Other industrial countries	−27·4	−18·7	−14·9	−2·2	2·5	1·7	−0·8	−5·4
Developing countries	30·6	−47·8	−86·4	−63·1	−33·3	−24·3	−40·7	0·3
By region :								
Africa	−2·2	−22·2	−21·5	−12·1	−8·0	−0·2	−8·8	−5·0
Asia	−14·5	−19·1	−17·4	−14·8	−4·3	−13·5	5·1	20·9
Europe	−15·6	−13·7	−8·0	−5·1	−2·9	−3·0	−2·0	0·9
Middle East	92·5	50·0	3·0	−20·2	−15·7	−2·8	−18·2	−5·2
Western Hemisphere	−29·8	−42·9	−42·4	−10·9	−2·5	−4·7	−16·9	−11·3
By analytical criteria :								
Fuel exporters	96·4	34·8	−18·2	−19·6	−5·4	2·3	−32·1	−3·9
Non-fuel exporters	−65·8	−82·3	−68·2	−43·5	−28·0	−26·6	−8·6	4·3
Market borrowers	−35·3	−71·5	−73·7	−29·3	−3·4	6·4	−0·8	20·6
Official borrowers	−9·1	−12·0	−10·5	−8·4	−9·7	−9·5	−8·7	−9·8
Other countries[a]	0·8	−3·4	2·7	3·1	4·8	2·3	3·1	5·7
Total[b]	−26·7	−67·1	−103·5	−77·3	−86·9	−70·0	−54·0	−37·3

[a] Covers estimated balances on current transactions only in convertible currencies of the USSR and non-member countries of Eastern Europe.

[b] Reflects errors, omissions, and asymmetries in reported balance of payments statistics on current account, plus balance of listed groups with countries not included.

Source : IMF *Annual Report* (1988)

position improved; there was a decline from US$54 billion in 1986 to US$ 37·3 billion in 1987.

The size of these deficits has meant, nevertheless, that the *normal* financial facilities available from the IMF have proved inadequate even though the total quotas have been increased substantially: between 1964 and 1988 quotas were raised from SDR14 billion to SDR89.9 billion. It has to be remembered also that the IMF is not a bank – or a development agency; its functions are primarily to do with sustaining an orderly system of international financial relationships, especially exchange rate arrangements, and the provision of relatively short-term finance to countries which have balance of payments problems. Some of the main changes that have taken place are examined below.

9.6.1.1 Changes in the structure of the IMF

Since the second amendment to the articles of agreement the structure of the Fund has been defined as consisting not only of a board of governors, an executive board, and a managing director and staff, but also a council if it is called into being by a decision of the board of governors with an 85 per cent majority of total voting power. To date, no such call has been made.

The roles of the board of governors and the executive board are broadly as described in Section 8.2.3. The interim committee, which was established by a resolution of the board of governors in 1974, has been given more of the responsibilities of the full board since its smaller number of members allows it to work more effectively. This group, comprising twenty-two governors, normally meets twice a year to review world economic conditions and the activities of the IMF. The highest authority of the Fund is still exercised by the board of governors, but the constitution of the interim committee is such that decisions taken there are usually ratified by the full board when it meets annually in the autumn.

9.6.1.24 New IMF facilities

Over the past decade it has been necessary for the Fund to play a more expanded role, principally because of the large current account imbalances identified in *Table 9.2*. The Fund's normal facilities were insufficient to meet the new demands, and so additional resources have been made available. *Figure 9.3* and *Table 9.3* display the main facilities currently available and show clearly the decline in relative importance of the credit

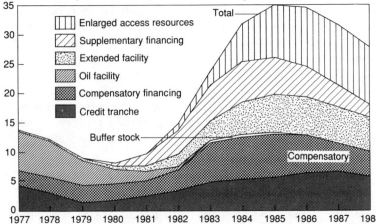

Figure 9.3 *Use of IMF's general resources 30 April 1977 – 88 (excluding SDR 584 million under structural adjustment facility)*

Source : IMF *Annual Report,* 1988

tranches, especially after 1980. The regular facilities provide only 20 per cent of the credit available from the Fund. The oil facility, set up in 1974 to assist countries which had current account difficulties because of higher oil prices, ceased to be available after 1983. Having reached a price of $ 36 a barrel at the beginning of 1981, oil prices began to fall in early 1982 and in April 1986 reached a low point of $ 10 a barrel. The decline in the price of oil in nominal as well as real terms made this clearly less of a problem. In addition to special borrowing facilities the Fund has renewed until 1993 the additional funding through the general arrangements to borrow (see Section 8.2.2) and which now amounts to SDR 17 billion.

The other facilities are as follows :

Compensating financing facility Set up in 1963, this line of credit was made available to countries which had exceptional balance of payments problems caused by special factors, such as a major crop failure, and beyond the control of a particular government. Although less significant it still provides about 15 per cent of funds.

Table 9.3

Outstanding IMF credit by facility and policy, 1982 – 88

	1982		1983		1984		1985		1986		1987		1988	
	mSDR	%	mSDR	%	mSDR	%	mSDR	%	mSDR	%	mSDR	%	mSDR	%
Regular facilities	3,206	21·7	4,721	20·0	5,197	16·4	5,511	15·8	6,315	18·2	6,575	20·8	5,732	20·6
Compensatory financing facility	3,643	24·6	6,837	29·0	7,304	23·0	7,490	21·4	6,430	18·6	4,779	15·1	4,342	15·6
Buffer stock financing facility	—	—	307	1·3	375	1·2	237	0·7	73	0·2	34	0·1	3	—
Oil facility	565	3·8	27	0·1	—	—	—	—	—	—	—	—	—	—
Extended fund facility	2,115	14·3	3,317	14·1	5,568	17·5	6,529	18·7	6,498	18·8	6,242	19·7	5,762	20·7
Supplementary financing facility	4,112	27·8	6,039	25·6	6,920	21·8	6,310	18·0	5,276	15·2	3,769	11·9	2,161	7·8
Enlarged access policy	1,160	7·8	2,342	9·9	6,378	20·1	8,896	25·4	10,047	29·0	10,247	32·4	9,829	35·3
Total	14,802		23,590		31,742		34,973		34,640		31,646		27,829	

Source : IMF Annual Report (1988)

Extended Fund facility This facility provides 20 per cent of credit and was established in 1974 to assist countries on a longer-term basis for supporting adjustment efforts through structural reform and appropriate macroeconomic policies. Borrowers are able to use the facility up to 140 per cent of their quota over a four-year period and with much more relaxed repayment conditions than the normal facilities. The availability of funds under this facility is conditional on appropriate policies being followed by the borrower.

Supplementary financing Providing about 8 per cent of funds, this facility, established in 1977, is intended to assist countries with longer-term problems in their balance of payments, and for which the normal facilities of the Fund are not adequate. As with the extended facility the Fund lays down conditions for borrowing.

Enlarged access resources By far the most important supplement to the Funds resources has been the enlarged access facility, available since March 1981. Both the enlarged access facility and the supplementary financing facility are available to members of the IMF only in conjunction with the use of resources in the upper credit tranches (i.e. they are special arrangements when normal credit lines are insufficient) and are for countries which are facing serious payments imbalances that are large in relation to their quotas. The enlarged access provision accounts for 35 per cent of credit available. The policy of the Fund is that access limits are to be regarded as limits and not entitlements, and provision of funds is conditional on the determination shown by a borrower to remedy its balance of payments problem. The IMF decided, in 1988, that the limit to enlarged access would be 440 per cent of a country's quota over a three-year period.

Structural adjustment facility This was established in March 1986 to provide balance of payments assistance to low-income developing countries. Loans are available for a three-year period in support of a three-year macroeconomic and structural adjustment programme. Repayments are in ten instalments beginning six years after the date of borrowing and completed at the end of the tenth year after borrowing. Interest is charged at 0·5 per cent p.a.

The funds made available under these supplementary schemes are obtained by the IMF through various borrowing arrangements with member countries such as West Germany, Japan and Saudi Arabia, as well as the Bank for International Settlements (BIS). Conditions for repayment of resources to the Fund vary according to the facility which has been used, with repayment in the form of SDRs or designated foreign currencies. For example, borrowings under the compensatory finance facility have to be repaid in quarterly instalments beginning three years and ending not later than five years after the date of the borrowings, whereas the enlarged access repayments are required twice a year beginning three and a half years and ending not later than seven years after the date of the borrowings. The extended Fund facility provides for a maximum of a ten-year repayment period after borrowing. The Fund is obliged to pay market-related rates of interest on its borrowings, and therefore members of the Fund which use borrowed resources pay an appropriate rate. For example, under the policy on enlarged access, the rate of interest charged to borrowers is the net cost to the Fund plus a margin of 0·20 per cent. In 1987 – 88 the rate of charge on enlarged access was 7·39 per cent.

It should be emphasized that private markets have remained the main source of financing for countries with balance of payments problems. However, to such countries the fact that the Fund has agreed domestic programmes as a condition for loans has often been the key factor in encouraging lending by banks and other private sector organizations. In this respect the importance of agreement with the IMF on access to its facilities is much greater for many borrowers than the actual size of the funds provided by the Fund would appear to indicate.

Despite the greater emphasis on additional facilities, it has been necessary for the ordinary financing arrangements to be enlarged by regular increases in quotas. The most recent review of quotas set up in March 1987 failed to conclude its review, and as a result the IMF board of governors requested fresh proposals for new quotas by April 1989; until that review the level of Fund quotas remained unchanged at SDR 89·99 billion.

9.6.1.3 Developments relating to the SDR

When the SDR was first introduced in 1970 its main purpose was to serve as an additional reserve asset because of a perceived shortage of gold and dollars. From 1974 onwards it evolved as a unit of account, first when its value was linked to a basket of currencies and then as the IMF denominated its growing balance of payments financing in terms of the SDR.

After the second amendment was ratified in April 1978, this process was speeded up because the concept of an official gold price was abandoned (the final step in eliminating gold from its central role in the Fund as a standard of value), the Fund's own unit of account became the SDR and members agreed that the SDR should become the principal reserve asset of the international monetary system.

Further practical steps were taken following the second amendment to make the SDR 'the principal reserve asset' :

(a) A new allocation of SDRs was made between 1979 and 1981 which increased the total to SDR 21 billion. No further issues have been made and at April 1988 this represents the cumulative total issued since the introduction of SDRs.

(b) SDRs could now be used more freely among participating countries : it became possible to use them to settle obligations without changing them first into currencies; they could be loaned to other countries; and they could be used as a security for a loan by another central bank or government.

However, it is essential for private sector as well as official transactions to be denominated in SDRs if they are to become the principal reserve asset. Although the earlier calculation of the value of the SDR in terms of a basket of sixteen currencies had the advantage of making it more stable in value than individual currencies, it had nevertheless certain shortcomings. One was that it might not be as attractive as some of the stronger currencies and so its general acceptability might suffer. Another is that its method of valuation was too complex and this would detract from its widespread adoption. In response to these problems the IMF decided from January 1981 to reduce the size of the basket of currencies determining the value of the SDR from sixteen to five and to simplify the calculation of the interest rate on the SDR. The five currencies chosen were the dollar, mark, French franc, yen, and sterling, weighted to broadly reflect their relative importance in international trade and finance. It was hoped that this simplification would enhance further the attractiveness of the SDR in both official and private transactions.

There were indications after 1979 that commercial banks and financial markets might use the SDR to denominate financial instruments created in the private sector capital markets. Some issues of securities denominated in SDRs were made in 1980 – 81 but none since. Nevertheless it is used as the unit of account not only by the IMF but also by a number of international organizations of modest importance, e.g. Arab Monetary Fund, Economic Community of West African States, Nordic Investment Bank. The International Air Transport Association uses movements of currencies against the SDR as a basis for reviewing cargo tariffs, and as we have already noted seven member countries peg their exchange rate to the SDR.

It is plain, however, that the innovation of SDRs has failed to develop as originally conceived. The allocations of SDRs by the IMF have been very limited, (no new issues since 1981) and consequently SDRs are only a small part of countries' reserves. The US dollar and the euro-currency markets were the main providers of additional liquidity, and therefore liquidity provided by the IMF was regarded as unnecessary or even potentially inflationary. Private sector use of the SDR as a unit of account or the basis for international transactions has been very limited because of the absence of SDR-denominated assets which could be purchased with SDR-denominated deposits. If the IMF had been a major borrower and issuer of SDR-denominated assets then the SDR might have been used more extensively.

9.6.2 THE US DOLLAR

We referred in Section 9.6.1 to the growing current account deficit of the USA, and *Table 9.2* shows this clearly : it moved from a current account surplus of $6.9 billion in 1981 to a deficit of $154 billion in 1987. This huge deficit can be explained by reference to the growth of demand within the USA which has drawn an increasing volume of imports. In the

early part of 1988, for example, the volume of imports was 83
per cent higher than in 1980 compared with an average import
growth for the rest of the world in the same period of 28 per
cent. Alternatively one might note that, relative to the growth
of domestic demand in the USA, imports were 41 per cent
greater in early 1988 than in 1980 – compared with, say, 7 per
cent higher for France and 17 per cent higher in West
Germany. One of the factors sustaining the growth of domestic
demand in the USA has been the very considerable federal
government budget deficit. Export growth over the same
period has shown an increase of only 36 per cent which,
although better than the world average growth of 28 per cent,
is clearly not sufficient to cover the large increase in import
demand. The demand for imported goods by the USA has been
sustained not only by the growth of incomes during the
economic expansion since 1982 but also by the considerable
appreciation of the US dollar in foreign exchange markets
between 1979 and 1985 (the depreciation of the dollar beginning in March 1985). During this period the dollar appreciated
by 55 per cent as an average against major currencies. In
particular, the exchange rate of the dollar against the Deutschmark and yen were such that US demand for goods from these
two countries must have been greatly stimulated. These rates
were as follows :

1979 (average)   *8 March 1985*   *7 October 1988*
US $1 = DM 1·83   US $1 = DM 3·39   US $1 = DM 1·86
US $1 = Y 219·00   US $1 = Y 261·30   US $1 = Y 133·20

It is clear from these data that the dollar appreciated against
the Deutschmark by 85 per cent and against the yen by 20 per
cent between 1979 and 1985. The position was reversed
towards the end of 1988, with a depreciation of 45 per cent and
49 per cent respectively.

Our discussion of the balance of payments in Section 7.1.1
showed that payments imbalances on the current account
would need to be offset by transactions in assets and liabilities
(the capital account); a deficit on the current account, as in the
case of the USA (and also the UK), is offset by inflows of funds
in the form of short-term and long-term capital. This has
indeed been happening to the USA, and much of the capital

funds moving to the USA have come from Japan. Our earlier analysis of balance of payments adjustment under floating exchange rates suggests that correction must come about through foreign exchange *depreciation* of the deficit country's currency relative to other countries. This could mean either a uniform, across-the-board depreciation of a greater depreciation against some currencies than others, i.e. some currencies in effect appreciate against the deficit country. In respect of the US dollar this might well require a general depreciation as well as much greater depreciation against the Deutschmark and the yen. This would make US exports generally cheaper in world markets but especially so in West Germany and Japan, and at the same time cause US imports to become generally more expensive in the USA but especially goods from West Germany and Japan. Without exchange rate depreciation the only alternative method of remedying the US trade deficit is for the US federal government to adopt contractionary economic policies aimed at reducing the rate of growth of domestic demand. Such policies might include raising federal taxes, cutting government expenditure, and raising interest rates in the USA.

In view of the above assessment one might ask why, therefore, the US situation is regarded as a problem. To summarize :

(a) The USA is the largest single economy in the world, accounting for about 40 per cent of the output of all the OECD countries. It is larger than the whole of the European Community combined. Changes in economic activity within the USA therefore have a significant effect on the level of exports of other countries and therefore affect the level of economic activity in most of the non-communist economies. If the USA were to solve its balance of trade problem by internal deflationary policies aimed at reducing USA demand for imports, then the effect on the exports of the rest of the world would be noticeable and serious. It could conceivably trigger recession in other countries.

(b) The chronic trade deficits have resulted in the USA becoming the major debtor country in the sense that other countries' savings have flowed to the USA, attracted by relatively high rates of interest and the apparent security of investment in the world's most powerful economy. As we noted earlier, these capital inflows have financed the current account deficits. It is usually assumed that although the ever-increasing indebtedness of the USA cannot continue indefinitely, the elimination of the imbalance should not be brought about by sudden and severe adjustment. One view is that the rising indebtedness might suddenly trigger a loss of confidence, with the consequential withdrawal of funds from the USA and massive sale of US dollars; the exchange rate for the dollar would collapse, and with it would collapse the value of dollar-denominated assets held by non-US residents. Such a fall in the value of wealth held outside the USA could itself trigger economic contraction on a wide scale.

(c) The need by the USA to finance the deficit by – in effect – foreign borrowing is regarded as a major factor sustaining high interest rates in the USA as well as other countries. Such high rates, it is held, are a disincentive to investment which is needed to sustain world economic growth.

(d) The growing indebtedness of the USA is regarded as unacceptable because it is draining savings away from other, less prosperous economies. One assertion is that the world's richest country is maintaining its high and raising standard of living by borrowing and thus depriving other countries – with very much lower living standards – of investible funds.

(e) A widely held view is that the USA current account deficit must be corrected but that the correction should produce 'a soft landing'. Essentially the recommendations consist of a combination of demand restraint within the USA, and a key component of this is a reduction in the federal government deficit, together with a moderated fall in the foreign exchange value of the US dollar in order to restrain import growth and boost exports (the depreciation of the dollar would cheapen US exports and raise the price of imports).

The essentials of the problem have been thoroughly analysed in the past few years; the difficulty has been to obtain international agreement on solutions. There have been several significant steps, as follows.

Plaza Agreement 1985 This agreement by the governments of five major economies (Japan, West Germany, France, UK, and the USA), known as the 'group of five', was that the dollar was overvalued (see *Table 9.6*) and that the central banks of the group of five should regulate the decline in the dollar's foreign exchange value by a policy of managed floating, i.e. foreign exchange market intervention by the central banks. It is clear from the data that the dollar began to depreciate steadily after March 1985.

Louvre Accord 1987 The finance ministers and central bank governors of Canada, France, West Germany, Japan, the UK, and the USA met in February 1987 (at the Louvre) and agreed to intensify efforts at economic policy coordination to promote more balanced economic growth and reduce existing imbalances. Since the Plaza Agreement the US current account deficit had continued to increase and the current account surpluses of West Germany and Japan also continued to rise substantially. The communique issued by the participants stated that 'surplus countries committed themselves to following policies designed to strengthen domestic demand and to reducing external surpluses' and 'deficit countries committed themselves to encourage steady, low-inflation growth while reducing their domestic imbalances and external deficits.' The accord also included agreement to 'foster stability of exchange rates around current levels'.

Venice Economic Declaration 1987 At an economic summit of the group of seven (Canada, France, West Germany, Italy, Japan, the UK, and the USA) in June 1987 in Venice, it was agreed to strengthen arrangements for multilateral surveillance and economic coordination. Of considerable importance, it was agreed that governments should develop medium-term economic objectives and projections for their economies which were mutually consistent, as well as using 'performance indicators' to determine whether there were significant deviations from an intended course that required remedial action.

The Louvre Accord and the Venice summit represent quite significant economic agreement because :

(a) There was the recognition that elimination of trade deficits can be accomplished by policy measures in both deficit *and* surplus economies, i.e. demand moderation in the deficit countries and demand stimulation in the surplus countries as well as regulated exchange rate adjustments.

(b) The setting of economic objectives and projections by individual countries would imply that the 'success' of economic policy could be tested and judged by other countries, and by implication that appropriate economic policies would need to be introduced if objectives were not being achieved.

Since the group of seven meeting in Venice there have been several statements by the group referring to the world economy and the need for intensified policy coordination. In 1987 there were three further statements after the Venice summit, maintaining the impetus towards greater policy coordination.

Toronto Economic Declaration 1988 In June 1988 another summit meeting of the group of seven extended the area of concern to include the overriding need to resist protectionism and strengthen the multilateral trading system; to develop a strategy for economic development and the debt problem of the less developed economies; and to deal with the world agricultural problem. The declaration recognized the special needs of the poorest developing countries and the proposals included concessional interest rates on debt as well as the adjustment of repayment periods.

The shift of emphasis of the Toronto declaration probably derives from :

(a) A recognition that by 1987 the fiscal position of the USA had shown improvement since the federal deficit had been reduced by the equivalent of 2 per cent of GNP; and West Germany, for example, had maintained an expansionary fiscal position since 1985.

(b) A diminishing of the current account imbalances by 1987 (see *Table 9.2*). The growth of the current account *deficit* of the USA was showing signs of moderating throughout 1987 and into 1988; the increase in the current account *surpluses* of Japan and West Germany was slowing markedly in 1987 and 1988.

(c) An awareness that the debt problem of the developing countries – particularly the group of fifteen heavily indebted nations [11] (see Section 8.2.2) required monitoring. Although the current balances of most developing countries had begun to improve after 1981, for many countries their ability to service

[11] Argentina, Bolivia, Brazil, Chile, Columbia, Ivory Coast, Ecuador, Mexico, Morocco, Nigeria, Peru, Philippines, Uruguay, Venezuela, Yugoslavia.

their heavy debts was less in 1987 than in 1982. Total debt too continued to increase from $633 billion in 1980 to $1,217 billion in 1987, of which about 40 per cent was owed by the fifteen heavily indebted countries.

9.7 Summary

(a) Under managed floating, exchange rates are free to move according to market forces but governments may intervene in an attempt to stabilize any short-term fluctuations. The characteristic features of an international monetary system based on floating are as follows :

Adjustment can now come about automatically via the exchange rate, although the success of this mechanism depends upon the elasticity of demand for imports and exports as far as the current account is concerned, and on the stability of capital flows for an overall balance of payments.

Liquidity is based less on the dollar or other key reserve assets and more on variety of currencies, since there is no obligation to peg individual currencies to any particular standard.

Cooperation seems to be less of an immediate necessity with market-determined exchange rates, but coordination of national policies still seems desirable if conflict and economic stagnation are to be avoided in the long run.

(b) In theory floating exchange rates should adjust to compensate for differences in domestic inflation rates. But the purchasing power parity theorem has not been a very successful explanation over short periods because in practice large discrepancies in real exchange rates have emerged. One reason is that current account flows no longer dominate the supply of and demand for currencies, and that capital transactions have assumed a greater relative importance. In this environment official intervention in the foreign exchange markets has less chance of achieving even short-term success, with the result that floating has become less managed in recent years.

(c) The general adoption of floating has also posed problems for the objective of economic and monetary union within the EC. It had been hoped that the removal of exchange rate fluctuations between EC currencies would constitute the first stage toward monetary union, but the widespread acceptance of floating has made this aim more difficult to achieve, although the European Monetary System has had some success in this respect.

(d) Both fixed and floating exchange rates have advantages and disadvantages, although the history of managed floating to date does cast doubt on some of the stronger claims originally made in favour of floating. However, floating has occurred previously, as in 1973, because of a breakdown in fixed exchange rates rather than as a result of a collective decision based on an assessment of its relative advantages. The success of floating should be judged in the light of the fact that it has usually operated under unfavourable circumstances, and thus the concerted adoption of floating exchange rates in more stable circumstances might well yield different results and evaluation.

(e) In recent years the stability of the international monetary system has been threatened by the debt problem of 'middle-income' countries such as Brazil and Argentina. Much of the indebtedness of these middle-income countries arose through borrowings in private sector capital markets, mainly the euro-currency markets, and although it was feared that the banks involved were seriously at risk it is becoming clear that rescheduling of debt by the banks with the debtor countries has been possible. Nevertheless the debtor countries continue to have a problem because the flow of private finance fell considerably between 1982 and 1984 after the emergence of the debt problem, and this fall in private flows of capital has not recovered. It is fortunate, however, that total debt has ceased to grow as fast, and since 1986 the total debt relative to country exports has fallen slightly. But it is still the case that such countries have considerable difficulty in servicing their debts and the debt problem continues to be serious. This was recognized in the Toronto Declaration.

(f) The USA trade deficit constitutes the other source of instability within the international monetary system. It is recognized that the current account deficit and associated capital inflows to the USA must eventually be corrected. The difficulty is to ensure that adjustment does not result in either world recession or financial collapse associated with a precipitate fall in the foreign exchange value of the dollar. There are indications that the US trade deficit is increasing at a lower

rate, and that inter-governmental cooperation has contributed
to an orderly decline in the dollar's foreign exchange value. It
continues to be a difficult problem in view of the role of the
dollar in international trade and finance, and the size of the US
economy.

Appendix 1 Exchange rate indexing

CALCULATION OF WEIGHTED EXCHANGE RATE INDEX

A simplified illustration allows us to demonstrate the importance of a weighted exchange rate in order to capture the effect of
changes in different exchange rates on the overall position. We
will assume that exchange rates with the rest of the world do
not change. The starting position for trade is as follows :

UK share of trade with West Germany	$= 40\%$
UK share of trade with USA	$= 15\%$
UK share with rest of world (ROW)	$= 45\%$

Exchange rates on 1 January

$$\pounds 1 = \$ 1\cdot18 \qquad \frac{1\cdot18}{1\cdot18} \times 100 = 100 \times 15\% = 15$$

$$\pounds 1 = DM\ 3\cdot5 \qquad \frac{3\cdot5}{3\cdot5} \times 100 = 100 \times 40\% = 40$$

$$\pounds 1 = ROW\ 1 \qquad \frac{1\cdot0}{1\cdot0} \times 100 = 100 \times 45\% = 45$$

Index for 1 January $= 100$

Exchange rates on 1 February

$$\pounds 1 = \$ 2\cdot00 \qquad \frac{2\cdot00}{1\cdot18} \times 100 = 111\cdot11 \times 15\% = 16\cdot66$$

$$\pounds 1 = DM\ 2\cdot8 \qquad \frac{2\cdot8}{3\cdot5} \times 100 = 80\cdot00 \times 40\% = 32\cdot00$$

$$\pounds 1 = ROW\ 1 \qquad \frac{1\cdot0}{1\cdot0} \times 100 = 100\cdot00 \times 45\% = 45\cdot00$$

Index for 1 February $= 93\cdot66$

By using a weighted average for the exchange rate we are able
to capture the much more important depreciation against the
Deutschmark, which swamps the appreciation against the

dollar. The overall position is therefore a sterling *depreciation*. If only the sterling – dollar rate were quoted, it would indicate an *appreciation* of the exchange rate.

REVISIONS TO THE CALCULATION OF THE EFFECTIVE EXCHANGE RATE

The 'old' exchange rate index (ERI) used weights derived from an IMF model, and these weights were becoming increasingly out of date. The IMF began publishing in July 1988 a new monthly series of nominal effective exchange rate indices for sixteen industrialized countries. The Bank of England has decided to make the IMF's new index the UK's 'official' exchange rate index. The main difference between the 'new' and the 'old' series is that the weights of the new are derived from trade flows in manufactured goods rather than trade in all goods based on 1977 trade flows, which was used for the old index. The base date for the new sterling ERI will be 1985 = 100 and the index came into operation on 3 January 1989. It is clear from *Figure 9.4 and Table 9.4* that the new index provides a similar picture to the old index but with some divergence.

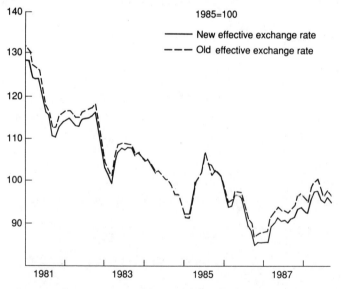

Figure 9.4 *Sterling effective exchange rate*

Source : Bank of England *Quarterly Bulletin,* Vol. 28, no. 4 (November 1988)

Table 9.4

'New' and 'old' indices of the sterling ERI, quarterly averages (1985 = 100)

		New	Old[a]
1985	Q1	92·9	92·1
	Q2	101·0	100·8
	Q3	104·6	104·9
	Q4	101·4	102·1
1986	Q1	95·0	96·1
	Q2	96·1	97·3
	Q3	90·2	92·0
	Q4	85·1	87·2
1987	Q1	86·7	89·3
	Q2	90·5	93·0
	Q3	90·5	92·9
	Q4	92·7	95·7
1988	Q1	93·5	96·4
	Q2	96·6	99·2
	Q3	95·2	97·0

[a] For comparison the old index has been rescaled to 1985 = 100.

Source : Bank of England Quarterly Bulletin, vol. 28, no. 4 (November 1988)

Appendix 2 Operation of a floating exchange rate in *Table 9.5*

Suppose at the beginning of year 1 in *Table 9.5* the exchange rate between the UK and West Germany (WG) is £1 = DM 3·00. During that year, however, the rate of inflation in the UK *relative* to that in WG is 10 per cent (e.g. inflation in the UK is 10 per cent p.a and in WG is zero; or is 15 per cent p.a in the UK and 5 per cent p.a. in WG). This would mean that at the end of year 1 a UK car would have a showroom price of £13,200 not £12,000. A West German car exported to the UK

Table 9.5

	General level of prices in UK relative to WG	Exchange rate	Price of UK car	Price of UK car in WG	Price of WG car in UK (DM price = DM 36,000)
Year 1	100·0	£1 = DM 3·00	£12,000	DM 36,000	£12,000
Year 2a	110·0	£1 = DM 3·00	£13,200	DM 39,600	£12,000
Year 2b	110·0	£1 = DM 2·727	£13,200	DM 36,000	£13,200

which sold for DM 36,000 in WG would still sell for £ 12,000 at
the exchange rate £ 1 = DM 3·00. Thus similar cars from WG
would be £ 1,200 cheaper than the UK-made car, and UK cars
would be selling for DM 39,600 in WG, i.e. DM 3,600 dearer
than the equivalent car made in WG (year 2a). Demand for
cars from WG would increase (UK imports) and demand for
UK cars would decline (UK exports), but this would also result
in an increase in UK residents' demand for Deutschmarks and
a decrease in West German residents' demand for the pound.

If the exchange rate for the two currencies is determined by
market forces then the price of Deutschmarks would rise and
the price of pounds would fall. The exchange rate (the price of
currencies in terms of each other) would move initially to, say,
£ 1 = DM 2·9, i.e. the Deutschmarks are becoming dearer, for
there are fewer per pound. This change in the exchange rate
would cause cars from WG to become dearer in the UK and
UK cars sold in WG would become cheaper. The change in the
exchange rate would continue automatically until the price
difference for cars had been eliminated. Such a situation would
apply when the exchange rate had moved to £ 1 = DM 2·727
(year 2b), when the UK car in WG would no longer be
uncompetitive and the WG car sold in the UK would no longer
have a price-competitive advantage. The levels of exports and
imports between the two countries would return to their
original positions, as would the balance of payments position
between the two countries.

Appendix 3 Exchange Rate Comparisons

Table 9.6 shows data for the sterling effective exchange rate as
well as for other currencies. The comparison of the effective
exchange rate and actual rates clearly demonstrates the value and
necessity for a weighted exchange rate. We can see from the
annual average figures that sterling's effective exchange rate
has fallen since 1975 (1975 = 100) and in 1987 it averaged
72.6 – depreciation of 27 per cent. But in recent years sterling
has appreciated against the US dollar but depreciated against
the major European currencies and also the Japanese yen. The
effective exchange rates for the Deutschmark, yen, Netherlands
guilder, and Swiss franc appreciated, whereas the French franc
and Italian lira (as well as the pound) have depreciated. One

should not be surprised at the offsetting movements of currencies, since if some currencies are appreciating then as a matter of arithmetic other currencies must be depreciating.

It should be noted that the Bank of England has, from January 1989, adopted a new effective exchange rate (see Appendix 1 to this chapter). This new index will continue to provide information on the relative movement in the average value of sterling, but it needs to be noted that the absolute value of the index is higher than the old index. In 1988 the old effective exchange rate had absolute values in the 70s but the new index is in the 90s. This change in these values does *not* mean that there has been an appreciation of sterling.

Table 9.6

Effective exchange rate indices and gold price

1975 average = 100; gold price US$ per fine ounce

	Sterling	US dollars	Belgian francs	Swiss francs	French francs	Italian lire	Netherlands guilders	Deutschmarks	Japanese yen	London gold price (at 3 p.m. fixing)
Annual average										
1983	83·2	124·8	92·4	151·2	69·6	51·2	117·1	127·5	148·4	423·27
1984	78·6	134·7	89·5	144·6	65·5	47·9	113·5	124·0	156·8	360·39
1985	78·3	140·7	90·1	143·2	66·1	45·1	114·0	123·8	160·7	317·33
1986	72·8	114·8	95·7	161·3	70·1	46·9	126·6	137·3	203·6	368·00
1987	72·6	101·2	100·2	173·8	71·8	47·6	135·6	147·7	220·0	446·53
Last working day										
1983	82·9	129·2	89·4	151·0	66·2	49·1	114·6	124·8	156·9	381·50
1984	73·0	145·0	88·6	138·9	63·5	46·8	109·9	120·0	155·2	308·30
1985	77·9	125·3	92·9	152·0	70·2	45·4	121·5	131·9	177·6	327·00
1986	69·2	107·9	98·6	168·6	71·1	48·8	132·9	145·3	207·3	399·90
1987	75·8	90·5	102·2	185·7	73·4	47·9	140·9	152·8	247·7	486·50
1988 July	76·5	98·6	97·5	166·7	69·0	45·1	131·8	143·1	241·0	436·80
Aug.	75·8	100·2	97·8	165·4	68·8	45·0	132·5	144·2	235·5	427·75
Sept.	75·9	99·6	97·8	164·6	68·5	44·8	132·4	143·8	239·0	396·70

Exchange rates against sterling and US dollars

Middle-market telegraphic transfer rates as recorded by the Bank of England during the late afternoon

	US dollars	Belgian francs		Swiss francs		French francs		Italian lire		Netherlands guilders		Deutschmarks		Japanese yen	
	£	£	$	£	$	£	$	£	$	£	$	£	$	£	$
Annual average															
1983	1.5158	77.47	51.16	3.1822	2.1012	11.5471	7.6266	2,301.61	1,520.19	4.3251	2.8558	3.8701	2.5551	359.93	237.43
1984	1.3364	76.96	57.78	3.1301	2.3507	11.6349	8.7399	2,339.14	1,757.10	4.2738	3.2103	3.7906	2.8470	316.80	237.55
1985	1.2976	76.34	59.31	3.1550	2.4543	11.5494	8.9758	2,462.69	1,907.28	4.2678	3.3171	3.7843	2.9407	307.08	238.30
1986	1.4672	65.47	44.63	2.6350	1.7963	10.1569	6.9222	2,185.67	1,489.75	3.5901	2.4470	3.1829	2.1694	246.80	168.33
1987	1.6392	61.12	37.35	2.4394	1.4917	9.8369	6.0107	2,122.66	1,296.65	3.3141	2.0257	2.9413	1.7977	236.50	144.67
Last working day															
1983	1.4520	80.70	55.58	3.1652	2.1800	12.0880	8.3250	2,397.25	1,651.00	4.4417	3.0590	3.9515	2.7215	336.27	231.60
1984	1.1580	73.17	63.19	3.0137	2.6025	11.1717	9.6475	2,238.42	1,933.00	4.1255	3.5625	3.6535	3.1550	291.30	251.55
1985	1.4455	72.40	50.08	2.9770	2.0595	10.8485	7.5050	2,412.54	1,669.00	3.4198	2.7540	3.5299	2.4420	289.39	200.20
1986	1.4837	59.38	40.02	2.3910	1.6115	9.4549	6.3725	1,985.19	1,338.00	3.2226	2.1720	2.8524	1.9225	234.72	158.20
1987	1.8870	61.99	32.85	2.3956	1.2695	10.0941	5.3175	2,187.03	1,159.00	3.3296	1.7645	2.9607	1.5690	228.33	121.00
1988 July	1.7115	67.04	39.17	2.6665	1.5580	10.7867	6.3025	2,361.87	1,380.00	3.6130	2.1110	3.2031	1.8715	227.29	132.80
Aug.	1.6810	66.18	39.37	2.6652	1.5855	10.7197	6.3770	2,346.68	1,396.00	3.5662	2.1215	3.1573	1.8782	229.66	146.62
Sept.	1.6860	66.39	39.38	2.6816	1.5995	10.7820	6.3950	2,359.98	1,399.75	3.5726	2.1190	3.1692	1.8797	226.88	134.57

Source: Bank of England *Quarterly Bulletin*, vol. 4 (November 1988)

A simple macroeconomic model

10.1 Introduction

In the remainder of the book we intend to examine macroeconomic theory and policy in order that the reader can appreciate how government decisions in the area of fiscal and monetary policy affect the economy in general and the banking and financial system in particular. But before we can understand the operation of macroeconomic management it is first necessary to examine a simple model within which some of the more fundamental macroeconomic relationships can be identified and explained.

The purpose of any model is to indentify and summarize the more important features of the problem under investigation. Economic models are particularly useful since millions of daily transactions are carried out in the real world and so some means must be found of expressing the essential characteristics of the problem at hand. A macroeconomic model by its very nature must be highly simplified since its purpose is to simulate what is happening in the economy as a whole. It is only on the basis of such a model that the government, which considers one of its basic functions to be the management of the economy, can predict what the effect will be of a change in one of its policies. However, the danger with relying upon such a model is that the necessity to summarize and simplify the more relevant economic relationships can lead to the omission or misrepresentation of some important features. This potential weakness has to be borne in mind when macroeconomic models are used as a basis for policy prescription.

The rest of this chapter will be concerned with developing

one particular model, known as the income – expenditure model, [1] which has frequently been used as a basis for explaining the operation of fiscal policy. Our basic model is developed from the circular flow relationship that was established in Chapter 1, and so the reader is recommended to refer to that chapter as a background for the present discussion. Readers who find the discussion too brief may wish to consult one of the many basic economics textbooks which cover this area. [2].

10.2 The basic model

Our basic model is developed from the circular flow approach which we adopted in Chapter 1. In Figure 1.1 we divided the economy into two sectors, households and firms, and we assumed that all the households' income earned in the current week was used to purchase the output of firms. Accordingly total expenditure E in the period under consideration was composed entirely of consumers' expenditure C, and total income Y in the community was identical to this expenditure. The assumptions can be expressed as follows:

income Y = expenditure E = consumers' expenditure C.

However, we did point out in Chapter 1 that the above summary is an over simplified representation of the real world, not least because it ignores the existence of the government and external sectors. We have explained elsewhere in this book that the government sector gives rise to taxation and expenditure flows (see Chapter 6) and that the external sector gives rise to export and import flows (see Chapter 7 and Appendix 2 to this chapter). At the same time we have to take account of the fact that some of the households' income will be channelled into saving, and that additional spending on the output of firms will arise from investment. How, then, can the circular flow be extended to include all these other flows ?

If we analyse all the uses to which income is put, then it is immediately obvious that for the economy as a whole consumers' expenditure on goods produced in the domestic circular flow is

[1] The model we are going to examine is one version of the income – expenditure model: other more complicated versions are often used in macroeconomics texts.

[2] See, for example, R. G. Lipsey, *Positive Economics* (Weidenfield and Nicolson); D. Begg, S. Fischer and R. Dornbusch *Economics* (McGraw-Hill)

only one element. Some income will be taken in direct taxation, such as income tax and so will not be available for other uses. The amount of income left over after deduction of this taxation is known as disposable income. This disposable income is not all directed into consumption on goods and services produced by firms in the domestic economy because some portion will be saved and some part will be used to purchase goods and services produced by firms in other countries (i.e. imports). Therefore we can classify the various uses of income as in *Figure 10.1.* [3] We can refer to taxation, saving, and imports as *leakages* from the

Figure 10.1

domestic circular flow since such flows are not immediately used to purchase goods and services produced in the domestic economy. However, these flows may be ultimately recycled into the domestic circular flow because governments invariably spend what they raise in taxation, because expenditure on investment goods is frequently financed out of current saving, and because other countries often spend on domestically produced goods and services at the same time as we purchase their products. But the point is that there is no *automatic* mechanism to ensure that taxation, saving, and import flows are immediately returned to the domestic circular flow.

If we examine all the categories of total expenditure in the economy, then consumption of domestic products is only one component. Aggregate expenditure also consists of government spending, exports, and investment, all of which contribute to the demand for domestically produced goods and services.

---

[3] In Chapter 1 we used C to refer to *total* consumption, i.e. consumption on domestically produced goods and services plus imports; here C refers to expenditure only on domestic products.

Therefore we may classify the various types of expenditure as in *Figure 10.2*. We can refer to government expenditure, investment, and exports as *injections* into the circular flow because

E
C=consumers' expenditure on domestic products
G=government expenditure
I=investment expenditure
X=exports

Figure 10.2

they add to consumers' expenditure on domestic products. This total expenditure is often referred to as *aggregate demand*, i.e. the total demand for goods and services in the economy which arises from consumption on domestic products, government expenditure, investment, and exports.

Now that we have identified the types of leakages and injections associated with the circular flow, we can begin to explain the assumptions that the basic model makes about the determinants of these various flows.

Consumers' domestic expenditure C is assumed to be related to income levels Y. This consumption relationship in its simplest form is often expressed as:

$$C = a + bY$$

where a is some constant consumption irrespective of income levels, and b is some fraction of additional income (known as the marginal propensity to consume) which would be less than 1 but greater than zero for the community as a whole. Many detailed studies have been carried out on the nature of the consumption relationship and all seem to agree that, for the community as a whole, consumption is related in some way to income.

Taxation T in the circular flow has been interpreted as income taxation and is the difference between gross and disposable income. Other forms of taxation may be introduced as well, but for the sake of simplicity we will confine our discussion to income taxation. It is taken for granted that such taxation is related to income levels because the amount taken in income tax varies directly with incomes.

Saving S in the economy is assumed to be related to income levels also, in a similar manner to consumption. The proportion of any additional income that is saved (the marginal propensity to save) will tend to vary according to the tastes and preferences of the individual, and one might expect the proportion that is saved to increase as income increases. For the community as a whole, total saving will tend to vary directly with the level of income.

Imports M will absorb a certain fraction of any additional income received by the community, the relevant proportion being known as the marginal propensity to import. The actual proportion will depend upon many factors, but whatever the fraction the basic model assumes that import spending is directly related to income. Again, this seems a justifiable assumption to make because the experience of the UK and other countries confirms that imports rise when incomes rise.

Government expenditure G is determined by political decisions, as we noted in Chapter 6. Accordingly, the model assumes that government spending is determined mainly by factors outside the circular flow. In other words, the level of government expenditure is assumed to be exogenous, i.e. given from outside the model. This is clearly an over simplification because, as was pointed out in Chapter 6, a considerable proportion of public expenditure in the modern economy is demand-determined, at least in the short term.

Investment expenditure I is also assumed to be exogenous in our model, with factors such as business confidence and the expectations of entrepreneurs being considered more important determinants of the level of investment than the current level of income. However, this may be an oversimplified assumption because the current level of economic activity will certainly influence business expectations and confidence. It is recognized, also, that investment may be influenced by interest rates, with fluctuations in the latter having a direct effect on the cost of borrowed funds and therefore on the profitability of potential investments. This relationship should be borne in mind when we examine monetary policy in the next two chapters.

Exports X from the domestic economy are related to income

levels in the rest of the world, along with other factors such as the exchange rate (see Section 7.2.1). The value of exports is assumed to be determined by factors outside the domestic circular flow and so is assumed to be exogenous in our model.

In summary, our basic model assumes that leakages from the circular flow (T,S,M) are determined within the model by income levels, and so can be described as endogenous. Injections of expenditure (G,I,X) are exogenous, however, because they are given from outside the model.

Now that we have classified the various sources of income and types of expenditure, as well as identifying the assumptions that the model makes about the nature of these flows, the next matter to discuss is the relationship between total income Y and aggregate expenditure E. In Figure 1.1 the reader will notice that income equals expenditure in the period under consideration. In fact income and expenditure also will be identical when we take into account all the various leakages and injections connected with the circular flow, because income and expenditure are simply two different ways of measuring the value of the same set of economic transactions. Expenditure by one party will be equivalent to income for another, and so total income must be equal to aggregate expenditure in the domestic circular flow. Indeed the national income accounts measure the value of goods and services produced in the economy (gross domestic product) by both an income and an expenditure method. [4] The use of these two methods of estimating gross domestic product (GDP) provides a cross-check on the accuracy of the recorded information. Income must equal expenditure when all the sources of income and types of expenditure are classified and measured.

We are now in a position to express our discussion in terms of a set of definitions :

$Y \equiv C + T + S + M$
$E \equiv C + G + I + X$
$Y \equiv E$
Therefore $C + T + S + M \equiv C + G + I + X$
and $T + S + M \equiv G + I + X$
$(G - T) + (I - S) + (X - M) \equiv 0$

[4] See Appendix 1 to this chapter for an illustration of this calculation.

Appendix 2 to this chapter explains how the last expression can be used as a basis for illustrating the flow-of-funds accounts, with each of the bracketed expressions representing the various sectors in the economy. But here the reader should notice that total injections $(G + I + X)$ must equal total leakages $(T + S + M)$. How, then, are these flows brought into balance in the model which we are investigating? It is at this point that the assumptions made about the nature of injections and leakages are relevant. For instance, imagine that there are increased injections into the circular flow in the form of investment, or government expenditure, or exports. Income will start to rise as a result of this additional spending, but leakages will rise also because taxation, saving, and imports are all related to the level of national income. In other words, extra spending automatically generates additional leakages from the circular flow. Accordingly, income and expenditure will increase as a result of additional injections of spending until once again total injections equal total leakages, but at a *higher* level of income and expenditure. On the other hand reduced injections will have a contractionary effect on income levels in the domestic circular flow. Leakages of saving, taxation, and imports will fall as income declines until once again total leakages equal total injections. In this case, however, the economy will operate at a *lower* level of income and expenditure.

So, it is variations in income levels which equate total injections and leakages, even though these flows are the results of the decisions of millions of different economic agents. This equality comes about in our basic model through leakages being directly related to income levels. The important question, however, is at what *level* of national income (and therefore national prosperity) will injections equal leakages and income equal expenditure? The answer to this question is of concern to government because it has responsibility for managing the economy in the interests of the community.

10.3 The multiplier

In the previous section we indicated the *direction* of changes in national income and aggregate demand when there were increased or reduced injections into the circular flow. The other crucial feature of the process is the *magnitude* of change in national income : if injections increased by £100 million, for example, would national income rise by the same amount?

We will investigate the magnitude of change in national income by first of all considering changes in government expenditure, one of the three categories of injections. Suppose the government spends an additional £100 million on the construction of a new motorway. This £100 million will be received by workers, contractors, suppliers, etc. who are engaged on building the motorway, and so the first-round effect will be an equivalent increase in national income of £100 million (remember, income must equal expenditure).

Let us suppose that the proportion of any additional income absorbed as leakages is 0·6. Therefore £60 million of the additional income will be channelled into taxation, saving, and imports, with the remaining £40 million being spent on consumer goods and services produced in the domestic economy. This extra consumers' expenditure will give rise to additional income of £40 million in those domestic industries producing the required goods and services. The second-round effect of the increased government expenditure will be a further increase in national income of £40 million.

Again some proportion (60 per cent) of this additional income will leak from the circular flow while the remainder is passed on as extra consumers' expenditure on domestic goods and services. This time £24 million (£40 million × 0·6) will be absorbed in leakages and £16 million will be received as additional income in the circular flow. The third-round effect of the increase in government expenditure will be a further increase of £16 million in national income.

The process will continue, and with each stage the amount of income passed on to others in the circular flow will be reduced by leakages of taxation, saving, and imports. The following increases in national income will take place after the initial increase in government expenditure of £100 million : £100 million, £40 million, £16 million, £6·4 million, £2·56 million, and so on. A simple formula exists for calculating the sum of such a series :

$$\text{total increase in income} = \frac{\text{initial expenditure}}{1 - \text{proportion of income spent on domestic Products}}$$

$$= \frac{£\,100\text{ million}}{1 - 0\cdot4}$$

$$= \frac{£\,100\text{ million}}{0\cdot6}$$

$$\simeq £\,167\text{ million}$$

This amount represents the total increase in national income following from the initial injection of government expenditure. Indeed the total increase in national income (£ 167 million) divided by the initial injection of expenditure (£ 100 million) is known as the *multiplier*. When leakages absorb 60 per cent of any additional income, therefore, the value of the multiplier is 1·67. [5] This value is simply the reciprocal of the proportion of income taken in leakages, i.e. $1/0\cdot6 = 1\cdot67$.

We are now in a position to see the significance of government expenditure and taxation flows in the determination of national income levels. An increase or decrease in government spending will stimulate or contract national income by an amount given by the value of the multiplier. A similar effect takes place when the government changes the rate at which taxation is levied because such changes alter the proportion of additional income which is absorbed by leakages. For instance, a cut in the basic rate of income tax would reduce the proportion of income taken in leakages and so would increase the value of the multiplier. Government spending and taxation will therefore have a magnified effect on total income and expenditure flows, thereby providing the fiscal authorities with a potential means for managing the economy.

We could examine the workings of the multiplier by considering changes in other injections into the circular flow. An increase in exports would be particularly beneficial in that the

---

[5] It was estimated that the value of the multiplier in the UK economy during 1986 was 1·35; see A.R. Prest and D.J. Coppock (ed. M.J. Artis), *The UK Economy*, 11th edn (Weidenfeld and Nicolson, 1986).

balance of payments would improve and at the same time national income will rise by an amount greater than the initial increase in exports. If we retain the assumption that leakages constitute 60 per cent of additional income, then a multiplier of 1·67 would apply to the increase in exports. The multiplier process would apply to additional investment expenditures also, but with both exports and investment expenditures the government has little direct control over the size of these flows. Certainly the government may exert an indirect influence on these injections (e.g. investment may be encouraged by lower interest rates), but the degree of control is not as powerful or certain as that which it exercises over government expenditure. Of course changes in national income can also be brought about by variations in the proportion of national income that is taken in imports and saving. Again, however, the authorities cannot control these leakages directly whereas they can vary tax rates through their own budgetary powers. Accordingly, variations in government spending and taxation might provide the best avenue for policies aimed at controlling the level of national income. This is not to say that other injections and leakages are less significant, only that they are less easy for governments to control.

10.4 Fiscal policy

Since the government has responsibility – either directly or indirectly – for the management of the economy, it is especially interested in the level of expenditure generated by the circular flow process. More precisely, the government has certain economic objectives that it would wish to achieve, and all are affected in some way by national income levels. The reader is referred to Chapter 12 for a more thorough discussion of the compatibility of these economic objectives. At this point, however, it is useful if we explain briefly what the principal economic objectives are and now their attainment is influenced by the level of national income.

Full employment Gross domestic product is a measure of the money value of the goods and services produced in the economy during a certain period of time. The *money* value of goods and service is derived from two components, quantity and price. [6] If an increase in national income is the result of an increase in the quantity of goods and services produced, then we would expect the level of employment to rise as more people are employed in the production of additional output. The employment objective may be attained, therefore, by increasing the quantity of goods and services produced. One obvious policy for the achievement of this objective is for government to stimulate aggregate demand by some means or other. One method may be through variations in government expenditure and taxation since these flows are under the direct control of the authorities.

Since the election of the Conservative government in 1979 the official attitude towards the achievement of full employment has shifted from the consensus which applied to previous Conservative and Labour governments. Although the present Conservative government would claim to be concerned about unemployment, it has argued that falling unemployment can only be achieved by (a) reducing the rate of inflation, since this would raise the *real* value of a given level of *money* spending in the economy, and (b) stimulating the operation of markets, especially the labour market, so that changes in the relative price of labour can come about more easily and thus 'price people into jobs'. Although the government would admit that in the short term a rise in aggregate demand stimulated by government fiscal policy would raise employment and output (quantity), in the longer term such fiscal relaxation would raise the rate of inflation (price) and not quantity; money GDP (price × quantity) would be rising but not output. These issues are still the basis for debate and controversy.

Stable prices Rapid inflation is regarded as undesirable for many reasons, not least because of the danger it poses for the stability of the economic and political system (see Chapter 12

---

[6] To make the point rather obviously, if a firm produces 1,000 units of soap powder per day and sells each for £1 then the value of goods produced is (price x quantity) £1,000. If output rises to 1,500 then value of output rises to £1,500. Alternatively a rise in the price per unit to £1·50 would also raise the value of the output to £1,500, but significantly in the latter case there would be no rise in production or employment; nor would there be any change in standard of living, since no extra output has become available. One might argue, therefore, that the preferred way in which GDP should rise is by virtue of a rise in the volume of output rather than in the level of prices.

for further discussion). Accordingly one of the objectives of government may be to achieve stable prices, or more realistically to reduce the rate at which prices are rising. But when governments expand aggregate demand in an attempt to secure the employment objective, there is a danger that the extra spending will increase prices rather than output. In theory it is conceivable for any increase in aggregate demand to raise output and employment levels as long as full employment of the labour force has not been reached. After full employment is reached, extra spending will only serve to add to the rate of inflation. In practice, however, bottlenecks in production are likely to develop well before this physical limit is reached, perhaps because of equipment and labour shortages in specific industries. In such circumstances the achievement of the prices objective may necessitate a reduction in aggregate demand through cuts in government expenditure and increased taxes.

Balance of payments equilibrium   For most countries the achievement of a balance of payments equilibrium is desirable because the authorities can then apply their economic policies solely for domestic purposes. We have argued earlier that the value of imports is related to the level of national income in the domestic economy and that the value of exports is related to aggregate demand abroad. Therefore an expansion of aggregate demand in the domestic economy which is not matched by comparable increases in other economies will result in a deterioration in the balance of payments. Conversely, a contraction in domestic national income relative to that in other countries may improve the balance of payments.

High rate of growth   The rate of growth is a measure of the increase in output over a period of time. But booms and slumps in economic activity occur periodically so that the relevant time period over which to measure economic growth is a number of years, e.g. the average rate of growth over ten years. Over such periods high growth rates, and rapid improvements in living standards, are dependent upon an increase in productive capacity rather than on temporary changes in the level of demand. However, investment is required to augment productive capacity, and policies to eliminate excessive fluctuations in aggregate demand may provide the best environment for high investment expenditures.

Our brief discussion of economic objectives and their relationship to the level of national income suggests that control over aggregate money demand is necessary if the government is to achieve all or some of these objectives. UK governments, until recently, have relied traditionally upon fiscal policy, i.e. variations in government expenditure and taxation, as the primary weapon to achieve its objectives. The income – expenditure model has been used as a framework for justifying this role for fiscal policy because government expenditure and taxation directly, and fairly reliably, influence national income levels. Up to the Second World War it was normal for governments to run a balanced budget. The only exception was in war periods when it became customary to meet part of the additional spending through borrowing. In the Victorian era, however, the burden of interest payments resulting from earlier wartime borrowing caused such concern that for some time budget surpluses were run in order to reduce the national debt. But the prolonged depression of the interwar period caused a reappraisal of the attitude of governments to their own budgetary position, with Keynes the most influential figure in advocating that budget deficits should be adopted in such circumstances. His argument was that aggregate demand could best be stimulated through fiscal expansion, and that in the prevailing conditions most of the increase in national income would feed through into output and therefore employment rather than inflation. After 1945 this philosophy became the conventional wisdom and governments accepted that they had a responsibility for macroeconomic management, predominantly through their own fiscal position. Budget deficits were regarded as a normal feature of economic management based on Keynesian principles. It is only relatively recently, as we have suggested earlier, that with the election of a Conservative government in 1979 this orthodoxy was challenged and reversed. Budget surpluses are now the norm and the emphasis is on repaying government debt rather than borrowing. Although at the political level it would seem that the Keynesian position has been relegated, at the theoretical (and practical) level it is maintained that fiscal policy can influence the achievement of the objectives of government policy. It has been argued that the Conservative government has in its policy changes (if not publicly voiced) moved towards a more Keynesian stance.

The preceding discussion suggests that the operation of Keynesian fiscal policy should pose few problems. But the typical situation facing a government has been what to do when the economy suffers from more than one problem simultaneously, e.g. unemployment *and* inflation. The coexistence of these two problems means that a choice must be made between an expansionary or contractionary budget depending on the government's preference : higher employment or stable prices. The response of most governments has been to manipulate the economy in order to secure some trade-off between the conflicting economic objectives. This question of trade-offs, and the 'fine-tuning' of the economy in order to achieve these objectives, will be examined further in Chapter 12.

Two other considerations relevant to the conduct of fiscal policy also should be mentioned. First, when governments want to make relatively large adjustments in their budgetary positions they may rely more upon changes in taxation than changes in public expenditures. Part of the explanation for this is that government spending tends to be planned over a number of years (e.g. hospitals, schools, and other capital expenditures take several years to complete, and governments are reluctant to dismiss teachers, policemen, and other employees for short-term economic reasons); consequently such expenditure tends to be fairly inflexible, especially downwards, in the short run. In contrast, tax rates are relatively easy to alter and so may be the more appropriate means to adjust fiscal policy when changing economic conditions require action. Secondly, when governments spend in excess of taxation receipts the budget deficit incurred will be reduced as income levels rise and taxation receipts subsequently increase. Thus part of the expense of an increase in government expenditure will be met by additional taxation receipts as national income and expenditure rise to higher levels than previously.

Now that we have outlined the basic operations of fiscal policy, it is desirable to conclude by pointing out some of the limitations of this approach to economic management :

(a) The achievement of a predetermined budgetary target may prove difficult because of the uncertainities involved in economic forecasting. It is the normal practice for the Treasury first to make an estimation of economic growth, inflation, public expenditure, and revenue receipts on the basis of unchanged fiscal policies. Then, if the general economic conclusions are considered unsatisfactory, a fiscal adjustment can be considered. But economic growth is subject to many influences, most of which are beyond the direct control of government, and relatively small errors in the Treasury's forecast can have quite large effects on actual revenue receipts and public expenditures. Between 1976 and 1986 the average error in the Treasury's forecasting of the PSBR (whether negative or positive) was £2·3 billion, and in the 1983 edition of the the Treasury's *Financial Statement and Budget Report* it was estimated that the average error in forecasting the public sector borrowing requirement for the year ahead was of the order of 1·5 per cent of GDP. Recently the size of the error has increased and the Treasury has greatly underestimated the negative PSBR (i.e. budget surplus). *Table 12.7* presents PSBR data since 1983.

(b) The supporters of fiscal policy as the principal macroeconomic policy defend their position by arguing that changes in government expenditure have a *direct* effect on economic activity. The argument is that government spending and taxation unambiguously influence total income and expenditure. But this approach tends to neglect the monetary effects of budgetary decisions. Earlier chapters (see Chapter 6 especially) have indicated how the financing of budget deficits (or surpluses) has implications for the size of the money supply and the level of interest rates, and it is to the relationship between these monetary variables and economic activity that we will turn in Chapter 11. However, *our* basic model may be criticized in advance of this discussion in so far as it ignores the monetary effects of fiscal decisions and so may overstate the case in favour of macroeconomic management through this route.

(c) The achievement of multiple economic objectives is especially difficult if the government relies exclusively upon one type of policy which operates essentially through the channel of aggregate demand. Additional policies may be required to complement fiscal policy if the government is to have a better chance of achieving its various objectives.

10.5 Summary

(a) In our basic model we established that total expenditure (or aggregate demand) derives from consumers' expenditure on domestically produced goods and services C, government expenditure G, investment I, and exports X; that national income Y consists of consumers' expenditure on domestically produced goods and services C, taxation T, saving S, and imports M; and that aggregate demand is equivalent to national income. From these relationships it was established that total leakages ($T + S + M$) must equal total injections ($G + I + X$).

(b) Since leakages are assumed to be related to income, and injections are assumed exogenous, then variations in income equate total income and expenditure flows in the circular flow model. The important question, however, is at what *level* of national income does income equal expenditure?

(c) Governments have a direct influence over the process of national income determination through their control over the flows of public expenditure G and taxation T. The management of the economy through fiscal policy is assisted by the multiplier which magnifies any injection of expenditures or leakages of income into or out of the circular flow.

(d) Fiscal policy may provide government with a potentially powerful method of managing the economy in order to achieve its macroeconomic objectives. However, government expenditure and taxation flows also exert an influence on monetary variables – and therefore affect economic activity – since the size and financing of the public sector borrowing requirement (negative or positive) are crucial elements in the determination of the money supply and interest rates.

Appendix 1 Calculation of GDP by expenditure method

The expenditure method of calculating the GDP is the most commonly presented. Extensive data for the UK are contained in *Table 10.1*. We may use the figures for 1987 to relate to the discussion in this chapter:

		£m
Consumers' expenditure	C	260,690
General government consumption	G	+ 85,773
Gross domestic capital formation (plus stocks)	I	+ 71,920

Table 10.1

Expenditure on the gross domestic product: at current prices (£m)

Final expenditure on goods and services at market prices

	Gross domestic product based measure (expenditure based measure) at market prices^a	Gross domestic product (expenditure based measure) at factor cost^a Total	Consumers' expenditure	General government consumption	Gross domestic fixed capital formation	Value of physical increase in stocks and work in progress	Exports of goods and services	Imports of goods and services	Taxes on expenditure	Subsidies
1980	231,209	200,453	288,833	137,896	49,022	41,561	-2,572	62,926	57,624	36,475	5,719
1981	254,832	218,736	315,253	153,566	55,457	41,304	-2,768	67,694	60,421	42,465	6,369
1982	277,607	236,951	345,642	168,545	60,446	44,824	-1,188	73,015	68,035	46,467	5,811
1983	303,218	260,027	381,113	184,619	65,873	48,615	1,465	80,541	77,895	49,460	6,269
1984	323,325	278,278	416,313	197,494	69,884	55,025	1,561	92,349	92,988	52,585	7,538
1985	353,730	304,208	452,896	215,267	73,995	60,283	569	102,782	99,166	56,724	7,202
1986	378,634	322,062	480,216	237,644	79,687	63,767	621	98,497	101,582	62,678	6,106
1987	413,743	351,413	525,788	260,690	85,773	70,846	1,074	107,405	112,045	68,173	5,843
1988 Q1^c	106,665	90,612	135,438	67,124	23,022	19,487	294	25,511	28,773	17,763	1,710
Q2^c	108,696	92,134	139,677	69,952	22,310	19,139	1,291	26,985	30,981	17,822	1,260
Q3^c	113,978	95,937	146,818	75,424	22,514	20,554	289,	28,037	32,840	19,335	1,294

^a Equals total final expenditure (TFE) on goods and services at market prices *less* imports of goods and services. TFE represents total spending flowing around the UK economy, but that includes spending on imports which is part of the output of other countries. TFE *minus* imports will thus measure spending on goods and services produced in the UK. This particular calculation measures expenditure at the prices prevailing in the shops, garages, etc., which of course includes the effect of taxes and subsidies.

^b The expression 'at factor cost' refers to the calculation of gross domestic product after the distorting effect of taxes and subsidies has been removed. Remember, the purpose of the calculation is to measure the 'true' value of output produced in the UK, and not a value which has been inflated or deflated by taxes and subsidies. Thus, gross domestic product at factor cost equals gross domestic product at market prices *less* taxes on expenditure *plus* subsidies. Within the national accounts we can identify therefore:

TFE − imports = GDP (market prices)

GDP (market prices) − taxes on expenditure + subsidies = GDP (at factor cost)

TFE might be regarded as a measure of total *spending power* flowing in the economy, whereas GDP at factor cost could represent the value of what is being *produced* within the UK.

^c Unadjusted.

Source : Monthly Digest of Statistics

Exports	X	+	107,405
Imports	M	–	112,045
Taxes on expenditure	T	–	68,173
Subsidies	S_b	+	5,843

$$351,413$$

These categories of expenditure do not correspond exactly with the simplifications in the text. For example, G above refers only to government consumption expenditure rather than *all* government expenditure, which would also include spending on fixed assets; this item is in fact included under gross domestic fixed capital formation.

In assessing how much is spent on *domestic* output we add the first four items. Spending on imports is then deducted because this represents spending on output produced by *other* countries. So

$$C + G + I + X - M$$

Because taxes on expenditure (i.e. VAT, customs and excise duties) artificially inflate the value of what is sold, we need to deduct T. On the other hand, subsidies (largely payments to farmers) reduce artificially the value of what is sold, and therefore this element S_b needs to be added back in. Thus the final calculation of the value of what was actually produced within the UK economy in 1987 is £351,413 million and is given by the relation.

$$C + G + I + X - M - T + S_b$$

Appendix 2 Circular flow model

For those readers who are familiar with the circular flow model outlined in Chapter 1, this appendix is intended to provide a slightly more rigorous approach to that which has already been developed in Sections 1.2 – 1.5.

Beginning with *Figure 1.3*, we can see that this system has all the major flows of expenditure and income incorporated within it. Looking first at expenditure flows, we can identify *total* expenditures within the economy as the sum of *consumption spending* by the personal sector; *investment spending* by the industrial and commercial sector; *investment and current spending* by the government, local authorities, and the public corporations, i.e.

the public sector; and the *net position with respect to imports and exports* ('net' since imports represent expenditure on output of another economy), i.e. the overseas sector.

Having identified the main sectors we can now include them in the circular flow approach adopted in *Figure 1.2*. All the sectors transact with another sector in some way, in the form of either production and sale of goods and services, or borrowing and lending (the production of financial assets and liabilities), or indeed both types of transaction. *Figure 10.3* and *Tables 10.2* and *10.3* illustrate these relationships. Beginning with the industrial and commercial sector (in *Figure 1.2* we simply call this sector 'firms'), these firms are paying out in each period (a year) £13,500 million which is largely wages and salaries to employees. A further £4,000 million is spent by this sector on the importation of necessary inputs from abroad (raw materials, etc.), as well as the £2,500 million spent on investment; and finally the firms pay £1,500 million corporation tax. In terms of market prices the industrial and commercial sector produces

Table 10.2

Total expenditure at market prices

(£m)

Domestic			
Consumption	10,000	C	
Investment	5,000	I	
Government			
Current spending	5,000	G	$C + I + G + X - M = E$
Exports	3,000	X	
Imports	−4,000	M	
	19,000		

Table 10.3

Income of the community

(£m)

Private consumption	10,000	C	
Private saving	500 ⎫	S	
Corporate saving	2,500 ⎬		
Income tax	3,000 ⎫		$C + S + T = Y$
Corporation tax	1,500 ⎬	T	
VAT	1,500 ⎭		
	19,000		

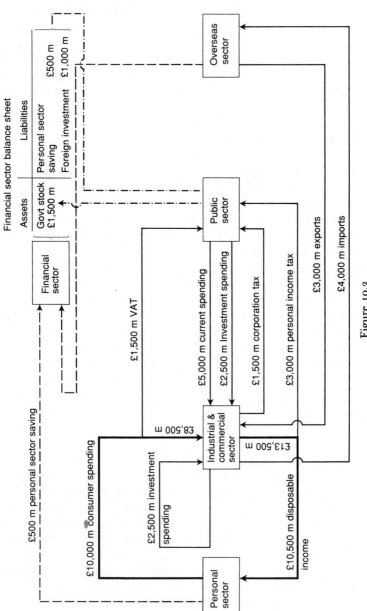

Figure 10.3

£10,000 million of consumer goods and services, and £5,000 million capital goods of which half is used by the sector itself and the other is purchased by the public sector. We have assumed for simplicity that the public sector's current spending of £5,000 million flows entirely into the industrial and commercial sector in return for goods and services. The personal sector earns in return for contributing to current production (no pensions are received by individuals in our model) a gross income of £13,500 million, and of this sum, £3,000 million is paid in income tax to the public sector. The personal sector's disposable income of £10,500 million is distributed between £10,000 million consumer purchases and £500 million saving. The public sector, as we have already seen, spends £7,500 million on current expenditure and capital goods. The receipts of this sector amount only £6,000 million, comprising £3,000 million income tax, £1,500 million corporation tax, and £1,500 million in VAT. It is evident that the public sector is running a deficit of £1,500 million. We have assumed that exports amount to £3,000 million and that imports are £4,000 million; the external sector has a surplus of £1,000 million (this does of course represent an unfavourable balance of payments for the country represented in the model). *Table 10.2* provides a summary of total expenditure as outlined at the beginning of the appendix.

Since spending also generates income for members of the community, we can also consider the income of the community as being disposed of in three ways: consumption, saving, and the payment of taxes. *Table 10.3* provides the alternative presentation.

Table 10.4 examines each of the sectors we identified at the beginning of the appendix. It will be noticed that the personal sector has a surplus of receipts over expenditure of £500 million, the public sector has a deficit of £1,500 million, the external sector has a surplus amounting to £1,000 million, and the industrial and commercial sector is in balance. However, the sums of the deficits and surpluses exactly offset one another so that all sectors together have neither a surplus nor a deficit. Nevertheless for an *individual* sector, as we have already seen in Section 1.3, this need not be the case since income can exceed expenditure and vice versa. Using the information and identit-

Table 10.4

(£m)

Personal sector		Industrial and commercial sector	
Gross income	13,500	Consumer spending	8,500
Income tax	3,000	Government current spending	5,000
Disposable income	10,500	Government investment	
Consumption	10,000	spending	2,500
		Private investment	2,500
Surplus	500	Exports	3,000
			21,500
		Factor payments	13,500
		Imports	4,000
		Corporations tax	1,500
		Investment	2,500
			21,500
		Surplus/deficit	Nil

Public sector		External sector	
Income tax	3,000	Exports (foreign spending)	3,000
Corporation tax	1,500	Imports (foreign receipts)	4,000
VAT	1,500		
	6,000		
Public sector current spending	5,000	Surplus	1,000
Investment	2,500		
	7,500		
Deficit	1,500		

Financial sector			
Liabilities		Assets	
Personal sector saving	500	Government stock	1,500
Foreign lending	1,000		
	1,500		1,500

ies of *Tables 10.2* and *10.3*, we can express some of these ideas
symbolically:

$$Y \equiv E \equiv C + I + G + X - M \equiv C + S + T$$

We can rearrange this to

$$Y \equiv E \equiv C + I + G + X \equiv C + S + T + M$$

and

$$Y - E \equiv (I + G + X) - (S + T + M) \equiv o$$

or

$$(I - S) + (G - T) + (X - M) = o$$

Since $Y \equiv E$ then $Y - E$ must be equal to zero, and the propositions
above follow from that identity. In the last equation you will
notice that the bracketed expressions approximate to our
sectors, the industrial and commercial as well as the personal
$(I - S)$,[7] the public sector $(G - T)$, and the external sector
$(X - M)$, and that although they must all sum to zero it does not
follow that each expression must be equal to zero. Thus
investment spending by firms may be greater or less than the
volume of saving, government spending may be greater or less
than tax receipts, and exports may be greater or less than
imports, but it must be the case that a deficit or surplus in one
sector is exactly offset in one or more of the other sectors. For
example, using the figures in *Table 10.2* and *10.3* ($£$ million):

$$(I - S) + (G - T) + (X - M) = o$$
$$(5,000 - 3,000) + (5,000 - 6,000) + (3,000 - 4,000) = o$$

If we return to *Table 10.4* we are able to examine how the
various sectors 'solved' the problem of their surpluses and
deficits, in the sense used earlier (Section 1.5). If a sector is not
in balance (i.e. $Y \neq E$) it has either to accumulate assets (the
surplus sector) or attempt to sell additional liabilities (the
deficit sector). In this illustration the personal sector channelled its surplus of $£$500 million to the financial sector (banks,
insurance companies, building societies, etc.)[8] and the remaining funds originated from the foreign sector which lent its
$£$1,000 million surplus derived from the excess of its exports

---

[7] $(I - S)$ incorporates the two sectors, since I represents the investment spending of the
industrial and commercial sector and S the saving of the personal sector.

[8] Composition of the financial sector is dealt with in Chapter 4.

over imports. The total funds were then used to purchase £1,500 million of government securities, thus allowing the public sector to cover its deficit.

Money and economic activity

The last two chapters of the book are primarily concerned with the problems and policies of macroeconomic management, with special emphasis being given to the role of monetary policy. Before we can look at the appropriate policies for macroeconomic management, we must first investigate the theoretical relationship between money and economic activity. Such a discussion is essential since it enables us to judge the degree to which the successful conduct of monetary policy can influence economic activity and thereby achieve economic objectives.

For quite a long time the prevailing view among economists had been that money does not affect the relative prices of commodities, but that it does determine the overall price level. These ideas, embodied in the so-called quantity theory of money, dominated economic thinking until the 1930s. Since then we have witnessed the development first of all of the Keynesian view of the importance of money, followed by the monetarist view which is at odds with the former and is closely associated with the original quantity theory. It is the aim of this chapter to examine these theoretical issues, especially the Keynesian versus monetarist debate, since theoretical controversy has had a profound influence on the attitude of most governments towards monetary policy as an approach to macroeconomic management.

11.1 The quantity theory

The quantity theory reflected the view of economists prior to the 1930s that changes in the quantity of money in existence do not have a permanent effect on the real sector of the economy (that is on output and employment levels), but do determine the general price level. The quantity theory is based on the following relationship, which is known as the equation of exchange :

$$MV = PT$$

where M is the quantity of money in the economy;
V is the velocity of circulation, or the average number of times a unit of money is used in a stated period;
P is the general price level, expressed as an index; and
T is the total number of transactions in the stated time period.

As expressed here, the relationship between MV and PT constitutes a truism, or identity, as can be illustrated by an example. Consider a simple economy consisting of one fisherman and one farmer. During a particular week the fisherman sells the farmer two fish at £4 per fish, and during the same week the farmer sells the fisherman eight loaves at £1 per loaf. So the total number of transactions will be ten, and the average price of each transaction is £16/10 = £1·60. Suppose the money stock consists of only eight £1 notes, then what will be the velocity of circulation of the money stock during the week under consideration? Of course some pound notes may be used more frequently than others, and some may not be used at all, but the velocity of circulation measures the *average* number of times a unit of currency is used. Since the value of transactions is £16 and the quantity of money is £8, the velocity of circulation is 2. We can express the above information as $M = £8$, $P = £1·60$, $V = 2$, $T = 10$, and so

$$MV = PT = £16$$

In fact MV *must* equal PT since both measure the same set of economic transactions in two different ways : indeed we can only observe P, T, and M, so V cannot be calculated independently of the rest of the variables in the equation, as can be seen in our example. Now if V and T are fixed, or are uninfluenced by M (i.e. V and T are independent of M), then the equation of exchange can be expressed as the quantity theory, which states that an increase/decrease in M will lead directly to an increase/decrease in P.

But why should T and V be fixed, or independent of M? Before the sustained economic recession of the inter-war years it

was thought that the economy automatically moved towards
full employment, even though periodic booms and slumps were
experienced at the time. Thus the total number of transactions
T in the economy can be taken to be fixed if full employment is
the norm, or alternatively the assumption that the quantity of
money has no permanent effect on the real sector of the
economy implies that T is independent of M. Consequently
there should be a definite relationship between the quantity of
money and the price level if the velocity of circulation can also
be shown to be independent of M.

Supporters of the quantity theory argued that V will be
influenced by the customs and payments practices prevailing at
the time, and that such arrangements change only slowly. If,
for example, workers are paid weekly, then a smaller amount of
money will be required compared with a monthly system of
payment; a worker will require to hold money balances to meet
his purchases only for a maximum of one week at any particular
point in time. But with monthly payment, money balances will
be held to meet expenditures up to one month in the future. So
although the quantity of money required will be larger in the
case of monthly payment, the velocity of circulation will be
lower than for weekly payment (assuming total spending is the
same). Therefore it was supposed that payments practices, and
other institutional arrangements which change only slowly over
time, have more influence on the velocity of circulation than
any temporary changes in M. Before the First World War there
may have been a good deal of truth in this assumption because
the financial system was relatively unsophisticated and financial innovation was taking place very slowly by today's standards. Indeed the statistical evidence that is available does
suggest that the relationship between the money stock M and
money national income PT was quite stable, in both the short
and the long term. But the prolonged depression of the
inter-war period upset this relationship, causing the quantity
theory to fall into disrepute. Money incomes actually fell quite
sharply during the early 1930s owing to a combination of falling prices and declining real incomes, but money growth
proved much more resilient. Therefore money supply measures
proved to be unreliable as an indicator of both money incomes
and prices.

11.2 Keynesian and monetarist views of money

The undermining of the credibility of the quantity theory during the depression years, together with the general failure of conventional economic doctrine to explain the events of the time, left a vacuum which was filled by the new theories of J. M. Keynes. Elements of the macroeconomic framework which he proposed were examined in Chapter 10. An important part of his contribution to theory was the analysis of the demand for money and its differences with the quantity theory view. It is to these ideas that we turn first. The monetarist attack on Keynes's ideas is considered next, and then some brief comments are made on the empirical issues which divide these schools of thought.

11.2.1 KEYNESIAN THEORY

The traditional Keynesian approach divides the demand for money into three elements : the transactions, precautionary, and speculative demands. Before discussing these elements in detail it might be useful to emphasize that the notion of 'the demand for money' – which may seem a curious concept – can be thought of as a demand to *hold* money.

The *transactions demand* is related to the function money performs as a medium of exchange in that a certain quantity of money balances is required by economic transactors simply to purchase the goods and services they expect to buy during the period in question. For example, a man may earn £100 per week and out of this he may plan to spend £70, and thus his transactions demand would be £70 in this particular week. What factors influence the size of the transactions demand? In most cases a man earning £300 per week would be expected to spend more than the man earning £100 per week, and so the transactions demand should be larger for the former. Furthermore, during periods of inflation money incomes will normally rise together with prices and so more money will be required simply to purchase the same collection of goods and services. For both these reasons, therefore, one would expect the transactions demand to be a function of money incomes.

In our example the man earning £100 per week plans to spend only £70; therefore he can save the remainder and purchase a range of financial assets which earn a rate of return. In this case, building society deposits or National Savings certificates are the most likely option, but for higher-income earners equities and government securities will be considered as well. However, such savings cannot immediately be turned into cash [1] since there is inconvenience, cost, and even uncertainty of value with some financial assets. Accordingly the man in our example may prefer to keep an additional fraction of his income as money balances in excess of his transactions demand, just in case something unexpected happens which necessitates immediate expenditure. For example, the man may travel to work each day by car and so carry an extra £20 with him just in case his vehicle breaks down and needs to be repaired at once. This *precautionary demand* for money will also be related to money incomes since : (a) the higher your regular income then normally the more expensive are the items you own, e.g. the Rolls-Royce is usually more expensive to repair than the Mini; (b) if money incomes rise due to inflation then the same items cost more to replace or repair.

If the level of money incomes in the economy is known, it might be possible to estimate the transactions and precautionary demand for money. The extent to which the money supply exceeds this combined transactions and precautionary demand determines the amount of money left over to satisfy the *speculative demand*. If the transactions and precautionary demands are estimated at £80 million during a certain time period, and the money supply is fixed at £100 million, then the speculative demand is £20 million. In Keynes's time it was mainly wealthy or high-income earning individuals who operated speculative balances, but in the modern economy this role has been assumed more by institutions which manage contractual savings held in pension funds, life assurance contracts, and the like. These speculative balances are available for the purchase of types of wealth such as financial assets, since wealth held as money, although it has the advantage of being perfectly liquid, earns no rate of return. Thus speculative balances will be held

---

[1] Of course cash is just one component of the money stock and money demand may take the form of a current account, for example.

in anticipation of the purchase of non-monetary assets at some future date. A crucial Keynesian assumption is that if holders of speculative money balances decide to hold their wealth in some other form, they are likely to purchase financial assets since these are taken to be closer substitutes for money than other types of assets. The idea of substitution has been examined in Section 2.4.2, but the reader is reminded by an example. Butter and margarine are close substitutes, and so any increase in the price of butter would be expected to lead to an increased demand for margarine as consumers substitute the latter for the relatively more expensive butter. In a similar way, the Keynesians argue that changes in rates of interest (price) bring about substitution between various financial assets, including money. Thus speculative balances are likely first of all to be spent on financial assets which are close substitutes for money, rather than on real assets such as land, buildings, and the like.

But why might potential buyers of financial assets delay their transactions and instead hold their wealth in a perfectly liquid form with a zero or low yield, e.g. cash or current account deposits? To answer this question it is necessary to refer back to Section 6.11.1, in which the relationship between the price of a financial asset, such as an undated bond, and its yield were explained. We concluded that there will be an inverse relationship between the market price of the bond and its true yield. In the case of dated bonds and other financial assets there will still be an inverse relationship between the market price and yield, but it will not be proportional. Now the holder of speculative balances not only has to consider the yield on close substitutes such as bonds, but he also has to take into account any prospective capital gains or losses which may accrue when buying the bond. If holders of speculative balances are of the general opinion that the price of bonds will fall in the near future (i.e. their yield will rise), then they will not purchase these assets now because they will suffer a capital loss if their expectations are borne out by experience. Instead they will prefer to remain liquid, and this will give rise to a speculative demand for *money* in preference to other forms of financial wealth. Thus the speculative demand for money will be strongly influenced by the expectations of the market as to the future course of financial asset prices.

What, then, are the implications of an increase in the money supply according to the Keynesian view of the demand for money? Since the 'Keynesian' sees no reason to expect money incomes to be directly affected by the increase in the money supply, we can assume that the transactions and precautionary demands remain unchanged at first. The extra money balances are therefore available as a direct form of wealth holding, or else they can be used to purchase those financial assets which are a close substitute. An increased demand for financial assets will lead to a rise in their price, and thus a fall in their yields. Consequently the first effect of an increase in the money supply is expected to be a decrease in interest rates. Of course market expectations may constrain the movements in interest rates since any increase in the money supply could simply be absorbed into speculative balances if the general opinion is that the price of financial assets will fall in the near future. Under these circumstances the rate of interest will not fall any further. But, apart from this possibility, an increase in the money supply should lead to a fall in interest rates, other things being equal.

11.2.2 MONETARIST THEORY

An alternative view is closely associated with the work of Milton Friedman from the middle 1950s onwards. Over this period an influential school of thought called monetarism has developed around his ideas and has come to challange the Keynesian orthodoxy as the dominant academic influence over monetary policy. Friedman's views are based essentially on the quantity theory relationship and depend crucially on statistical evidence which purports to show that velocity is relatively stable and predictable especially over long time periods. However, he has elaborated on the simple quantity theory to provide a more sophisticated framework for the explanation of a link between monetary growth and inflation. The velocity concept is developed as a demand for money relationship.[2] Friedman argues that money is just *one* form in which wealth can be held, other forms including bonds, equities, *and* physical

[2] See M. Friedman, 'The quantity theory of money – a restatement', *Studies in the Quantity Theory of Money* (1956).

goods such as houses, property, and even consumer durables. The actual proportion in which each individual holds his wealth depends upon the relative yields he receives on the whole range of assets, and upon his individual tastes and preferences. The yields concerned may be of the direct money kind, as is the case with equities and bonds, but may be implicit in the form of services or benefits received, as with owner-occupied houses. The individual receives an implicit yield on money because of its convenience value as a means of payment. Thus the demand for money is seen to depend upon the relative yield or attraction of money and a wide range of other assets, and so 'money' is taken to be an equal substitute for all these other types of assets.

Since the demand for money is related to several variables, according to Friedman and the monetarists, then it may be difficult to measure the precise effect of a change in one of these variables on the demand for money. However, the basic argument of the monetarist is that money is a unique asset which is not a close substitute for any particular range of assets, but instead is a substitute for all assets both real and financial. Thus the *substitutability of money* for other assets is one crucial area of difference between the Keynesians and monetarists: whereas the former argue that money is a close substitute for financial assets, the latter claim that money is a substitute for all assets.

How does this demand for money specification affect the relationship between money and prices? A key assumption is that the money supply is exogenous – uninfluenced by economic activity – but is controllable by the monetary authorities. Any increase or decrease in the money stock is thus directly attributable to the activities of the central bank. The transmission process through to money incomes and prices is then determined by the interaction between money supply and demand. An increased supply of money will encourage economic transactors to substitute other forms of wealth for money as the convenience yield on these extra money balances will be exceeded by the potential yields on the wide range of alternative assets. Because the demand for money is fairly stable there should be a reasonably predictable effect in terms of increased demand for other assets, which may be real or financial.

Although the supply of these assets – and therefore economic activity – may respond at first, eventually the increase in the money stock feeds through to prices. The final result is just as the simple quantity theory states, except that the monetarist view explains the process by reference to a stable demand for money function and an exogenously determined money stock which is under the control of the monetary authorities.

11.2.3 EMPIRICAL CONTROVERSY

The Keynesian and monetarist views seem to lead to very different conclusions as far as monetary policy is concerned. But it is first necessary to consult the available empirical evidence on the relevant theoretical issues before we turn to their recommendations for the conduct of monetary policy. Investigations here have focused on two aspects of the debate.

One difference between the two views is that Keynesians believe money is a close substitute for financial assets, whereas the monetarists argue that money is not a particularly close substitute for any specific range of assets. The Keynesians would therefore expect a close relationship between the demand for money and the yield (rate of interest) on near-money substitutes, but the monetarist would not expect a significant relationship because of the belief that money is a substitute for all assets alike. The empirical evidence does suggest that there is a definite relationship between the demand for money and the interest rate on near-money substitutes, *but* it is not as strong as the Keynesian theory suggests. Therefore the extreme versions of both theories do not seem to be supported by the empirical evidence on the demand for money, although measurement is complicated by various definitional and conceptual problems. For example, what definition of money is taken and which financial asset(s) is it best to use in the investigations? For these and other reasons, the empirical evidence on the demand for money does not provide conclusive evidence in support of the extreme versions of either of the two theories.

Secondly, the claim that there is a strong correlation between changes in the money stock on the one hand and changes in money incomes and prices on the other is central to the monetarist case. Statistical evidence does show support for a link, although it may not be as precise as some of the stronger

monetarist claims have suggested. The graph in *Figure 11.1* is
useful because it illustrates the relationship between the real

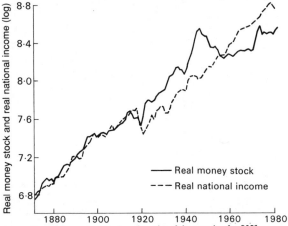

Figure 11.1 *Real money stock and real national income in the UK*

Source : 'Monetary trends in the United Kingdom', Bank of England Panel
of Academic Consultants paper no. 22

money stock and real national income over the long term,
(more than 100 years), which is equivalent to comparing the
actual money stock with nominal national income. Monetarist
theory argues that the two lines on the graph should more or
less coincide over long periods, showing that any increase in the
money stock in excess of that needed to finance real output
growth will be dissipated in price rises. Up to about 1920 this
appeared to be the case, but thereafter the link was more
tenuous. For example in the inter-war period the real/nominal
money stock grew much more quickly than real/nominal
national income, only for this trend to be reversed after the war.
Using more recent data which provide a similar comparison,
Figure 11.2 plots real money stock and real GDP for the period
1979 – 87. This is, of course, a much shorter period than that
represented in *Figure 11.1,* but it does show that the growth of
the real money stock has been consistently faster than the
growth of real GDP. Whatever the factors underlying the
different growth rates, it is consistent with the uneven relationship emerging in the inter-war years. The high growth of the
real money stock after 1979 compared with the growth of real
GDP is partly reflected in the high rate of inflation during the

Figure 11.2 *Real money stock and real GDP, 1979 – 87*

Source : derived from data in : *Economic Trends;* Bank of England *Quarterly Bulletin*

1980s – an annual average of 9.3 per cent, compared with 2 per cent growth of real GDP.

But even if all participants accepted that there is a close link between the money stock, money incomes, and prices, this would not prove that changes in the money stock caused changes in money income and prices. Indeed the causality might run the other way. This is where the monetarist assumption of an exogenous money supply plays such a vital role. If an exogenously determined money stock can be taken for granted, then movements in money incomes and prices would not influence the money stock and so the causality must run in the direction presumed by monetarists. In practice there are strong grounds for believing that the money stock is not entirely exogenous. Therefore monetarists have resorted to the claim that governments can exert control over the money stock if they are determined enough, and in so doing will bring about the desired effect on money incomes and prices.

11.3 The role of monetary policy

Our preceding discussion has concentrated upon the two major views of the importance of money, and this section intends to clarify their implication for the direction and significance of monetary policy. Indeed we will see that the outcome of the Keynesian view is that monetary policy should be directed at interest rates, rather than the money supply, but that in any case monetary policy should be subsidiary to fiscal policy. On the other hand, the monetarist recommends that control of the money supply should be the major concern of the monetary authorities and that such a policy is of paramount importance for the conduct of macroeconomic policy.

11.3.1 KEYNESIAN VIEW

We have already established the Keynesian view that an increase in the money supply will lead to the purchase of financial assets. Further, these purchases are expcted to lead to an increase in the price of financial assets and a fall in their yields (i.e. interest rates). However, this process now needs to be spelled out a little more clearly if we are to gain insight into the effectiveness of the increase in money supply on the level of interest rates. It is first necessary to recognize that some financial assets are closer substitutes for money than other financial assets, and so are the more likely to be immediately affected by a change in the money supply. Therefore any adjustment which comes about as a result of an increase in the money supply will probably take place first of all through purchases of short-term, highly liquid financial assets such as Treasury bills and bank bills. As a consequence the prices of these assets will begin to rise, i.e. their yields fall. Other economic transactors are now assumed to compare the declining yield on bills with the (now relatively higher) yield on close substitutes such as short-dated bonds. Rational behaviour would dictate that substitution of short-dated bonds for the relatively less attractive bills will now take place, and so the price of these bonds will begin to rise as investors increase their demand for them and the yield on these assets will begin to decline. The Keynesian view would emphasize that the original increase in the quantity of money will have a ripple effect spreading through the whole financial market until eventually even the less liquid financial assets such as equities are affected. At each stage, yields will fall as economic transactors adjust to the 'disturbance' through the purchase of close substitutes.

The overall effect of the above process should be a fall in interest rates throughout the whole spectrum of financial assets. But precisely because the effect is dispersed through the whole market the Keynesian argues that, unless there is a massive increase in the money supply, the impact on interest rates in general may be relatively small. Furthermore, the process may be unpredictable as far as individual yields are concerned because the movement in the prices of financial assets is subject to the variable and uncertain expectations of the market.

How will the change in interest rates affect economic activity? The Keynesian answers this question in terms of the income – expenditure model of Chapter 10. To summarize: the level of economic activity is determined by the level of injections and withdrawals into the circular flow of income. Keynesians assume that investment expenditures are the more likely to be influenced by changes in interest rates, since raising money to purchase capital goods – perhaps through the issue of equities or through borrowing from the banks – is more attractive when interest rates are lower. It thus becomes a matter of the sensitivity of investment to changes in interest rates, i.e. what is the interest-elasticity of investment?

In the early post-war years it was believed that investment expenditures were not very responsive to changes in interest rates, and most of the empirical evidence at the time, seemed to support this view. The Keynesian concludes, therefore, that an increase in the money supply would not have a marked effect on economic activity since: (a) the money supply only influences economic activity indirectly via interest rates, and the latter may not be significantly affected anyway because all parts of the financial market bear the burden of adjustment; and (b) investment expenditures may not be very sensitive to changes in interest rates. So, the Keynesian argues that monetary policy will be more effective if the authorities aim to control interest rates directly, rather than indirectly through the money supply. Furthermore, monetary policy is not as crucial as fiscal policy because the latter has a *direct* impact on economic activity via government expenditure and taxation, whereas monetary policy only affects economic activity *indirectly* via the tenuous link between interest rates and investment. Indeed, some Keynesians went so far as to say that money is unimportant since it only exerts an influence on economic activity via interest rates, and then without much success.

11.3.2 MONETARIST VIEW

The assumption that money is a substitute for all assets, both real and financial, leads the monetarists to conclude that an increase in the money supply brings about *directly* an increase in prices as a consequence of increased purchases of all types of assets. Also Friedman and others have undertaken many detailed empirical studies to investigate whether changes in the money supply are a cause of fluctuations in national incomes and prices. Their results purport to show that, in different time periods and in different countries, changes in the money stock precede changes in money incomes and prices. Based on this theoretical and empirical approach the consensus view would be that not only do increases in the money supply cause changes in the price level but fluctuations in the money supply are a major source of economic instability; both can have an impact nationally and internationally.[3]

Unfortunately, empirical evidence rarely leads to the resolution of economic debates, primarily because the economist cannot control his experiments in such a way as to isolate the effect of one variable (e.g. the money supply) on others (e.g. money incomes). Apart from some of the empirical problems mentioned earlier, a fundamental point is whether correlation, no matter how good it might be, proves causality. For example there is very good correlation between the arrival of swallows and summer, but no one suggests that the presence of swallows causes summer. Similarly, the fact that the increases in the money supply precede increases in money incomes does not prove causality. Professor Kaldor has pointed out[4] that an increase in the note issue precedes the Christmas spending spree, to facilitate the extra demand for transactions balances,

[3] M. Friedman, 'The role of monetary policy,' *American Economic Review* (March 1968).
[4] N. Kaldor, 'The new monetarism,' *Lloyds Bank Review* (July 1970).

but the absence of such an increase would not prevent the spending boom. Instead the given money stock might be used more intensively (i.e. a rise in V) as notes, coin, and bank deposits are exchanged more frequently. So, despite the detailed and extensive studies of the monetarists, there is still disagreement as to whether the money supply is the prime cause of fluctuations in money incomes and prices.

Although the monetarists claim that there is a direct link between the money supply and money incomes, they do point out that variable and unpredictable lags exist. Indeed, US studies indicate that the lag may vary between six months and two years. Perhaps paradoxically, it is argued that the money supply should *not* be manipulated by the monetary authorities on a short-term basis because the existence of such lags would make the effect of monetary policy uncertain, although powerful. The best policy, according to the monetarists, is for the authorities to aim for a *steady* growth in the money supply in order that economic growth can be accommodated without undesirable fluctuations in money incomes and prices.

The Keynesian versus monetarist debate, at the practical level, gives conflicting advice to governments on the role and importance of monetary policy. The ambiguity of the empirical work and research does little to resolve matters. Keynesians argue that the interest rate is the most important variable for the monetary authorities to control, but that monetary policy should be subsidiary to fiscal policy. In contrast the monetarists argue that a steady growth in the money supply is the best policy to follow, and that monetary policy directed to this purpose is of paramount importance. Certainly the Keynesian view provided the academic basis for the conduct of monetary policy in the period from the Second World War up to the late 1960s, with the influential Radcliffe Report (1959) supporting this general approach in the UK.

However the 1970s and early 1980s witnessed a change in opinion towards the monetarist view, especially in respect of government policy in the UK. UK governments since 1976 adopted explicit monetary targets, and with the Conservative election victory in 1979 came a strong commitment to controlling the money supply. Although a succession of Conservative governments since 1979 has expressed a firm belief in monetary methods of managing the economy, with the emphasis on controlling inflation, it is fair to say that the empirical justification for much of this policy has been thin. In particular, establishing a close and sustained relationship between money and nominal income or prices has been especially elusive. It may well be the case – as some commentators have observed, perhaps unduly cynically – that the economic and political situation in 1979 was such that it mattered little what the government tried to control as long as they showed determination and resolve to control something; the money supply happened to be both a convenient and a relevant variable at that time.

11.4 Summary

(a) An appreciation of why governments follow certain types of economic policies requires an understanding of the theories which influence the decisions of the policy-maker. Thus the relationship between money and economic activity is of crucial importance to the direction and emphasis of monetary policy.

(b) The original quantity theory suggested that the major impact of the money supply is on the general price level, but this crude theory fell into disrepute during the inter-war years with the absence of any well-defined link between money and prices. Nevertheless the relationship between the money supply and price has received continued attention, with the monetarists trying to provide theoretical and empirical support for the argument that changes in the money supply cause fluctuations in money incomes and prices.

(c) The Keynesian and monetarist views provide opposing theories of the importance of money upon which the authorities can base their policies. The Keynesians argue that money is a close substitute for financial assets, so they see an increase in the money supply resulting in an increase in the price of financial assets and a fall in the yield received. In contrast, the monetarists argue that money is a substitute for all assets, so they see an increase in the money supply resulting in an increase in prices in general, not just in the price of financial assets.

(d) These divergent views on the demand for money lead to very different policy conclusions. The Keynesian view implies that the money supply has its major effect on economic activity via the impact of interest rates on investment expenditures. The Keynesian then considers the implications in terms of the income – expenditure model of Chapter 10, with any increase in investment bringing about a magnified increase in national income through the workings of the multiplier. However, the Keynesian sees the effect on economic activity as being unpredictable and indirect, and instead attaches more significance to fiscal policy.

The monetarist position is that control of the money supply is essential for the successful conduct of macroeconomic policy since they see a direct link between the money supply and prices. But they argue that the money supply should not be manipulated on a short-term basis because of the variable and unpredictable lag which exists before prices and money incomes are affected.

It is therefore a background of academic controversy which provides the theoretical framework for the conduct of macroeconomic policy in general, and for monetary policy in particular.

Macroeconomic management and the conduct of monetary policy

12.1 Macroeconomic objectives

The major macroeconomic objectives are usually summarized as:

(a) High employment of the labour force
(b) Stable prices
(c) Balance of payments equilibrium
(d) A satisfactory rate of growth.

However, this list may be far from complete since most governments have objectives in other areas, notably the distribution of income and wealth. Nevertheless it is very difficult to achieve even the major objectives listed above, either because some of them conflict in practice or because the policy tools are insufficient in number or effectiveness to complete the task adequately. Thus the policy-maker is invariably in the position where he has certain aspirations in terms of macroeconomic objectives, but he has to decide which are to be given priority. Obviously such choices are political decisions, which will involve social as well as economic considerations, but it is first necessary to establish the nature of the trade-offs between macroeconomic objectives so that the policy-maker is well aware of the sacrifices involved. The economist would seem to have two crucial roles:

(a) To identify and measure the trade-offs that exist between economic objectives so that the policy-maker is made aware of how much of one must be given up to get more of another, e.g. 2 per cent more inflation or 0.5 per cent less unemployment.

(b) To search for the most appropriate policy-tools which will enable the government to achieve its economic objectives more satisfactorily.

There would be no need for a choice between economic objectives if they were all uniformly related to one controllable variable. Chapter 10 explained that although the four macro-economic objectives listed earlier are each related in some manner to the level of demand, the relationship is by no means uniform or in the same direction. Output and employment may be improved at least temporarily through using fiscal policy to expand aggregate demand, but at the same time there is an increased likelihood that inflation will be exacerbated by such an injection of spending. Furthermore, a higher level of demand will probably result in an increase in the value of imports, implying that the balance of payments objective may also conflict with the employment objective. So fiscal policy on its own cannot be relied upon to achieve all the macroeconomic objectives simultaneously since it operates essentially through the channel of aggregate demand. In fact it is generally the case that the achievement of more than one independent policy objective requires the adoption of a combination of policy tools.

We will investigate the nature of the trade-offs between macroeconomic objectives in the UK economy from the 1950s onwards. In this period not only did the nature of the trade-offs change but at the same time the policy-makers came to attach more or less importance to particular objectives.

During most of the 1950s and 1960s UK governments as a whole concentrated predominantly upon the employment object-ive, with the balance of payments frequently exerting a cons-traint on the achievement of this goal. Indeed the problem was that fiscal and monetary policies designed to stimulate employ-ment often resulted in a deterioration in the balance of pay-ments under the then existing fixed exchange rate system. Specifically, an expansion of demand would result in a reduc-tion in unemployment but would also lead to a balance of payments deficit as imports increased. This was largely a reflection of Britain's uncompetitiveness in world trade. One possible solution was that fiscal policy could be used exclusively for the management of the level of employment, and monetary policy could be directed at raising interest rates to attract capital inflows and thereby offset the increase in imports in the balance of payments accounts. Unfortunately such capital inflows tend to be very volatile in nature, as we have seen in earlier chapters, and this is one reason why this option did not provide a permanent or reliable solution. Instead more reliance was attached to expenditure-reducing policies (see Section 7.2.3) as a solution to the balance of payments problems, and this involved the use of both fiscal *and* monetary policies to bring the expansion of demand to a sudden end. Consequently the policy of expanding and then contracting demand, which came to be known as 'stop – go', was a result of the direct conflict between the employment and balance of payments objectives since control over the level of aggregate demand was relied upon in order to achieve both goals.

The use of fiscal and monetary policies to influence the level of demand also has implications for the prices and growth objectives. An expansion of demand can give rise to inflationary pressures, and the frequent *expansion* and *contraction* of demand (stop – go) provide an inappropriate environment for invest-ment spending by business and therefore economic growth. In fact the more immediate objectives for most of the 1950s and 1960s were employment and the balance of payments. Our earlier discussion suggests that: (a) a trade-off might need to be established between these two objectives, and (b) additional policy tools might need to be used to achieve a more desirable combination of objectives. In case (a), it could be concluded that equilibrium in the balance of payments might only have been accomplished with the existing policies by accepting higher levels of unemployment. In case (b), the availability of additional policy tools for the achievement of balance of payments equilibrium was limited. Indeed the adjustable peg system was operated in such a way that the exchange rate was rarely used as a means of adjustment, and import restrictions were not allowed under the Bretton Woods agreement.

During the same period it was also alleged that there was a trade-off between unemployment and inflation, which came to be known as the Phillips curve. This trade-off was based on the original observations by Professor A. W. Phillips of the relation-ship between the rate of change of money wage rates and unemployment levels over long periods of time going back as far as 1861. *Figure 12.1* gives an example of a Phillips curve, with the horizontal axis measuring the level of unemployment. On the vertical axis is plotted the recorded rate of increase of money wage rates, and it may be assumed that the rate of

Figure 12.1 *A hypothetical Phillips curve*

inflation can be closely associated with these rates of wage change because wages are usually the largest component of costs. To the extent that a growth in productivity allows a certain increase in money wages to take place without price increases, then this productivity growth can be deducted from actual wage rises to calculate price increases. For example, with 2 per cent productivity growth, a 4 per cent rate of wage increase can be associated with an inflation rate of 2 per cent. When such adjustments are made, the Phillips curve apparently gives the policy-maker a choice between employment and stable prices; more of one can only be gained at the expense of the other. For example, our hypothetical Phillips curve shows that a 4 per cent per annum wage increase (equivalent to 2 per cent inflation with a 2 per cent productivity growth) is associated with a 3 per cent unemployment rate, and that a 9 per cent annum wage increase (equivalent to 7 per cent inflation) is associated with a 2 per cent unemployment rate. In other words, a reduction in unemployment is associated with a certain increase in the rate of inflation. By the early 1960s, therefore, it had become accepted that fiscal and monetary policies could only be used to reduce unemployment at the expense of a deterioration in the balance of payments *and* a higher rate of inflation.

Figure 12.2 illustrates a Phillips relationship using data for the UK between 1953 and 1967. The data do appear to confirm the view that there was a relationship between the level of unemployment and the rate of change of prices. However, unemployment and inflation data after 1967 shows an almost total absence of the typical Phillips relationship. *Table 12.1* provides inflation and unemployment data from 1953 to 1988 and is divided into three sub-periods; 1953 – 67; 1968-75; and 1976 – 88. In the first period, as we have seen in *Figure 12.2*, there does appear to be some degree of relationship between unemployment and the rate of price inflation. Unemployment is relatively very low and so is the rate of inflation. In the second period, however, the relationship – if such there be – seems to be one of relatively

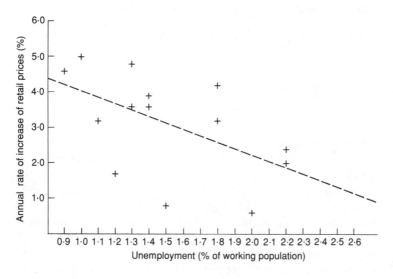

Figure 12.2 *Rate of change of retail prices and percentage unemployment in the UK,*
1953 – 67

Table 12.1

Rate of change of retail prices and percentage unemployment in the UK,
1953 – 88

1953 – 67	Change in prices (%)	Unemployment (%)		Change in prices (%)	Unemployment (%)
1953	3·0	1·5	1961	3·6	1·4
1954	1·7	1·2	1962	4·2	1·8
1955	4·6	0·9	1963	2·0	2·2
1956	5·0	1·0	1964	3·2	1·1
1957	3·6	1·3	1965	4·8	1·3
1958	3·2	1·8	1966	3·9	1·4
1959	0·6	2·0	1967	2·4	2·2
1960	0·8	1·5			

1953 – 67 : average unemployment 1·5%; average rate of inflation 3·1% p.a.

1968 – 75

1968	4·5	2·3	1972	7·2	3·3
1969	5·6	2·3	1973	9·1	2·3
1970	6·3	2·4	1974	16·0	2·3
1971	9·4	3·0	1975	25·0	3·6

1968 – 75 : average unemployment 2·69% average rate of inflation 10·39% p.a.

1976 – 88

1976	16·5	5·0	1983	4·6	11·7
1977	16·4	5·3	1984	4·8	11·6
1978	8·1	5·2	1985	6·1	11·8
1979	13·0	4·8	1986	3·6	11·8
1980	18·2	6·2	1987	4·2	10·2
1981	11·8	9·4	1988	5·6	8·0
1982	8·7	10·9			

1976 – 88 : average unemployment 8·6%; average rate of inflation 9·35% p.a.

Source : *Economic Trends*, Annual Supplement.

stable unemployment but sharply accelerating inflation, with average unemployment higher than in the previous period. In the third period, average unemployment is higher still but the rate of inflation is declining. In the first and third periods there does seem to be a Phillips relationship, but whether the relationship is causal, and in which direction, are very debateable. It is equally convincing that although the level of unemployment may have an effect on price inflation, there may well be other factors of greater short-term impact, for example, the incorporation of previous price increases into current wage bargaining, regardless of the level of unemployment. Nevertheless, if one plots unemployment against data showing the acceleration or deceleration of price inflation then a trade-off does re-emerge, which is consistent with a monetarist view of the economy; lower levels of unemployment which are below the natural, market-determined, rate can only be achieved with the consequence of an *acceleration* of the rate of inflation.

So far we have discussed the existence of trade-offs between the employment and balance of payments objectives, and between employment and changes in prices. Furthermore, we have noted that in the UK during most of the 1950s and 1960s employment and the balance of payments were considered to be the most important macroeconomic objectives by both Labour and Conservative governments. But by the late 1960s world inflation had gathered pace to such an extent that most governments came to regard this as the major problem confronting them. Moreover, high inflation rates were and are of particular concern because of the danger that the monetary and financial systems might collapse as conventional money no longer becomes accepted as the medium of exchange. Past experience in Germany and other countries in the inter-war years suggests that hyper-inflation can ultimately lead to the collapse of the economic and political system as well. Accordingly, the prices objective became more important in most economies, and by the middle of the 1970s it had replaced full employment as the principal objective of the UK government.

The traditional Keynesian approach has tended to regard unemployment and inflation as being inversely related, as is depicted by the shape of the Phillips curve. Indeed the implication of the Phillips curve relationship was taken to be that control of demand via fiscal and monetary policies allowed the government to operate the economy at full capacity, yielding high employment but rising prices; or at lower levels of demand, producing more stable prices but higher unemployment. But the coexistence after 1967 of high unemployment *and* inflation cast doubt on both the usefulness of the Phillips curve as a representation of a trade-off, and on the excess demand explanation of inflation. It was against this background of 'stagflation' that monetarism increasingly became more influential, providing as it did an alternative explanation of the economic problems of the time as well as a potential remedy.

The coincidence of rising inflation *and* unemployment, in spite of Keynesian-type policies to maintain aggregate demand, cast doubt on the continued effectiveness of conventional economic policies during the 1970s. Monetarists argued that excessive growth in the money stock was the root cause of the inflationary problem, and that any trade-off between inflation and unemployment was at best temporary. It was claimed that a 'natural' rate of unemployment existed in an economy at any particular time, determined by such things as the state of technology and any impediments to the free movement of labour such as restrictive work practices. Any attempt to reduce unemployment below this rate was sure to fail, according to monetarists, and would bring about higher inflation. This particular view has become one of the central tenets of the present Conservative government's economic policy.

Our commentary suggests that the nature of the trade-offs between economic objectives may change over time, and that the policy-maker needs to be advised of such changes when deciding upon the preferred combination of objectives. Another issue which needs to be considered is whether or not new policy tools can be found to enable the authorities to achieve their objectives more effectively, and to this we will turn next.

Incomes policies were first adopted in the UK in the late 1940s but became a regular feature during the 1960s. The argument was that fiscal and monetary policies could be used to achieve the government's objectives as regards full employment and the balance of payments (although such policies were not very successful in that they gave rise to stop – go), and that incomes policies could be used to contain the inflationary consequences. Indeed, increasing concern over inflation led to the operation of more or less continuous incomes policies during the 1970s. Moreover, succeeding governments tried to operate the economy at lower levels of demand and therefore at higher levels of unemployment in order to reduce inflationary pressures. The search for new policies led additionally to the widespread adoption of monetary targets in most economies, including the UK, apparently giving some acceptance of the monetarist claim that inflation is a consequence of a rapid growth in the money supply. The conduct of monetary policy, and its changing emphasis over time, will be discussed further in Section 12.4.4.

Since 1972 in the UK there has been available an additional means for the achievement of the balance of payments objective : the adoption of floating exchange rates. This enables easier adjustment to take place, although in practice the balance of payments has at times continued to pose problems for the UK economy. The urgency of such problems, however, is not usually as acute under floating, since the government is no longer obliged to defend a fixed exchange rate and to direct domestic policies to this purpose. (see Section 9.5).

The discussion so far is intended to highlight the point that macroeconomic objectives often conflict, and that the policy-maker has to choose the most desirable combination. Also the nature of the trade-offs may change over time, as may the choices of the policy-maker. The economist's role in all this is essentially to make the policy-maker aware of these trade-offs and to advise him of the suitability of alternative policy tools for the achievement of objectives.

12.2 The framework of macroeconomic management

Our discussion in Section 12.1 broadly indicated how fiscal, monetary, and incomes policies might be used to achieve some combination of macroeconomic objectives. In this section we intend to explain how such policies involve the relationship between objectives, targets, and instruments.

Objectives have been defined already in Section 12.1, where it was stated that priorities are decided by the policy-maker in line with political, social, and other considerations. In the subsequent discussions we intend to concentrate upon employment, prices, and the balance of payments as the most relevant objectives. This approach seems to be consistent with UK post-war experience since policy-makers have tended to concentrate their attention upon the more short-term objectives rather than on strategies aimed specifically at longer-term growth.

Targets (or intermediate variables) are the variables through which government actions have an influence on macroeconomic objectives. The relevant fiscal targets are the levels of government expenditure G and taxation T, each of which the government tries to control via instruments. But both these target variables are also influenced by variables outside the direct control of the authorities. For example, government expenditure on unemployment benefits is related to the number of people out of work; state pensions are related to the number of people over retirement age; and taxation receipts are influenced by the incomes of the community (via direct taxes) and by prices (via indirect taxes). With monetary policy the target variables may consist of some measures of the money supply or interest rates. But again the monetary authorities do not control these variables directly; instead they are able to exert influence over their chosen targets via their control of instruments.

Instruments (or techniques) enable the authorities to influence target variables. In the case of fiscal policy the major instruments are changes in tax rates and allowances, and variations in expenditure plans. Chapter 6 has already explained the role of the Budget and the Public Expenditure White Paper in this context. It is through changes in instruments that the fiscal authorities influence the levels of taxation and government expenditure, the two target variables. A variety of instruments are available for the conduct of monetary policy, such as reserve requirements, special deposits, open market operations, and the central bank discount rate. These instruments can be directed at the two monetary targets, the money supply and interest rates.

Table 12.2 uses fiscal and monetary policies as illustrations of the difference between objectives, targets, and instruments. But it should be remembered that these two policies are not to be

Table 12.2

Some of the major objectives, targets, and instruments

Objectives	Targets	Instruments
Prices	Fiscal :	
Employment	Taxation receipts	Tax rates
Balance of	Government expenditure	Expenditure plans
payments	Monetary :	
	Money supply	Reserve requirements
	Interest rates	Open market operations
	Volume of credit	Special deposits
	Exchange rate	Central bank discount rate
		Directives

treated as mutually exclusive : the fiscal position often has important ramifications for the conduct of monetary policy.

Our discussion of macroeconomic management emphasizes that the link between instruments and objectives is by no means direct or precise. Accordingly we can identify two necessary conditions which must be fulfilled before macroeconomic policies are likely to be successful :

(a) Macroeconomic objectives must be sensitive to changes in target variables.

(b) The authorities must be able to control target variables via instruments.

For any type of policy to be successful *both* of these conditions need to be satisfied or else the policy instruments under consideration will fail to give an adequate degree of control over macroeconomic objectives. For example, it may be of little value that the authorities are able to control interest rates via monetary instruments if the relevant objectives are not very sensitive to changes in interest rates.

Another consideration is that the process of economic management, involving the use of instruments to achieve objectives via some set of intermediate target variables, is subject to delay and uncertainty because of the existence of various lags. In the following discussion we will identify the major lags, with special reference to fiscal and monetary policy.

The recognition lag Effective economic management would require the authorities to take action as soon as a disturbance occurs which is judged to have an adverse impact on the desired combination of macroeconomic objectives. But in practice a certain period of time may elapse before the authorities are able to recognize that a problem exists. One reason for this is that suitable up-to-date information on employment, prices, etc. may not be immediately available, partly because it takes time for such data to be collated. Furthermore, the authorities will require sets of consistent data before they accept that action is required. Bank base rates were raised in the UK during 1988 from 8·5 per cent at the beginning of the year to 13·0 per cent by the end. The Chancellor of the Exchequer's intention was to cut back consumer spending. During 1988 there was considerable uncertainty as to whether a slowing down of spending was taking place. For these and other reasons, there may be a recognition lag before the fiscal and monetary authorities consider activating their policy instruments to cope with what is perceived as a change in circumstances.

The administration lag Even when the authorities recognize that action is required, there may be a further lag before the available instruments are brought into action. In the conduct of fiscal policy the government has to receive Parliamentary approval before proposed changes in taxation or public expenditure can be made effective, and obviously the planning of a Budget and its acceptance by Parliament is a time-consuming process. The administration lag should not be as long for monetary policy since formal Parliamentary approval is not required. However, delays may occur if the authorities have failed to make contingency plans to meet the change in circumstances, and consequently prolonged discussion may be necessary before a decision is made to use particular instruments in a certain way. But the monetary authorities in most advanced countries normally do make such contingency plans, and therefore the administration lag is unlikely to be excessive.

The operation lag More time may elapse before the activated policy instruments exert their full impact on targets and then employment, prices, and the other macroeconomic objectives. A lag exists between the change in instruments and their effect on intermediate target variables. With monetary policy, for example, the money supply may not decrease immediately following a decision to make open market sales of public sector debt to the non-bank sector. Instead, the money supply might contract over a period of time as the banking sector adjusts stage by stage to successive sales of gilt-edged securities. In the conduct of fiscal policy, several months may pass – due to the delay in adjusting individuals' tax codes – before a change in personal taxation influences the tax paid by the community. Another lag, for example, is that between changes in instruments and the achievement of the employment and prices objectives. For instance, employment and prices may react slowly to variations in the money supply or interest rates. Indeed, the monetarists argue that frequent manipulation of the money supply is a mistaken policy because of the long and variable lag before prices are affected. Thus the monetarists recommend a steady growth in the money supply. To refer again to the rise in interest rates in 1988, the cost of personal and business borrowing is approaching levels which in real terms (after taking away the effects of inflation) are high. In view of the uncertain lagged response of spending to changes in interest rates (real or nominal), there is an element of speculation in considering the size and timing of this change in interest rates and the effect on borrowing, spending, inflation, and the balance of trade.

The overall conclusion to be drawn from this discussion is that the various lags can complicate the business of macroeconomic management, and may even make it counter-productive. One common criticism of the UK government during the 1950s and 1960s was that fiscal and monetary policy were conducted in such a way that these policies ultimately exerted their full influence at the wrong time. It was suggested that the authorities tried to manipulate aggregate demand – primarily through fiscal policy – in order to achieve their desired combination of economic objectives but, because of the lags mentioned earlier, such policies exerted their full effect much later when economic conditions had changed as a result of the fluctuations in the business cycle. To give an extreme example, fiscal policies designed to increase employment might take effect after a year, when, say, the economy had begun to move out of the recession. The stimulus to demand would be felt during a period of expansion and so would exacerbate any inflationary pressures which might be building up. Moreover, it was argued that contractionary policies introduced during boom periods to reduce the growth in imports and inflationary pressures had their full effect when the economy had begun to move into recession. Therefore the contraction in demand engineered by the government only succeeded in adding to the unemployment problem. The manipulation of aggregate demand by the government, and in particular the fairly frequent changes in policy instruments, became known as *fine-tuning*. By the end of the 1960s many economists were critical of this policy of fine-tuning on the grounds that it added to rather than reduced the instability of the economy.

12.3 Monetary instruments and control : UK experience to 1979

In the remainder of this chapter our attention is focused on the means by which control has been exercised by the monetary authorities, and the problems connected with such control. The emphasis in Chapters 4 and 5 was on the theoretical aspects of monetary control, whereas here we attempt to place the problem in the context of UK experience since 1945.

Between 1945 and 1951, the immediate post-war period, it would be no exaggeration to suggest that the authorities viewed monetary policy instruments as rather limited in their effectiveness. The problems of physical shortages and the volume of highly liquid financial assets accumulated during the war (high incomes during the war period, with few goods and services to be bought, led to high savings) probably meant that attempts to regulate the economy by monetary means would have failed.

The Labour government lost office in 1951, however, to be replaced by a Conservative one, and with this change came a different approach to economic policy which included the revival of monetary methods of control – in particular the manipulation of bank rate and associated interest rates. Suffice to say that it became evident fairly soon that the existing monetary techniques of regulation were not sufficiently effective, and in 1957 a committee was set up by the Chancellor of the Exchequer to inquire into the working of the monetary and credit system in the UK. This committee – commonly known as the Radcliffe Committee after its chairman – produced a report in August 1959. This report, together with the minutes and memoranda of evidence, provided a considerable volume of information about the workings of the financial system in the UK as well as some of the views of monetary authorities (the Bank of England and the Treasury) as to how the system might be regulated. Of special interest was the Radcliffe Committee's view that control of the banking system was exercisable via the liquidity ratio and the supply of Treasury bills, and not through regulating the supply of cash (see Section 5.6). Another view expressed was that the stock of money *per se* was not of prime importance and should not be the prime target of the authorities; rather the authorities should concentrate on the liquidity of the whole system. The reader is referred to Appendix 1 to this chapter for further discussion of this emphasis on liquidity.

Although the general tenor of the Radcliffe Report cast some doubt on the strength of monetary methods of control – at least in the way they were being used at the time – monetary and fiscal instruments of control continued to be used to regulate the economy. During the 1960s, however, the use of market methods of monetary regulation (e.g. open market operations, shifts in interest rates) to influence the major part of the banking system (the primary banks) became of even more questionable value. There were a number of reasons for this, some of which have been uncovered earlier in the book :

(a) The support operations in the gilt-edged market were proving to be an awkward commitment for the authorities. The gilt-edged market and the foreign exchange market were, and are, influenced by each other, so that a deterioration in the balance of payments tended to produce a weakness in the gilt-edged market. If the authorities intervened in the gilt-edged market to support prices, they would be tending to *add* to the liquidity of the banking system. But a deterioration in the balance of payments position was usually followed by economic policies designed to *curtail* credit and spending, and therefore support operations in the gilt-edged market would be somewhat counter-productive and inconsistent with overall economic policy. Such support operations would involve the Bank of England buying gilt-edged and thus tending to expand the liquidity and lending potential of the banking system. Furthermore, the authorities did not control the supply of all the eligible liquid assets which could count towards the banks' liquidity ratio. We have seen earlier that the banks were able to substitute other liquid assets (money at call, commercial bills) as the supply of Treasury bills contracted.

(b) The rapid growth of the secondary banking sector meant that unsatisfied demand for credit from the primary banks could be met by the secondary banks; this sector not being subject to the liquidity ratio requirements. Squeezing the primary banks simply pushed some customers into the secondary sector. Indeed, the setting up of secondary banking subsidiaries by the primary banks is indicative of the slippage that was occurring.

The response of the authorities to the inadequacy of market methods of control was to introduce, and increasingly rely upon, non-market methods of regulation. The call for special deposits was used on fifteen occasions between June 1960 and the end of 1966. Other methods of regulation used by the authorities were 'moral suasion' and direct controls. Moral suasion by the Bank of England was frequently directed at the *nature* of banking business (qualitative directives) rather than the overall *level* of business (quantitative directives) to which, say, the call for special deposits would be aimed. The Governor of the Bank of England on a number of occasions requested the banks to refrain from certain types of lending in favour of others.

A direct control introduced in the 1960s was the use of the lending ceiling, i.e. a direct control on *credit* rather than, say, bank deposits. The banks were asked to prevent lending rising above the level prevailing at the time. This lending ceiling was reinforced by a further statement by the Bank in November 1968 which gave the banks four months' notice to reduce their lending to 98 per cent of the mid November 1967 level. At the end of May 1969 the Bank curtly announced that the banks had not complied with the earlier request for the attainment of the lower lending ceiling and that therefore the Bank intended to halve the rate of interest payable on special deposits for as long as the banks exceeded the lending ceiling. This penal arrangement came into effect from 2 June and would have cost the clearing banks about £150,000 per week as a result of the lost interest.

It is hardly surprising that the clearing banks found the use of both moral suasion and direct controls particularly irksome. Moral suasion caused the banks to discriminate between customers in a manner unrelated to their ordinary business relations : a customer who happened to be an exporter was eligible for funds, but an equally good customer who, say, imported manufactured consumer goods was deprived of necessary funds. The firm application of market methods of control would have yielded a rise in interest rates which would have provided, albeit more slowly, the allocative mechanism rather than the banks having to discriminate against one customer in favour of another. In addition, the banks claimed that the authorities' monetary measures – particularly prior to 1964 – tended to restrict mainly the clearing banks, whereas other financial intermediaries (secondary banks, building societies, insurance companies, etc.) were relatively untouched. Thus it was argued that the non-market methods of control were discriminatory, limited in their application, and somewhat clumsy as instruments, producing distortions and inequities within the financial system. It is probable that both the authorities and the banking system felt the need for an alternative approach to monetary management, and after wide-ranging discussions between the Bank and financial intermediaries, the arrangements embodied in the document *Competition and Credit Control* became operative on 16 September 1971. These changes are of considerable interest because they represented a major step towards the deregulation of the UK financial system – a process which is still continuing. The proposals and subsequent amendments also provide us with a case study of central bank policy-making in respect of both monetary control (macroeconomic policy) and prudential regulation. As we shall see, the private sector financial system proved highly adaptable to the new system and that in itself provides us with insight into the problems of banking regulation.

12.3.1 COMPETITION AND CREDIT CONTROL

Our approach to these changes may be divided conveniently into the two parts : the competition and the credit control aspects of the new arrangements.

Competition The proposals included a number of reforms which were intended to stimulate competition in the financial system and also to remove some of the discriminatory aspects of the previous methods of regulation :

(a) The new reserve ratio arrangements[1] were to apply across the whole of the banking system and not merely to the London clearing banks.

(b) The special deposits (and after 1973 the supplementary special deposits) scheme would be applied to all banks and the larger finance houses.

---

[1] The details of the reserve requirements have been presented in Section 4.5.3 and the reader should refer to this section.

(c) The collective agreement between the London and Scottish clearing banks on interest rates would be abandoned. The banks would be expected to compete with each other in both the attraction of deposits and the making of loans.

(d) The discount houses agreed to abandon their collectively agreed price for the weekly Treasury bill issue, but they would continue to apply for a quantity of bills sufficient to cover the tender.[2]

(e) The larger finance houses were expected to adhere to a slightly lower reserve ratio than the banks (10 per cent rather than 12.5 per cent) but the reserve asset requirements would be the same as for the banks. Some of the finance houses chose to apply for bank status (under the Protection of Depositors Act) and these finance houses would observe therefore the same reserve requirements as the other banks.

(f) The Bank ceased to *support* the gilt-edged market but would sell gilt-edged when the market could absorb stock satisfactorily. If the market were weak, the authorities intended simply to withdraw rather than give support until it strengthened again, when gilt-edged sales would be resumed. Such a change of tactics in the gilt-edged market did not preclude intervention, but such intervention would be in accordance with the authorities' own requirements rather than in response to particular market changes. It should be realized that this change of tactics in the gilt-edged market is consistent with the objective of greater competitiveness since it allowed greater freedom for market forces to determine prices, and therefore yields, on government stock and close substitutes. For the authorities to have maintained their 1960s approach to the gilt-edged market would have been inconsistent with the other aspect of policy : flexibility of interest rates through greater competitiveness amongst banking and other financial intermediaries.

Credit control The arrangements in this area were as follows :

(a) The quantitative lending controls were abolished and the liquidity and cash ratio requirements as devices for regulating

---

[2] The competition and credit control arrangements which were applied to the discount houses may be found in the Bank of England *Quarterly Bulletin*, vol. 13, no. 3 (November 1973), p. 306.

credit were to be replaced by the reserve asset ratio (this will be considered further).

(b) The authorities declared their intention of relying more on interest rate changes as a means of regulating both the direction (allocation) and volume of credit available. This represents quite a significant change because it signals that the authorities were inclined to let market forces have a greater influence on the volume of credit (and therefore the stock of money; see Chapter 5) as well as the recipients of credit.

(c) Special deposits would continue to be used as a means of regulation, but the Bank indicated that in the future it would consider using special deposits in a more flexible way. The Bank stated that a call for special deposits might be related either to domestic or overseas sterling deposits and that the percentage-rate of call might be different for domestic and overseas sterling deposits. One reason for such differentiation was that some banks, e.g. the secondary banks, were and are much more dependent on foreign business, and such business is based on finer margins. A uniform call for special deposits, it was argued, could upset their foreign business very substantially. A further reason was that the Bank might wish to influence the net inflow of funds to the UK by means of either a different application in respect of the type of deposits, or a different rate of call. In practice, the Bank of England ceased using special deposits after 1980.

The introduction of competition and credit control triggered off a considerable amount of comment and criticism from the City as well as from within academic circles. Furthermore, events since the new scheme was introduced cast some doubt on the underlying approach as a basis for monetary management. We shall look now at some of the comments which have been made and attempt an evaluation of the scheme before going on to discuss subsequent developments.

12.3.2 COMPETITION AND CREDIT CONTROL AND THE AFTERMATH : A CASE STUDY

It will be remembered that one of the intentions of competition and credit control was to increase competitiveness by eliminating the discrimination against the London and Scottish clearing banks which had existed under the old methods of control. Arguably the new arrangements simply replaced one form of discrimination with another, since the reserve assets ratio might be congenial to one type of bank but not to another. Furthermore, the imposition of *any* reserve asset ratio is a potential distortion within the banking system. It is certainly the case that in September 1971 the finance houses, for example, were holding a mix of assets which was unsuitable, since their reserve asset ratio in October 1971 was 1·7 per cent whereas it was to be 10 per cent. Similarly, the group of banks classified as 'other UK banks' had a reserve ratio of 9·9 per cent in October 1971 and thus had to build up their reserve assets (by approximately an extra £25 million) in order to comply with the new arrangements.

A further distortion stems from the nature of the assets selected by the Bank to be eligible as part of the reserve asset ratio. One basic question which was asked concerns the rationale for the assets selected: in particular, the exclusion of bills eligible for re-discount at the Bank of England (in excess of 2 per cent of eligible liabilities) and also refinanceable export credit seems curious since these assets are just as liquid as those classified as reserve assets.

One view of the new reserve ratio scheme was that it was to form the basis of a return to market methods of regulation and, in particular, the traditional use associated with open market operations in the bond market – bond sales generating a contraction of bank deposits by a multiple derived from the reserve asset ratio. It is unlikely that this was ever the intention since even a casual examination of the reserve assets reveals that the prescribed ratio fails to satisfy the criteria laid down in Chapter 5, namely that the reserve assets should be capable of tight control by the Bank of England and that the banking system should be unable to generate reserve assets. For example, the banking system could expand deposits and reserve assets by purchases from the non-bank public of some of the public sector assets eligible for inclusion in the calculation of the reserve asset ratio. It is more likely that the authorities took the view that they could exercise some control over the banking system by inducing the non-bank public to move into public sector debt by increasing the attractiveness of such debt through higher interest rates, and at the same time depress the growth of bank advances as a further consequence of higher interest rates.

The original proposals – and subsequent amendments – are unclear as to the underlying theoretical position adopted by the Bank. After 1971, the speeches made both by the Governor and by the Chief Cashier of the Bank of England did not clarify the position sufficiently. An important question was whether the authorities' chosen monetary target was to be the money stock (which definition?), sterling deposits of an original maturity of two years and under, (the main eligible liability under the reserve ratio scheme), or the level and structure of interest rates. As we saw in Chapter 6, it is not possible to regulate both interest rates *and* the money stock. In 1978, a lecture delivered by the Governor of the Bank of England did make clear that the Bank had moved away from interest rates as a target in favour of sterling M3.

It is possible to draw some conclusions about the effect of competition and credit control in the years after 1971, although it is not an easy matter to make firm judgements about either aspect of the competition and credit control policy. Nevertheless, we shall attempt to draw some inferences from the events of subsequent years.

After the reconstruction of their balance sheets, the London clearing banks found that their reserve asset ratio was well in excess of the minimum 12·5 per cent, and this gave considerable scope for increased lending between October 1971 and the end of 1974. London clearing bank sterling advances rose by almost £8,000 million. Other banks with comfortable reserve ratios in October 1971 increased their lending faster than the London clearing banks, but the size of their operations was very much smaller. The authorities, however, viewed the massive expansion in lending and the money stock with some anxiety and, as a result, during 1972 they were allowing interest rates to rise – a policy consistent with the ethos of competition and credit control. The interest rates quoted in *Table 12.3* indicate the effect of this approach.

By the end of 1973, interest rates in the UK had reached historically high (nominal) levels, and yet it is clear that the authorities' use of this instrument as a means of curtailing bank credit was ineffectual. It should be pointed out, however, that

Table 12.3

Selected UK interest rates, 1972 – 74 (%)

	Bank rate MLR	Treasury bill rate	Local authority (3 month)	War loan 3½ %
28 January 1972	5	4·35	4·69	8·14
30 June 1972	6	5·64	7·56	9·48
29 December 1972	9	8·31	8·75	9·81
29 June 1973	7·5	6·96	8·12	10·33
28 December 1973	13	12·42	16·06	12·26
28 June 1974	11·75	11·24	13·38	15·37
27 December 1974	11·5	10·99	13·25	17·45

Source : Bank of England *Statistical Abstract,* no. 1.

although nominal interest rates were relatively high by the end of 1973 (and were to rise even higher in 1974 and 1975), the real rate of interest was not. This was because the rate of inflation between 1970 and 1975 was not only rising but was expected to rise still further. In line with such expectations, potential lenders would have been unhappy to observe nominal interest rates failing to rise sufficiently as inflation increased. We can use a simple arithmetic illustration. By deducting the inflation rate from the nominal interest rates we obtain a rough idea of the real rate which lenders obtain. For example, if a loan of £100 is made for one year at a rate of interest of 10 per cent, and the rate of inflation during that year is 5 per cent, at the end of the year the £100 loan has lost 5 per cent of its value during the year (i.e. the lender can only buy £95 worth of goods at the end of the year compared with his real spending power at the beginning of the year). Furthermore, the interest he receives at the end of the year also has depreciated in value compared with the nominal return negotiated at the beginning of the year. The lender has only £110 − (5/100) 110 = £104·50 of spending power and not £110. Thus in inflationary conditions, and when inflation is expected to continue or to rise, the nominal interest rate is likely to rise in order that the real return to lenders is not whittled away by the inflationary process. Borrowers, on the other hand, may benefit considerably from inflation if the real value of their borrowing is reduced, i.e. at the end of the term of the loan they repay a nominal amount (principal plus interest) which may be substantially less in real terms than the original sum borrowed. Thus an inflationary situation might act as a stimulus to certain kinds of borrower. It is an interesting speculation as to the increase in nominal interest rates which would have been required during the early 1970s effectively to damp down the growth in advances and the stock of money.

Evidence that competition and credit control was not working satisfactorily can be deduced from the introduction in 1973 of a powerful *non-market* method of bank regulation. This was the supplementary special deposit scheme. The scheme, announced on 17 December 1973, established a specific rate of growth for interest-bearing eligible liabilities initially for the period November 1973 to May 1974. The rate of growth chosen by the Bank was 8 per cent and the deposits base selected was calculated as the average for each bank and finance house on the make-up days of the last three months of 1973. If a bank or finance house moderated its growth of interest-bearing eligible liabilities (IBELs) to that required, then there would be no penalty. Growth in excess of 8 per cent, however, would result in a sliding scale of supplementary deposits required by the Bank of England. It is clear from the figures in *Table 12.4* that the supplementary special deposit scheme would make excess

Table 12.4

IBEL growth	Supplementary deposit call
8 per cent	nil
9 per cent	5 per cent of excess deposits
10 – 11 per cent	25 per cent of excess deposits
over 11 per cent	50 per cent of excess deposits

growth of IBELs rather costly to the banks and finance houses which were obliged to make such supplementary deposits. These deposits did not bear interest, whereas the banks of course would be paying interest to their own depositors. The scheme was extended for a further six months at the end of April 1974 and the permitted growth of IBELs was 1·5 per cent per month. From 1974 onwards the scheme was temporarily suspended and reactivated on two further occasions (November 1976 to August 1977, and June 1978 to June 1980), and the detailed operation was altered as well.

This instrument of control had two features which are of particular interest. It was a flexible scheme (the permitted growth could be varied, the excess growth percentages could be altered, the size of the supplementary deposit could be changed) and one which had a potentially strong influence on the growth of bank deposits. Any bank or finance house near to the penal growth limit would be likely to adjust its deposit interest rate downwards to depress the inflow of funds. It is notable also that the supplementary deposit scheme was a non-market method of control dealing directly with bank liabilities in a rather blunt way. The introduction of this scheme implied that market methods of regulating the banking system – an implicit feature of the ethos of competition and credit control – were deemed to be functioning ineffectively by December 1973. A much stronger and swifter instrument was required.

Although the supplementary special deposit scheme seemed to provide a powerful weapon for the authorities, it did detract from the objective of encouraging competitiveness and the removal of distortions. When operational, the scheme imposed an arbitrary limit to the growth of interest-bearing deposits for banks and finance houses but not for *all* financial intermediaries. In other words, the financial intermediaries not covered by the competition and credit control arrangements, e.g. building societies, would be able to offer attractive interest rates to depositors/investors and thus draw funds from the banking system and the finance houses. The scheme thus provided a penalty to one part of the financial system and thereby a boost to the remainder. It was in its last period of operation from June 1978 to June 1980 that some of these distortions became more apparent and paved the way for the abandonment of the scheme.

At the end of the first fifteen months of the operation of competition and credit control, the Bank expressed the view that the 'creation of conditions conducive to greater competition between the banks has been attained'.[3] There were certainly signs that the banking system was competing more vigorously than before, and particularly through the medium of price, ie. the banks and discount houses abandoned their cartel agreements on interest rates. Although such agreements were put aside, it is difficult to measure the effect of competitiveness by observing the prices (interest rates) prevailing. The fact that the major banks' business operations are very similar means

[3] Bank of England *Report*, p. 5, year ended 28 February 1973.

that they are subject to the same market pressures and therefore their responses will often coincide.

A significant consequence of the introduction of competition and credit control was the closer links which developed between the primary and secondary banking systems. We have seen already that the primary banks had moved directly into the secondary banking field as well as through their own subsidiaries. The uniform application of competition and credit control to all banks and finance companies meant that the primary banks could operate directly in the secondary markets and the associated money markets on a much larger scale. After the changes in 1971 it is very noticeable that the primary banks' holdings of sterling CDs particularly, but also interbank deposits, increased very considerably.

Undeniably, the introduction of competition and credit control provided a fillip to greater competition, but there were other factors which were contributing to greater competitive ness in the British financial system. In particular, the growth of the Euro-currency market resulted not only in an extension of banking activities but also in the setting up and the growth of overseas banks in the UK. Such banks were active in the market but were becoming increasingly interested in extending their business activities in sterling, i.e. competing with British banks within the UK. Our earlier discussion of secondary banking referred to the successful development of term lending to meet UK residents' needs, particularly companies, and this exemplifies the opportunities open to foreign banks with offices in the UK. It is likely, furthermore, that operating in the Euro-dollar market gave appropriate experience to many banks which could have been the foundation for operations in the other parallel markets which began to develop in the 1960s.

Although competition and credit control was explicitly intended to stimulate competition in the banking system, it is evident from the intervention of the authorities since 1971 that they were not prepared to accept the full implication associated with the competitive ethos.

A further illustration of the Bank's reluctance to see the full consequences of competition is linked to the behaviour of interest rates and the money stock M3. During 1972 and the early part of 1973 banks were attempting to satisfy their reserve requirements by bidding for funds in the parallel markets which would then be put out at call to the discount houses (money at call was an eligible reserve asset). As a result of this vigorous bidding the rates of interest on deposits rose, but the rates of interest on bank lending tended to lag behind. (Changes in bank base rates, and therefore lending rates, have as their proximate cause an *administrative* decision of the banks, i.e. they are not immediately market-determined). The result of this situation was a process called round-tripping, or the merry-go-round, whereby it was profitable for some of the banks' customers to borrow (or fully utilize their advance facilities) at, say, base rate plus $1^1/2$ per cent, and redeposit the same funds with another bank, either as a time deposit or more likely as a sterling CD. The consequence of this round-tripping for banks' balance sheets was a simultaneous rise in advances and deposits. Thus M3 rose entirely as a consequence of the arbitrage opportunities. The authorities clearly did not like this process and introduced measures in the Budget of 1973 to reduce the attractiveness of sterling CDs by removing the capital gains exemption and also by introducing a new tax deposit account offering competitive interest rates to companies who wished to make deposits against future corporation tax liability. But it was the introduction of the supplementary special deposit scheme in December 1973 which effectively clamped down on round-tripping, since the scheme, it will be recalled, could penalize the attracting of deposits by the banks. At the same time as the introduction of the new scheme, the banks agreed to adjust their base rates swiftly as market conditions changed.

The greater flexibility of interest rates after 1971 and their independence from the officially determined rate, i.e. bank rate, resulted in the old bank rate being replaced in October 1972 by the minimum lending rate (MLR). The immediate cause of this change was that the Treasury bill rate rose above bank rate in September 1972 and this meant that bank rate could not be a penal borrowing rate for the discount houses. The flexibility of short-term interest rates, including the Treasury bill rate, was one of the consequences of the greater competitiveness. Bank rate, however, was an administered interest rate and therefore 'sticky'. The MLR which was introduced could not be less than the prevailing Treasury bill rate because of the nature of its calculation. The MLR was calculated as the average Treasury bill discount rate *plus* 1/2 per cent and then rounded to the nearest 1/4 per cent above. The MLR calculation resulted in its being a market-determined rate, except on those occasions when the authorities chose to suspend the method of calculation and fix the MLR administratively. In May 1978 the Bank of England abandoned the MLR mechanism, whilst retaining the term MLR, and returned to the old bank rate procedure whereby the discount rate became, once again, an administratively determined interest rate. One of the reasons for this reversion was that the authorities wished to exercise, whenever possible, tighter control of the key rates of interest in the economy, in an environment in which control of the money supply was becoming an increasingly more important aspect of monetary policy.

The *Competition and Credit Control* document alluded to the possible discrimination which might be needed to protect savings banks and building societies against the loss of deposits stemming from the greater competitive opportunities of the banks. Because of the effect on the cost of mortgages and its political implications, in September 1973 the Bank asked the banks to observe a limit of $9\frac{1}{2}$ per cent interest rate on deposits under £10,000. When interest rates began to fall in the early part of 1975, the $9\frac{1}{2}$ per cent ceiling became redundant and it was withdrawn on 8 February 1975. Apart from the evident discrimination against the small saver (those who had time deposits with the banks which were less than £10,000), this application of an interest rate ceiling was clearly a distortion and a deliberate attempt to prevent the effect of competition extending to certain financial intermediaries.

12.3.3 THE BREAKDOWN OF COMPETITION AND CREDIT CONTROL
The preceding discussion has highlighted the fact that in the difficult economic conditions of the 1970s competition and credit control, together with its various qualifications and amendments, had limited success as a framework for monetary control. Indeed it could be argued that the boost to bank liquidity resulting from its introduction was one of the factors

contributing to the explosive growth in bank lending and the subsequent rise in inflation from around 6 per cent in mid 1972 to almost 20 per cent by late 1974 (and even higher in 1975). However, it would be unfair to put too much blame on monetary control arrangements alone for the rising inflationary trend experienced throughout most of the 1970s, because fiscal policy and general international economic conditions (such as the first oil shock) played important parts as well. But the greater attention given towards controlling monetary targets from the second half of the 1970s onwards led to pressure for changes in monetary control arrangements consistent with this emphasis. This was particularly the case when a Conservative government assumed office in 1979 with monetary targets as the cornerstone of its overall economic strategy.

The supplementary special deposits scheme – which came to be known as the 'corset' because of its restrictive impact on deposit creation – had become the major feature of the monetary control arrangements. But direct controls such as this inevitably produce distortions to the operation of the financial system and encourage methods of avoiding the effects. Moreover, it is often the case that when one loophole is closed, another is found and used. This was to be the case with the corset, especially in its last period of operation from June 1978 to June 1980. The avoidance that took place had the effect of diverting the financing of spending from the controlled parts of banking activity to areas uncontrolled by the corset arrangements. Two principal forms of such 'disintermediation' (so called because ultimate borrowers and lenders bypass the normal intermediation process of banks and may even undertake business directly with one another) were the acceptance bill 'leak' and the Euro-sterling 'leak'.

The acceptance bill leak When the corset ceiling was in danger of being breached, it was not in the interest of the relevant bank to meet increased corporate sector loan demand through the usual channels of term loans and overdraft facilities since the additional interest-bearing deposits necessary to finance this activity would add to the total of IBELs. An alternative route was through bank acceptances, which are bills of exchange accepted within the banking system, i.e. a bank provides a financial guarantee against default by the issuer of the bill in return for a fee. Such bank acceptances are not included in an individual bank's advances and did not require extra IBELs as long as the bank did not provide the money to the borrower by purchasing (i.e. discounting) the bill. From the point of view of the banking system as a whole, only those bank acceptances which were purchased by the non-bank private sector did not contribute to the banking sector's total of IBELs *or* to sterling M3 because the acceptance of bills by a bank is not recorded as a deposit liability in its balance sheet. Therefore if banks persuaded their corporate customers to borrow through issuing bills of exchange, this had the effect of circumventing the corset controls as long as banks left the actual provision of finance by purchases of these bills in the non-bank sector.

The Euro-sterling leak Since the corset arrangement could be applied only to banks based in the UK, one distortion which arose during its operation from June 1978 to June 1980 (a period which coincided with the relaxation and eventual abolition of exchange controls, with the effect that transfers of funds into and out of the UK became much easier to conduct) was that banks overseas, especially the subsidiaries of UK banks, could attract sterling deposits from lenders in the domestic economy. This type of business was stimulated because the corset discouraged domestic banks from bidding for interest-bearing deposits, with the result that domestic interest rates were depressed to a lower level than that being offered by foreign-based banks in the Euro-sterling market. This Euro-sterling borrowing by, say, a subsidiary of a London clearing bank in Paris would not be counted as part of the parent bank's IBELs. The transfer of sterling deposits to the Euro-sterling market would also depress sterling M3, although it could rise from this lower level if Euro-sterling deposits found their way back into the UK banking system. The latter might occur if the funds were on-lent to UK borrowers or if the Euro-sterling interest rate differential was narrowed or eliminated with the result that Euro-sterling deposits were transferred back to banks based in the UK.

These types of activity were excluded from the definition of eligible liabilities and at the same time were in general omitted from sterling M3. So not only were distortions being caused in the financial system which were inconsistent with the free competition objectives of competition and credit control, but such diverted financial flows went unrecorded in the official monetary target. Sterling M3 was becoming therefore a less reliable indicator of actual monetary conditions.

12.4 Monetary management : a Conservative government

The emergence of unsatisfactory side-effects of the corset after its reintroduction in June 1978 coincided with the election in 1979 of a Conservative government which elevated monetary targets to a central role in economic policy. Indeed their medium-term financial strategy had as its central element a progressive reduction in money supply growth over a four-year period in order to reduce inflation. The Chancellor of the Exchequer recognized some of the distorting effects of the corset on both the financial system and the official monetary statistics and so he abandoned the scheme from June 1980.

The abandonment of the corset arrangements served to remove the restrictions on conventional forms of bank lending. Therefore financial flows which had been pushed into forms such as acceptance credits or Euro-sterling lending were now rerouted back into more orthodox types of financial activity that was recorded in eligible liabilities and sterling M3. This 'reintermediation', as it became known, had the opposite effect to the introduction of the controls in that it artificially boosted the growth in the official monetary statistic in the immediate period after the abolition of the corset. But the scale of the reintermediation surprised even the monetary authorities; in 1980 sterling M3 grew by 5 per cent in July and 2·9 per cent in August compared with an *annual* target range of only 7 to 11 per cent, with the result that measured monetary growth was pushed higher above the official target range than expected.

The revelation that underlying monetary growth was much higher than previously anticipated caused concern to the authorities, who were now committed to monetary targets. An obvious response was to raise interest rates, i.e. to rely on market methods of control. Previously the authorities had been reluctant to raise interest rates to levels sufficient to choke off excessive lending and preferred instead 'non-market' methods of control such as the corset which had by then shown themselves to be defective in many respects. Some of the more fervent monetarist commentators argued not only that interest rates should be used more flexibly as an instrument of policy to achieve progressively lower monetary targets, but that the techniques and operation of monetary policy should be over-hauled to facilitate the process. This was the monetary base control debate which led the authorities to issue a Green Paper (i.e. a consultative document seeking the view of interested partners) on monetary controls.[4] A substantial part of this document was devoted to a discussion of the previous methods of operation. It is to these criticisms and the response of the government that we turn now.

12.4.1 THE MONETARY BASE CONTROL DEBATE

The concept of the monetary base should be familiar from the discussion in Chapter 5 when we examined the relationship between the cash base of the banking system and the level of bank deposits. The monetary base is simply the ultimate means of liquidity in the economy in the form of notes and coin issued by the central bank and bankers' balances at the Bank of England. The principle behind monetary base control is that banks keep a certain proportion of their deposits (which constitute the main element in the 'money supply') in base money, either because there is a mandatory requirement on them to do so *or* for prudential reasons. The mandatory requirement would be some form of cash ratio along the lines suggested by Section 5.2.1. But even without a mandatory requirement, banks would choose to hold some proportion of their assets in a liquid form in order to meet actual and potential claims for cash from the public, settlement of inter-bank indebtedness, and transactions with the central bank. Since the monetary authorities are responsible for issuing base money, they should in theory be able to exert control over the growth of bank deposits and the money supply, given that the banks' balance sheets cannot exceed some multiple, mandatory or voluntary, of their base money.

In practice, tight control of the money supply would require that: (a) the authorities can actually control the monetary base with some precision; (b) there is a stable or predictable

[4] *Monetary Control*, Cmnd 7858 (March 1980).

relationship between the cash base and the level of bank deposits; and (c) the banking system as a whole is unable to relieve its cash shortage by obtaining cash from the public or monetary authorities when subject to a tightening of monetary policy. If all of these requirements are not met, then close control of monetary aggregates such as sterling M3 may be difficult to achieve, at least in the short term via monetary base control. We will return to these conditions later after first summarizing the technical aspects of the Bank of England's approach to monetary policy in the period from the introduction of competition and credit control.

The Bank of England has never in the past attempted to control the growth of bank deposits through the combination of a cash ratio and limitations on the cash available to the banking system. Both before and during competition and credit control the Bank was always prepared to provide the cash requested by the banking system *but* at interest rates of the Bank's own choosing. As was explained in Section 4.8.3, the Bank would use the Treasury bill issue to ensure that money market conditions were consistent with its view of how short-tem interest rates should move. Typically, the Bank would have created a shortage of funds by over-issuing Treasury bills but would then relieve that shortage via the discount market at interest rates deemed consistent with monetary control, e.g. a tighter monetary policy would require higher interest rates. These money market rates would affect other lending and borrowing rates and so were presumed to have some effect on the level of bank lending. This approach relied upon the fact that the London clearing banks had to maintain 1·5 per cent to their eligible liabilities as bankers' deposits at the Bank of England; consequently they were obliged to build up their cash reserves to this level after the Bank operated in the money market to create a shortage of cash in the banking system. Thus under competition and credit control the effective fulcrum of monetary policy was this 1·5 per cent ratio and not the reserve assets ratio.

The Bank's tactics in the money market were an integral part of its overall policy of attempting to control monetary aggregates by setting interest rates at what it considered to be an appropriate level. The reader is reminded here of the accounting relationship explained in Section 5·5 between, principally, the PSBR, bank lending, sales of public sector debt to the non-bank private sector, and the money stock. The Bank's approach was that, given the PSBR, variations in interest rates could be used to influence both bank lending and sales of government securities mainly in the form of gilt-edged stock. Not only did the Bank try and influence short-term interest rates via its money market operations, but at the same time it would fix tap prices for new issues of gilt-edged stocks at levels (and therefore interest rates) it thought appropriate for sufficient sales consistent with the needs of monetary control. These tactics were not independent of each other because the gilt-edged market came to regard short-term interest rates as an indicator of likely movements in bond yields and prices. Of course, these operations on both short-term and long-term (bonds) interest rates could be reinforced by changes in minimum lending rate, which had an immediate effect on money market and bond market rates and to which other administered rates such as bank base rates and building society rates were linked.

Supporters of monetary base control have argued that this general policy of attempting to control the money supply by pegging interest rates was misplaced and unsuccessful. The result, it was claimed, was devices such as the 'corset' which served mainly to distort monetary statistics and at best had only a temporary effect on monetary growth. Instead, they recommended that the Bank should control the monetary base and let interest rates move to the level consistent with this base.

At this stage it may be worth pointing out how monetary base control might work and some of the problems that could be encountered in its operation. Variations in the monetary base, which essentially arise from cash transactions between the government and non-government sectors, come about for several major reasons. A positive PSBR adds to the cash base since government disbursements exceed revenue receipts, but on the other hand sales of government debt have the opposite effect since cash flows to the government in payment for securities. Additionally, exchange rate intervention by the authorities will give rise to cash transactions between the government and non-government sectors as explained in Section 5·3. Given the

PSBR and the absence of exchange rate intervention, the Bank of England's attempts to control the monetary base would have to depend on sufficient sales of government securities. This might require a change in the methods of debt management since the Bank would have to sell a certain amount of debt at whatever price and therefore interest rates were necessary, perhaps by issuing gilt-edged securities through the auction method described in Section 6.11.1.

What would be the reaction of the banking system to pressure on the monetary base? Clearly, much would depend on the precise details of the system adopted, but two general points can be made. First, interest rates might become more volatile not only because of changes in the marketing of government debt but also because banks would have to adjust their cash and lending positions in response to the authorities' efforts to control the monetary base. An attempt by banks to raise cash from within the banking system or from the public could push up short-term interest rates. At the same time, bank lending might be contained only at the expense of large variations in interest rates which in turn might not be very effective in the short term if borrowers believe that the changes are only temporary. Indeed, the overdraft system is not suited to an arrangement under which banks have to make sudden adjustments to their lending because banks have little control over the extent to which these facilities are used by customers once they have been granted. Secondly, certain institutional arrangements might have to change. In particular, it might be difficult to reconcile the essential lender of last resort function of the central bank with the need to contain the monetary base. Also there could be pressure to end or modify the overdraft system in favour of forms of bank lending such as term loans which in principle are easier to control in the short term.

Now that we have outlined how a system of monetary base control might work, we will discuss some of the key issues of dispute regarding its potential effectiveness. For this purpose we will frame our discussion in terms of the three key requirements identified earlier:

(a) It may be difficult to control the monetary base with precision. The Green Paper was sceptical about some of the technical factors which could make short-term control very difficult, e.g. daily shifts into and out of central government balances and fluctuations in the public's demand for cash would both complicate control of the monetary base. Also, exchange rate intervention by the authorities as a means of smoothing excessive fluctuations in the exchange markets might be inconsistent with close control of the monetary base because such intervention has an effect on that base. Apart from these difficulties, attempts to control the monetary base could result in greater volatility of interest rates.

(b) Even so, it is uncertain as to whether there will be a stable or predictable relationship between the monetary base and bank deposits unless some mandatory relationship is imposed which, like all such types of non-voluntary restriction, could have the effect of distorting competition between different banks according to their type of business *and* might lead to the diversion of monetary flows outside the controlled area. To avoid discrimination a mandatory ratio might need to distinguish between retail deposits, which are more risky because of their susceptibility to quick withdrawal, and wholesale deposits, which are large, usually for fixed terms, and therefore are matched by banks against assets with similar characteristics. Because of this matching, little cash is needed for prudential reasons with wholesale deposits and so it might be fairer to exempt these from a mandatory ratio.

(c) Finally, it is uncertain as to the extent to which banks can obtain cash from the public or government (via lender of last resort facilities) when the authorities seek to tighten monetary control under a monetary base system. For example, banks may be able to induce the public to hold less cash by offering them a better return on bank deposits. Indeed a bank which was faced with a need to attract extra cash might consider offering a rate of return on current accounts so that customers would have an extra incentive to minimize their withdrawals of cash for normal transactions purposes. The ability of banks to attract cash in this way might frustrate attempts by the authorities to control the monetary base because open market operations to reduce the cash reserves of the banking system could be offset by a reduced holding of cash by the public.

There is also a problem regarding the role of the central bank as lender of last resort to the banking system. This function is crucial to general confidence in the financial system because it effectively means that the Bank of England will not allow a liquidity shortage to develop which could threaten the collapse of parts or all of the banking network. But rigid application of monetary base control might force banks into a cash shortage which could endanger their solvency. Thus a potential conflict exists between the Bank's role as lender of last resort and operator of monetary policy in the form of monetary base control. The decision as to when and in what circumstances the Bank provides cash to the banking system could influence the extent to which monetary base control might be effective as a means of monetary control.

Some of these doubts were reflected in a statement[5] made by the Bank on 24 November 1980. Also it was emphasized that movement to either a mandatory or a non-mandatory system of monetary base control would require more information and experience to be gained about the banks' demand for cash. Various changes were made to monetary control arrangements subsequently, one of which would generate information on the banks' operational demand for cash, but adoption of monetary base control was rejected for the time being at least. The new arrangements, their operation to date, and the general conduct of monetary policy in this period are examined next.

12.4.2 MONETARY CONTROL ARRANGEMENTS SINCE 1979

Although the publication of the Green Paper *Monetary Control* aroused considerable debate, its main element was not implemented. Nonetheless, in the increasingly competitive and deregulated environment of the financial markets, some system of Bank of England supervision was needed. The Treasury and Bank of England consulted with the interested parties and in August 1981 introduced changes both in the way interest rate decisions are made and disseminated to the financial markets and in the minimum reserve requirements previously imposed on banks. The main changes affecting the conduct of monetary policy were as follows:

(a) The practice of announcing in advance a minimum rate at which the Bank would supply liquidity to the banking system

[5] See the Bank of England *Quarterly Bulletin*, vol. 20, no. 4 (December 1980).

via the discount houses was discontinued. Thus minimum lending rate was terminated, although the authorities reserved the right to announce in advance the minimum rate which for a short period ahead the Bank would apply to its lending in the money market.

(b) Instead, the Bank aimed to keep short-term interest rates within an unpublished band which would be moved from time to time as conditions changed. The procedure for carrying this out has been described in some detail in Secion 4.8.3. It relied upon the discount houses offering or buying various bills – predominantly commercial bills, but Treasury bills as well – and the Bank responding to these bids and offers at dealing rates of its own choosing. This operational procedure was designed to give market participants a greater role in determining short-term interest rates.

(c) The minimum reserve assets ratio was abolished, as was the requirement on the London clearing banks to hold 1.5 per cent of their eligible liabilities with the Bank in non-interest-bearing form. This was replaced by a uniform requirement on *all* banks and licensed deposit-takers to hold 0.5 per cent of their eligible liabilities with the Bank. [6] In addition the clearers will hold at the Bank whatever operational balances they think necessary.

(d) The scheme for supplementary special deposits lapsed but the special deposits scheme remains in place and, if activated, will apply to all institutions with eligible liabilities (ELs) of £10 million or more, with calls set as a percentage of ELs. To date no such calls have been made.

Clearly the arrangements were designed to reduce the distortions caused by the competition and credit control arrangements and to make interest rates more responsive to changing market conditions. On the first of these there can be little doubt that the new arrangements represent a significant improvement. The abolition of the minimum reserve assets ratio and the corset means that some types of banking institutions or activities are no longer penalized at the expense of others, with the result that actual monetary data provide more reliable information than they did at times in the past. Even so, it could be argued that the application of a 0.45 per cent cash ratio to all

---

[6] In December 1988 it was 0.45 per cent of eligible liabilities.

banks does mean that a distortion, albeit modest, exists between their activities and those of non-bank financial intermediaries such as building societies which are an increasingly powerful force in the personal credit market, but are exempted from the arrangements.

Although short-term interest rates do have an added degree of flexibility now that MLR has been abolished, it is of course still the case that the monetary authorities largely dictate whether and to what degree any changes should be made. However, money market participants have a role in anticipating such changes under the new system, even though this does not guarantee that the authorities will be satisfied with the speed or extent of adjustment. A couple of examples might illustrate the point. The first real test for the market system of short-term interest rate determination arose in September 1981. At the time, sterling was losing ground uncomfortably quickly against other currencies, threatening the government's inflation objective since import costs would rise. Although the Bank wanted to push rates up in order to show its concern over the situation – for which the appropriate tactic for the Bank was to refuse offers of bills from the discount houses at the prevailing rates – dealings in the early part of the month failed to produce any increase in market rates and the exchange rate continued its slide. Part of the difficulty was that for seasonal reasons there was plenty of liquidity in the money markets and therefore the discount houses were not aggressive sellers of bills. In the end the Bank had to revert on 14 September to the old tactic (used before the new arrangements became operational) of draining liquidity, leaving the market short at the morning's dealings and then lending above prevailing rates in the afternoon. Only in this way could the authorities obtain the sharp, substantial rise in interest rates which they wanted. Accordingly money market intervention rates were pushed up by a sufficient amount to trigger a 2 per cent rise in clearing bank base rates to 14 per cent. During mid 1982 the situation was reversed in that the authorities wished interest rates to decline, and on this occasion the result was achieved in an orderly manner. Although money market rates were initially quite firm the Bank steadily reduced its intervention rates, pulling market rates in the same direction. This prompted successive 0.5 per cent cuts in base rates, and by the third one the intentions of the monetary authorities were so clear to market participants that base rates were changed before official rates became fully compatible. At the time there were persistent shortages of liquidity in the markets and so the discount houses were having to sell bills to the authorities. Because the Bank was taking these bills at increasingly higher prices (lower interest rates) the discount houses were obviously making a profit and so were quite satisfied with the outcome. This greatly facilitated the smoothness of the process.

Since the introduction of the new money market arrangements it would seem that they have worked well. The Bank is able to sustain an influence over short-term interest rates without appearing to dominate the market through the administrative imposition of the old bank rate. However, it might well be argued that in the absence of foreign exchange controls and the general freeing of international money flows, the Bank of England might in fact have little choice in its methods of operation in the money market. The change in the fiscal position of the central government which we examined in Chapter 6 provides an underlying strengthening of the Bank's position in the money market, since the fall in the central government's borrowing requirement (CGBR) is likely, on balance, to tighten conditions in the money market. As we have seen, by the second half of 1987 the central government's financial deficit had yielded to a surplus and with it the CGBR had changed to a position of net repayment. The contrast is clear when we compare April to June of 1987 with the same period in 1988. The CGBR contributed £4 billion to the cash position of the money market in 1987II whereas it accounted only £0.1 billion in 1988II. Market operators are aware of such factors as the underlying budgetary position as well as the authorities' attitude towards, say, the exchange rate. This means that market participants can anticipate the Bank's view of events and act accordingly. The Bank can therefore appear to follow the market and adjust its own dealing rates. Since 1981 there has only been one occasion when the system did not work and that was in January 1985. During the early part of that month there were anxieties and uncertainties about the sterling exchange rate and with it uncertainties about the immediate changes in short-term interest rates. To provide a clear position for market operators the Bank announced on 14 January 1985 that, for that day, Bank lending to the discount houses would be at a minimum lending rate of 12 per cent. Clearing bank base rates moved up to 12 per cent and subsequent increases in interest rates took place at the initiative of the market, with the Bank endorsing the changes through its money market operations.

The new arrangements and their subsequent operation have disappointed some of the monetarist critics of UK monetary policy who wanted to see a move towards monetary base control. But the Conservative government's early experience with monetary targetry convinced them that too rigid a stance might be inappropriate, and could be damaging in some circumstances, so the reforms which have been made are relatively cautious compared with some of the suggestions put forward. The adoption of money supply targets in the UK, particularly from 1979, represents a new phase in the conduct of monetary policy and the experience to date merits more detailed treatment.

12.4.3 A STRATEGY FOR THE MEDIUM TERM

It is widely regarded that the policy of targeting monetary aggregates such as sterling M3 or M4 is a key feature of the Conservative government's period of office since 1979. But it could be argued that the first experience was even earlier because in 1967 the IMF imposed a domestic credit expansion (DCE)[7] target as a condition for granting standby loan facilities in the aftermath of the sterling crisis and the subsequent devaluation. During the early 1970s the monetary authorities – the Treasury and Bank of England – did use an unpublished M3 objective as one of the factors affecting the interpretation of overall economic conditions, but it was not until 1976 that monetary targets were officially presented on a

---

[7] In Section 5.4 we saw that the balance of payments position can affect the domestic money stock. DCE was a calculation of the expansion of domestic credit *after taking into account any changes in the money stock as a result of the balance payments position.* DCE was thus a measure intended to show changes in the money supply caused by *domestic* pressures leading to a change in the credit component of the money supply. DCE is no longer used as an official indicator.

regular basis. A financial crisis caused by rapidly expanding government borrowing, a deterioration in the balance of payments, and yet another run on sterling persuaded the Labour government of the time to introduce a monetary target in an attempt to improve confidence in the financial markets. But this, together with a rise in short-term interest rates to 15 per cent, did not solve the underlying problem, and once again a loan had to be negotiated from the IMF. As one of the conditions the IMF imposed a DCE target and the UK authorities added as well a subsidiary sterling M3 target range for the 1976 – 77 financial year. Early experience with such targetry seems to have been successful, as can be seen from *Table 2.5.* Both the DCE and sterling M3 targets were met easily in 1976 – 77, and in the 1977 – 78 financial year a preferred range for sterling M3 was added to the DCE limits set out earlier by the IMF. In this period the DCE target was once again achieved with comfort, but sterling M3 over shot its target range. The reason for this divergent behaviour was a restoration of external confidence in the UK which led to heavy flows of sterling and intervention by the authorities to moderate the appreciation of the pound. This is just the set of circumstances that inflates sterling M3 (but has no effect on DCE). Indeed the intervention to contain sterling's rise (which was causing concern for the external competitiveness of British industry) jeopardized restraint on the domestic money supply to such an extent that it has to be abandoned. From April 1978 a slightly reduced target range of 8 – 12 per cent annualized. was set for sterling M3 and when the Conservatives gained office in May 1979 the target period was extended to October of that year. Actual growth turned out just at the top of the target range for the period as a whole, aided by the effectiveness of the corset in containing measured monetary growth despite an accelerating inflationary trend.

Macroeconomic strategy was radically revised when the new Conservative government gained office. The approach was much more monetarist than anything seen before and had as its centrepiece a progressive reduction in monetary growth and public sector borrowing over time as the preferred means whereby inflation would be reduced and the conditions put in place for a sustainable increase in output. Initially a 7 – 11 per cent target range was set for sterling M3 in the first statement of the medium–term financial strategy (MTFS) in March 1980 [8] with a progressive reduction to 4 – 8 per cent planned by the 1983 – 84 financial year. It was made clear that interest rate adjustments would be made according to whether monetary growth was proceeding satisfactorily, with other considerations taking a subsidiary role. In practice, the first year's experience under the MTFS was very disappointing for the government, especially in view of the fact, that monetary growth had been

Table 12.5

A chronological record of monetary targetry in the UK

Period	Target variables	Target range	Out-turn
April 1976 – April 1977	M3	12%	9.5%
1976 – 77 financial year	DCE	+£9 billion	+£4.4 billion
April 1976 – April 1977	£M3	9 – 13%	8%
1977 – 78 financial year	DCE	+£7.7 billion	+£3.8 billion
	£M3	9 – 13%	16%
April 1978 – October 1979	£M3	8 – 12% annualized	12%
October 1979 – April 1980	£M3	7 – 11% annualized	7%
February 1980 – February 1981	£M3	7 – 11% annualized	20%
Februrary 1981 – February 1982	£M3	6 – 10% annualized	14.5%
February 1982 – February 1983	M1		11%
	£M3	8 – 12%	10%
	PSL2	annualized	9%
February 1983 – April 1984	M1		14%
	£M3	7 – 11%	9.5%
	PSL2	annualized	13%
February 1984 – April 1985	£M3	6 – 10%	11.6%
	M0	4 – 8% annualized	5.5%
April 1985 – April 1986	£M3	5 – 9%	19.5%
	M0	3 – 7%	3.4%
April 1986 – April 1987	£M3	11 – 15%	20.5%
	M0	2 – 6%	4.8%
April 1987 – April 1988	M0	2 – 6%	6.3%
April 1988 – April 1989	M0	1 – 5%	

Source : Bank of England *Quarterly Bulletin; Financial Statement and Budget Report.*

[8]See *Financial Statement and Budget Report, 1980 – 81.*

contained to the bottom of the 7 – 11 per cent target range set
for a six-month period prior to its launching – although a rise in
short-term interest rates to an unprecedented 17 per cent had
been made to achieve this. During 1980 much of the acceleration in monetary growth could be put down to reintermediation
following the ending of the corset arrangements, but even so it
was clear that underlying growth was running beyond the
target range. If the authorities had followed through their new
approach, a further rise in interest rates would have had to
have been made. But all the other economic and financial
conditions suggested that monetary conditions were quite tight:
the sterling exchange rate was gaining ground rapidly, supported by rising oil prices as well as high interest rates, and at one
stage exceeded the post-1967 devaluation level of $2.40; the
domestic economy was moving sharply into recession, prompted
by a cutback in inventories on a scale not seen since the war:
and by autumn 1980 there were signs of marked slowing down
of wage and price pressures. In response the monetary authorities cut interest rates – to 16 per cent in July 1980, 14 per cent
in November, and 12 per cent in March 1981 – despite an
overshoot on the monetary aggregate.

After this experience the government chose to be more flexible
in determining its interest rate response to the behaviour of the
money supply. To summarize the view of the Bank on events up
to mid 1980: The apparent relationship between M3 and
nominal incomes, in the shorter term, begin to display alarming
properties. Pressing policy to the point where the monetary
target might have been achieved would seemingly have risked
unacceptably severe and immediate consequences for the real
economy, consequences that were unintended and strategically
damaging. [9]

A target range was set for the 1981 – 82 financial year at a 1 per
cent lower level than in the previous year – in line with the
progressive reduction set out in the MTFS – but once again it
was exceeded by a considerable margin. One of the reasons was
that in the recessionary conditions most companies were forced
borrowers because of a sharp fall in profitability, and so they
were not able as a group to make significant reductions in their

bank borrowing until economic conditions improved. By the 1982 Budget the less rigid attitude to monetary targetry became expressed formally in terms of an extension of the monetary variables covered and a raising rather than lowering of the official target range.

In addition to sterling M3 one more broad (PSL2) and one narrow (M1) measure of money were introduced as targets, each with the same range for the 1982 – 83 financial year. The Chancellor emphasized that none would assume exclusive importance for monetary policy purposes, but that all three would be monitored along with monetary conditions in general, including the *exchange rate*. This latter qualification was shown to be important because when sterling came under pressure in the late autumn of 1982 the Chancellor's response was to raise interest rates, initially by 1 per cent, with rises in the Bank's intervention rates leading the way. For the year as a whole, all three monetary aggregates were contained within the target range.

It should be noted that disappointment with the relationship between particular monetary targets and final economic objectives – for example inflation fell from a peak of over 20 per cent in 1980 to a low point under 5 per cent in 1983, despite sterling M3 growth well above target over this period – led to the examination of other monetary series as potentially better indicators. Indeed the introduction of M1 and PSL2 as additional target variables to sterling M3 in 1982 shows the development of official thinking. Since then, emphasis has been put on finding a suitable narrow definition of money on which to base policy decisions. One reason is that much of the empirical work in other countries on the relationship between 'money', national income, and prices has been based on 'narrow' definitions and indeed the US authorities, for example, chose such a measure for their targetry when they adopted a more aggressive monetary stance in late 1979 (although subsequently they were to place just as much emphasis on wider monetary aggregates as well). M1 was adopted in the UK as a target variable because it was thought potentially useful as a 'narrow' indicator, but it now has a large interest-bearing component currently amounting to about 25 per cent of the total. As such, it is not a good measure of transactions-related balances and, indeed, could be said to have some of the characteristics of broad money. This was one of the reasons why the Chancellor introduced a new series called M2 (see Section 2.4.3.1) following his Budget statement in March 1981, designed specifically as a measure of transactions balances, but because statistics on M2 had been available only for a short time it was considered unwise to place too much policy emphasis on it in the early stages.

Accordingly in October 1983 it was announced that the wide monetary base (Mo) would receive more attention because a long statistical series is available for it (unlike for M2) and yet it covers mainly notes and coin with the public and is not subject to the same distortions as M1. It was made clear that it was not intended to signal the introduction of some form of monetary base control (see Section 12.4.1).

In Budget statements the Chancellor had maintained the emphasis on both narrow and broad monetary aggregates (M1, £M3 and PSL2) as well as adjusting downwards the target range. However, from 1984 there was a switch from M1 to Mo as a target as well as using £M3. It is clear, however, from *Table 12.5* that the growth of £M3 was persistently well above the target range but growth of Mo seemed to be satisfactorily contained. The Chancellor took the view in October 1985 that although the growth of £M3 was in excess of the target, the fall in the inflation rate (it had fallen from 17.8 per cent p.a. in 1980 to 6.1 per cent p.a. in 1985 and was set to fall to 3.4 per cent p.a. in 1986) was such that excess £M3 growth was not damaging to the government's inflation objective. In 1987 the use of M3 as a monetary target ceased and only Mo remained since 'Mo has continued to be a reliable indicator of monetary conditions.'

12.4.3.1 Overfunding

Until the £M3 target was downgraded by the Chancellor in 1985, the containment of the growth of £M3 was only achieved by a combination of interest rates and a technique known as *overfunding*. Overfunding can be described as a situation in which debt management policies are geared to selling greater amounts of debt to the non-bank private sector – mainly in the form of gilts – than are necessary simply to meet the government's borrowing requirement. This has a contractionary effect on monetary growth which may be necessary to achieve specified monetary targets if bank lending is growing at a faster pace than these targets. The latter had been the case for much of the period since 1979, although at first measured monetary growth was allowed to take the strain as we have seen earlier. Why should bank lending have grown strongly? A large part of the explanation lies with changes in the pattern of corporate finances which have taken place over recent years. Up to the early 1970s corporate borrowers had provided a considerable part of their financial needs by borrowing long term through fixed-interest markets (for example, in the form of debentures). This type of borrowing does not push up monetary growth because it is financed mainly by other parts of the non-bank private sector, such as insurance companies and pension funds. By the late 1970s the inflationary conditions of the period had made the corporate debt market unattractive both to borrowers and lenders – borrowers were reluctant to take money at fixed rates well over 10 per cent for periods of twenty years or more, whereas lenders had faced substantial capital losses on their debenture portfolios because of the rising trend in interest rates over the previous ten years – and so companies resorted to borrowing more from the banks, usually on a medium-term variable basis. Of course the switch from fixed-interest borrowing from the debt markets to greater reliance on loans from the banking system had the effect of raising the growth in monetary measures such as sterling M3.

When the monetary authorities overfund, larger shortages in the money markets are created which have to be relieved. The typical practice had been for the Bank to purchase commercial bills from the banking system via the discount houses. Effectively this means that the authorities were replacing bank lending to the corporate sector with short-term lending of their own via the accumulation of commercial bills. And the funds for this were provided by additional sales of gilts, National Savings, etc. to the non-bank sector. The net result is that measured monetary growth turns out lower than it otherwise would be, even though the process might be regarded as a little cosmetic.

Table 12.6 provides an indication of the extent of overfunding particularly since 1981; figures with a positive sign in column 4

Table 12.6

Overfunding, bank lending, 1979 – 1988

	PSBR	Sales of debt to non-bank private sector	Bank lending to UK private sector	Overfunding (2 – 1)
1979 – 80	+ 9,925	– 9,149	+ 9,330	– 776
1980 – 81	+ 13,216	– 10,889	+ 9,248	– 2,327
1981 – 82	+ 8,632	– 11,334	+ 14,928	+ 2,702
1982 – 83	+ 8,864	– 8,440	+ 14,354	– 424
1983 – 84	+ 9,729	– 12,552	+ 15,387	+ 2,823
1984 – 85	+ 10,112	– 12,401	+ 18,589	+ 2,289
1985 – 86	+ 5,795	– 6,601	+ 21,389	+ 806
1986 – 87	+ 3,347	– 1,457	+ 30,344	– 1,890
1987 – 88	– 6,242	– 569	+ 44,728	+ 6,811

Source : Bank of England Quarterly Bulletin, various issues.

indicate overfunding because sales of debt to the non-bank private sector will have exceeded the PSBR. Column 3 shows the additions to bank lending to the private sector in each of the financial years. These figures show clearly how bank lending expanded after 1980. In order to restrain the growth of £M3 there was an associated increase in sales of debt to the non-bank private sector, as shown in column 2. The ending of the policy of overfunding is equally visible after 1985. The emergence of the budget surplus and net repayment of debt by the public sector after 1986 presents an interesting situation. On the basis of the unadjusted figures for 1987 – 88 the debt *redemption* of £6,242 million represents the opposite effect of the public sector's need to borrow; that is, using the approach explained in Chapter 5, this would represent a pressure to reduce the growth of the money supply, and together with debt sales to the non-bank private sector of £569 million the overall effect is equivalent to heavy overfunding.

The decision by the Bank to cease overfunding derives from the acknowledgement that the rapid growth in £M3 did not seem inconsistent with declining inflation. In other words, it was a recognition that a sufficiently close relationship between changes in £M3 and inflation (or growth in money incomes) did not exist for the purpose of monetary policy and targeting. Furthermore, in simple theory the technique of overfunding should have had the effect of raising yields on long-term financial assets relative to short-term assets. If such were the case then this would reinforce the tendency for the corporate

sector to borrow from the banks rather than in the capital
market, thus encouraging the growth of the money stock rather
than dampening it. Finally, the technique of overfunding had
the effect of systematically draining cash from the banking
system which the Bank then had to alleviate through its open
market operation in the *bill* market. This resulted in a steady
rise in the holding of commercial bills by the Bank of England
and in effect distorted the balance of assets held by the
non-government sector. The relative scarcity of such assets
would tend to push up yields on short-dated assets. Overfunding might therefore represent a preordained element in the
decision-making of market operators which, if sufficiently large,
would represent a reduction of the influence of 'free market
forces' on short-term interest rates and correspondingly a rise in
the indirect influence of the Bank. At its simplest, however, it
would seem that overfunding – whilst having an accounting
impact on the published money supply figures – did little more
than drain funds from one sector (the non-bank private sector)
and recycle it back to another (the banking sector).

12.4.4 AN ASSESSMENT

It is evident that although the government has sustained a
reference to the medium-term financial strategy in each *Financial Statement and Budget Report* (FSBR), in fact that strategy – at
least in respect of *monetary* targetry – has changed since 1979,
even though the underlying objective of policy has been
maintained, namely the reduction in the rate of inflation. Since
the inception of the MTFS a continuing component of that
strategy has been targets for the public sector borrowing
requirement. The PSBR is, strictly speaking, a part of government fiscal policy but it has had a high profile in the MTFS for
two reasons at least. First, control and reduction of the PSBR
(roughly the difference between public sector spending and
receipts; see Chapter 6) would require tight control of public
expenditure, and was a strong element in the Conservative
government's thinking. Indeed, in its Public Expenditure
White Paper in 1979 the government proclaimed that public
expenditure was at the root of all Britain's economic difficulties
and should therefore be reduced. Secondly, it could be argued
from an accounting framework that changes in the PSBR

would result in changes in the money supply. Chapter 5 and especially Section 5.4 illustrate this possibility, particularly where a public sector borrowing requirement has to be financed by the banking system. A more subtle analysis of the effect of the PSBR on the money supply was that sales of government debt to the non-government sector in order to finance the PSBR would make private sector portfolios unbalanced in that they would be less liquid. In order to maintain the balance, asset holders would increase their *demand to hold money* and the banking system would respond by supplying the necessary money balances. The government's policy, as we have seen, has been towards market methods of regulating the banking system and particularly by the use of interest rates. However, our earlier description (see *Table 12.6,* column 3) shows that the banking system's ability to expand credit in these conditions seems to have been unconstrained and therefore its ability to meet the demand for money by the non-government sector was also unconstrained. It has also been argued by the government that the size of the PSBR was directly related to the level of interest rates; a high PSBR would lead to higher interest rates, whereas a small or negative PSBR would lead to lower interest rates. [10] Early MTFS references to the PSBR were couched in terms of reducing the size of the PSBR as a proportion of GDP, but with the buoyancy of government revenues the 1988 MTFS declared that an absolute (not a ratio) target is a *zero* PSBR over the medium term, accepting that there are likely to be fluctuations around zero from year to year.

A further change in the content of the MTFS was instituted in the 1985 statement. This was the inclusion of figures for money GDP in the table showing money supply targets, with the declaration that 'the government's overriding aim will be to maintain monetary conditions consistent with a declining growth rate of money GDP and inflation. Short-term interest rates will be held at the levels needed to achieve this.' The MTFS statements in subsequent years continued to make reference to reducing the rate of growth of money GDP, *Table 12.7* shows the anticipated changes in money GDP in the

[10] The PSBR began to move into surplus in late 1986 or early 1987 and this negative borrowing requirement has been subsequently termed the public sector debt repayment (PSDR), on the assumption that the surplus is used to redeem public sector debt.

Table 12.7

Percentage changes in money GDP

MTFS	1985 – 86	1986 – 87	1987 – 88	1988 – 89	1989 – 90
1985	8¹/₂	6¹/₂	5³/₄	5	5¹/₂
1986	9¹/₂	6³/₄	6¹/₂	6	6
1987		6	7¹/₂	6¹/₂	6¹/₂
1988			9³/₄	7¹/₂	

Source : various. *Financial Statement and Budget Reports*

MTFS statements from 1985. The out-turn, in fact, has been higher rates of money GDP growth than expected and, not surprisingly, the subsequent MTFS expectations have been revised slightly. The emphasis on money GDP growth coincides with the dropping of £M3 as a monetary target. One reason for this, which we considered earlier, was a recognition that the link between a monetary target (£M3) and the objective of policy (the rate of inflation or growth of money incomes) had become significantly less tight (see the quotation in Section 12.4.3). In view of such a change, the maintenance of a particular target becomes not only fruitless but even injurious for the management of the economy. For example, in such uncertain conditions it would be possible for a government to find that a given tightening of monetary policy in one year has a much greater and unexpected effect than the same policy change in another. Contemporary debate had included the recommendation that as a consequence of the change in the underlying relationships, money GDP should become a target rather than a broad monetary aggregate such as M3. It was argued that to establish money GDP targets would represent a clear statement about the government's commitment to bear down on inflation since a given rate of growth of money GDP combined with, say, 'excessive' increase in money wages leading to a higher rate of inflation would result in a fall in real GDP, falling profits, and rising unemployment. [11] A determined approach in this situation would indicate a resolve by

---

[11] Thus, for example, a target growth of money GDP of 8 per cent p.a. combined with an inflation rate of 8 per cent p.a. would mean that output would not grow at all. If inflation were, say, 10 per cent p.a. then this would imply a fall in output of about 2 per cent. On the other hand, if inflationary pressures eased to, say, 4 per cent p.a. then this would allow a rise in output of about 4 per cent p.a. and with it rising employment and living standards.

government not to validate the underlying inflationary situation by permitting *money* GDP to expand.

A most significant element in the government's strategy has been the sterling exchange rate. In the first FSBR the government's view of the exchange rate appeared to be that it was determined by market forces, but subsequent FSBRs, have changed the emphasis to suggest that the exchange rate has become a target of policy rather than a variable over which the government had little direct control. The emerging approach of the Chancellor was that the exchange rate could move (appreciation or depreciation) because of changes which were either internal or external to the UK economy. In particular, if monetary conditions within the UK were too slack, e.g. monetary growth was too high or interest rates were too low, then the expectation would be for the exchange rate to depreciate. The converse would be, presumably, that if internal monetary conditions were too tight then the exchange rate would appreciate. Domestic monetary policy would be adjusted in the light of such exchange rate movements. External factors might include a change in economic policy in the USA or a movement in commodity prices such as oil. A tightening of monetary policy in the USA would tend to cause the US dollar to appreciate (or slow its decline) and thus affect the sterling exchange rate in the opposite direction. Such a movement in the sterling exchange rate could affect the domestic economy and therefore monetary policy would need to take this into account. Certainly the implication would be that exchange rate movements caused by internal factors would require a clear response, e.g. higher or lower interest rates; the response to changes in external factors might be rather less certain.

The government's view about the link between the exchange rate and its important policy objective, inflation, is that an appreciation of the exchange rate reduces the sterling price of imports and raises the foreign currency price of exports. The former has a direct bearing on lowering the cost of materials and finished goods, and therefore a direct effect on the retail price index (the most commonly used measure of inflation). The latter effect, whilst making UK exports less competitive, does have the consequence (it is argued) of pushing UK firms which operate in export markets to raise their productivity as well as being restrained in the size of wage awards to their labour force. In a similar way, the lower price of imports puts pressure on UK firms which are competing with foreign goods in the home market to raise their productivity and also be restrained in their wage offers to their employees. Thus the exchange rate could be regarded as an anti-inflation weapon. The scheme of things might be represented as in *Figure 12.3*. These relationships seem clear and coherent and on the face of

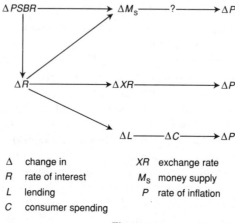

Δ	change in	XR	exchange rate
R	rate of interest	M_S	money supply
L	lending	P	rate of inflation
C	consumer spending		

Figure 12.3

it should provide the basis of a fairly simple style of management of economic policy. Reality is, however, more complex and the relationships may not offer the degree of certainty which policy-makers and governments require. There are a number of points which can be made.

First, the PSBR, which has held a central place in government thinking, is an unreliable policy target. To be of value, a policy instrument or target should be predictable and controllable. Since 1975 the government's forecasts of the PSBR have been prone to very large errors. The FSBR contains forecasts for the PSBR in the year ahead, and *Table 12.8*, shows the FSBR forecasts as well as the out-turn. The size of the errors in the forecasts is impressive. The errors in forecasting the absolute size of the PSBR has, of course, resulted in errors in the forecast of PSBR/GDP ratios. There are two main reasons why the forecast of PSBR is difficult: one is that the PSBR is the

Table 12.8

PSBR : forecast and out-turn (£m)

	Out-turn	Forecast at March Budget	Absolute error	Error/out-turn (3/1) (%)
1983 – 84	9,717	8,200	1,517	15·6
1984 – 85	10,098	7,200	2,898	28·6
1985 – 86	5,658	7,100	– 1,442	25·5
1986 – 87	3,457	7,000	– 3,543	102·5
1987 – 88	– 3,621	3,900	– 7,521	207·7
1988 – 89	– 14,000	– 3,200	– 10,800	77·0

Source : Financial Statement and Budget Report; Financial Statistics.

difference between two very large aggregates, public spending
and receipts. Predicting changes in these two aggregates is also
difficult because of their components. The second reason is that
PSBR forecasts (and PSBR/GDP ratios) cannot be reliable
unless the forecast for inflation is also accurate. This is because
the rate of inflation will affect: the rate of growth of *money* GDP;
the growth of government spending (a very high proportion of
government spending is wages and salaries); and the growth of
government tax revenues. If, therefore, policy changes were to
be based on the *forecasts* of the PSBR then clearly such policy
changes may well incorporate quite serious mistakes, and one
could make a case for neglectng or rejecting the PSBR entirely
as a policy target.

Secondly, much of the success of policy seems to hinge on the
use of interest rates. Interest rates are expected to have an
impact on borrowing (and indirectly the money supply) and
thus spending, and also to have an effect on the exchange rate.
The Governor of the Bank of England made it quite plain in a
lecture given in May 1987 that in the Bank's view the only
effective instrument of monetary policy is the short-term interest rate. The fundamental question, therefore, is how effective it
is. The Bank's position as represented by the Governor seems to
be that although the rate of interest should, in principle, affect
the demand for credit via changes in the cost of borrowing, in
practice – evidenced by the data – it would appear that the
cost of borrowing effect has been weak. In particular, the
household sector has proved very resilient in its borrowing
through mortgage finance; such borrowing is partly sustained
by the above-average rise in the value of houses and the growth

in household income. The corporate sector, on the other hand, may be influenced by interest rates not so much in the level of their borrowing as in the *source* of such borrowing – the banks or the capital market. The effect of changes in interest rates on the value of wealth holdings is also recognized by the Bank, but this too is regarded as an uncertain response. Equally doubtful is the consequence of a change in the flow of income between borrowers and depositors with the building societies and banks. For example, a rise in interest rates will transfer income from net borrowers to net depositors, and since the two groups are unlikely to have the same spending patterns there will be some effect on consumer spending.

There would seem to be much firmer conviction about the effect of changes in interest rates on the exchange rate; in normal circumstances a rise in UK interest rates *relative to other countries* would cause the exchange rate to appreciate and a fall in interest rates to lead to a depreciation. But here again, the effects can be perverse if the financial markets' expectations are greatly different from the view of the authorities. Additionally there could be circumstances, for example, in which inflows of foreign funds are substantial and pushing up the exchange rate with the implied requirement of a cut in domestic interest rates. Such a fall might, however, be inconsistent with the anti-inflationary stance adopted internally. The only way round such a dilemma would be for the Bank to intervene in the foreign exchange market to try to push the exchange rate in the desired direction, whilst leaving the authorities free to use interest rates for domestic purposes. The difficulty here is that a single central bank would find such solitary foreign exchange intervention hard to sustain, partly because the size of the flows of funds through the foreign exchange market is so large that no central bank could maintain intervention for very long. The Bank of England's reserves are only around $50 billion, which represents a very small fraction of the flow of funds through the foreign exchange market. A further difficulty might be that in trying to maintain a particular exchange rate band the Bank is obliged on occasions to sell sterling to prevent excessive appreciation. The domestic monetary consequences of this action (see Section 5.4) could be the expansion of the domestic money stock. A typical response of the Bank in order to neutralize such expansion would be to sell debt, but this would of course tend to push up interest rates, and that in turn could exacerbate the pressure on the exchange rate as foreign funds were further attracted by higher rates.

One of the fundamental difficulties about using the rate of interest to change household and corporate behaviour is that the authorities only exercise influence over *nominal* interest rates. But why might this be a problem? Rational behaviour by households and businesses would require them to consider not nominal interest rates but *real* interest rates. As we saw in Section 6.13, if the rate of inflation is, say, equal to the rate of interest over a particular period then the holder of a financial asset will have gained nothing in real terms by holding his wealth in that particular form. Inflation will have reduced the real value of his wealth by an amount equal to the interest received. Clearly, if the rate of inflation exceeds the rate of interest then a wealth-holder will lose part of his wealth in real terms. For example, if the rate of interest is 10 per cent p.a. and the rate of inflation in that year is 12 per cent then the real rate of return is negative since the wealth-holder will lose roughly $12 - 10 = 2$ per cent of the value of his wealth.[12] Similarly, one might argue that a business, when considering an investment project such as the purchase of a piece of plant or equipment, would be weighing up the relative merits of investing funds in the capital equipment compared with holding such funds in a risk-free form such as a bank deposit. If the equipment were purchased then it would have a life into the future and would, therefore, be producing goods into the future. If inflation emerged as a problem then the firm could sustain the *real* value of its investment in the equipment by raising the price of the goods produced by the machine. Thus, a rational firm would wish to determine the *real* rate of return (i.e. having discounted for inflation) on its alternative investment of funds in the form of a bank deposit.

[12] The correct calculation would be $\frac{110}{112} \times 100 - 100 = -1.78$ per cent. It is important to recognize that the denominator (the rate of inflation) should really be the *expected* rate of inflation, since the purchase of an asset is done with the expectation of a *future* income. The rational individual, therefore, should really do this calculation using a forecasted inflation rate. The data used to construct *Figure 12.4* are *actual* inflation rates, i.e. after the event. This is really incorrect, but unfortunately there is no adequate way of determining the expected rate of inflation in the minds of the decision-makers, whether they be households or business.

In *Figure 12.4* we have plotted for illustrative purposes and for simplicity the nominal and real rates of return on $2^1/_2$ per cent consols.[13] The data which we have used (consols yield and the rate of inflation measured by the retail price index) do reveal several interesting features;

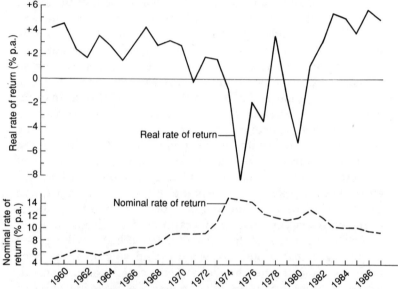

Figure 12.4 *Nominal and real rate of return on $2\frac{1}{2}$ per cent consols 1959 – 87*

(a) As we suggested in Chapter 6, the nominal rate of return on financial assets does shadow fairly closely the rate of inflation. If the rate of inflation increases then the nominal rate of return on financial assets also rises. This relationship could be caused by a number of factors, but it nevertheless confirms what we would expect; that for rational investors the nominal rate of return 'should' match movements in inflation. If this does not happen then lenders will experience a diminution in the real value of their capital which, one might presume, in the long run they would find unacceptable.

(b) Over the long run the holder of an asset such as consols would have received a positive rate of return even though in

[13] Consols are undated government bonds, i.e. they have no redemption date and are unlikely to be redeemed. Because of this characteristic their yield is uncomplicated by capital gains or losses to redemption date, and so can be regarded as a good measure of the long-term rate of interest.

some years the real rate of return had been negative. Between 1959 and 1987 the average annual *real* flat yield was 1·7 per cent (this ignores capital losses).

(c) From the point of view of government policy and the adjustment of interest rates in order to influence economic behaviour of households and firms, the graph reveals that as real rates of return fall or rise, the nominal rate of return is moving in the opposite direction. This is significant because, for example, between 1973 and 1978 the level of interest rates reached historically high levels and it would have seemed that the stance of monetary policy was 'tight'. But the graph of the real rate of return reveals that during that period the real rate of return was negative. Far from borrowers paying income to lenders, lenders were in effect subsidizing borrowers since the indebtedness of a borrower in *real terms* would have fallen between 1973 and 1978. In other words, although borrowing seemed costly in nominal terms, in fact it was quite the reverse.

(d) The difficulty for the authorities is that they cannot be sure about the movement of the real rate of interest and in that case they cannot be certain whether monetary policy is 'tight' or 'slack'. During 1973 – 74 it was relatively slack when measured by the real rate of interest. By contrast, in 1981 – 88 the real rate of return was itself rising to historically high levels whereas the observable rate of interest (the nominal rate) was actually falling; monetary policy was 'tight'.

The third point to be made on the scheme of *Figure 12.3* concerns deficits. In Chapter 7 we discussed the balance of payments of the UK and noted the growing deficits on trade since 1982 and the emergence of an overall current account deficit in 1986 of £175 million, rising to almost £15 billion in 1988. Notwithstanding any doubts about the reliability of the data, it does seem clear that the trading position has deteriorated rapidly as the economy has moved out of recession and expanded very rapidly. This deficit has had its counterpart in the capital account (transactions in assets and liabilities) section of the balance of payments, and it is evident that part of the deficit has been financed by inflows of relatively short-term bank deposits rather than long-term capital. The deficits within the current account are expected to continue into 1989 and beyond. One reason for this expectation is the sheer size of the deficit relative to GDP; it is in that respect even larger than the USA deficit and likely to diminish slowly.

Conventional analysis would argue that the UK deficit (and indeed that of the USA) will be corrected ultimately by a substantial depreciation of the exchange rate. But in view of the discussion above this would raise serious problems for the management of the domestic economy. In the November 1988 Bank of England *Quarterly Bulletin*, the Bank expressed anxiety about the increased inflationary pressure within the UK during 1988. If, as the Bank suggests, the only monetary instrument available is the short-term rate of interest (and the government's approach to fiscal policy is *not* to use it as a regulatory device; indeed, the preference is to reduce the level of income taxation) then the appropriate response is to increase interest rates sufficiently until there is some monetary response within the economy which begins to neutralize the inflationary pressure. During 1988 this was exactly the stance adopted by the Chancellor; from the end of May to the end of November, short-term rates rose from about $7^1/_2$ per cent p.a. to almost 13 per cent p.a. The dilemma is that such high interest rates may well sustain a high foreign exchange value of sterling and in that case the correction of the balance of payments cannot begin. Indeed, a high foreign exchange value of sterling will do the reverse by maintaining the uncompetitiveness of UK exports and the attractiveness of foreign imports. If cost-inflation were to emerge as a significant element in the inflation process then balance of payments adjustment would be further delayed as interest rates are kept high.

To some economists, this dilemma arises partly because of a reluctance to introduce other instruments of policy, following the 'rule' that there is a need for as many instruments as there are objectives. At the present time it seems that economic policy objectives rely heavily on one instrument – the short-term interest rate – whose influence is as limited and uncertain as is the control over it.

12.5 Summary

(a) Governments have certain objectives in such areas as employment, prices, the balance of payments, and growth, but these objectives may prove to be incompatible in practice. The policy-maker will have to take account of economic, social, and political considerations in deciding which combination of objectives is both feasible and desirable. The economist has two major functions in this respect : (a) to identify and measure the trade-offs that exist between economic objectives so that the policy-maker is made aware of how much of one must be given up to get more of another; and (b) to search for the most appropriate policy tools which will enable the government to achieve its macroeconomic objectives more satisfactorily.

(b) Macroeconomic management is concerned with the relationship between instruments, targets, and objectives. The government has at its disposal instruments which can be directed at chosen target variables, and movements in these variables are expected in turn to help bring about the desired economic objectives. Successful macroeconomic management will require that : (a) macroeconomic objectives are *sensitive* to changes in target variables; and (b) the authorities are able to *control* target variables via instruments. The satisfaction of *both* these conditions is necessary for the effective operation of fiscal, monetary, and other macroeconomic policies.

(c) We suggested that control of the banking system, including the secondary banks, was becoming a growing problem for the Bank of England. In the 1960s the Bank had to rely increasingly on non-market methods of control – methods which were not popular with the primary banks. In 1971, following discussions with the financial institutions, the Bank devised competition and credit control. This scheme introduced a new reserve asset ratio (replacing the liquidity ratio) which applied to all the banks, and it was hoped that other features of the scheme would stimulate competition in the financial area as well as allowing the Bank of England to exercise control over the financial sector by market, rather than non-market, methods of control. One important element in this approach was that the supply of credit to end users should be determined by price, i.e. the rate of interest borrowers were prepared to pay, rather than central bank non-market regulation.

(d) Events since 1971, we suggested, have indicated that the new scheme was not entirely successful from the point of view of credit control and the Bank had to move back to the use of non-market methods of regulation such as the 'corset'. But in 1980 the authorities issued a statement implying that market methods of control would resume their central role, and subsequently changes have been introduced to make this effective.

(e) The primary instrument of control which the authorities regard as central to monetary policy is the short-term rate of interest, determined in the money markets. This is consistent with the changes introduced in August 1980, and which continue. There may be some doubt whether a single instrument, whose control and impact are regarded as uncertain by the Bank of England, can be relied on to assist the government in achieving its macroeconomic targets. It is certainly arguable that the subsidence of inflation since the early 1980s has had little to do with the manipulation of monetary aggregates or the rate of interest but has been much more related to rising unemployment, falling commodity prices, and an overvalued pound.

Appendix 1 Liquidity

There are a number of strands running through the debate about liquidity; an illustration should be useful. Suppose there are two individuals who have the same income and identical circumstances of family and other commitments, and the only significant difference between them is the nature of their wealth holdings. Both individuals were fortunate to inherit a substantial sum and they invested it in the manner displayed in *Table 12.9*. Clearly individual A has a 'balanced portfolio' weighted towards fairly secure financial assets such as building society accounts and unit trusts. Even the less capital-certain assets, government securities, are weighted towards the short-dated end. Individual B has bought a tract of land in the Scottish Highlands which has virtually no other use than for light grazing. If we consider the idea of liquidity as the ease with which an asset can be converted into spending power, then we can make a rough evaluation of the two individuals' liquidity. It is probably correct that most would describe individual A as being the more liquid, especially in view of the substantial holdings of building society deposits. Other aspects or interpretations of liquidity may be also introduced. To what extent are

Table 12.9

Individual A Net income p.a.	£	Individual B Net income p.a.	£
Employment	16,000	Employment	16,000
Investments	4,000	Investments	4,000
	20,000		20,000

Wealth		*Wealth*	
House	80,000	House	80,000
Building society accounts	20,000	Land in Scottish Highlands (suitable	
Unit trusts	5,000	only for light	
TSB shares	2,000	grazing)	50,000
Government bonds :			130,000
Short-dated	15,000		
Medium-dated	6,000		
Long-dated	2,000		
	130,000		

the wealth holdings marketable? Are there risks of capital loss as a result of converting the assets into spending power? How serious is the 'forced-sale' risk? Are the assets secure from a significant risk of default? Do the assets provide the holder with a hedge against inflation?

It was the view held by the Radcliffe Committee, and for which there is evidence, that the degree of liquidity and variations in liquidity may well affect *the ratio of spending out of current income.*[14] To return to our illustration; is it likely that the two individuals will spend the same fraction of their net income on consumer goods, or is it probably the case that individual A will spend a higher fraction? The reasoning behind such a possibility might be that since he has such a substantial part of his wealth which is very secure and liquid he can 'risk' spending a higher fraction of what he earns on consumer goods, because if he makes a mistake in his budgeting he can cash part of his very liquid assets and use the funds to supplement his budget. Individual B would find this much more difficult to do because of the relative illiquidity of his assets.

[14] In the economic theory discussed in Chapter 10 this is termed the *propensity to consume,* and the size of the propensity to consume affects the size of the *multiplier.*

An important characteristic of assets is that their degree of liquidity may change over time. This can be a result of both the micro – and the macroeconomic changes in the economy. A rise in consumer demand for compact discs weakens the profitability of firms dependent on old technology, whereas those firms producing the new product will have their profitability in the future enhanced. The value of these companies' shares will change to reflect the turn of events. At the macroeconomic level a general slow-down in economic activity is likely to affect share values across the board; a rise in interest rates, for example, is likely to have an immediate impact on the prices of government and other fixed-interest assets. Significantly, the government is capable of affecting liquidity through changes in economic policy. We saw in Chapter 6 that the price of consols was inversely related to the level of interest rates. This relationship implies that if the government were to engineer a rise in interest rates then this would reduce asset values; household liquidity would fall and with it spending. If the relationship is sufficiently close and strong then this could be a vehicle for monetary policy having an impact on economic activity. The corporate sector of the economy also holds a range of financial assets. As with households, this portfolio provides firms with liquidity, and it is also a group of assets whose value can change through government economic policy. Thus monetary policy may have an influence on business spending on fixed capital assets.

Many economists at the time of the Radcliffe Committee investigation, and also today, hold the view that concentrating government attention on the stock of money as a policy target is mistaken because :

(a) What matters for many households and firms as an influence on their spending is their liquidity.

(b) In a modern financial system, financial intermediaries such as banks are able to generate money in the form of bank deposits in response to the need for it; the supply of money is largely *demand-determined*. If households or firms require to hold more money then they will attempt to convert liquid assets into money, and the banking system – a profit-seeking group of firms – will be happy to oblige. What matters therefore is the stock of liquidity of households and firms and not the stock of money.

(c) Central bank control of the money stock is likely to be very difficult to achieve, and this has certainly been the UK experience.

(d) Governments and central banks can influence liquidity more easily than the money stock.

Additional reading

The reader who wishes to pursue topics in more depth should find the following references useful :

The British Financial System, J. Revell, Macmillan Press Ltd.

The Economics of Money and Banking, L.V. Chandler and S.M. Goldfield, 9th edn., Harper International Edition.

The Evolution of the International Monetary System 1945-88, B. Tew, Hutchinson.

The Economic System in the UK, D. Morris (ed.), 3rd edn., Oxford University Press.

Economics, D. Begg *et al.,* 2nd edn., McGraw-Hill.

Bank reviews and bulletins :

Bank of England *Quarterly Bulletin.*

Barclays Bank *Economic Review.*

Financial Statistics, HMSO.

Glossary

Arbitrage The opportunities for arbitrage arise when there are differences in the prices or yields on similar assets in different markets. An arbitrage operation would consist of the buying of such assets in the 'cheaper' market and selling in the 'dearer' market. As a result of such activity the difference in prices or yields in the markets would thus narrow or disappear. Arbitrage occurs in such markets as the foreign currency and securities markets.

Adjustable Peg System A system in which exchange rates are fixed but are subject to periodic revaluations/devaluations. Such a system was set up at Bretton Woods in 1944 and operated in the international monetary system during the period 1945-73.

Accepting House Otherwise known as merchant banks whose original role was the accepting (endorsing) bills of exchange. Such firms – e.g. : Hill Samuel; Baring Brothers; – have diversified their functions and are much involved in corporate financial advice.

Aggregate Demand The total money demand for goods and services produced in the economy which arises from consumption of domestic products, government expenditure, investment, and exports.

Bank for International Settlements (B.I.S.) An international institution set up in 1930 with the intention of providing banking facilities for central banks. The so-called Group of Ten countries are represented on the Board of Directors, along with Switzerland, and the Board meets regularly at Basle.

Bank Rate An administratively determined rate of interest which the Bank of England charged for its lending to the discount houses. Bank rate was operational until October 1972 when it was replaced by Minimum Lending Rate. After the August 1981 changes a more market related system of lending to the banking system via the discount houses was adopted, based on money market intervention rates.

Bear Market A market in assets which is characterised by a sustained fall in prices, perhaps because of the change in expectations of market operators.

Bill of Exchange The bill of exchange (or commercial bill) used to be the most important method of financing international trade. The bill of exchange is rather similar to a post-dated cheque except that the bill is drawn by the trader providing the goods (and therefore in effect credit to say, a foreign importer) and 'accepted' by the recipient of the goods by writing his name on the bill. The exporter thus has a promise to pay – an I.O.U. – which may be for three months ahead. The exporter may choose to wait for payment from the importer, or he may arrange with the importer for the bill to be 'accepted' by a London accepting house, or clearing bank. Once such a bill has been accepted, the exporter is able to sell the bill to a discount house or even his own bank, at a discount of course. The bank or discount house may then hold the bill until maturity and finally take payment from the importer. Bills which have been accepted by an acceptance house or bank are termed 'bank bills' and 'fine bank bills' are those which have been accepted by banks or accepting houses of the highest reputation and probity. A 'trade bill' is a bill of exchange which has simply been accepted by a trader. With the growth of international banking links the bill of exchange has become much less important as a means of international finance. The commercial bill – issued by companies to raise short term finance – has gained in importance in recent years, largely as a result of changes in the way the Bank of England provides assistance to the money markets.

Blue Chip The term used to describe assets – usually company shares – which are regarded as a solid and safe financial investment e.g. ICI, Glaxo.

Bulldog Security Fixed interest securities denominated in sterling which are issued by sovereign states other than the UK.

Bull Market The opposite of a bear market, i.e. a market which is characterised by expectations of rising prices or continued rise in prices.

Business Cycle Periodic fluctuations in economic activity which give rise to variations in output and employment.

Call Money Loans to the discount houses which are available to the lending bank on demand and are secured, the security usually being *Treasury bills, commercial bills,* or *certificates of deposit.*

Call Option A contact which confers the right on the holder to buy a limited number of shares in the future at a specific price, and within a particular time period.

Capital is a stock of goods which have been produced and then used to produce more goods (or services). Capital thus refers to such things as machines, tools, buildings.

Cash Ratio Prior to September 1971 and the introduction of *Competition* and *Credit Control,* the clearing banks were obliged to hold 8 per cent of their deposits in the form of cash held as notes and coin and balances with the Bank of England. This figure of 8 per cent was known as the cash ratio. In September 1971 the old cash ratio was abolished but the London clearing banks, and only they, were obliged to hold 1 1/2 per cent of their eligible liabilities as balances at the Bank of England. After the August 1981 changes all large banks were required to deposit a certain proportion of their eligible liabilities at the Bank of England, currently 0.45 per cent.

CD Certificate of deposit. An instrument issued by a bank which acknowledges that there has been a deposit of funds for a period of weeks to several years and at a particular rate of interest. Such certificates are usually saleable in the secondary market. The discount houses are large dealers in CDs.

Chinese Wall A concept which relates to the requirement of those financial firms (market makers) which deal in shares on their own account and who also advise private clients. The chinese wall (which is usually regarded as rather thin) represents the need for information *not* to move between the two parts of the organization representing the two functions. The barrier, albeit it this, is expected to protect the client from the financial firm exploiting its inside knowledge derived from its relationship with the client.

Commercial paper Securities or certificates issued by companies as a means of short-term borrowing, having maturities of between one week and a year. Commercial paper, issued in large denominations, enables corporate borrowers and investors to deal directly with each other, usually with the assistance of the banks enabling the transaction to take place but *not* themselves providing the funds.

Consolidated Fund The central government's cash account which includes all revenue and expenditure items.

Consols A short form used to describe UK government Consolidated Stock. These are old securities which have no stated redemption date. Such securities are sometimes referred to as undated stocks or irredeemable stocks. Because these securities have a redemption date which might be regarded as being at some infinite date in the future, the calculated yield on these assets is regarded as a good measure of the long-term rate of interest.

Consortium Banks These are banks which are owned by other banks, but no one bank has a majority shareholding. The Bank of England's classification includes the proviso that at least one of the shareholders is an overseas bank. The Midland Bank, for example, has interests in twelve consortium banks. The bulk of the business undertaken by such banks is in foreign currencies i.e part of the Euro-currency market. Their business tends to be specialized both geographically as well as in kind.

Corset See Supplementary Special Deposits.

Coupon This is the warrant (authorization) attached to a security which has to be presented to the issuing authority (company or government) for payment of the earnings on the security. Thus the coupon rate is sometimes used to describe the nominal return on fixed interest-bearing securities.

Cover The avoidance of currency risk, i.e. unfavourable changes in the foreign exchange rate, by using the futures markets.

Cross-Elasticity of Demand The degree of responsiveness of the demand for a product. For example, a 10 per cent rise in the price of butter may result in a 5 per cent rise in the quantity of margarine demanded. The relationship may be expressed by calculating :

$$\frac{\text{Proportionate change in quantity demanded (good X)}}{\text{Proportionate change in price (good Y)}}$$

Debenture A security issued by a company in exchange for a loan. The debenture may be secured for the creditor against specified assets of the company or the whole of the assets of the company.

Discount House One of nine companies in the City whose main business activity is dealing in short-dated assets such as bills of exchange which they buy and sell at a discount.

Domestic Credit Expansion D.C.E. was introduced in 1968 in the U.K. and is a measure of the change in the money supply which takes into account changes in the balance of payments position.

Dow Jones Index This is an index of share prices in the New York Stock Exchange and similar to the FT Ordinary Share Index.

ECU European Currency Unit. A composite unit of account which is derived from a weighted average of the European currencies forming exchange rate mechanism of the European Monetary System (E.M.S). The ECU is the official unit of account for the European Community. It has no physical existence but, like the SDR, is used for accounting purposes and the transfer of credits and debits. Private sector bank deposits and securities, travellers' cheques, insurance policies, have been denominated in ECUs.

Effective Exchange Rate A measure of the exchange value of a currency under the system of floating exchange rates. The Effective Exchange Rate of a currency is a weighted average of changes in its exchange value against other currencies.

Equity Capital An expression often used in the context of the provision of new funds for a company by the purchase of ordinary shares issued by the company. Ordinary shares are frequently called 'equities'.

Equity Capital for Industry Equity Capital for Industry (E.C.I.) was set up in May 1976 on initiative from 'the City' and support from the Bank of England. Part of the initial capital of E.C.I. was provided by F.F.I.

E.R.M The Exchange Rate Mechanism by which members of the European Monetary System (E.M.S) ensure the foreign exchange rate stability of their respective currencies through foreign exchange market intervention.

Euro-Bond Market A general term which refers to the international market which raises long-term funds in various capital markets and in different currencies. The development of the Euro-bond market is associated with the Euro-dollar and Euro-currency markets. International banks are involved in the issue of Euro-bonds, and about three-quarters of such bonds are in U.S. dollars.

Euro-commercial paper Short-term, negotiable bearer-certificates issued outside the USA in denominations of not less than $500,000.

Euro-commercial Paper Facility Like a NIF this provides for the borrower to issue short-term paper, but it is not backed by a commitment from banks and usually allows for more flexible maturities. (See Euro-commercial paper)

Euro-Dollar Deposit A Euro-dollar deposit is a U.S. dollar bank deposit which is held outside the U.S.A. Such deposits may arise through trade, e.g. sales of goods in the U.S.A. by, say, a German firm, or by the sale of U.S.A. securities held by a non-resident of the U.S.A. Since such dollar deposits are held by non-Europeans as well as Europeans, the term 'Euro-dollar' is a slight misnomer. The main dealers in Euro-dollars (as well as other foreign currencies) are the U.K. banks (mainly the secondary banks) as well as foreign banks based in London. The Euro-dollar and Euro-currency markets are involved with the bidding and the lending of such deposits either to another bank or the final user, e.g. a U.K. firm wishing to purchase capital equipment in the U.S.A.

European Investment Bank (E.I.B.) An E.E.C. institution set up in 1958 to act as a source of project finance primarily within the E.E.C. The main source of funds is bonds and loans raised on international capital markets, supported by capital subscribed by members of the E.E.C.

European Monetary Cooperation Fund (E.M.C.F.) An E.E.C. institution formed in 1973 to supervise the snake arrangements, i.e. to record the currency transactions between the central banks of the participating countries and to administer the financing arrangements.

European Monetary System (E.M.S.) The proposals originally made at Bremen in July 1978 for a system of fixed exchange rates within the E.E.C. supported by a joint fund for intervention in foreign exchange markets.

European Monetary Union (E.M.U.) The proposal that a common currency, supported by a new central bank, should be introduced within the E.E.C.

Exchange Equalisation Account A Treasury account established in 1932 to hold the U.K.'s official reserves of gold and foreign currency. The Exchange Equalisation Account is used by the Bank of England to intervene in foreign exchange markets.

Finance Corporation for Industry (F.C.I.) F.C.I. was established in 1945 by the Bank of England and the London and Scottish Clearing Banks. In contrast to the I.C.F.C., the F.C.I. is intended to provide term loans to finance large-scale industrial projects.

Finance for Industry Finance for Industry (F.F.I.) is a holding company for the *Industrial and Commercial Finance Corporation* (I.C.F.C.) and the *Finance Corporation for Industry* (F.C.I.). It was set up in 1973 and is jointly owned by the Bank of England (15 per cent) and the London and Scottish Clearing Banks (85 per cent).

Fixed Exchange Rate System A system whereby the exchange value of currencies is fixed in terms of some common standard such as gold.

Forward Dealing A general term used to describe the striking of contracts for some future completion which provides some protection against variations of prices of commodities, currencies, or other assets.

Free-Floating Exchange Rate System A system whereby the exchange value of currencies is determined by market forces and one in which monetary authorities do not intervene to influence exchange rates.

FRN Floating Rate Note. Loan stock which has a variable yield determined by market rates of interest such as London Inter-bank Offer Rate (LIBOR).

Funding Funding operations by the Bank of England involve the selling of longer dated securities to the non-government sector and the buying of shorter dated assets – usually Treasury bills. One effect of a funding operation is to make the average maturity of the national debt greater, as well as the non-government sector 'less liquid'. Funding operations have, in the past, often been intended to reduce the liquidity of the banking system and its capacity to lend.

Futures Contracts for the future sale or purchase of assets representing commodities, currencies, or other assets.

General Agreements to Borrow (G.A.B.) An arrangement whereby the Group of Ten (and later Switzerland) provide supplementary resources to the I.M.F. for drawings by members of the Group of Ten. The G.A.B. were established in 1961 and the facilities provided were used extensively by the U.K. and the U.S.A. under the prevailing adjustable peg system.

General Government Expenditure Central and local government expenditure.

Gilt-Edged Securities A common term used to describe British Government fixed interest securities.

Gilts A popular term given to describe British Government securities. Also termed gilt-edged securities, originating from the gilded edges of the early certificates and implying a very secure asset.

Gross Domestic Product (G.D.P.) A measure of the value of the output of goods and services produced in the domestic economy.

Group of Ten : Belgium, Canada, France, Germany, Holland, Italy, Japan, U.K., U.S.A. and Sweden. Switzerland subsequently became an honorary member, making eleven countries in total.

IBELS Interest-bearing eligible liabilities. See Supplementary Special Deposits scheme and Chapter 7.

Index-Linked Gilts Available since 1981, these gilt-edged securities have their nominal value linked to the Retail Price Index over the life of the security. By this means the capital value of the security is protected against the effect of inflation. These securities usually have a relatively low coupon rate which is applied to the *current* value of the security.

Industrial and Commercial Finance Corporation (I.C.F.C.) This body was set up in 1945 jointly by the Bank of England and London and Scottish Clearing Banks. The main purpose of the I.C.F.C. is to provide long-term finance to companies unable by virtue of their small size to make use of the new issue market.

Injections Spending arising from government expenditure, investment, and exports which stimulates the level of aggregate demand.

Insider Dealing Dealing in shares based on information about a company which is not generally available, e.g. a decision about a take-over bid, which enables the individual or company which undertakes the transaction to make an illicit capital profit. Such transactions may well be more likely within those firms which are both market operators and dealers for clinets. (See Chinese Wall)

Instruments Variables which the government is able to change in order to influence target variables.

Inter-bank Deposit Bank deposits which form part of the wholesale market, and which are used by banks – mainly the non-clearing banks – to offset the ebbs and flows of inter-bank indebtedness. Inter-bank deposits are denominated in both sterling and foreign currencies. Such deposits assist the secondary banks in the business of matching the maturity structure of their assets and liabilities.

International Development Association An international institution established in 1960 to assist the World Bank in its lending activities. It has granted loans on more favourable terms (e.g. for longer periods and at lower interest rates) to less-developed countries, i.e. it is a soft-loan fund.

International Finance Corporation An international institution established in 1956 to assist the World Bank in its lending activities. The International Finance Corporation supplements the World Bank's activities by making available assistance on a commercial basis to private enterprises within less-developed countries.

International Liquidity Assets which are internationally acceptable in the settlement of debts.

International Monetary Fund (I.M.F.) An institution set up at the Bretton Woods Conference in 1944 to supervise the international monetary system.

Investment A commonly used word which has a precise meaning in economics. The term refers to the purchase of new *capital*, e.g. the buying of a machine. 'Investment' in stocks and shares (sometimes called 'financial investment') is simply the purchase of financial or paper assets and need not relate to the production of new capital goods.

Junk Bonds Bonds issued, often to finance a take-over, which are based on the security of the assets of the target company. Using such bonds which may well be underwritten by large financial institutions, this enables take-overs of large companies by relatively small ones.

Key Currency A currency which is an important medium of international exchange and is held widely as official reserves by domestic monetary authorities. The U.S.A. dollar became the key currency under the adjustable system of exchange rates during the period 1945-73.

Leakages Flows of taxation, saving, and import spending, which are not immediately passed on in the circular flow of income.

Legal Tender This is a property which money possesses if the money-substance must by law be accepted as a means of settling a debt. In the U.K., Bank of England notes are legal tender but the coins issued by the Royal Mint are legal tender only up to limited amounts. It is clear from this definition of legal tender that bank deposits do not have this property even though such deposits are the most important means for settling debt in the U.K.

LIBID London Inter-bank Bid Rate.

LIBOR London Inter-bank Offer Rate.

Lifeboat Operation Following a confidence crisis in respect of a number of secondary banks in 1973 and 1974, the Bank of England and the London and Scottish Clearing Banks established a committee under the chairmanship of the Deputy Governor of the Bank of England which would consider requests for financial support from such secondary banks who were experiencing rapid withdrawals of deposits.

London Inter-bank Bid Rate (LIBID) is the rate at which certain highly rated banks bid for funds in the inter-bank market.

London Inter-bank Offer Rate (LIBOR) is the rate at which most banks can obtain funds in the inter-bank market. (See Inter-bank deposit.)

Managed Floating A system whereby the exchange value of currencies is determined by market forces but in which domestic monetary authorities use their reserves of domestic and foreign currencies to influence exchange rates.

Market Maker A financial firm whose status in the market for particular assets requires it to make a market in such assets, e.g. gilts, by setting buying and selling prices for those assets and declaring those prices through the Stock Exchange automated quotation system. Market makers came into existence after the Big Bang in October 1986 and effectively replaced the jobbers which operated under the old system.

Minimum Lending Rate The M.L.R. replaced Bank rate as the lending rate for assistance to the discount houses. Until May 1978 the M.L.R. was a market-determined rate which was calculated according to the formula : average rate of discount on Treasury bills + 0.5 percentage point and rounded up to the nearest 0.25 per cent. On May 25, 1978 the Bank of England announced that M.L.R. would be set administratively, in effect the 'old' Bank rate arrangement. It was abolished in August 1981 and replaced by the intervention rate method of giving assistance to the discount houses and thereby the banking system.

Multiplier The ratio of the increase in income to the increase in injections which brought it forth.

National Debt The accumulated debt of central government which increases when there is a central government borrowing requirement.

National Debt Commissioners A government body which has

been traditionally responsible for investing the National Insurance Funds and the Ordinary deposit accounts of the National and Trustee Savings Banks. Until 1973 all these funds were automatically invested in central government debt, but since then the Commissioners have been granted wider investment powers.

National Income Accounts The accounts which record the value of transactions within the domestic economy.

National Insurance Funds A central government account into which are paid the National Insurance contributions made by employers and employees and out of which National Insurance benefits are financed.

National Loans Fund The central government account which records transactions involving changes in its financial assets and liabilities.

Near-Money Near-money (sometimes referred to as 'quasi-money') assets refers to those assets which, whilst not performing the means-of-payment function of money, have some of the other characteristics of money, e.g. store of value, medium of exchange. Thus, for example, building society deposits, trade credit, bills of exchange, could be regarded as near-money assets.

NIF See Note Issuance Facility

Note Issuance Facility This is a medium-facility which enables the borrower to issue a series of short-term notes known as euronotes. The facility is usually backed or underwritten by a commitment from a group of banks to ensure that the borrower will have access to funds when they are required.

Objectives The ends to which economic policies are directed e.g. a certain level of employment.

OPEC A cartel of oil producing countries which attempts to set prices for crude oil by setting production quotas for its members. It came to prominence in the early 1970s when it organized a fourfold increase in the price of oil during the first oil shock of 1973.

Open Market Operations The buying and selling of securities (government securities) with the intention of influencing the cash and liquidity base of the banking system and in turn the capacity to lend by the banks. Open market operations are also likely to influence both the level and structure of interest rates.

Organization of Petroleum Exporting Countries (O.P.E.C.) Oil producing and exporting countries which have experienced massive balance of payments surpluses since the four-fold increase in oil prices in 1973.

Parallel Money Markets This broad term refers to the borrowing and lending (short-term) – largely between the banks – arising from the ebb and flow of funds between the banks. The claims which are associated with these parallel (or complementary) markets are certificates of deposit, inter-bank deposits, short-term loans to local authorities, Euro-currencies, finance house deposits.

Price-Elasticity of Demand The degree of responsiveness of the demand for a product to a change in its price. For example a 10 per cent rise in the price of milk may result in a 2 per cent fall in the quantity demanded. A convenient way of expressing the relationship is to calculate :

$$\frac{\text{Proportionate change in quantity demanded}}{\text{Proportionate change in price}}$$

Thus in the illustration used above, the numerical value of the price-elasticity of demand would be :

$$\frac{2}{12} = 0.2$$

Prudential Controls As a result of the secondary banking crisis of 1973-74 the Bank of England together with the London and Scottish clearing banks prepared a joint paper (published in the Bank of England *Quarterly Bulletin,* September 1975, volume 15, No. 3) which set out the broad principles for the assessment of banks' balance sheets. These principles have been developed subsequently and until the Banking Acts prudential control was on an informal basis. The Johnson Matthey bank affair, for example, ensured that prudential controls would have to be established on a tighter, legal basis. This framework is incorporated largely in the Banking Act.

PSBR Public sector borrowing requirement : the balance of borrowing required by the public sector (central and local government, and public corporations) after taking account of expenditures and receipts.

PSDR Public sector debt repayment : a term which has arisen in recent years as a result of the emergence of *net receipts* of the public sector which has enabled the public sector to be a net redeemer of its debt.

Public Expenditure The expenditure of central government, local authorities, and public corporations which has to be financed by borrowing or taxation.

Public Sector Central government, local authorities, and public corporations.

Quantity Theory of Money A theory which states that changes in the quantity of money bring about variations in the price level.

Real interest rates The rate of return on lending after taking account of the effect of inflation on the interest payments received by the lender. The real rate of interest can be calculated approximately by subtracting the annual rate of inflation from the annualised rate of interest. In some years this has produced a negative figure indicating that the lender has lost real income as a result of inflation rates being higher than interest rates.

Retail Deposits Usually regarded as the sum of current accounts and deposit accounts. The use of the expression 'retail' implies that the size of such accounts is relatively small and that the term of the deposit is short. *(See wholesale deposits.)*

Retail Price Index An index designed to indicate the general level of prices of goods and services in the U.K. economy. Changes in the Retail Price Index are often used as a measure of the rate of inflation.

Sight Deposits Deposits which are transferable or withdrawable on demand without interest penalty (or interest indemnity). Thus, for example, an individual's current account would represent a sight deposit.

Snake Arrangements which restricted the degree of fluctuation between the exchange rates of some European countries, even though these currencies floated as a group against all other currencies. Superseded by the European Monetary System in 1979.

Special Deposits The Special Deposit scheme was announced in 1958. The device involved the mandatory depositing of additional cash with the Bank of England by the London and Scottish Clearing Banks as a percentage of their total deposits. The banks received interest on such deposits in line with the current Treasury bill rate, but these Special Deposits did not count as part of the banks cash and liquidity ratios. Changes in the call for Special Deposits were intended to influence the capacity of the banks to lend. After 1971 and the introduction of *Competition and Credit Control* the Special Deposit scheme applied to all banks.

Special Drawings Rights (S.D.R.s) And additional source of international liquidity introduced by the I.M.F. in 1970. The S.D.R. is a book-keeping entry in the Special Drawing Account of the I.M.F. which, when activated, can be utilized by member countries seeking to finance payments imbalances.

Sterling Balances Sterling bank deposits, money market liabilities, British government stocks, and Treasury bills held by overseas residents.

Supplementary Special Deposits This scheme was introduced in December 1973 and became known as the 'corset'. The target of this scheme was not the assets of the banks but their interest-bearing eligible liabilities : a device which aimed at directly influencing the size of these liabilities.

Tap Stocks These are gilt-edged stocks which are held by the Issue Department of the Bank of England and are known, by the Stock Market, to be available for sale by the Government Broker on behalf of the Bank of England. The tap stocks will vary over time as new issues of stock are made by the Bank, most of this stock being absorbed by the Issue Department and then used as the next tap stock. The Bank usually has a medium-dated and long-dated tap stock available. The prices at which such stocks are sold by the Bank are taken as important market indicators.

Targets The variables which governments hope to influence through the instruments at their disposal e.g. a certain growth in the money supply may be the target to which monetary instruments are directed.

Term Lending This usually refers to medium and long-term lending by banks to, say, companies. The secondary banks in the U.K. were vigorous in the development of this form of lending, but in the 1970s the clearing banks expanded this form of business – particularly loans of between five and seven years.

Time Deposits Deposits which usually may not be transferred or withdrawn without notice or interest penalty. An individual's deposit account represents such a deposit but in the U.K. the notice of withdrawal may be waived with a consequent loss of interest for the period of notice which has been waived.

Unfunding Unfunding involves the Bank of England selling shorter dated assets – especially Treasury bills – and buying longer dated securities. Such an operation reduces the average maturity of the national debt, and makes the non-government sector 'more liquid'. Unfunding operations are usually intended to raise the liquidity of the banking system and raise its capacity to lend.

Wholesale Deposits These refer to deposits of relatively large denomination placed with banks by large firms and financial intermediaries. The term of the deposit varies, as does the rate of interest on such deposits. Such deposits not only include deposits in excess of £10,000 obtained through bank branches but also deposits obtained through the issue of *certificates of deposit*.

Wilson Committee This is the abbreviated name for the 'Committee to Review the Functioning of Financial Institutions' which was set up in January 1977 under the chairmanship of Sir Harold Wilson.

Withholding tax Tax levied on the income on assets (dividends or interest) paid to non-residents. If such a tax payer has a similar tax liability on such funds once re-patriated, then the original tax paid is usually reclaimable.

World Bank (The International Bank for Reconstruction and Development) The sister institution of the I.M.F. which began operations in 1946. The World Bank assists economic development in the poorer countries of the world through making commercial loans to governments and governmental agencies.

Index